D0765256

Recasting the Vote

Recasting the Vote

HOW

WOMEN OF COLOR

TRANSFORMED

THE SUFFRAGE

MOVEMENT

CATHLEEN D. CAHILL

THE UNIVERSITY OF

NORTH CAROLINA PRESS

Chapel Hill

This book was published with the assistance of the
Greensboro Women's Fund of the University of North Carolina Press.
Founding contributors: Linda Arnold Carlisle, Sally Schindel Cone,
Anne Faircloth, Bonnie McElveen Hunter, Linda Bullard Jennings,
Janice J. Kerley (in honor of Margaret Supplee Smith),
Nancy Rouzer May, and Betty Hughes Nichols.

© 2020 Cathleen D. Cahill
Manufactured in the United States of America
Designed by Rich Hendel
Set in Quadraat
by Tseng Information Systems, Inc.

The University of North Carolina Press has been a
member of the Green Press Initiative since 2003.

Cover illustrations: (top left) Gertrude Simmons Bonnin (Zitkala-Ša),
from Houghton, *Our Debt to the Red Man*; (top right) Mabel Lee, courtesy Library of
Congress Prints and Photographs Division; (bottom, left to right) Mrs. Charles E. Peck,
Mrs. James L. Laidlaw, Anna Howard Shaw, Mabel Lee, Mrs. Frank Stratton,
and Lee Lia Beck, from the *New York Tribune*, April 11, 1912.

Library of Congress Cataloging-in-Publication Data
Names: Cahill, Cathleen D., author.
Title: Recasting the vote : how women of color transformed
the suffrage movement / Cathleen D. Cahill.
Description: Chapel Hill : The University of North Carolina Press, [2020] |
Includes bibliographical references and index.
Identifiers: LCCN 2020018378 | ISBN 9781469659329 (cloth) | ISBN 9781469659336 (ebook)
Subjects: LCSH: Women—Suffrage—United States—History. | Suffragists—United States—
History. | Minority women activists—United States—History. | Feminism—United States—History.
Classification: LCC JK1896 .C25 2020 | DDC 324.6/23092520973—dc23
LC record available at https://lccn.loc.gov/2020018378

Portions of chapters 6 and 9 originally appeared in somewhat different form in Cathleen D.
Cahill, "Marie Louise Bottineau Baldwin: Indigenizing the Federal Indian Service," in
"The Society of American Indians and Its Legacies," ed. Chadwick Allen and Beth H. Piatote,
special combined issue on the Society of American Indians, *Studies in American Indian Literatures*
25, no. 2, and *American Indian Quarterly* 37, no. 3 (Summer 2013): 63–86. Portions of chapters
14, 16, 17, and 20 originally appeared in somewhat different form in Cathleen D. Cahill,
"'Our Democracy and the American Indian': Citizenship, Sovereignty, and the Native Vote
in the 1920s," *Journal of Women's History* 32, no. 1 (2020): 41–51. Copyright © 2020 Journal
of Women's History. Reprinted with permission by Johns Hopkins University Press.

For Cecilia and Lincoln

[CONTENTS]

[ILLUSTRATIONS]

Recasting the Vote

[INTRODUCTION]

On a bright March day in 1913, Marie Louise Bottineau Baldwin stood on the lawn of the U.S. Capitol. She had come to participate in a historic event. Although the city thronged with people who planned to attend Woodrow Wilson's inauguration as the twenty-eighth president of the United States, Bottineau Baldwin had other priorities: she and thousands of other women had marshaled themselves for the first national woman suffrage parade.

Above her, the white Capitol dome gleamed in the sunlight against a brilliantly blue sky. Along the dome's railing, spectators with the best view in town appeared as small specks.[1] At the very top stood the bronze Statue of Freedom, nineteen feet tall, her classical robes flowing and the eagle feathers on her cap splayed visibly against the sky. The statue was part of a long tradition of female allegorical figures representing America—the feathers symbolized the continent as a "wild" Indian woman, while the robes signaled the classical tradition of "civilization" with which European colonists clothed their New World.[2]

Bottineau Baldwin was also wearing a robe, but hers was the black regalia of the Washington College of Law. She stood with her fellow lawyers and students wearing dark mortarboard hats from which hung short, thick tassels. She wore no feathered headdress nor braids, beadwork, or buckskin—nothing that would have marked her as an Indian to the non-Native Americans gathered along the Pennsylvania Avenue parade route. In marching as a lawyer, she asserted her place as a modern Native woman, rejecting the widely held notion that Indians were relics of the past. As a result, most people did not realize that an Anishinaabe woman was taking part in the march that day.[3]

Mrs. Wu stood out as a more visible participant in the procession. She wore a striking "embroidered gown of pale blue" and rode on the float representing nations of the world working toward woman suffrage. One report stated that she and her husband were students at George Washington University and that she held "Baby Wu [in] a white robe embroidered with little golden dragons."[4] A photograph of the float depicts a Chinese woman in a richly patterned dress, but instead of a baby, she carries the flag of the new Chinese republic with its five horizontal stripes.[5] Chinese names puzzled American reporters, who seldom bothered to confirm their accuracy or spelling. Exactly who Mrs. Wu was remains uncertain. It is possible that Wu was not even her real name.

She was there for a reason, however: to invoke the women of the Chinese Revolution of 1911 who had inspired American suffragists. The republican revo-

Crowd braking parade up at 9th St. Mch 3 1913

TAYLOR-WASH. D.C

This photograph suggests the diversity of the suffrage movement hiding in plain sight. Part of the first section of the March 3, 1913, Washington, D.C., suffrage parade, "The World-Wide Movement for Woman Suffrage," this float carried a Chinese suffragist (far right, reported as Mrs. Wu) proudly carrying the first flag of the new Chinese Republic. Her presence indicates American suffragists' fascination with the Chinese Revolution and the transnational currents of suffrage conversations. (Courtesy Library of Congress Prints and Photographs Division, Washington, D.C.)

lutionaries' support of women's rights fascinated the American public, as did reports that Chinese women had won the franchise. Wu's float was in the first section of the parade, labeled "The World-Wide Movement for Woman Suffrage." Most of the foreign nations in her section were represented by white American women in costumes, but as the press eagerly announced, "China was represented by a real Chinese woman."[6]

Carrie Williams Clifford marched in the "Homemakers" section. She was surrounded by women uniformly dressed in white shawls and caps. African American women like Clifford had insisted that they be included in the parade despite fierce resistance to their presence. They took their places throughout the procession as representatives of different professions, including artists, musicians, teachers, and doctors. Black women also marched with the individual state delegations of Illinois, Michigan, and New York, while a large body of students from Howard University marched in the college section.[7] Clifford was proud of all of them. They "are to be congratulated that so many of them had the courage of their convictions," she later wrote, "and that they made such an admirable showing in the first great national parade."[8]

It had indeed required conviction. White parade organizers feared that Afri-

INTRODUCTION

can Americans' participation would alienate southern whites, whose support they deemed essential to the suffrage cause. The leaders of the march eventually relented, but only after proposing that the African American contingent appear at the back of the parade. But Clifford and her fellow black suffragists insisted on participating on an equal basis. Recognizing the historic nature of the moment, they understood that black women's visible presence symbolized their claims to full belonging in the nation.

To highlight women's achievements as well as the righteousness of their cause, parade organizers drew on a vast library of symbols familiar to most Americans. At the head of the procession, the famous white suffragist and lawyer Inez Milholland sat astride her white horse as a black groom held its reins. She wore a delicate white lace dress and sported long white gloves and white riding boots. A diadem topped with a large star wreathed her dark hair, while a white cape covered her shoulders and flowed down over the horse's haunches. Milholland rode in front of a float emblazoned with the words "We demand an amendment to the Constitution of the United States of America Enfranchising the Women of this Country."[9] The whiteness of her outfit as well as her renowned beauty were intended to reinforce the high ideals of the movement. To underscore that message, marchers carried banners such as the one that read "Forward out of Darkness, Leave Behind the Night, Forward out of Error, Forward into Light."

Inez Milholland and women like her have been the predominant image of the suffrage movement. But that image conceals the full history of the fight for the vote in the United States. This book uncovers the vibrant and varied stories of a wide range of women who demanded their democratic rights as Americans while also fighting for equality as women of color.[10] They participated in many pivotal events from suffrage history—not only in the first national parade but in countless other efforts before and after. Scratch the surface just a bit and their stories shine through, suggesting vast lodes of activism and courage, contention and complexity.

In the decades leading up to 1920, diverse women from across the nation and its territories were deeply involved in movements for suffrage and citizenship rights. These issues engaged all parts of the American public; the movement was forged in myriad places and in multiple languages. At the Carlisle Indian Industrial School, students held debates on the suffrage question, and the senior class of 1914 acted out a futuristic scenario that imagined the world as run by militant British feminist Emmeline Pankhurst. *The Crisis*, the journal of the National Association for the Advancement of Colored People, regularly published articles on the woman suffrage question and devoted special issues to the matter.[11] Chinese American student newspapers also covered the topic. Elite Native Hawaiian (Kanaka Maoli) and Anglo women formed a joint woman suffrage club in

Honolulu after the United States annexed the Island Kingdom. And politicians held forth in both Spanish and English at the New Mexico state constitutional convention as they debated the inclusion of woman suffrage along with language protections for the Spanish-speaking citizens of the state.

Recasting the Vote looks to these examples and many others to explore the broad range of suffrage activism and other political activity by women of color. The book focuses especially on six such women: Gertrude Simmons Bonnin, a Yankton Dakota (Sioux) writer who used the pen name Zitkala-Ša; Mabel Ping-Hua Lee, a Chinese-born longtime resident of New York City; Carrie Williams Clifford, an Ohio-born African American woman living in Washington, D.C.; Marie Louise Bottineau Baldwin, a woman of Turtle Mountain Chippewa and French heritage from North Dakota; New Mexican politician Adelina "Nina" Luna Otero-Warren; and Laura Cornelius Kellogg, a Wisconsin Oneida author and activist. The narrative is built around their stories but also touches on others, including Pearl Mark Loo, Aurora Lucero, Soledad Chávez de Chacón, Ida B. Wells-Barnett, Mary Church Terrell, and Addie Hunton. Telling their stories collectively reveals a richer and more holistic history of the woman suffrage movement.

These suffragists of color did not come to the movement from the same places as such well-documented activists as Alice Paul, Carrie Chapman Catt, and Anna Howard Shaw, nor did their paths lead to the same ends afterward. Indeed, the full suffrage story is a complex one, and no single trajectory fits the experience of all women. The suffragists examined in this book intersected with the predominantly white national and state organizations that focused on legislative solutions to the disenfranchisement of women. But many feminists of color also fought outside of those organizations, struggling parallel to and sometimes against them. Their movements had their own genealogies that ran through black churches,[12] Indigenous governments,[13] and labor movements.[14] Though this book focuses on women who did engage with the familiar organizers and events of the suffrage movement, these other important stories also deserve greater attention. Some of these women are well-known political activists, though rarely described as suffragists; others are seldom recognized outside of their communities, which have worked hard to keep their histories alive.[15]

The well-deserved charge of racism aimed at the suffrage movement has perhaps served to elide the presence of women of color in suffrage histories. To be sure, women of color did face intense racism. But they still actively shaped the movement's history, specifically through their participation in suffrage activities and in the multiple ways white Americans—pro- and anti-suffragists alike—invoked ideas about race and gender in suffrage debates.[16] Women of color understood the need for white allies to influence other white Americans. The suffragists in this book expended much energy writing and speaking to white suffragists and female voters and educating them about the issues faced by their nonwhite counterparts. Their persistence and insistence on their rights forced white suffragists to acknowledge them. At times, white women worked alongside marginalized women as genuine allies; at other times, they only grudgingly granted women of color recognition for their efforts; at still other times, they opposed them outright.

Popular interest in suffragists of color amplified their voices far beyond their numbers. White suffrage advocates and the broader white public used images of nonwhite women and men to debate women's rights, often in different ways. But in many cases, women of color were able to leverage stereotypes to increase their influence. The press often sought interviews with them, and they received invitations to address college students, women's clubs, and missionary organizations. These opportunities provided platforms that they used to present their visions of the nation and their place in it.

Women of color also bore different relationships to U.S. citizenship. This meant that once they gained a public platform, they often had to instruct their audiences about their legal status. Each group had a particular historical relationship to the United States, one that dramatically shaped their suffrage work and their political strategies. This also meant that the ratification of the Nineteenth Amendment in 1920 meant different things to different groups of women.

Citizenship in the United States followed a complicated path. Throughout the antebellum period, citizenship was connected to whiteness, a status confirmed by the *Dred Scott* decision. After the Mexican-American War of 1846–48, the Treaty of Guadalupe Hidalgo offered citizenship to former Mexican citizens who swore allegiance to the United States, making them legally white. The Fourteenth Amendment expanded citizenship to include all people born in the United States regardless of race, color, or previous condition of servitude, emphatically expanding the category to include African Americans. But the amendment excluded "Indians not taxed" from birthright citizenship, ostensibly recognizing the sovereignty of Native nations. At that very moment, however, the federal government was attempting to destroy that sovereignty by placing Native people under federal wardship and developing coercive policies to incorporate individual Indian people into the U.S. citizenry. Racists also fanned fears about Asian immigrants, leading to the Chinese Exclusion Act of 1882, which severely limited immigration from China and denied Chinese immigrants the option of naturalization. Women from each of these groups therefore had a distinct relationship to citizenship that shaped their suffrage activism.[17]

These multiple relationships to citizenship and suffrage also mean that this book does not end in 1920 with the ratification of the Nineteenth Amendment. Instead, it considers that year as a pivot when the status of some women changed. The Nineteenth Amendment enfranchised white women nationwide as well as northern and western black women and some Hispanas. But many Native women remained legal wards of the government; southern black women and many Mexican Americans faced disenfranchisement under Jim Crow; and immigration laws deliberately excluded Chinese women.[18]

Recasting the Vote is not merely an additive project. The stories of the women at the heart of this book challenge us to contemplate how our narrative of the suffrage struggle changes when we see it from different perspectives—especially when we move beyond the black/white binary and put different groups in conversation. Chinese, Native, Hispanic, and African American women fought for suffrage as part of a constellation of political activities. Their political awakenings emerged from their engagement with the concerns of their own communities as well as their anti-racist activism, fights for justice, and struggles for sovereignty and nation-building. They saw the campaign for women's right to vote as addressing some of the specific concerns of their communities; they also saw it as a means of finding allies in other causes. Few scholars have analyzed these women of color as suffragists, however, because their stories do not fit the traditional narrative of the fight for women's rights, which is built around middle-class white women. For example, Indigenous women's feminism often grew out of their struggle for tribal sovereignty; Chinese women hoped to use their votes to resist oppression in the United States, but also looked across the Pacific to build the new Chinese republic; and Hispanic women's battle for inclusion largely centered on language rights.

Many of these women were elites in their own communities, and their economic resources helped them engage suffrage conversations in places such as college campuses, women's reform organizations, and literary circles. While they generally had less economic privilege than their white counterparts, this still placed them in a different position than many of their community members. So despite their class advantages, they nonetheless struggled against the sexual *and* racial limits of American society, including within the women's rights movement.

This book is composed of four parts. Part 1 highlights the backgrounds of the women whose experiences structure the narrative. These stories are key to understanding how they became politicized and looked to voting rights as an instrument in their struggle for broader civil and human rights. It is impossible to separate their fight against racial injustice from their quest for enfranchisement. This section, set largely at the turn of the twentieth century, reveals the intersection of their identities as women and women of color—what Mary Church Terrell called a "doubled cross."[19] It sketches the state of play of suffrage legislation as western states led the nation in fully enfranchising primarily white women with a string of victories between 1910 and 1914. Some familiar names and stories of suffrage activism appear here but as background to women of color and their experiences.

In 1913 suffragists revived the strategy of amending the U.S. Constitution. Part 2 takes up the story of women's activism after that shift. In the eventful years between 1913 and 1917, a rising phalanx of white supremacists captured the levers of the federal government, including the office of the president. This had an immediate impact on women of color, especially black women, forcing them to reconfigure their activism. For many, the struggle over citizenship rights for their communities took priority, though none stopped fighting for suffrage. During this period, the major national suffrage organization split, offering women different strategies. Some continued to focus on state-by-state legislation, while others backed federal constitutional change. Against this backdrop, suffragists of color occasionally engaged with white suffragists but primarily worked within their own community organizations, focusing on their most relevant issues and concerns.

As Part 3 demonstrates, the entry of the United States into World War I changed the political landscape once again as suffrage activists balanced their demands for greater democracy at home with the war abroad. The settings and events of this period are familiar to many, but the standard narrative looks quite different when centered on stories of women and men of color who were in those same places and for whom the war also offered new arguments. Pointing to the contributions of their communities, especially through military service, they insisted that the United States live up to its rhetoric of democracy. White suffragists also pointed to the hypocrisy of fighting for freedom overseas when women were disenfranchised at home. But once again, for women of color, that hypocrisy affected their entire communities in very different ways.

Part 4 begins when the Nineteenth Amendment was ratified on August 18, 1920. People celebrated women winning the vote, but the reality was more complicated. The amendment did not guarantee all women the right to vote—it simply stated that sex could no longer be used as a reason for denying them the franchise. Many states turned to other methods for restricting the ballot, just as they had for men of color for many years. Those left behind vigorously pointed this out to celebrating white women, but their appeals received mixed responses. Meanwhile, those women of color who were able to vote embraced their new status and worked to make their concerns felt through the exercise of that right and participation in party organizations. As a result, the following decade was marked by great possibility and crushing disappointment. Those years saw the first women of color in the nation elected to office but also witnessed the evolution of Jim Crow laws to repress the political power of women of color.

The epilogue follows the book's central actors through the end of their lives while also revealing the legacy of their stories through a meditation on why women like these have so often been left outside the narrative, both by white suffragists who memorialized their own accomplishments and to a lesser extent by professional historians since. Nevertheless, these suffragists of color and their communities understood the power of history. They very deliberately placed their thoughts and stories in the historical record. They wrote and published, they collected and curated, they constructed and conserved to ensure that their histories and especially the histories of their communities would not be forgotten. They insisted that their contributions to the nation's history mattered, and it is because of their work that we can recover a sense of how they continue to matter today.

PART I

Prelude and Parades
1890–1913

CHAPTER 1

Woman versus the Indian

Gertrude Simmons Bonnin

During the summer of 1890, fourteen-year-old Gertrude Simmons (later Bonnin), or Gertie, as she was known, was on an extended visit home to the Yankton Sioux Reservation in southeastern South Dakota. The young Yankton Dakota girl had left home for a boarding school when she was only eight years old. She had been raised by her mother in what she later described as an idyllic traditional childhood, but one which was also desperately poor. The missionaries from White's Institute in Indiana had lured her away with promises of bright red apples.[1] Her mother had not wanted her to go, and indeed, Gertie had been miserable at school. But she was also unhappy during the visit home. It had been three years since she had been back, and everything had changed. "I seemed to hang in the heart of chaos, beyond the touch or voice of human aid," she remembered. Her brother was too old to understand her sorrow, and her mother, who had never been "on the inside of a schoolhouse," could not comfort her. "I was neither a wee girl nor a tall one, neither a wild Indian nor a tame one. This deplorable situation was the effect of my brief course in the East, and the unsatisfactory 'teenth' in a girl's years." Her mother mourned for her, but their relationship was strained, the result of Gertie having left at such a young age. Her sense of not belonging at home was precisely what federal policy makers hoped to achieve with the boarding school policies that they implemented in the late nineteenth century.[2]

Another traveler to South Dakota that summer was Susan B. Anthony, leading light of the suffrage movement, who came to canvass the state along with two young workers for the cause, Anna Howard Shaw and Carrie Chapman Catt. They represented the National American Woman Suffrage Association, or NAWSA (pronounced Nah-saw), which suffragists had formed in 1890 by merging two earlier organizations and healing a twenty-year split in the movement. They were campaigning for the woman suffrage referendum that was on the ballot for the state's fall elections. They recognized the vote in South Dakota as part of their broader movement to enfranchise white women on a state-by-state basis, a strategy that had been particularly successful in western states and territories, beginning with the Wyoming Territory in 1869.

A few months later, the year 1890 became an infamous one in the history of American conquest. In the deep cold of late December, U.S. cavalry troops were placed on high alert by officials alarmed by large groups of Lakota people who had gathered for the Ghost Dance. Intercepting Big Foot's band of Lakota camped along Wounded Knee Creek, the cavalry took up positions on the high ground and readied their weapons. As they aggressively disarmed the Lakota men, a scuffle broke out and the cavalry opened fire into the camp, killing almost three hundred men, women, and children. Their bodies were thrown into a mass grave while a photographer documented the gruesome scene.

A young girl's difficult summer back from school, a suffragists' speaking tour, and a horrific mass killing may seem unrelated other than having occurred in the same time and place. Thinking about them together, however, reveals that people of color were always at the heart of the debates over suffrage. In large part this was because women of color were generating important ideas about women's rights and their place in the nation. But it was also because white suffragists constantly invoked race in their speeches, writings, and activism.

After the Civil War, as the federal government consolidated its conquest of Native nations in the American West, Native children like Gertie often bore the brunt of the offensive as they were taken from their communities to be raised by strangers. Seeking to "break up the tribal relation," policy makers argued that removing Native children from their "uncivilized" parents and placing them in federally run or missionary-run boarding schools was "a kindly cruel surgery that hurts that it may save."[3] Child removal policies were part and parcel of a larger plan to destroy Native nations and incorporate Indigenous people into the American citizenry as individuals. By 1902 the government operated twenty-five off-reservation boarding schools, dozens of on-reservation boarding schools, and hundreds of day schools. Their mission was to educate Native children in "civilized" ways, teaching the men to be farmers and the women to be housewives who would raise the next generation of Native children as American citizens.[4]

Policy makers developed a variety of other programs that supported the goal of "Americanizing the First American," as Gertrude Simmons Bonnin would later call it. Their most important objective was to break up the political power and land bases that Native nations held in common under their treaty rights. The General Allotment Act of 1887, also known as the Dawes Act, divided communally held reservation lands and assigned parcels to individuals while selling off the "excess" to white settlers. Congress also passed a series of other laws and orders attacking Native cultures and political structures. These policies outlawed sacred dances and other religious ceremonies, dissolved tribal governments, coerced men to cut their hair, and policed marriage practices.

All of this was in service of opening up Indigenous land for white settlers. Indeed, South Dakota, the state that surrounded Gertie's Yankton Reservation, was a new name for an old place, ironically drawn from the people whom white settlers were seeking to replace. Initially part of what the United States called the Dakota Territory, by 1889 it had been split into two, with Congress approving the petitions for the statehood of North and South Dakota. That same year, with the Sioux Agreement, the government had divided the Great Sioux Reservation, which constituted roughly a third of western South Dakota, into six smaller reservations tied to specific bands. With the Dawes Act already in place, whites assumed that as Indians received their allotments in fee simple, those reservations would disappear and their members would become U.S. citizens indistinguishable from their white neighbors — or, if Indians were unable to adjust to the new circumstances, they would die out and disappear.[5]

The first elections in the new state in 1890 reflected this vision of settlement and assimilation. That summer was the hottest and driest on record, but despite the weather, speakers feverishly canvassed the state. The white male voters of South Dakota were considering a number of questions that year, including moving the state capital and raising the state debt limit from $100,000 to $500,000 to encourage internal improvements.

The ballot included two referenda about voting: one asking voters whether to enfranchise women and the other supporting the enfranchisement of Indians who had separated from their Native nations.[6] Both turned on the question of belonging and the mechanisms of assimilation. While race was not mentioned in the former, everyone assumed it meant white women, just as sex was not mentioned in the latter, but everyone assumed it meant Native men. The status of Native women was largely ignored in the debate over the referenda.

Americans used the right to vote to encourage the destruction of tribal communities and to measure the advancement of "civilization": until Native people renounced their tribal connection, they were ineligible to vote. This was written into the U.S. Constitution, including in the Fourteenth Amendment, which distinguished "Indians not taxed" from those who willingly participated in the U.S. system as possessive individuals. Earlier territories that had achieved statehood, like Michigan and Wisconsin, had followed the same approach. Those state constitutions had granted suffrage rights to many people of mixed Indigenous and French descent who appeared "civilized."[7]

In South Dakota, it seemed that individual allotment of the reservations would happen in the very near future, making the question of Native suffrage a fairly immediate one. The authors of the South Dakota referendum had used very convoluted language, however, which created great confusion at the ballot box. Voters were asked to respond in the affirmative or the negative to the statement "No Indian who sustains tribal relations, receives support in whole or in part from the government of the United States, or holds untaxable land in severalty, shall be permitted to vote at any election held under this constitution."[8] Newspaper editors carefully explained that those who did not want "uncivilized" Indians who were living in "tribal relations" to vote should support this statement affirmatively, while a response of "no" would sink the restrictive clause and allow all Indians to vote.[9]

Initially, white women's suffrage seemed like a sure winner. South Dakotans had originally wanted to write it into the constitution they had sent to Congress for approval, but the territorial governor had convinced them that it would hurt their chances for statehood. So instead they agreed to hold a referendum on woman suffrage in the new state's first election. The agriculturalists who made up the Farmers' Alliance and the Knights of Labor had invited the venerable Susan B. Anthony to campaign in their state, promising that their party would include a suffrage plank in the platform. But politics intervened. When the Alliance and the Knights joined the new Independent Party, they left the women's suffrage plank out of their platform, claiming it was too controversial. Nevertheless, Anthony had already made plans to campaign and had also invited Carrie Chapman Catt and Anna Howard Shaw to join her. It was to be Catt's and Shaw's first national campaign, and they were eager to work with their hero, Aunt Susan, who had been leading the suffrage fight for decades. And so they went. In the future, the two young women would shepherd the Nineteenth Amendment into the Constitution. But in 1890 they were fairly green apprentices just starting the work.[10]

Catt and Shaw found it outrageous that despite white women's self-sufficiency and contributions to the territory's settlement, they could not vote. Catt in particular emphasized the difficulties white women faced as they helped transform Lakota and Dakota lands into American space. "The state contains thousands of women farmers," she reported, "young women, spinsters and widows who came here a few years ago, took up claims, improved them and are now full-fledged agriculturalists."[11] Young families, after working all day, drove for miles in heavy lumber wagons just to see her talk. She was struck by the women's youth and that most had a babe in arms.[12] On one occasion, she invited them to lay their bundles down on the floor behind her; she lectured with a dozen babies slumbering at her back. Other women impressed Catt with their ingenuity and strength, like the two who found her on the road with a broken wagon wheel and improvised a fix before accompanying her to her meeting. Or the widow with six children who pitched hay all day, cooked dinner, and milked the cows before hitching her team to drive to Catt's lecture.

The suffragists experienced many moments of outrage during the campaign. Spurned by the Farmers' Alliance, they attended the Republican Party's convention. Generally, Republicans supported woman suffrage, but in South Dakota the party did not offer the women a warm welcome. The convention floor was packed with men from across the state, including several Native men—according to Shaw, they were wearing blankets and sporting feathers in their hair. And to her great indignation, the white male politicians greeted them respectfully and gave them seats near the front of the room. The white women, she remarked, received no such courtesy. Relegated to the back of the room, Catt had to stand on a chair to see above the crowd and report the convention's proceedings to the other women.[13]

White suffragists had long contrasted white womanhood, which they saw as the highest form of civilization, with uncivilized, crude manhood as a rhetorical tactic. In South Dakota, they noted that Native men were not the only men the state's politicians had elevated over women. There were also Russian-born men who spoke no English but wore sashes mocking Susan B. Anthony, Shaw indignantly remembered. They, too, had been enfranchised before native-born white women. Although the question of woman suffrage and suffrage for Native people had been left to referenda after statehood, South Dakota's constitution had allowed for so-called alien suffrage, the enfranchisement of noncitizen immigrants who had declared their intent to become citizens—"first-papers" voters, they were called. By 1900 eleven states had similar laws, down from a high of twenty-two in the 1870s. While the suffragists did not mention that law specifically, the actions of the Russian immigrants (whether citizens or not) who flaunted their voting rights particularly galled them.[14]

When the election was held in November, white suffragists were further outraged by the results. Though voters rejected both referenda, it appeared that more men in South Dakota were willing to enfranchise Indians than women. Newspapers interpreted this as an accident due to the confusing language of the referendum. Appearing on the ballot as a negative statement ("No Indian who sustains tribal relations . . . shall be permitted to vote"), it required voters to cast an affirmative vote. But many South Dakotans voted no, thus casting a vote for enfranchising all Native people in the state, both "civilized" and "uncivilized." "The voters of Pennington County labored under the same mistake in regard to the Indian franchise as did the people of this county," lamented the *Daily Deadwood Pioneer Times*. "As a result, Pennington casts a majority in favor of the Indians possessing the right of suffrage."[15]

Rather than seeing their struggles as similar, white suffragists read the results as an insult. Shaw told of encountering Indian men wrapped in blankets who spoke in Lakota and was furious that South Dakota's white men seemed more willing to enfranchise them than the white women of the state. Native women seem to have been forgotten in the conversation.

But there was little love in South Dakota for Native people.

The Ghost Dance was a ceremony that promised to return the Indigenous world to the days before white settlers had come. It had spread eastward from Paiute country in Nevada to the Lakota. The dance held out hope and balm for people who had witnessed their world being torn apart and offered a way to reverse those ravages. Many bands, smaller groups within the Lakota usually bound together by kinship, moved away from the government agencies to the remote corners of the reservations. There they could dance in peace, away from federal officials' eyes and draconian rules against religious ceremonies. Those same officials, many of them ignorant of the Native cultures they sought to destroy, were afraid that the gatherings to dance were pretexts to prepare for war. Reporters fanned the fear throughout November and December 1890 with headlines describing the Ghost Dancers as gathering for an attack.

Everyone was on edge.

Just a few days after Christmas, orders went out to the U.S. Seventh Cavalry to bring the bands back to the agency on the Standing Rock Reservation. The Seventh held a grudge against the Lakota due to the Battle of the Greasy Grass, known to white Americans as the Battle of Little Big Horn. There, in 1876, the nation's centennial year, the Lakota had defeated the troops of the Seventh and killed their commander, General George Armstrong Custer. Fourteen years later at Wounded Knee, eleven of the Seventh's same nineteen officers were in the field.

When they reached Lakota leader Big Foot's camp, the band was already heading back to the local agency. Yet the soldiers still ordered the men to assemble about fifty yards away from the camp and demanded that a small group of Lakota return and retrieve all the guns. They complied, bringing back a few rifles, but the officers were not convinced that the collection represented all the Lakota weapons and sent white soldiers down into the camp to look for more. The Lakota men being held at the council grounds could see the soldiers going into tepees where they tore open bundles and scattered people's belongings. Claiming Lakota women were hiding guns, soldiers body-searched some of them, throwing them down and looking under their skirts.

During the search one Lakota man refused to give up his gun. It was said that he was deaf or did not hear or understand the order. In the struggle, the gun went off, and the men of the Seventh found a pretext to unleash their anger.

From the ridge above, the soldiers opened fire with the four Hotchkiss guns they had aimed down at the people's homes.[16] As a hail of revolving cannon fire shredded the tepee covers, women and children fled. Some ran to Wounded Knee Creek, where those who were not cut down by shrapnel and bullets hid beneath the banks. Most sought shelter in a ravine that ran west and south of the camp. Their husbands, sons, and fathers, having relinquished most of their weapons, initially bore the brunt of the violence, standing together in the council ground. Though they fought back in hand-to-hand combat and with knives and a few guns grabbed from the pile of confiscated weapons, within the first ten minutes eighty-three of the Lakota men had been slain. Only half that number escaped into the ravine, where they desperately tried to protect the women and children from the cavalry who advanced to hunt them down. Rough Feather's wife remembered the terror as she ran to a "cut bank and lay down there. I saw some of the other Indians running up the coulee so I ran with them, but the soldiers kept shooting at us and the bullets flew all around us." Lakota leader American Horse also related the horror of the scene: "The women as they were fleeing with their babes on their backs were killed together, shot right through and the women who were very heavy with child were also killed."

As the stutter of the guns slowed to a stop, smoke cleared, and men stood panting from their murderous exertions, the scene became clear. The bodies of almost three hundred Lakota people lay on the bloody snow. Over half of them were women and children, killed as they had fled and tried to hide. The army's own records support this as one officer reported that the bodies of one woman, two young girls, and a ten-year-old boy were found three miles from the camp. They had been shot at such close range that there were powder burns on their skin and clothing. Though the officers later claimed they tried to avoid killing women, they excused themselves by employing racial slurs: the soldiers "could not discern the distinction between bucks and squaws." But that did not explain the murder of children.[17]

It was a massacre, but that was not how the press reported it. The next morning, headlines nationwide blamed the dead. "Red Treachery," proclaimed a Massachusetts newspaper. The *Morning Oregonian* of Portland declared the victims "The Scheming Reds." Journalists gleefully welcomed a fight and delighted in the deaths of the Indians. "Hot Times at Pine Ridge," Chicago's *Daily Inter Ocean* ghoulishly reported. "Indian War at Last," blared the *Boston Daily Advertiser*.[18]

Anna Howard Shaw contemplated the violence at Wounded Knee together with the results of the November referenda in South Dakota as she wrote her speech "Indians versus Women" for the second annual conference of NAWSA, convened in February 1891 in Washington, D.C.

NAWSA resulted from the reunification of the nation's two major suffrage organizations, the American Woman Suffrage Association (AWSA) and the National Woman Suffrage Association (NWSA). The two groups had split almost twenty years earlier over the question of African American men's suffrage rights. Outraged that the Fifteenth Amendment had excluded women from enfranchisement, Susan B. Anthony and Elizabeth Cady Stanton turned against black allies who had been by their side for many years, including even Frederick Douglass, who had been at Seneca Falls in 1848 and put his name to the Declaration of Sentiments calling for women's rights. Stanton and Anthony abandoned the earlier national organization, the Equal Rights Association, and formed the NWSA. They reached out to racist Democrats, campaigning in Kansas in 1867 on the explicit statement that white women were racially superior and deserved the vote before black men.[19] Other white suffrage leaders like Lucy Stone defended the strategy of prioritizing black men's voting rights and formed the AWSA. Led by Stone and her husband, Henry Blackwell, AWSA argued that the fight was gradual and celebrated black men's gains as part of the process. While a small number of black suffragists participated in NWSA, many more of them joined the AWSA. Frances Ellen Watkins Harper, for example, attended AWSA meetings and spoke from its platforms.[20]

Anna Howard Shaw was part of the next generation that hoped to heal the split between NWSA and AWSA and revive the movement's momentum. But if members of this generation—whose political views had not been formed by the abolitionist movement and the Civil War—believed that the question of suffrage and race had been settled, they were wrong. It remained at the center of discussions. Shaw indicated that white suffragists were still thinking in racial terms when she gave her speech the title "Indians versus Women." It was a strange oration, full of contradictions as Shaw tried to reconcile the horrific violence against Native people, especially women and children at Wounded Knee, with her indignation that Native men seemed to enjoy greater support than white women for suffrage in South Dakota. Using a strategy she would employ again and again, she set up a contrast between the disrespect that educated, native-born white women received from white men and the solicitousness with which those men treated nonwhite men, Indian men in blankets, and Russian immigrants who spoke no English. Outraged at the idea that the white men of South Dakota were more willing to enfranchise Indian men than white women, she mused that perhaps it was because Indian men could threaten violence. "He goes on the warpath. Then what does the Indian get? He gets what our Government takes to him." This was a strange conclusion given the recent massacre at Wounded Knee. She did, however, admit that the government owed Native people a debt—"he gets something, though he does not get half that belongs to him"—and further acknowledged "when this last unholy, unrighteous war was waged on those plains know that the war was never begun by the Indians, never dreamed of by them."[21]

Shaw did not end there. She went on to meditate on the backbreaking and lonely work white women had done to improve homesteads on the windy plains. In the end, they had no property rights to the transformation they had wrought. Nor, she pointed out, did they have legal rights to their children in the new state. Surely their work of settlement, of transformation, had earned them full rights of citizenship; this was, after all, the promise of the American West. Shaw wanted it to apply to women as well.

Yet Shaw also expressed sympathy for Native women. To righteous applause and hisses, she described the plight of the women and children shot down by the Seventh Cavalry. Custer's former unit had "murdered" them, she asserted. Like white women, they, too, had grievances; they, too, lost their children; they, too, lacked a say in government. Native women likely would have disagreed that the legal restrictions on white women were the same as the genocidal violence they faced, but Shaw spent little time on the thought. In the next breath she returned to white women and derided Native men. "Now I do not wish to say that Indians should not have rights, and ought not to have recognition; but it is exceedingly marvelous how little an Indian, or any other kind of a man, needs to know before he may be regarded as a valuable citizen, and how much a woman needs to know before she becomes any kind of citizen whatever." The tension in Shaw's speech around sex and race would infuse her career and was one that dogged many white suffragists who could not separate their racial privilege from their gender disadvantage.

Anna Julia Cooper was dismayed by Shaw's speech. Cooper, an African American activist and public school teacher in Washington, D.C., may have attended the NAWSA conference, or she could have read Shaw's speech when it was published in the *Woman's Tribune*.[22] Either way, she was frustrated that once again, white women were vilifying people of color in order to make claims for their own benefit. Cooper was working on her book *A Voice from the South*, which she would publish the following year (1892). It included her thoughts in a chapter that she called "Woman versus the Indian," reversing Shaw's formulation and commenting directly on her ideas.

Cooper began with a strategy black suffragists often used: appealing to white women's better nature as a way of holding them to a higher standard than they were living up to in reality. She opened the chapter describing Shaw as "broad and just and liberal in principle" and praising her and Susan B. Anthony for the stand they had taken in defense of racial equality during the "color ripple" that shook a women's club in Kentucky, the Wimodaughsis Club. Cooper recounted how the organization's secretary, a white woman, had refused to allow a black woman to enroll in one of the club's classes. Shaw, with Anthony's support, had threatened to resign from the club's presidency, refusing to "lend her influence to such unreasonable and uncharitable discrimination."[23]

But, Cooper went on, it was precisely because she thought so highly of Shaw and Anthony that Shaw's speech rankled her. Certainly white suffrage leaders faced tensions balancing the concerns of black women and southern white women who constantly threatened to quit the movement if black women were included, but Shaw and Anthony had proven themselves to be of nobler stuff, of grander vision, standing on higher ground. Indeed, Cooper believed that women had "a real and special influence" on society, and when they bullied or were contemptuous of those weaker than themselves, as men did, they caused real damage.[24] She called on white leaders like Shaw to do better, arguing that they must fight for all women, not just themselves. The Woman's Movement, the "Reform of our day," was, she insisted, the embodiment of universal good. "It is not the intelligent woman vs. the ignorant woman; nor the white woman vs. the black, the brown, and the red, — it is not even the cause of woman vs. man." No, she asserted, it was larger than that; it was a fight for "the final triumph of all right over might, the supremacy of the moral forces of reason and justice and love in the government of the nation." Anything less was "hitching our wagon to something much lower than a star."[25]

Gertie Simmons Bonnin shared Cooper's insistence that race and sex could not be separated because they intersected in the experiences of women of color. She had witnessed the results of the November 1890 election from the Yankton Reservation in South Dakota. On December 18, she boarded a train and returned to her school in Wabash, Indiana. It was just eleven days later that American troops perpetrated the massacre at Wounded Knee on the Standing Rock Sioux reservation, on the other side of the state from her home at Yankton.[26] The newspaper coverage of Wounded Knee was neither the first nor the last time Gertie would encounter anti-Indian prejudice. Five years later, she enrolled at Earlham College, a Quaker-run school that by 1895 admitted both Native and African American students. But despite the college's progressive reputation, at the time of her enrollment, she was the only Indigenous student among almost five hundred peers. At the same time, the Quaker emphasis on spiritual equality meant that women and their ideas were also welcomed at the institution. This setting melded with her Lakota upbringing to solidify her ideas about women's capabilities and strengthen her desire for equality, forging a foundation that informed her politics for the rest of her life.[27]

Early in the winter of her freshman year, Bonnin crafted a speech on the rights of women for the school's oratorical contest. Unfortunately, the content of the speech has been lost, though the title, "Side by Side," strongly suggests her vision of sex equality. Competing against both men and women as well as many upperclassmen, she remained undaunted. The school's paper, The Earlhamite, reported, "Her delivery was pleasing, and her voice, though not strong, was clear and distinct." The panel of judges composed of Earlham alumni was certainly impressed. They named her the winner. Her classmates, thrilled that one of their own had bested the upperclassmen, threw a reception in her honor, while the seniors, stunned at their loss, "retired to the library . . . and consoled themselves with oranges."[28] They soon rallied, however, and became Bonnin's enthusiastic supporters when she represented Earlham in the statewide competition in Indianapolis.

Bonnin seized the opportunity to speak to a large audience in a state capital. Her speech on women's rights had been a compelling and important topic, but not as close to her heart as the rights of Native people. She took the bold step of rewriting "Side by Side" into a meditation on the relationship of Indigenous people to white Americans and a call for Native rights. She reminded the crowd of the violent dispossession of Native people: "The White Man's bullet decimates his tribes and drives him from his home." Despite that history, she called for reconciliation through assimilation but also asserted an Indigenous right to belong. We come "seeking by a new birthright to unite with yours our claim to a common country," she offered.[29]

Sadly, her experience in Indianapolis reinforced why such a speech was necessary. "Here again was strong prejudice against my people," she wearily remembered. Held in a large opera house, the contest was intense, the different student bodies warring and wrangling among themselves over the reputations of their schools. They derisively mocked Earlham's representative, and "the slurs against the Indian" burned "like a dry fever within my breast." After the orations, as she stood on the stage in front of a "vast ocean of eyes" waiting for the verdict, some "college rowdies" unfurled a large white banner "with a drawing of the most forlorn Indian girl on it. Under this they had printed in bold black letters words that ridiculed the college which was represented by a 'squaw.'" It was a mean, ugly word. Standing exposed she gritted her teeth, glaring into the crowd while the flag waved "insolently" in front of her. She recalled a stab of glee when she was awarded one of the two prizes of the night; the students holding the flag hurriedly rolled it up. But the pleasure drained out of her as she left the crowd as quickly as possible and returned to her room alone.[30]

The students who deployed the term "squaw" attacked Bonnin not just as a Native person but as a Native woman. In her struggles for equality she could not ignore the question of race to focus solely on gender. This was a false dichotomy that she would constantly call on white audiences to recognize.

Though it failed, the 1890 South Dakota referendum on woman suffrage was one of many such efforts in the West, of which several succeeded. First came territorial victories that required only legislative, not voter, approval. The Wyoming Territory inaugurated the movement, enfranchising women in 1869, followed by the Utah (1870) and Washington (1883) Territories. As with the Farmers' Alliance in South Dakota, the influence of third parties and Populist energy led to the next successes, with suffrage gaining legislative victories in Colorado (1893) and Idaho (1896).

A referendum in California failed in 1896, and as in South Dakota, Shaw and Catt blamed men of color and immigrants, in this case the Chinese. Shaw angrily declared that "every Chinese vote was against us," though very few Chinese men were among the thousands of male voters who rejected the referendum.[31] Catt likewise complained of uninformed "Chinese voters, in 'pigtails' and sandals, at the polling booths" as they cast "their votes to deny self-government to American women." Assessing the failed campaigns of that decade years later, Catt likewise blamed nonwhite men for almost all of them. "There had been hours for the Indian, the Russian, the German, the Chinese, the foreigner, the saloon, hours when each had decided the limits of woman's sphere, but no woman's hour had come."[32]

Despite the mixed success of the western campaigns of the 1890s, the leaders of NAWSA recognized that the strategy of winning suffrage state by state was working. To capitalize on that energy, they chose to have their annual conference in Portland, Oregon, in 1905. It was the first NAWSA meeting west of the Mississippi Valley. They had been invited to the city to have their conference correspond with Portland's World's Fair, extravagantly called the Lewis and Clark Centennial and American Pacific Exposition and Oriental Fair.[33]

The fair celebrated the course of American empire, linking the transcontinental expansion of the United States to its Pacific possessions. In his speech requesting congressional funding for the fair, Oregon representative Binger Hermann emphasized the importance of Lewis and Clark's 1804–6 expedition for establishing America's claim on the Pacific Coast, a claim that, a century later, placed the United States at an advantage in trade. He pointed to a continuous colonial pursuit stretching from the role of Lewis and Clark in claiming the Pacific Northwest for the United States to the recent actions establishing territorial "stepping stones" across the Pacific: Hawaii, Guam, and the Philippines.[34] For any visitors who remained unclear about the meaning of the name, the fair's entrance, a Roman imperial–style colonnade, was emblazoned with the words "Westward the Course of Empire Takes Its Way." Both Asians and Indians were invoked at the fair. Eager to tap the markets in the Far East, Hermann suggested that the steamships on the Pacific would soon bring Chinese people carrying Chinese goods. He also referenced Native women, describing the "nucleus" of the first settlement in Oregon as consisting of white men from the Lewis and Clark and Astoria expeditions "living with Indian women of the country."[35]

Oregon suffragists also invoked people of color, specifically Sacagawea, who had been part of the Lewis and Clark expedition. They turned her into a symbol of women's equality for their cause. In 1902 a local Oregonian, Eva Emery Dye, rewrote a history of the expedition that credited Sacagawea as its navigator and "princess." Dye had also founded the Sacagawea Statue Association and raised funds for a sculpture to be displayed at the fair. The piece, created by Alice Cooper, another white woman, featured a young woman (modeled after contemporary Shoshone girls) in a buckskin dress with a buffalo robe around her shoulders and carrying a baby on her back. She looks west, extending her arm in that direction while stepping forward.

Susan B. Anthony and Anna Howard Shaw, in town for the NAWSA conference, were invited to be guests of honor at the statue's unveiling. Both gave speeches. Shaw, now president of NAWSA, waxed eloquent about Sacagawea:

> Forerunner of civilization, great leader of men, patient and motherly woman, we bow our hearts to do you honor! Your tribe is fast disappearing from the land of your fathers. May we, the daughters of an alien race who slew your people and usurped your country, learn the lessons of calm endurance, of patient persistence and unfaltering courage exemplified in your life, in our efforts to lead men through the Pass of justice, which goes over the mountains of prejudice and conservatism to the broad land of the perfect freedom of a true republic; one in which men and women together shall in perfect

equality solve the problems of a nation that knows no caste, no race, no sex in opportunity, in responsibility or in justice![36]

In Shaw's vision of the future, Native women were foremothers only, since their nations were "fast disappearing"—in the future, few if any would remain to participate in that equal society.[37] Had Shaw forgotten about the actual Native men who were campaigning for the vote in South Dakota in 1890? Perhaps she believed the rhetoric of the federal Indian Office and various "Friends of the Indian" who were arguing that, as a result of the federal government's assimilation programs, especially its system of boarding schools and efforts to divide communally held reservation land into individually owned allotments, Indians were melting into the American citizenry, to disappear within a generation.

Many national organizers from NAWSA would stay on in Oregon to lead the state suffrage campaign in 1906. That year would be a disappointment, but Oregon women tried again six years later and were successful. Their victory signaled a turning tide in the West. The shift was led by women in Washington State in 1910. Though the territorial legislature had granted women the right to vote in Washington, it had not been written into the state's constitution and required another vote. In 1911 women in California creatively used elements of popular culture, redeploying them in an exuberant campaign for the vote. Their golden posters adorned department store windows while they motored around the Golden State in modern automobiles raising awareness of their cause. Along with Oregon, Arizona and Kansas came into the fold in 1912. Kansas had also involved a particularly colorful campaign, with the state's golden sunflowers becoming a national symbol of suffrage. Two years later Montana and Nevada joined the pantheon of states—all in the West—granting full suffrage to women. This left only New Mexico, one of the newest states in the region, as an outlier on the issue of woman suffrage.

The West became the beacon of inspiration for the rest of the nation, and suffragists drew their strategies from activists in the region. But their successes often applied only to white women. In early 1916, the Woman's Journal, NAWSA's magazine, printed a list of populations excluded from suffrage in each state. On one hand, it sought to shock readers that some white women were disenfranchised along with the disabled, criminal, and nonwhite. But it also indicated that suffragists knew very clearly who was denied the vote. In many western states this explicitly meant Native people, usually described as "Indians who have not severed tribal relations." Such laws applied to Native people in the territory of Alaska and the states of Arizona, Minnesota, Montana, New Mexico, North Dakota, Oklahoma, Washington, and Wisconsin as well as the non-western states of Maine, Michigan, and Mississippi.[38]

Today we are very aware of how Jim Crow voting laws targeted African American men through poll taxes and literacy tests but are less familiar with how other states borrowed these strategies to disenfranchise their "undesirable" populations as well.[39] Take, for example, California, which had passed woman suffrage but continued to block "idiots, insane, embezzlers of public moneys, those convicted of infamous crime, [and] persons unable to read and write in English." The latter category aimed directly at the state's Chinese population but could also apply to Spanish speakers and Indigenous people who spoke their tribal languages. Arizona used a similar formulation, and Montana's exclusions mirrored Arizona's almost exactly, suggesting the borrowing of legal codes across states.[40] Wyoming blocked "persons unable to read the State Constitution." The territory of Hawaii also focused on excluding Asian immigrants but protected the weakened though continued power of Native Hawaiians with its laws against "idiots, insane, felons, those unable to speak, read and write the English or Hawaiian language, [and] women." New Mexico similarly protected its Catholic Spanish-speaking population, which held political power in the state, by declaring that the right to vote "shall not be restricted, abridged, or impaired, on account of religion, race, language or color, or inability to speak, read or write the English or Spanish language," even as it excluded Indians living in tribal relations. Several eastern states also used English-only clauses to disenfranchise immigrants, but in the West, these were primarily aimed at the Chinese men who had arrived during the gold rush and built the nation's railroads.[41]

It may have come as a surprise, then, how central the Chinese became to American suffragists' strategies in 1912.

[CHAPTER 2]
Our Sisters in China Are Free
Mabel Ping-Hua Lee

The shadows were just starting to slide across New York's Washington Square Park on the evening of May 5, 1912, when a company of fifty women on horseback trotted smartly around the east side of the park's triumphal arch. Their arrival was the signal that the great suffrage procession, the largest in the nation's history, had begun. They led the parade of 17,000 women up Fifth Avenue. On their heads they wore tricornered hats reminiscent of the American Revolution topped with knots of purple, green, and white ribbons, the colors of Harriet Stanton Blatch's Women's Political Union. The women in the cavalcade represented the finest of New York society as well as prominent suffrage activists.

Among them was Mabel Ping-Hua Lee, the Chinese suffragist whose presence had been much anticipated in the papers for weeks beforehand.[1] Lee's appearance at the front of the parade was not an accident. Organizers had invited her to be there to remind viewers of the recent revolution in China and the enfranchisement of women that they believed it had inaugurated.[2] Lee herself was pleased with the opportunity to draw the United States' attention to events in China, as she hoped to challenge Americans' stereotypes about the backwardness of her nation.

In the United States, 1912 became the year of the Chinese suffragist. Americans closely watched the unfolding of the Chinese Revolution, focusing on the participation of Chinese women and the women's rights being championed by the republican revolutionaries under Dr. Sun Yat-sen. White suffragists seized upon these news stories to support their cause by using them to shame American men. They looked for Chinese women living in the United States who could tell them more about events in China. Those women, some American-born but most of them immigrants barred from naturalized citizenship, drew on transpacific conversations to educate their white sisters about the women's movement in China. Having captured their attention, Chinese women used the opportunity to raise their concerns about the United States' policies toward China. As a result, Chinese and Chinese American women were unexpectedly visible in American suffrage debates and events.

During the fall of 1911 and into 1912, Sun Yat-sen's Tongmenghui, or Revolutionary Alliance, battled the Quing Empire, overthrew that 268-year-old dynasty, and established the Chinese republic. Chinese women, especially students, had been early supporters of the Revolutionary Alliance. They worked in underground revolutionary networks, recruiting other students, writing powerful articles and manifestos, carrying secret messages, and serving as spies. Many of them were attracted by Sun and the Alliance's emphasis on women's rights. When open conflict broke out, they raised money and provided medical assistance for the troops, and one woman, Tang Qunying, even formed a military organization called the Women's Northern Attack Brigade with two of her friends. During the Wuchang Uprising, Tang led the famous "women's army" into battle, helping capture Nanking (Nanjing).[3] Americans were astonished to see pictures of these "Chinese amazons" under resounding headlines like "The Chinaman's Better Half? Wideawake Woman Is Encouraging the Rebellion against the Manchus."[4]

These Chinese women were elated when Sun Yat-sen became provisional president of the new nation at the beginning of 1912. He had long supported women's rights and had promised them suffrage as soon as the revolution suc-ceeded. In February, Chinese suffragists, including Tang Qunying, had two meet-ings with Sun in Nanking. They presented him with funds they had raised for the new nation and inquired about his promises. They reminded him of their ser-vice to the nation as soldiers, mothers, and citizens. He graciously accepted the money but avoided making a strong statement in favor of immediate suffrage. It was an important matter, he agreed, but out of his hands. He urged the women to qualify themselves for the vote by educating themselves as to the government and laws. When women were ready, he had no doubt that they would be given the vote. His acknowledgment of the importance of woman suffrage and his assur-ances that it would be granted went out across the world. The *Salt Lake Tribune*, for example, reported "Chinese President Plans Reforms: Women Want Electoral Franchise." Chinese women were optimistic.[5]

White suffragists in the United States closely followed the news from China. Rumors that Chinese women had been enfranchised reached New York on a blustery March day in 1912. A number of the city's women were gathered at the Women's Industrial Exhibition at the Beaux Arts–inspired New Grand Central Palace, which for the next half a century would serve as the city's main exhibition hall. In the expansive showrooms on the second and third floors, attendees were marveling at the latest products for the modern woman. Electric vacuums and other labor-saving devices for housewives sat next to displays announcing fash-ionable hairstyles, fancy perfumes, and luscious looking cosmetics, which only recently had been deemed acceptable for respectable women. Local suffragists had set up shop in the hall, insisting that the vote was also an essential feature of modern womanhood. They outfitted their booth with bold posters designed to attract the passing crowds to the table, where women pressed pamphlets into their hands and urged them to buy suffrage buttons.[6]

In the midst of the expo, rumors that Chinese women had won the right to vote flashed over the wires. Florence Ivins,[7] a suffrage booth volunteer whose husband would soon become a curator at the Metropolitan Museum of Art and who thus may have known a thing or two about displays, seized the moment. She quickly made up a poster declaring "The People of China Have Enfranchised Their Women" and hung it to be seen by all. Crowds surged to the table, and the suffragists did a brisk business in buttons—even, they claimed, to some anti-suffragists. They attributed the crowds' run on their booth to the "indignation felt by American women" who felt poorly treated in comparison. Indeed, the white suffragists themselves were "glad, but irritated, too," by the news.[8]

The irritation felt by white suffragists stemmed from Americans' most contempt toward China and Chinese immigrants to the United States. These attitudes had arisen in California as white workers derided Chinese men who they believed were taking their jobs; they were also shaped by wider ideas about the difference between the Occident and the Orient. The Workingmen's Party, founded by Irish immigrant Denis Kearney in 1876, had castigated Chinese men as "coolie labor," contract workers who were just above slaves—a powerful metaphor for Americans still reeling from the Civil War and emancipation. These "enslaved" Chinese men, they contemptuously sneered, frequented prostitutes, Chinese girls sold for that immoral purpose by their own countrymen—this instead of establishing and supporting "normal" families like proud, independent American men. Even worse, they accused the Chinese of undercutting wages because they could live on "rice and rats" while real Americans required meat and bread for their families.[9]

These ideas had a long life. For decades, describing the odd un-Americanness of the Chinese had been a minor industry for politicians, journalists, missionaries, nascent social scientists, and assorted hacks. They described Chinese men as effeminate, slavish, and the political inferiors of white Americans; meanwhile, Chinese women were characterized as drudges or prostitutes whose bound feet indicated their cowed nature. In 1902 Samuel Gompers, president of the American Federation of Labor, bluntly repeated these notions in a pamphlet titled *Meat vs. Rice—American Manhood vs. Asiatic Coolieism. Which Shall Survive?*[10]

The politicians perpetuating these ideas argued that China was too different and its people too foreign to become citizens of a modern democracy—so foreign, in fact, that the Chinese became the first nationality that Congress banned from immigrating. The Page Act of 1875 had been explicitly aimed at Chinese people. Passed just seven years after the ratification of the Fourteenth Amendment, the act plainly intended to reduce the number of Chinese immigrants to the United States. It contained two elements: one banned unfree "coolie labor," while the second aimed to exclude prostitutes. The latter was directed primarily at Chinese women, as most Americans and especially immigration officials held the "presumption that every Chinese woman is a prostitute." Given the new articulation of birthright citizenship, the notion of Chinese prostitutes bearing children on U.S. soil might have alarmed white Americans. Representative

Horace Page of California, who had introduced the bill, drew on these stereotypes when he argued that the Chinese were "a class of people wholly unworthy
to be entrusted with the right of American citizenship."[11]

The Page Act was augmented in 1882 by the Chinese Exclusion Act, which
effectively banned the vast majority of Chinese immigration to the United States.
The act granted only very specific exemptions to "every Chinese person other
than a laborer," which in practice meant merchants, teachers, students, and ministers. The law was renewed every ten years until 1924, when it was made permanent as part of that year's restrictive National Origins Act.[12]

Mabel Lee's family history spanned this xenophobic era and was shaped by it.
Her father, Lee Towe, arrived in California in 1874 when he was twelve years old.
He disembarked in San Francisco, a city that would soon ring with the fervent
anti-Chinese speeches of the California Workingmen's Party. But he also found
some sympathetic Americans. He enrolled in church-sponsored English classes
at the Tenth Avenue Baptist Church in Oakland and soon converted to Christianity.[13] He briefly returned to Canton, where he studied theology at the Graves'
Theological Seminary, and met and married Lai Beck. When he returned to the
United States, he was admitted because as a missionary he was exempted from
the restriction laws. Lai Beck and their daughter Mabel remained in China. In
1901, Lai Beck applied for immigration papers as a teacher and also received an
exemption. She and Mabel sailed to California to join her husband.[14] The family
briefly settled in San Francisco, where Mabel attended public schools.[15] Within
a year they had moved north to Washington State, where Lee Towe took charge
of the Chinese mission of the First Baptist Church of Spokane. Their brief so-
journ in Spokane held both joys and sorrows for the family: Lee Towe celebrated
his ordination at the church, while Lai Beck gave birth to a son who died soon
after delivery. This was the second time that she had borne a son who died in infancy, an experience that must have been devastating. Years later Mabel still remembered her brothers, even though they had been in the world for only a short
time.[16]

Soon the Baptist Church moved the family to New York City. Although most
of the Chinese immigrants in the United States lived in the West, by 1910 there
were roughly 4,500 Chinese people in New York City.[17] The majority of those were
men who had moved east after western opportunities in mining and railroads
dried up and they were violently run out of many communities by white mobs.[18]
The Chinese Exclusion Act was also changing the demographics of the nation.
Baptist missionaries reported that they noticed "a steady decrease in the Chinese
population" as the law cut off new immigration. They also pointed out "a notice-
able movement eastward which accelerates the depletion of the Chinese population of California. In the Atlantic States, on the contrary, there was an absolute
gain of 141 per cent."[19] The Lee family was part of this movement.

In New York Lee Towe began to work at the Morningstar Mission on Mott Street. It was in the middle of Chinatown, situated just east of the city's courts. The Chinese Consolidated Benevolent Association anchored the neighborhood at 6 Mott Street and a Chinese Theater opened its doors at 5–7 Doyers. Chinese restaurants and shops quickly sprang up around these institutions and spilled over into Pell Street, which ran perpendicular to Mott and Doyers.[20] This U-shaped series of streets became a magnet that attracted the curious, including reporters like Jacob Riis and Louis Beck who recorded their impressions for uptown audiences. While sometimes sympathetic, their reports mostly reinforced long-held stereotypes that Chinese men were secretive and exotic, dangerous opium smokers who might lure white women to their underground dens. They described Chinese women as scarce, almost nonexistent, making Chinatown a strange community of bachelors.[21]

With China and its people held in such low regard by most Americans, white suffragists were embarrassed that Chinese republicans had enfranchised women before the most modern nation in the world. As one suffragist grumbled, the ongoing disenfranchisement of white women was "a discredit to the men of this country." Anna Howard Shaw, now president of NAWSA, knew of the Revolutionary Alliance's support for women's rights and had been predicting such a victory in China. However, she had also been known to make anti-Chinese statements herself as when in 1896 she had blamed Chinese men in California for the defeat of a suffrage referendum in that state.[22] Her previous reservations notwithstanding, Shaw immediately set out to celebrate Chinese women's achievements and to use white Americans' bewilderment and chagrin over the events in China as a weapon in the fight for suffrage.[23]

Across the nation, from Portland, Oregon, to Cincinnati and Boston, white activists joined with Chinese suffragists to publicize China's achievement and contrast it with women's voting rights in America.[24] On April 10, 1912, just a few weeks after the news reached the United States, Shaw, along with Alva Belmont, "probably the wealthiest suffragette in the world," and Harriet Laidlaw, chairman of the Manhattan branch of the Woman Suffrage Party, gathered for a meeting with a group of Chinese suffragists at the Peking Restaurant at the corner of Seventh Avenue and Forty-Seventh Street. At least five members of the Chinese community attended: Grace Yip Typond, wife of a powerful merchant; Pearl Mark Loo (Mai Zhouyi), a teacher and missionary in Chinatown; Rev. Lee Towe, minister of the Morningside Mission; Lee's wife, Lee Lai Beck; and their daughter Mabel. They were joined by Mrs. Charles Peck, a white missionary who worked with them in Chinatown.[25]

Reporting on the meeting, the press fell into the old tropes of describing Chinese women as cowed and helpless. Journalists held up Mrs. Peck, the white missionary, as the driving force of the meeting. "I am not a suffragist myself,"

WOMEN SUFFRAGISTS AND THEIR CHINESE ALLIES.
Left to right—Mrs. Loo Jin holding Miss Ying Long, Dr. George Kirchwey, Miss Fung Li, Mrs. Charles E. Peck, Mrs. James I.
Laidlaw, Dr. Anna H. Shaw, Miss Mabel Lee, Mrs. Frank Stratton and Mrs. Lee Towe.

White suffragists across the nation sought out Chinese suffragists to learn more about the role of women in the Chinese Revolution of 1911. Suffragists like Pearl Mark Loo (Mai Zhouyi), Mabel Lee, and Lee Lia Beck, pictured here with national suffrage leaders in New York City, also used the opportunity to advocate for the issues faced by Chinese American communities. (New York Tribune, April 11, 1912)

she declared, but she admitted that she could get no one else to help her with her mission in Chinatown and thus accepted the suffragists' offer to meet. Reporters sympathized, painting a picture of the heroic white missionary as the brains behind efforts to uplift the Chinese women from ignorance and poverty. They suggested that the Chinese women were isolated in their homes by patriarchal custom, shunned by American society, and dependent on Mrs. Peck to help them. They had never been out in public before, one reporter stated, and "had unbounded faith in Mrs. Peck's word."[26]

The Chinese women at the meeting would likely have have found such a description of their ignorance grating, as it certainly did not fit their actual experiences. The Chinese women came prepared with political speeches and had dressed their children in suffrage colors. One little girl wore a lavender and blue coat that sported a row of "Votes for Women" buttons across the front.[27]

The Chinese women at the meeting doubtless appreciated Mrs. Peck's help and her wider connections, but they were by no means helpless or hapless. They were a well-educated group whose husbands and fathers were leaders in their community. Like many middle-class white women, they focused their efforts on the uplift of the poor. They had previously organized themselves as the Chinese Women's Club for Mutual Encouragement and sponsored a series of fundraisers for Chinese famine victims. For example, working with the YWCA, they created

PRELUDE AND PARADES, 1890–1913

tableaux of six historical scenes in the life of Chinese women, showing progress from the "conservative past" to the "modern present." Afterward, the costumed players served Chinese tea in special teacups that they gave to the audience members as souvenirs.[28]

Soon the room at the Peking grew crowded with women in large hats. They sat at tables between elaborately painted square pillars and under ornate lanterns. The decor allowed the white women to feel a tingle of the exotic without actually going to Chinatown, where they imagined the buildings and basements were full of salacious misdeeds. The honored guests took their places on the speaker's platform: Rev. Lee Towe, Lee Lai Beck, and Mabel Lee were on the left; on the other side of the platform Anna Howard Shaw sat next to Harriet Laidlaw, who was presiding over the meeting.[29]

Some of the guests at the Peking were likely disappointed by Reverend Lee's short hair, suit, and tie, but Mabel and her mother were outfitted in what the New York Herald was delighted to call "their Oriental finery." More than one white suffragist must also have compared the generational difference between the unbound feet of Mabel and those of her mother, whose feet were encased in tiny arched slippers. To some, Lee Lai Beck's bound feet reinforced their ideas about traditional Chinese women. She may have had bound feet and may have rendered her name the Chinese way, with surname first, but Lee Lai Beck also chose to leave the house to attend the suffrage meeting and supported her daughter's public speech. The Lees had chosen a modern path for their daughter. Likely influenced by her conversion to Christianity, but also by criticism from Chinese women's activists, Mabel's mother did not bind her daughter's feet. Both parents also encouraged her education in both Chinese and Western traditions. She attended public school, first at PS #1 on Henry Street, just a few blocks from her family's apartment on Bayard Street in Chinatown. She excelled in her studies and soon transferred to the prestigious Erasmus Hall High School in Brooklyn, where she was the only Chinese student in her class.[30]

All of the Chinese women who spoke that afternoon considered themselves modern, progressive ladies. They drew on ongoing social debates in both the United States and China to formulate solutions to the problems faced by their communities. Despite that, they all had the term "alien" listed next to their names in the U.S. census. Having been born in China, none were eligible to become U.S. citizens, no matter how long they lived in America.[31]

The Chinese women spoke of the women's movement in China while also calling their audience's attention to the difficulties faced by the Chinese community in the United States. Grace Typond, the wife of a powerful leader in Chinatown, spoke on the lack of educational opportunities for Chinese women in the city. Pearl Mark Loo called for U.S. citizenship for Chinese women, likely sharing with the audience her own harrowing tale of having been detained for months by the Immigration and Naturalization Service in San Francisco despite her education and white missionary traveling companions.[32] Before coming to the United States she had lived in Canton and worked as a teacher. She had been involved in the women's movement there and served as the editor of the *Lingnan Women's Journal*. She believed education was essential to both women's rights and the strength of a nation, be it China or the United States. "The key to a country's prosperity lies in its women's propensity for learning," she insisted.[33]

Mabel Lee spoke next. In introducing Lee, Harriet Laidlaw announced that she had been admitted to Barnard College for the fall. The young woman stood confidently on the stage in a long coat with a high mandarin collar. Her parents, sitting behind her, were pleased and supportive as she addressed some of the most famous women in America.

Mabel Lee was proud of being Chinese and excited about the new nation presaged by the recent revolution in China. Nonetheless, she still had many thoughts on the treatment of the Chinese in the United States, especially Chinese women. She spoke eloquently on the topic, concluding with a plea for equality and a condemnation of the racism that limited Chinese women in the United States.[34] She appealed to the suffragists' devotion to sex equality, pointing out that these racist restrictions hit Chinese women hardest of all. "All women are recognized in New York, excepting Chinese Women," she reminded them. "She is not included in your educational institutions. Your social and recreational centers do not include her. How can she learn! How can you have half of your people in utter darkness, and the other half in light!" In contrast, she proudly pointed to the new Chinese government's efforts to promote female education and suffrage. For Chinese women, suffrage was important, and they were clearly in support of it, but they also recognized that unlike their white sisters, the political arena was not the only site from which they were excluded, nor was their exclusion solely on the basis of their sex.[35]

Whether or not this message got through, white suffragists welcomed the chance to work with the women of Chinatown, and together they laid plans for the Chinese women's participation in the upcoming "Votes for Women" parade scheduled for May 4, 1912.

Harriet Stanton Blatch, daughter of Elizabeth Cady Stanton and head of the Women's Political Union, had taken on the gargantuan task of organizing the parade. A good friend of radical British suffragist Emmeline Pankhurst, Blatch was not afraid to aim high or make waves. In England, she had watched suffragettes chain themselves to fences, smash shop windows, and initiate hunger strikes. She was not deterred by bad publicity. "Ridicule, ridicule, ridicule, blessed be ridicule," she once declared. She had begun planning the 1912 parade immediately after the suffrage parade in 1911 had seen an unprecedented turnout of 3,000 marchers that garnered them some much sought after publicity.[36]

Only a few years earlier, public spectacles like parades were beyond the pale for respectable suffragists. The more conservative organizations had objected to them as too militant and too radical. City leaders in New York agreed. In 1908, they refused to issue a parade permit to a group of suffragists, but twenty-three women marched anyway. Just two years later, four hundred women insisted on their rights by parading in the streets and using floats for the first time.

These tactics worked. The press, which had ignored suffragist activities in New York, suddenly found them newsworthy. Any publicity meant more successful fundraising. Blatch's budget increased sevenfold during those years. More money allowed her to rent an office, hire staff and organizers, and eventually start her own suffrage newspaper. This era saw the birth of modern advertising, and suffragists like Blatch eagerly borrowed ideas from department stores and corporations to sell their cause. For the 1912 parade, she wanted an event that would be so large, so well organized, so provocative that no one could ignore it. "The enemy must be converted through his eyes," she strategized. "He must see uniformity of dress. He must realize . . . the discipline of the individual, of the group, of the whole from start to finish."[37]

As the day of the parade approached, women from across the city's boroughs, in neighboring counties, and even over state lines furiously made preparations. Volunteers arrived at headquarters ready to send out press releases, stuff envelopes for direct mailings, and wrap magazines in brown paper. They sewed letters onto banners for marchers to carry. They encouraged participants to buy the special twenty-eight-cent parade hats available at local department stores and to pick out white dresses to wear with them. Blatch dispatched an army of young women to the streets, deliberately choosing those who were young, "pretty," and white so as to garner more attention. She assigned them to drumming up publicity for the parade and encouraging other girls to participate, which they did with gusto. Carrying news bags stuffed with suffrage literature, they drew attention to themselves and their cause. Some marched up and down the sidewalk behind a hand organ player; others stood on street corners holding parasols emblazoned with "Votes for Women." Still others put on their white dresses, pinned on their suffrage sashes, and went out into the city parks. Standing under banners, they enjoined young working girls on their lunch breaks to join the parade.

The press helped generate excitement as well by focusing on the women from Chinatown, especially young Mabel Lee. For weeks reporters had touted her upcoming role in papers from New York to Atlanta to Topeka: "Chinese Girl in Parade," announced many. "Chinese Girl Wants Vote," stated others.[38] A number of newspapers around the Midwest went with less-flattering headlines, such as "Suffragettes on Parade: Cavalrymen, Negroes and Chinese in Line." Such copy asserted that those marching were not respectable (white) women, perhaps not even women at all.[39] The morning of the parade, readers of the *New York Times* awoke to find a reminder emblazoned in large print: "Chinese Women to Ride."[40] Throughout the afternoon of May 4, women arrived at Washington Square. As

Mabel Lee rode in the opening cavalcade of the 1912 New York City suffrage parade. Her presence was highly anticipated, and newspapers across the country ran illustrated stories about her. This photograph was featured in a montage of images in the Washington Post. Other women from New York's Chinatown also participated in the parade, celebrating Chinese women's rights and defying American stereotypes about foot-bound and passive Chinese women. (Washington Post, May 6, 1912)

MISS MABEL LEE.

the start time approached, the magnitude of the event became clear. Marchers crowded streets around the park, looking for large signs bearing the letter that marked each group's position. Crowds also pushed into the neighborhood to gawk. Organizers were thrilled that the day presented perfect weather.

At precisely 5 p.m., the marchers set out. Mabel Lee was one of the first women to head up Fifth Avenue with the opening cavalcade. Dressed in her dark riding costume with her hair pulled back under her hat, she looked down from her horse upon packed sidewalks, twenty people deep in some places. Spectators crowded stoops and leaned from the windows. Women excitedly waved their handkerchiefs and scarves, and boys shouted. Young men with their hats tilted aggressively to the side made suggestive comments. The crowd looked back at her, some peering at her feet in curiosity. A newspaper photographer moved up close to her horse's neck and snapped a picture, capturing her confident pose as she sat tall and held the reins low and firm.

As Lee rode up the avenue, the largest women's parade ever seen in America followed in her wake. After she and her mounted sisters came the representatives of the Women's Political Union in their parade hats with purple, green, and white sashes across their chests demanding "Votes for Women" and carrying a large banner in the same colors. Behind them marched their president, Harriet Stanton Blatch, and Alice J. G. Perkins, both resplendent in their college caps and robes: Blatch in Vassar College's pink and gray and Perkins in the blue and white of Columbia University.

Then in perfect order from the side streets surged other groups of women. From along Washington Square North came the lobbyists urging the state senate in Albany to pass suffrage legislation. Next marched the educators, their appearance eliciting excited shouts as students along the route recognized their teachers.[41] At East Ninth Street the professional women joined in: lawyers, doctors, musicians, writers, artists, librarians, lecturers, and social workers. From the west side of Ninth Street came industrial workers: dressmakers, milliners, shirtwaist makers, and laundry and domestic laborers. From Tenth Street poured businesswomen, managers, buyers, tearoom proprietors, bookkeepers and secretaries, stenographers and telephone operators.

Banners and standards punctuated the parade as each group proudly asserted its professional identity. Teachers hoisted the tree of learning and printers the tree of knowledge. Other workingwomen unfurled flags adorned with trade symbols: a sewing machine waved above the dressmakers, a hat over the milliners, and a kettle over the cooks. Many held aloft banners bearing the names of historic figures in their fields: doctors honored Dr. Mary Putnam Jacobi while nurses celebrated Florence Nightingale and Clara Barton. Writers bore the names of Louisa May Alcott and Harriet Beecher Stowe.

Large banners billowed across the route emblazoned with bold phrases: "We prepare children for the world. We ask to prepare the world for our children!" "More ballots, less bullets!" "Of the twenty States having the fewest illiterate children women vote in eighteen." "All this is the natural consequence of teaching girls to read." Women's bands enthusiastically sounded trumpets, trombones, and tubas as they walked among the marching groups, rendering patriotic airs with up-tempo beats.[42] The strains of suffrage songs rose from the marchers' throats as their boots kept time on the pavement.

The marching women were followed by carriages adorned with yellow buttercups pulled by teams wearing plumes of yellow feathers and driven by coachmen dressed in yellow and black holding yellow reins. These carried the elderly suffrage pioneers too frail to march as well as two "future voters," Harriet Blatch's young granddaughters. The oldest surviving suffragist in the country at eighty-six, Rev. Antoinette Brown Blackwell, followed in a car trimmed in lavender.

Behind the pioneers came the successes. Representatives from western suffrage states proudly marched. Special trains had carried a large contingent from California, whose voters had granted women the vote the previous year. Foreign women with the franchise marched here, too, women from Denmark and Finland, and Swedes who stood out in their red and white dresses.

Next came perhaps the most anticipated group: the women from Chinatown. Pearl Mark Loo and others from the Twelfth Assembly District proudly represented the new Chinese nation. Loo led the group, bearing aloft the flag of the

Republic of China with its red, yellow, blue, white, and black horizontal stripes celebrating the five main ethnic groups of the new nation.[43] Most of the women wore Chinese coats and caps, and several carried banners.[44] "Light from China," read one, cleverly throwing Americans' words back at them, rejecting the appellation "benighted heathens" or a people in darkness. There were reports of a second banner that read "Women vote in China, but are classed with criminals and paupers in New York." Mabel Lee's mother, Lai Beck, was there, too, but rode in a car, unable to walk the route of the parade.[45] The *New York Times* reminded spectators that her "tiny, unfranchised feet" were just out of sight. The press's obsessive focus on the women's feet suggested that the problem lay in a hidebound culture that crippled women and denied them the freedom of movement available to American women, even if they lacked the vote. The Chinese women countered by appearing in public and asserting with their banners that the problem was not how Chinese men treated their women but how the people of the United States viewed the Chinese.[46]

Deliberately positioned directly behind the Chinese women marched Anna Howard Shaw, president of NAWSA. In her college cap and velvet-trimmed robe she solemnly held aloft a turquoise banner with golden fringe that declared, "NAWSA Catching Up with China."[47] While on the face of things Shaw's banner was complimentary to China, it also challenged New Yorkers to right the role reversal that had placed China in an enlightened position and the United States in the backward one. Only by enfranchising American women could the United States maintain its purported superiority.[48]

African American women, too, had carefully choreographed their part in the parade. They donned black dresses topped with striking yellow sashes, reversing the organizers' call to wear light frocks. Some carried American flags while others waved yellow and black pennants. But reporters treated black women very differently from the highly publicized Chinese women whose names and pictures they circulated around the nation. They virtually ignored the black women. Some reporters briefly noted their presence but refused to differentiate them, lumping them together as nameless "negresses." The *New York Times* deigned only to comment that their leader was a "great fighter," without further details.[49]

African American readers may have assumed that the great fighter was Irene L. Moorman, president of the Negro Women's Business League who also presided over the "colored" branch of the Political Equality Association. Parade planners had reached out to her and other prominent black women in the city but for different reasons from the ones with which they had approached the Chinese women. Unlike Chinese men, black men had the right to vote in New York State, and their ballots could help pass the state suffrage legislation. Moorman and other African American female activists in the city had been invited to join white suffrage groups in 1910. She was wary at first: she recognized that white suffragists' goals might not always align with hers, but she also saw that she could

WOMAN'S JOURNAL

OFFICIAL ORGAN OF THE NATIONAL AMERICAN WOMAN SUFFRAGE ASSOCIATION

VOL. XLIII NO. 19   SATURDAY, MAY 11, 1912   **FIVE CENTS**

GREAT SUFFRAGE PARADE

500,000 Crowd to See the Biggest Procession of Organized Womanhood Ever Held in this Country

ONE VIEW OF THE PARADE   REV. ANNA HOWARD SHAW AND HER BANNER

The Woman's Journal, mouthpiece of the National American Woman Suffrage Association, published this image of its president, Anna Howard Shaw, on the cover of its May 11 issue about the 1912 New York City parade. Shaw carried her banner, which read "NAWSA Catching Up with China," directly behind the contingent of women from Chinatown, literally and metaphorically placing white women behind Chinese women who had reportedly been enfranchised by the Republic of China. (Courtesy Schlesinger Library, Radcliffe Institute, Harvard University, Cambridge, Mass.)

gain powerful allies.[50] African American votes in New York City did not translate into respect from the press, however. The brief mentions about African Americans in contrast to the many articles highlighting Chinese women's participation suggest white America's racial hierarchies at the turn of the century. Still, Chinese women were not immune to the press's derision. None of the women in the parade would have been surprised by the dismissive articles that circulated over the wires questioning their reputations and using their race to mock them; those tactics were par for the course. One article picked up by a number of midwestern papers defamed white suffragists who, the reporter concluded, "ran long on lingerie and French heels." "Likewise, there were suffragettes of every shade. . . . These parti-colored advocates of equal suffrage, however, paled to insignificance beside the doughty Miss Tinker and her cavalcade of equestriennes," he wrote, referring to one of the suffragist leaders.[51]

The parade rolled on. Women from non-suffrage states, including Connecticut, Kansas, Maryland, Massachusetts, Nebraska, and New Hampshire, motored down the avenue in their automobiles. Embracing the new transportation technology, their presence behind the wheel also reminded spectators that they were modern women, independent, strong, and deserving of the vote. Marching a bit behind the autos were members of the Woman Suffrage Party who also touted the modern nature of their cause with new technology: electricity. Although Blatch anticipated that the parade would end before dark, they hoped to use their Greek lights, small eight-cent fireworks, which would bathe their whole division in red light as their grand marshal led them on with a battery-operated light on the end of her baton, symbolic of the light of women voters' influence on politics.[52]

And still more women came. Marchers representing a myriad of New York organizations surged forward: the Equal Franchise Society, the Legislative League, and county suffrage organizations. The women of the College League appeared in their caps and mortarboards. Next came unions full of workingwomen: the Wage Earner's League and the Women's Trade Union League. Many women working in the uptown department stores could not make it to Washington Square by 5 p.m., so they joined the parade at a prearranged point at Twenty-Seventh Street, where they poured into the route with Alva Belmont's Political Equality Association, waving blue banners as they came.

Following them came the men. Young collegians from the Ivy League schools of Columbia, Princeton, Harvard, and Yale were joined by fellows who worked for liberal causes or whose family connections to suffragists motivated them to march as allies. There was hardly a moment of the parade when gibes, catcalls, and hisses were absent, but the crowds' jeers grew louder as the men passed. "Henpecked" was a great favorite and thrown out with frequency. "Men who wished this curse upon you?" shouted one man loudly. "Can't youse fellows get a wife?" called one wag. "Who's minding the babies?" yelled another. The marching men refrained from responding to the shouts in kind. Instead, they enjoyed the affirmations they received from many of the young women on the route. To drown out the heckling, the men burst into the old Civil War tune "Tramp, Tramp, Tramp," its lyrics rewritten to reflect the suffrage fight:

Tramp, tramp, tramp, we're onward marching,
Good luck comrades, on the way!
And beneath the golden glow
Of the suffrage flag, we know
You will join us on the next election day!

The men finished their march to the ringing cheers of women who had completed the route. Bringing up the rear, and somewhat reluctantly included, were the scarlet-banded Socialists, reportedly singing the "Marseillaise."[53]

The parade came to an end at Carnegie Hall on Seventh Avenue and Fifty-Seventh Street. Crowds of marchers and spectators roiled together in some chaos on the street, blocking it tight. Photographers' flashes lit up the growing darkness, illuminating undulating flags and banners, hats and horses. Arriving first, Mabel Lee and the other horsewomen were met by grooms who attached leads to the horses' bridles, allowing the riders to dismount. A large number of marchers descended on the local restaurants for dinner. Suffrage banners and colorful hats and sashes hanging over the backs of chairs could be seen through the windows for blocks.[54]

Did the Chinese and African American women stay on there, or did they head back to their neighborhoods? Perhaps they joined the crowd who squeezed into Carnegie Hall to listen to speeches from the national and state suffrage leaders who had organized the parade. Police directed marchers into the hall, and when it filled, people crowded around and listened to the young suffragists dispatched throughout the neighborhood to give street corner addresses through megaphones. Inside, parade marshals turned ushers and directed women to seats and stage as the organist played them in to Wagner's "Pilgrim's Chorus." Three hundred of the women took their seats in the green and white camping chairs arranged on the stage under a golden yellow canopy. Behind them a row of Greek columns stood linked with a chain of green leaves. Potted palms and daisies rounded out the decorations.

In front of the crowd, exhausted but triumphant, sat the three speakers, Harriet Stanton Blatch, Anna Howard Shaw, and Anna Garlin Spencer. Blatch spoke and castigated both political parties for failing to support suffrage and then sat to thundering applause. Anna Garlin Spencer stood and first invoked their foremothers, women she had worked with as a young suffragist. Looking forward, she urged women to pursue a political agenda that helped "socialize the state" and clean up society. She insisted on better education for every child and called for policies ensuring that all children had the leisure to learn.

If they were in the crowd, the Chinese suffragists would have applauded this as an agenda they shared. But they would have recognized echoes of anti-Chinese propaganda in Spencer's insistence that the appointment of female judges and governors could "wipe out white slavery and cleanse the dark places" of their cities. The Chinese neighborhoods were the ones often painted as the "dark places" that threatened young white women and needed cleaning or purging. The women knew those ideas helped lead to Chinese exclusion and animated anti-Chinese campaigns, race riots, and murders.

The audience was appropriately warmed up for the formidable Dr. Shaw. Rising, she drew her audience's attention to the Chinese explicitly. Catching up the banner she had carried in the parade, Shaw began. America had had the chance to lead the world in enfranchising women, but now the oldest nation in the world has beaten us, she reminded her audience, her words carrying harsh judgment for America's men. It was a theme she would repeat in speeches with the banner over the course of the summer. Shaw was pleased with the day's success and encouraged her troops to keep fighting. "You are tired," she said, "but you have a joy that does not recognize fatigue. You go to bed weary this night, but you will rise to-morrow with a greater determination than ever." [55]

Throughout that summer and into the fall election season, women's winning of the vote in China stayed at the center of conversations in both pro- and anti-suffrage circles.[56] Shaw liked the impact of the banner she had carried in the parade and continued to flourish it at her speeches. Preparing to head to the Democratic convention in Baltimore in the fall, she spoke to a reporter. "If the Democratic party wants to catch up with China," she said, "they can give women the vote. China has waked up. Will they?" Reporters noted she was flaunting her "saucy banner,"[57] and quipped, "The Reverend Anna Howard Shaw has said she wishes she 'had been born with a queue.'"[58]

In her Equal Suffrage Song Sheaf, which she dedicated to Shaw, Eugénie M. Rayé-Smith included the song "Bring It to Pass in the Year," set to the tune of "Bring Back My Bonnie to Me." Its verses revealed suffragists' excitement over the news from China:

> Last night as we listened and waited,
> A message came over the sea,
> It wished us good luck and it stated,
> Our sisters in China are free.[59]

Anti-suffrage activists found that they had to address this line of argument. In Ohio and Michigan, where woman suffrage was to be on the ballot in the fall, Chinese women were frequently invoked. The antis decided their best strategy was to admit that some Chinese women had been enfranchised, but only those passing property and educational qualifications. Those limitations, they scoffed, were undemocratic. Signing her letter to the editor "A Woman Who Does Not," one anti argued, "The woman vote in China is very much a joke. It is, in reality, a vote of the aristocracy—is that what the Michigan suffragists want to introduce into this country?"[60] Under the headline "American Women Do Not Want to Catch Up with China," Mrs. Robert McVicker of Ohio asserted the suffragists "know very well that the vote in China is the vote of the aristocracy—something that would never be tolerated in this country."[61] They had apparently forgotten or merely overlooked similarly undemocratic measures in the United States, including literacy tests, understanding clauses, and poll taxes.

The stories about Chinese suffragists kept rolling in as fall approached. Especially prominent was the coverage of Carrie Chapman Catt's world suffrage tour. Catt, the president of the International Woman Suffrage Alliance, had embarked on her journey after attending the organization's meeting in Stockholm, Sweden. Catt wrote detailed descriptions of her travels and the women she met for the *Woman's Journal*, NAWSA's Boston-based suffrage magazine. Reporters like Ida Husted Harper distilled her reports into articles for newspapers such as the *New York Tribune*, feature pieces that were then republished throughout the nation.[62]

In September, Catt arrived in China. She was determined to learn the truth as to whether the new republican government had enfranchised women. The chaos and internal power struggles that had followed the revolution left Americans confused as to what was true. In Hong Kong, dozens of people, American and Dutch officials as well as Chinese supporters of the republic, assured her that there was no truth to the rumors that the new nation had enfranchised women. She and her traveling companion, Dr. Aletta Jacobs, set out for Canton, ninety miles from Hong Kong. As a stronghold of the republican government, they assumed there would be suffragists there. The unsettled situation in China became increasingly clear as they traveled upriver. The boat line announced that all precautions were being taken to protect the passengers, including stationing armed watchmen on deck. They read of pirates looting an American missionary station they passed and saw the patrol boats that had been called in for protection. Riding in sedan chairs from the docks to their hotel in Canton, they witnessed guards holding rifles on every street and found their hotel equally vigilant.[63]

As they set out to search for suffragists in the city, the hotel manager insisted that they take a guide as a precaution against foul play. Again climbing into sedan chairs, the only available transportation, Catt and Jacobs doggedly followed the clues in their letters of introduction. They decided to search for the Guangdong Provincial Assembly to learn of any suffrage legislation firsthand, but no one seemed to know where it met. Each person they encountered "gave us other names and clues, and these we chased up and down from north to south and east to west of the six square miles of Canton, in and out of its narrow streets, over bridges and through gateways, always in the midst of hurrying, scurrying throngs." For two days they scoured the city.[64]

Finally, the Dutch consul-general directed the pair to an old and hastily re-

THE TRUTH ABOUT SUFFRAGE IN CHINA By CARRIE CHAPMAN CATT

President of The International
Suffrage Alliance

MRS. CATT AND DR ALETTA JACOBS AT RECEPTION GIVEN BY CHINESE SUFFRAGISTS

Carrie Chapman Catt, president of the International Suffrage Alliance (and later president of NAWSA), illustrated her article in the November 16, 1912, issue of The Woman's Journal with this image of a suffrage meeting honoring her and Aletta Jacobs's visit to Shanghai. They also visited suffragists in Canton (Guangzhou) and Nanking (Nanjing). They met Zhang Mojun (Sophia Chang), founder and president of one of the first suffrage organizations in Shanghai, and Tang Qunying, leader of the "women's army." (Courtesy Schlesinger Library, Radcliffe Institute, Harvard University, Cambridge, Mass.)

paired building. They went inside and climbed into a gallery above the assembly hall. There Catt saw a sight that warmed her heart: ten women sitting as members of the assembly. The heat, the humidity, and her fatigue were forgotten as she looked upon the proceedings from the gallery. She was struck by the clothing of the assembly members. Some men wore European-style dress while others wore long light-colored gowns, and the women wore black outfits with trousers. She observed that two of the women had bound feet, but the building itself struck her as Western with "nothing Chinese nor even oriental about it." The proceedings were orderly and efficient as the legislators made their case and then stood to indicate their vote. The women, she noticed, did not always vote the same way. In the headline for an article she later wrote for the *Woman's Journal* she trumpeted, "The New China: She Sits in the Gallery and Looks Down on China's Ten Women Legislators, Who Had Been Called a Myth." [65] It was, she and Jacobs agreed, the most wonderful day of their lives.

In Shanghai and Nanking, Catt was thrilled to find more suffragists, though they could not vote. In Shanghai, she took tea with a committee of ten representing the two hundred members of the Chinese Ladies Mutual Helping Society (or the Shenzhou Women's United Assistance Society), an organization founded by a woman named Zhang Mojun (Sophia Chang) and which counted Sun Yat-sen's wife as a member.[66] It is possible that there were also representatives of the more radical women's organization led by Tang Qunying, as "one demure, tiny-footed little woman was pointed out as having carried many bombs into China from

Japan." Either way, Catt was delighted during the two hours they spent together. They told her about their organization and its goal of getting the vote for women and helping to prepare them for suffrage by working toward education.

Two days later they held a reception in Catt's honor at the Chang Su Ho Gardens. Some 350 men and women gathered for the event. Catt sat with her heart swelling with pride as she listened to Zhang Mojun address the audience. She was thrilled that "our cause had found so noble a leader in this far-away land." When Catt rose to address the crowd, she was also impressed with the interpreter, a young woman who had just returned from studying in the United States. The crowd applauded "with exactly the same spirit as in our own meetings," she observed, exulting at the display of international agreement. After the talks, they retired for tea in the garden, where the group gave her a banner to be presented at the next International Woman Suffrage Alliance. It was made of red silk, the Chinese color of happiness, they explained. It was bordered with white, and in the center they had embroidered a Chinese suffrage motto in white Chinese characters: "Helping each other / All of one mind."[67]

On her way home, when Catt's steamer paused to refuel in Honolulu, Hawaii Territory, she entered a place where many of the political currents from East and West swirled together and combined with the Indigenous politics of the islands. Catt thought of suffrage from the point of view of a white woman from the eastern United States, believing that all women shared her ideas. But in Hawaii, women connected the fight for suffrage with political struggles that differed from those on which Catt was focused, including Indigenous Hawaiian sovereignty and the power struggle in the new Chinese republic.

While in Honolulu, Catt was invited to address the Women's Equal Suffrage Association of Hawaii, which was primarily composed of elite Indigenous Hawaiian (Kanaka Maoli) women as well as a few white women. Catt, blithely unaware of the local politics, gave a speech reflecting the frustration white suffragists on the mainland felt when they saw foreign-born men (Italians in her example) voting before they did. For Kanaka Maoli women, however, the analogous foreign-born men were white Americans. Catt encouraged them to organize as a branch of NAWSA, which they did, and Hawaii sent representatives to NAWSA's annual conference the following year.[68]

Catt imagined women of different groups as unified in their fight, but they came to the suffrage struggle for many reasons. The Native Hawaiian women supported the cause as part of their effort to regain the political power they had lost after U.S. annexation. In 1893 white planters had overthrown Queen Lili'uokalani, ruler of the Kingdom of Hawaii. A few years later the United States annexed the islands. In the Organic Act of 1900 that made the islands a territory, Congress limited suffrage to white and Kanaka Maoli men despite the protestations of suffragists like Susan B. Anthony. She argued that the annexation was meant to give Native Hawaiians "the benefits of the most advanced civilization," which she argued was measured by "the approach of women toward the ideal of equal rights with men." Kanaka Maoli women would have pointed out to Anthony that they had already enjoyed equality with men, as Hawaiian society was more divided by status than gender. U.S. annexation in fact meant a loss of power for elite women.[69]

Many of the Hawaiian women Catt addressed had been very active in the anti-annexation movement and had turned to suffrage after the U.S. takeover. Their desire to recover the political power they lost in the overthrow meant that they were the most vocal group in the islands advocating that position. White women were more ambivalent. Congress had removed the property requirements on male voting with the result that Native Hawaiians were the largest group of voters on the islands. It was this demographic reality that made white planters and their wives worry that enfranchising women meant augmenting Native Hawaiian political power. Moreover, many of the white women descended from or were themselves Christian missionaries and believed that women's proper place was in the domestic rather than the political sphere.[70]

The Kanaka Maoli women who invited Catt also represented the multiracial population of Hawaii. Many of them descended from elite Indigenous Hawaiians who had intermarried with immigrants to the islands but continued to identify as Kanaka Maoli. They were led by Wilhelmine K. Widemann Dowsett, the daughter of a Hawaiian mother of chief rank and a German planter father. Some of the women were also of Kanaka Maoli and Chinese descent, like Emma ʻAima Aiʻi Nāwahī, whose mother was a Hawaiian princess and whose father was a Chinese sugar miller.

Despite the fact that some of the Kanaka Maoli women like Nāwahī were descended from Chinese settlers, the Women's Equal Suffrage Association of Hawaii did not seem interested in inviting Chinese suffragists from Honolulu's Chinatown. Perhaps this was because the territory's Organic Act had excluded Chinese people from suffrage rights, as Asians were "ineligible to naturalization."[71] It seems unlikely that the women were unaware of the Chinese activists. In June, a few months before Catt's visit, Honolulu's English-language papers carried a series of articles about a court case involving "Chinese suffragettes" and the editor of a local Chinese newspaper. Some four hundred members of the Chinese community turned out to watch the trial in which editor Chung You Hung of the Wah Hing Publishing Company sued a "bevy of Chinese suffragettes." He claimed that "he was attacked and violently beaten" by the women, who had approached him in his office and demanded he sign an apology for an insulting piece he had written. When he refused, their leader, Mrs. Lum Yip, yelled, "Strike him," and the women had proceeded to beat him with their umbrellas, rip his shirt, grab his "private parts," and choke him about the neck until, dizzy from the assault, he agreed to write out an apology.[72]

The seven women, whom papers described as "leaders of the Chinese woman suffrage organization," filed a countersuit. They arrived at the courthouse defiant with "umbrellas in their hands," even as a broken umbrella was admitted into evidence as proof of their assault.[73] Nonetheless, they represented themselves as respectable women and emphasized that they were wives of local leaders who had lived in Hawaii for some time, thirty years in the case of the "leader" Lum Chang Tai or Mrs. Lum Yip, wife of Lum Yip Kee, also known as the "Poi King."[74]

Under examination it became clear that this incident was part of the wider debates over the Chinese Revolution and women's rights that circulated throughout the Pacific world. It is worth remembering that Sun Yat-sen had been raised and educated in Hawaii. The first staunch supporters and donors of the Revolutionary Alliance were members of the Chinese diaspora in the Island Kingdom, including the husbands of the women on trial. It turns out that editor Chung was a supporter of Yuan Shikai, the man who had replaced Sun Yat-sen as provisional president of the Republic of China. Yuan had a much less favorable view of women's participation in governance, and with his support the Chinese parliament refused to add women's voting rights to the new constitution. Chung likely supported this position. He admitted that in his original article he had referred to the Honolulu Moon Kee Society and the Tong Ming Society (likely meaning Sun's Tongmenghui) as "monkey clubs" and "dog clubs." He also confirmed that he had described their members as "whores." He insisted, however, that he had not been referring to his attackers specifically when he used that language.[75]

The women responded to his insults by echoing the actions of Tang Qunying's radical Chinese suffrage group, the Alliance for Women's Political Participation. When Chinese suffragists in Nanking learned of their betrayal by Yuan Shikai and parliament, they were outraged. Tang along with nineteen other women of the alliance stormed the floor of the Chinese national legislature, breaking windows and chairs, attacking lawmakers, and demanding their rights. The Chinese suffragists in Honolulu followed the Alliance's example when Chung had attacked their position.[76] Whatever their motivations, they were found guilty of assault, paid their fines, and returned home.

The currents of revolution and women's rights moved both east and west across the Pacific. Just as Mabel Lee and the women who spoke at the Peking were aware of the political events in China, so were the Chinese women in Hawaii. They were part of much larger transpacific conversations that influenced the women's movements in many places.

Carrie Chapman Catt was a part of this as well. In November 1912, she returned to New York City. She opened up her home at 2 West Eighty-Sixth Street to display the banner she had been gifted in Shanghai and to speak to American suffragists and the press about her experiences. By now, it was clear that the revolutionary promise of woman suffrage had been broken and the Chinese women were in for a longer fight for their political rights. Catt relayed their story to her American audience. She related how they had been promised equality with men but then told that the moment was not right. Frustrated, they had turned to militancy, breaking windows in the chambers of the Chinese National Committee.[77] Catt was not a militant—campaigns of window smashing like those in Britain and China did not appeal to her—but, she admitted, "everyone who was familiar with the movement would be compelled to admit that the work of the militant suffragists in England had given the movement a boon throughout the world," including in China.[78]

Catt was invoking the actions of Chinese suffragists in Nanking just as the women of the Chinese umbrella brigade in Honolulu had. Bringing their story back to New York, she participated, as had Mabel Lee, in extending the influence of the women in the Chinese Revolution around the globe from Nanking to Honolulu to New York and many places in between. Women's rights activists from many different places often shared ideas and strategies but could also deploy stories of other suffragists to further their own causes. Only time would tell if the claims of shared sisterhood could stand up to the intersecting motivations that compelled women to join the suffrage movement.

[CHAPTER 3]
Tierra e Idioma
Nina Otero-Warren

María Adelina Isabel Emilia "Nina" Luna Otero was almost two years old when her father, Manuel Otero, was murdered on an August morning in 1883. He had inherited his father's share of the massive Bartolomé Baca (Estancia) land grant in the New Mexico Territory as well as the 35,000 sheep on its many ranches. With the arrival of the railroad in New Mexico in 1881, Anglos poured into the state and began challenging the land grants that Hispano families had held since the Spanish crown had granted them during their conquest of the Indigenous lands of northern Mexico. By the nineteenth century, many land grants were held communally by families who lived in towns surrounded by agricultural fields fed by acequias, or communally built and maintained irrigation ditches. Control of springs and water sources was key to holding large swaths of arid rangeland. Communities also held surrounding pastureland and mountains in common for grazing sheep and gathering resources. But some land grants, like those of the Oteros, were held by a patrón who had families working for him as vaqueros or ranch hands.[1] The Oteros' Estancia Ranch was located at the site of a large lake fed by natural springs—an area known as Antelope Springs for the thousands of antelope that watered there alongside the Oteros' sheep herds. Around it grew thick grass, shade trees, and flowering shrubs.

James and Joel Whitney, sons of a Massachusetts paper mill magnate who had become controlling partners in the Silver City, Deming, and Pacific Railroad, bought a portion of the grant and challenged the boundaries of the other land grant holders, including Manuel Otero. In 1883 James Whitney and his men arrived at the Estancia Ranch where Pablo Baca, an Otero vaquero, was living with his family. The Whitney brothers planned to run off the "squatters," telling a skeptical Baca that the New Mexico Supreme Court had settled the claim in their favor. They made themselves comfortable in the ranch house, where they spent the night drinking whiskey and playing poker.

Alerted to their presence, Manuel Otero arrived the next morning along with his brother-in-law Dr. Edward C. Henríquez, Carlos Armijo, and two vaqueros. James Whitney met them at the door with a rifle in hand. Otero remained polite and shook hands with the unexpected visitors before entering the house to discuss the dispute. Talk soon became heated, however, as Otero demanded that Whitney prove his claim. In response, Whitney drew his pistol and shot Otero point-blank in the chest. All of the remaining men went for their guns; in the barrage, Whitney was hit three times in the side, hand, and jaw but ultimately survived. One of his men was killed instantly. When the shooting stopped, Dr. Henríquez, his arm wounded, went to check on his brother-in-law. Otero's collarbone had been shattered, and his carotid artery torn open. Henríquez frantically tried to stop the bleeding while sending for a justice of the peace to take statements. Otero managed to give a statement and sign it before dying.

Despite deep anger in New Mexico, a judge released Whitney on bail and allowed him to leave for California. He would not come to trial for two more years. When he did, he was acquitted on the grounds of self-defense. Otero's relatives believed that Whitney had bribed the judge to charge the jury strongly in Whitney's favor.

Nuevomexicanos mourned for Manuel Otero, remembered by a fellow citizen as "one of New Mexico's promising young men—cultured, kind and noble. He died manfully contending for his rights, and his death is chargeable to the perpetrators of the system of land grant swindles that have for years crushed out the progressive industries of New Mexico and are now striking at the lives of her best and truest citizens." Indeed, in this period, the courts were systematically favoring Anglo challenges to Hispanic land grant claims. More Hispanic claims were overturned than upheld, and Anglo lawyers grew rich bringing cases and fraudulently taking land. This assault on Hispanic land ownership and political power was an unavoidable fact of life among Hispanos in the New Mexico Territory. The need to protect their rights framed every other political issue.[2]

The New Mexico Territory had come into the Union in 1848 after the Mexican-American War. The Treaty of Guadalupe Hidalgo laid out specific rights for former Mexican citizens in the territory. If they chose to stay and swore allegiance to the United States, their rights would be protected. The treaty recognized them as legally white, a key classification that would offer some important citizenship protections.[3] The place of Native people in those lands—which had, after all, been theirs before the Spanish arrived—was more complicated. The treaty did not give any rights to the "bárbaros" or "uncivilized" Indians like the Comanche and Apache, whose powerful military forces resisted settler encroachment in Mexico and the United States—in fact, the treaty required that the United States police the new border to prevent Native incursions into Mexico. Although the United States recognized the Spanish land grant rights of "civilized" Indians such as the Pueblos (though not their original Indigenous claims to the land), a series of unratified treaties in the 1850s reassessed their status and placed them in the undifferentiated category of Indians, making them federal wards.[4]

As the United States began to transform the region into U.S. space, it recognized that while it might claim those lands in name, the vast territory was in reality primarily under the control of Indigenous nations. The 1850 U.S. Census counted approximately 100,000 former Mexican citizens divided among New

Mexico, Texas, and California. New Mexico was home to 61,547, of whom 95 percent had been born within Nuevo México, making them the largest U.S. territorial population. To maintain their claims, federal officials turned to these Spanish-speaking populations and partnered with them. Initially the vast majority of citizens in the former Mexican territory, these Hispanos wielded political power and demanded that their Spanish language as well as their property rights be respected. Territorial and state legislative sessions in California, Colorado, and New Mexico hired interpreters and published their proceedings and legal codes in both Spanish and English. In California, however, population shifts due to the gold rush and anti–foreign miner laws rapidly weakened Spanish speakers' political power. In Colorado that power remained concentrated in the southernmost counties of Las Animas, Conejas, Costilla, and Huérfano. But in New Mexico, the political power of Spanish speakers remained strong into the twentieth century.[5]

This demographic advantage in territorial politics was a disadvantage nationally. Prejudice against Spanish-speaking Catholic populations as well as substantial Native resistance to incorporation resulted in Congress refusing to allow the territories of New Mexico and Arizona to become states. They remained territories for more than sixty years, decades longer than previously admitted states. Only military campaigns against the Navajo and Apache and the arrival of railroads in New Mexico in the 1870s and 1880s began to tip the demographic scales. The iron rails brought Anglo settlers who coveted the vast land holdings of Hispanic and Native communities. They also did not recognize the communal nature of many of the Hispanic land grants—or simply rejected them—just as they reviled Indigenous people's communal land holding. As part of a litigious culture, they demanded written proof of grant claims that were often held far away in archives in Mexico or Spain. Many Hispanic land claims, like the Oteros' Estancia Ranch, were lost in court or to extrajudicial violence.[6]

After her husband's murder, Eloisa Luna Otero was left with two young children, a son and a daughter, with another son on the way. She was also aware of Anglos' growing influence. Like many wealthy Hispanos who wanted to ensure that their children would speak English as well as Spanish, she sought an English-speaking companion and governess for her children. Traveling to Pittsburgh, Pennsylvania, Otero hired Mary Elizabeth Doyle, a twenty-four-year-old Irish orphan who had been working in a convent in the city. Otero and the young woman, whom the family called Teta, returned to New Mexico, and the governess lived with them for many years.

In 1884 Eloisa married Alfred M. Bergere, an aspiring businessman of Italian and French descent who had migrated to New Mexico from England. He joined the family at Los Lunas, the ancestral home south of Albuquerque. Eloisa was also from a powerful old Hispanic lineage and had her own income from land grants and several thousand head of sheep, which Alfred now managed for her.

Eloisa and Alfred eventually had nine children together, Nina's half sisters and brothers.

Otero-Warren remembered these years at Los Lunas very fondly. In her book *Old Spain in Our Southwest* she described the seasonal rhythms and self-sufficiency of the hacienda. She played with her siblings and watched as women spun and wove wool, men brought in the harvests, and everyone worshipped in the family chapel. She received some private tutoring and then attended St. Vincent's Academy in Albuquerque. In 1892, when she was eleven years old, the family sent Nina to the Maryville College of the Sacred Heart in St. Louis. Hispano families had been sending their children to be educated in St. Louis for many years, especially since the opening of the Santa Fe Trail in 1826 connected New Mexico with the Missouri city. The Catholic presence in St. Louis and its proximity made it an excellent choice. Maryville College was primarily a finishing school, though girls were trained to be teachers. Nina returned to New Mexico in 1894 having greatly strengthened her English-language skills.[7]

When Eloisa Otero's cousin Miguel Otero was appointed territorial governor by President William McKinley in 1897, he procured Alfred Bergere a position as a judicial clerk. The job took the family to Santa Fe, the largest city in the territory with almost 8,000 people. There Nina and her siblings became part of the capital's active social life. Their ties to the powerful politicians Solomon Luna, who was their mother's brother, and Miguel Otero ensured their high social position in the city. According to Nina's biographer Charlotte Whaley, Nina was "high-spirited and independent [and] liked being the center of attention, and the quickness of her mind delighted her parents and friends."[8] She was thrilled with the family's move and was soon attending balls and parties, beginning with Governor Otero's inaugural celebrations in June. Over the next few years, she remained active in the city's social life.

In 1907, Nina Otero was twenty-six years old and still unmarried. But that year, she met a handsome cavalry officer named Rawson Warren. He was a graduate of Stanford University and had received his master's degree at New York University. After joining the army in 1899, he was stationed in the newly acquired territory of the Philippines, which the United States had just won from Spain in the Spanish-American War. By 1907 he was reassigned to a post in the Southwest.

Both Warren and Otero loved riding horses—she refused to ride sidesaddle and was known for jumping fences—and seemed well matched. With the blessing of her family, Otero married Warren after a courtship of a few months. Although Rawson was not Catholic, they held the ceremony in the sacristy of the St. Francis Cathedral. He signed the requisite papers stating that he would agree to raise their children as Catholics. Soon after the wedding, they moved to Rawson's post at Fort Wingate on the western side of the state near the Navajo reservation.

Being an army officer's wife was difficult for Otero-Warren. She missed her

Adelina "Nina" Otero-Warren was a member of a politically powerful Hispano (Spanish-speaking New Mexican) family. A suffrage leader who would later serve as state chair of the National Woman's Party, she helped make Spanish a language of suffrage by insisting that campaign literature, speeches, and outreach be made in both Spanish and English. (Bain News Service, 1923, courtesy Library of Congress Prints and Photographs Division, Washington, D.C.)

large family and close friends in Santa Fe. She was bored and felt stifled by the rigid social strictures that followed her husband's rank. She made a few friends at Fort Wingate, but then Warren was transferred to Utah, where she had to start over again. The wives of senior officers discussed everything she said and did, and she seems to have given them fodder for their gossip. At one point, while Warren was away on duty, she took out his stallion despite his expressly forbidding her to do so. During the ride, the horse reared, threw back its head, and broke her nose. On another occasion, at a party for the fort, she broke social rules and danced with a private. Her biographer observes that the more constraints put upon her, the more rebellious she became, but the final strain for the marriage may have been something else. She later confided to close friends that Warren had a common-law wife and two children in the Philippines. This was too much for her, and she left him after two years of marriage.[9]

Although she returned to the family home in Santa Fe, she did not drop her married name; she remained Otero-Warren for the rest of her life. She also referred to herself as a widow. These choices allowed her to elide the fact of her divorce (or possibly annulment), which was not respectable in either the English- or Spanish-speaking community. Her Anglo surname also likely opened doors to her in a state where Anglos were growing in power, while the Otero name allowed her to display her ongoing pride in her Spanish heritage.[10]

Otero-Warren returned to Santa Fe in 1910 in the midst of the state constitutional convention. After decades of refusals, Congress had passed an enabling act that would allow the territory to submit a request for statehood. For Hispanos, the key question was how their language rights would be protected. Otero-Warren also involved herself in the question of women's rights, especially the right of suffrage. These two issues would become intertwined and play out in complex ways in the years that followed, with elite Hispanas like Otero-Warren at the heart of the debate.

The enabling act passed by Congress divided the New Mexico Territory into two potential states, New Mexico and Arizona, allowing the citizens of the two territories to submit constitutions for congressional approval. The act also contained a model for the New Mexico constitution that included two troubling articles: one stipulated that English would be the language of instruction in public schools; the second asserted that members of juries and candidates for office must be proficient in English.[11]

Spanish-speaking New Mexicans, including women, spoke out in defense of their language rights. Otero-Warren's cousin Aurora Lucero was a student at the New Mexico Normal School, the teachers college in her hometown of Las Vegas, New Mexico.[12] She addressed the issue at the State Educational Association meeting in December. On the last evening, the conference concluded with the state interscholastic oratorical contest at the Las Vegas opera house. Open to the public, the contest featured high school and college students from across the state. Lucero made a passionate defense of Spanish-language rights. Often referred to by scholars as "A Plea for the Spanish Language," the title as reported in newspapers was "Shall the Spanish Language Be Taught in the Schools of New Mexico?" or "Defensa de Nuestro Idioma" (Defense of our language), a direct response to the English-only clauses in the enabling act.[13]

Lucero began by invoking the constitutional convention. "It seems beyond all doubt that New Mexico is soon to take her place as one of the states in the grand sisterhood of commonwealths of this mighty union." But, she warned, the English-language requirement that Congress and the president proposed threatened "to break into fragments at a single blow" the Spanish language, "this strong and marvelous link in the chain of events which has connected and held together the history of the Old and the New World."[14] Lucero would often use this claim to the long history of Spanish speakers in the Americas in both her language and suffrage advocacy. Moreover, she charged, such efforts on the part of national politicians were an "unwarranted interference of Congress" with the "natural rights" of Spanish-speaking citizens. Those rights were protected by the U.S. Constitution, and it would be inconsistent of Congress and an insult to "single out New Mexico" with legislators' English-only demands.

Anglo-Americans mostly assumed that Spanish-speaking New Mexicans were ignorant, disloyal, and incompetent. Those stereotypes had been a major factor in the refusal to let New Mexico become a state. White suffragists held these views as well. When in 1876 Susan B. Anthony had gone on a suffrage speaking tour through the largely Hispanic counties in southern Colorado, she described her audiences as a "densely ignorant class of foreigners" rather than U.S. citizens under the Treaty of Guadalupe Hidalgo. Using familiar rhetoric that marginalized nonwhite men and asserting the greater fitness of white women to vote, Anthony complained, "It was to these men that an American woman, her grandfather a soldier in the Revolution, appealed for the right of women to representation in this government." Anthony later blamed Hispanos for the defeat of Colorado's suffrage referendum, even though their ballots were but a small fraction of the total number of negative votes.[15]

It was precisely these kinds of stereotypes about Hispanics to which Lucero responded in her speech. She instead insisted on their European heritage and offered examples of the benefits that a bilingual state would offer the nation. In so doing, she demonstrated the political acumen that she would bring to the suffrage fight. Spanish Americans were loyal citizens of the nation, she asserted, pointing to their military service in the Civil War, Spanish-American War, and Indian Wars as proof of their "love for the 'Stars and Stripes.'" She also described the cultural contributions of Spanish writers, including Lope de Vegas, Calderón, Enrique Pérez Escriche, Emilio Castellar, and, of course, Cervantes—whom she deemed the equals of Chaucer, Dryden, Milton, Byron, and Webster—and warned that they would lose their influence if New Mexican schools became English-only. She also observed that Spanish was spoken in many countries with which the United States had diplomatic and economic relations. Indeed, she claimed, next to English, Spanish was the most widely spoken language in the world. "If we would cultivate their friendship and good will, get them to do business with us, admit us into their society, we should be able to greet them with a 'Cómo está usted?' as well as that they should be able to greet us with a 'How do you do?'" Bilingual education would make New Mexicans the perfect economic and political ambassadors to Latin American countries as well as help the United States with newly acquired territories like the Philippines and Puerto Rico.

Besides these practical reasons, there was tradition. Spanish was "the language of our fathers" and would therefore be "the language of our own children and our children's children," she insisted. She proudly linked it to the history of Western civilization as the language that "saved Europe from the fate of the Roman Empire" and that was spoken by the men who gave "a New World to civilization" while bringing Christianity to the Incas and Aztecs, reminding her listeners that they too were descended from "civilized" Europeans. She rallied her audience with a rousing assertion of patriotism but also cultural pride in bilingualism: "We are American citizens, it is true, and our conduct places our loyalty and patriotism above reproach. We want to learn the language of our country, and are doing so; but we do not need on that account, to deny either our origin or our race or our language or our traditions or our history or our ancestry, because we are not ashamed of them, and we will not do it, because we are proud of them."[16]

The judges at the oratorical contest awarded Lucero third place for her speech, but it went on to have a larger impact as it was reprinted in newspapers across the state and even into Texas. Her original address had been given in English and was printed in English-language papers,[17] but it appeared in a Spanish-language version as well. This likely originated with *La Voz del Pueblo* (The voice of the people), the newspaper for which her father, the soon-to-be first secretary of state of New Mexico, was an editor. Other Spanish-language papers such as *La Estrellita de Las Cruces* and *La Revista Católica* reprinted the speech along with favorable commentary. *La Voz del Pueblo* proudly reported that a number of "caballeros" (gentlemen) from New Mexico sent Aurora Lucero notes of gratitude and that she had also received letters from Washington, D.C., from the Spanish ambassador and the chairman of the Buró de las Repúblicas Latinas (likely the Pan-American Union).[18]

Lucero's passionate defense of the Spanish language echoed the tenor of the New Mexico Constitutional Convention as Spanish speakers used their political power to resist the English-only directives from Congress. Thirty-two of the one hundred male delegates to the state convention were Spanish speakers, leading a reporter for the *New York Sun* to dismiss the proceedings as "some bull fight in a Mexican village."[19] But unlike the *Sun*'s reporter, New Mexicans knew that Spanish speakers were important constituents with political power and that the convention must therefore address them respectfully. Nina Otero-Warren's uncle Solomon Luna was a powerful Republican delegate in a state where the GOP dominated politics—seventy-one of the one hundred delegates were Republican. Spanish speakers were also among the elected leadership of the convention: George W. Armijo was chief clerk, and Cesario Pedregon was selected as interpreter. Solomon Luna was appointed chairman of the extremely important committee on committees, which established the twenty-seven committees that were each assigned a specific section of the constitution to draft. All this bore directly on the question of suffrage in New Mexico.[20]

At the turn of the twentieth century, New Mexico had only a very small women's suffrage movement. In 1910, the National American Woman Suffrage Association had two women on its subscription list for New Mexico, but one was recorded as dead and the other was in a Silver City tuberculosis sanatorium.[21] The woman in Silver City may still have been there in 1911 when the Cottage

Tuberculosis Sanatorium decorated a float for the local Fourth of July parade that mocked suffrage. A dozen men from the institution rode as "suffragettes" in dresses and bonnets, complete with a sign demanding "votes for women." The float drew "the one good laugh of the day," reported the *Silver City Enterprise*. Another paper joked, "So well were the boys gotten up in their female garb that scarcely a spectator could be found who did not swear that there were three or four girls in the party." The men also carried a sign denoting them as "Bullock's Indians," referencing Dr. Bullock, the head of the sanatorium, and suggesting an increasingly familiar trope linking suffragists with "wild" Indian women. Indeed, New Mexican men sometimes deployed such stereotypes linking race and gender to critique suffragists and maintain racial lines. These could show up in surprising places. An article about a chicken show in the New Mexico newspaper *Las Vegas Optic*, for example, opened with "Cackle-cackle-cackle, gluck, gluck, gluck, cu-cu-cu-ac-dahcut, gobble-gobble-gobble. This is not a Chinese college yell, neither is it a section of the convention at a meeting of the suffrage-yets."[22]

But the women of New Mexico were undeterred. While they may not have been active in NAWSA, local clubwomen, including Otero-Warren, advocated in favor of woman suffrage during the constitutional debates of 1910. The state association of women's clubs had confederated the year before as the New Mexico Federation of Women's Clubs with several hundred members. Most of the members were Anglo, though a number of Hispanas joined the Santa Fe branch.[23] The association sent a petition to the convention in favor of woman suffrage. Many of these supporters were also members of the growing Woman's Christian Temperance Union. These prohibitionist women also made a strong showing at the convention. Interested in addressing civic, educational, and cultural affairs, the clubwomen had reason to believe that the men of the convention would be open to woman suffrage, since women had already been elected as superintendents of public schools in two New Mexican counties (Colfax and Roosevelt) and the governor had appointed a woman, Lola C. Armijo, to the office of territorial librarian.[24]

While earlier historians, perhaps drawing on white suffragists like Susan B. Anthony, characterized Spanish-speaking voters as more conservative on the woman suffrage issue, Joan Jensen's examination of newspaper accounts and memoirs about the convention suggests that "attitudes ranged" and did not break down along ethno-racial lines. That earlier characterization was perhaps a legacy of blaming men of color for keeping the vote from white women. A small Anglo minority supported full suffrage, while a few Anglos and Hispanos opposed suffrage altogether. The vast majority of Anglo and Hispanic men at the convention, including the influential Solomon Luna, favored limited school suffrage for women. That majority carried the day, and women were granted the right to vote in school elections if they met the qualifications of male voters. If a majority of the qualified voters of any school district presented a petition against woman suffrage, however, it could be suspended. The constitution also stipulated that school elections would be held at a different time from other elections. Women could run for the office of county school superintendent as well as school director or member of the board of education. But unlike women in the other western states who had full suffrage, New Mexican women were barred from voting on other candidates and questions.[25]

The Hispanic men of the convention were focused first and foremost on the voting rights and educational rights of Spanish-speaking citizens. Faced with aggressive Anglo dispossession and growing political influence, they worked to keep their rights strongly protected. They were especially concerned by the number of white Texas Democrats who had settled in the southeastern part of the state, known as "Little Texas," because they were aware of how Texans had used Jim Crow laws to disenfranchise people of color.[26] Rejecting Congress's suggestion to write an English-only constitution, the men of the convention included Section 3 of Article VII to protect the right of a citizen to vote regardless of "religion, race, language or color" and regardless of "inability to handle effectively either the English or Spanish languages 'except as may be otherwise provided in this constitution.'" Those exceptions included idiots, insane persons, felons, or "Indians not taxed," which disenfranchised Native people residing on reservations, meaning a majority of them. Residency was also denied to students and members of the military from out of state. Section 10 of Article XII stated that "children of Spanish descent" would never be denied the right of admission to public schools nor ever "classed in separate schools, but shall forever enjoy perfect equality with other children in all public schools."[27]

In order to protect these rights from future Anglo majorities, they made it extremely difficult to change the state constitution. To amend it would require three-fourths of the members of each house and three-fourths of the electorate of the whole state with not less than two-thirds of those voting in each county for ratification.

The same New Mexico constitution that accomplished the goal of protecting Hispanos' language and culture also meant that any effort to achieve full woman suffrage at the state level would be extremely challenging. It set the terms for the suffrage struggle in New Mexico in the years to come. As a result, a federal constitutional amendment came to be seen as the best strategy for New Mexican women to gain the right to vote. Nina Otero-Warren and Aurora Lucero made sure that the concerns of Hispanic women did not fall by the wayside in that fight. They continued to help shape the New Mexican movement, ensuring that Spanish would also be a language of woman suffrage.

[CHAPTER 4]
Race Rhymes
Carrie Williams Clifford

By 1912, Carrie Williams Clifford had built a strong reputation in the black community as a "noted suffragist." Throughout 1912 she organized meetings about women's voting rights in Washington, D.C., and traveled to speak on the topic in other cities, including in Brooklyn, where she addressed the borough's Equal Suffrage League.[1] At the turn of the new year in 1913, Clifford and Mrs. Bell I. Riley had argued the affirmative in a debate on the woman suffrage question against two male attorneys at a fundraiser for the John Wesley AME Zion Church in Washington.[2] She made her case for women's enfranchisement by drawing on ideas about women's difference, especially their capacity as mothers. "It is the great mother-heart reaching out to save her children from war, famine, and pestilence; from death, degradation, and destruction," she wrote, "that induces [a woman] to demand 'Votes for Women,' knowing well that fundamentally it is really a campaign for 'Votes for Children.'"[3] For black women, the sources of death, degradation, and destruction were not abstract concepts but the direct result of white supremacy. Concern about the racial violence aimed at their communities made their decision to fight for the vote quite different from that of their white sisters.

Before 1912, specific evidence of Clifford's suffrage activism is not visible in the historical documents. There is, however, a great deal of evidence of her other political work that reveals the concerns that motivated her to join the suffrage struggle. Clifford directed her considerable intellect and energy toward fighting what her friend W. E. B. Du Bois had termed "the problem of the color line."[4] Wielding words as her weapons, she brought black women's specific concerns into those conversations. She helped found a number of organizations committed to fighting anti-black violence and came to recognize the need for suffrage rights during those battles. In order to understand Clifford's political agenda and how suffrage fit into it, therefore, it is essential to recognize how she became politicized and what her goals were.

Carrie Williams was born in the midst of the Civil War in the free state of Ohio. Her maternal grandparents, Charles and Martha Allen, had been slaves in Alabama who managed to purchase their freedom after the War of 1812. They moved north to Chillicothe, Ohio, where they arrived "poor in all save health and ambition" but built the first brick house "owned by a colored man" in the city.[5] Their

Carrie Williams Clifford was the founder and first president of the Ohio Federation of Colored Women's Clubs. Clifford advocated for woman suffrage as a strategy for addressing issues facing the African American community, especially racial prejudice and violence. She used this image, which emphasizes her respectable class status, to illustrate her first book of poetry, Race Rhymes (1911). (Frontispiece from Clifford, Race Rhymes)

daughter Mary E. Allen married Joshua T. Williams, and they had Carrie in 1862. The family soon moved to Columbus, where Carrie graduated from the integrated public high school. She briefly taught in Parkersburg, West Virginia, but returned to work in her mother's hairdressing business and was proud that she had learned a trade.

For most African Americans, especially the majority who lived in the South, the decades that coincided with Carrie Williams's early life began with great hope founded on emancipation, citizenship, and black male suffrage rights. But the white supremacist backlash to those changes began immediately and grew steadily after 1877 when the federal government abandoned the cause of justice in the South. As white "redeemer" governments took over southern state legislatures, they passed Jim Crow laws that legally designated African Americans as second-class citizens and began to segregate public spaces—public transportation systems, schools, hospitals, restrooms, drinking fountains, and even graveyards—by race. Emulating the Mississippi legislature of 1890, southern states also implemented laws to disenfranchise African Americans without technically defying the Fifteenth Amendment through targeted poll taxes and literacy clauses. In 1896, the Supreme Court upheld a system of legal segregation in the infamous *Plessy v. Ferguson* case.[6]

Growing up in Columbus, Ohio, Carrie Williams was sheltered from those injustices, and her own experiences initially shaped her vision of the possibilities for black Americans. It was an optimistic vision but also a conservative one, based on ideas about hard work and respectability drawn from her life in Columbus: she had attended integrated public schools, her parents and grandparents owned their own homes, and her mother ran a thriving and highly respected hairdressing establishment in the main business block of the city and additionally owned a three-story brick investment property. Her mother was also dedicated to rendering service to others of her race, as Carrie put it, especially by employing and training young black women. For Carrie, her mother proved that "the character of the woman mattered, and not the color. . . . In the business world, at least, color cuts absolutely no figure," and her example shaped Carrie's future political activism.[7]

In 1886, Carrie married William H. Clifford, a rising politician from Cleveland. He served in a variety of Republican organizations and was elected state representative for Cuyahoga County in the Seventy-First (1894–95) and Seventy-Third (1898–99) General Assemblies. She supported his political efforts as a member of the Republican Women's Executive Committee of Cleveland.[8] She also facilitated their social life as a hostess. The Cliffords were well known in Cleveland's African American society, and visitors including Booker T. Washington and W. E. B. Du Bois dined at their home. They also had a growing family: Joshua Williams, named after Carrie's father, was born in 1886, and Maurice Cecil followed two years later.[9]

Upon marrying, Clifford had been excited to move to a city where she believed "colored people had always enjoyed marked school privileges," but she was disappointed not to find a strong literary society in Cleveland. She and Harriet Price, a local schoolteacher, soon founded the Minerva Reading Club.[10] Inspired by Mary Church Terrell, Clifford and Price attended the 1899 National Association of Colored Women's (NACW) meeting in Chicago, where Clifford was elected third recording secretary. This position brought her into the circles of prominent feminist thinkers who would influence her activism, especially Ida B. Wells. For example, as an officer, she received an invitation to lunch with Jane Addams. The offer was relayed by none other than Wells, who escorted the invitees to Hull House.[11]

The NACW itself had been a direct result of Wells's activism and would shape Clifford's work. In 1892, while living in Memphis, Wells had witnessed the lynching of her good friends, storekeepers whose cooperative business was undercutting a white competitor. Like virtually all African Americans, Wells knew that white southern men justified lynching by claiming that "savage" black men posed a danger to white women. But the lynching of Wells's friends had nothing to do with rape and everything to do with economic competition.

Wells, co-owner of a newspaper, the *Memphis Free Speech*, put her journalistic skills to use. She published an editorial demonstrating that rape was rarely the reason that drove whites to inflict violent deaths on black men. Rather, she concluded, the violence was used by white men to keep black communities terrified and under their control. And even in those cases where perpetrators claimed rape, she added, perhaps white women had in fact engaged in consensual intimacy with black men that white men could not countenance.[12]

The white community of Memphis was outraged. While Wells was out of town the leading white businessmen of the city threatened her coeditor with death but settled on running him out of town. They threatened Wells also, warning her "that bodily harm awaited her" if she returned. They took possession of the press and sold it. The assaults and threats proved her point: violence against black men and women was about maintaining white supremacy.[13]

Exiled from her home, Wells went on a speaking tour in the Northeast. Black women throughout the region were moved to action by her story. In Boston and New York, women raised money for Wells to rebuild the newspaper, but she used it to publish a fuller account of her article in pamphlet form. With *Southern Horrors* (1892) she hoped her words and her research would convince white Americans that the tales white southerners told about black men were false and that those same white men were the perpetrators of the true horrors.

Her ordeal also inspired black women to form clubs that began to push back against that narrative. In 1896 they organized a national meeting in Washington, D.C., and joined together as the National Association of Colored Women. Led by powerful thinkers like Josephine Ruffin, Mary Church Terrell, and Margaret Washington, the NACW took up the task of challenging the stereotypes white Americans were perpetuating about African Americans, especially depictions of black women as "savage" and always sexually available.

Black women had been fighting this stereotype for a long time. Abolitionist Harriet Jacobs had made it clear in her 1861 autobiography, *Incidents in the Life of a Slave Girl*, that under slavery, black women had been forced into sexual relationships and that mixed-race children across the South were the result of white men's assaults on enslaved women. The elite and middle-class women of the NACW hoped to disprove these stereotypes by living their lives according to the norms of respectability that were presumed to apply only to white women. They embraced ideas about middle-class womanhood that emphasized purity, piety, domesticity, and women's maternal role. They dressed modestly, wore their hair fashionably, and worked to better their community, especially through projects that helped to uplift women and children. They hoped this behavior would prove that they were ladies—a designation generally denied to black women. They still protested the sexual assaults faced by black women but tended to talk circumspectly about them.[14]

This all appealed to Carrie Clifford, as did the NACW's intellectual community.[15] Joining was the beginning of a long activist career for her. By 1901 she had founded the Ohio Federation of Colored Women's Clubs (OFCWC) and was elected its first president. She was extremely proud of this position and continued to use the title for many years.[16]

The OFCWC's motto was "Deeds, Not Words," but Clifford's position opened opportunities for her to use words to advance the issues important to black women. She founded, funded, and edited the *Queen's Garden*, a newspaper to "maintain the cause of the women of the race in Ohio."[17] She also published poetry while editing the women's department for the *Cleveland Journal* and serving as a contributing editor to *Alexander's Magazine*.[18] In a 1902 interview in *Colored American Magazine*, a monthly published in Boston, she informed readers "that the work of the NACW is the movement of the hour, and that if we are true to it and true to ourselves, it will prove one of the greatest factors in the solution of the race problem, and in wiping out of race prejudice," the two issues she saw as impeding African American civil rights and equality.[19] She cared passionately about defending those rights. In her 1905 presidential address to over one hundred OFCWC delegates, she spoke on the theme "The Rights of Humanity Are Worth Fighting For."[20] She saw in the federation the "thorough organization, co-operation and working together for the good that we may expect to become powerful and able to demand our rights as citizens of this republic."[21]

As OFCWC president, Clifford turned to history to highlight black women's contributions to the nation and the race. In 1900, she edited *Sowing for Others to Reap*, seeking to "call the attention of the people everywhere" to the "grand work" of the organization.[22] The writers addressed black women's solutions to "the Negro Problem." They emphasized self-representation and respectability, political activism, and education. They drew ideas from W. E. B. Du Bois and Booker T. Washington, but also from Margaret Washington and Mary Church Terrell. They quoted the Bible, European poets, philosophers, and each other as they developed their theories of political action.[23]

Clifford understood the power of the written word to inspire change. In the introduction to *Sowing for Others to Reap* she wrote, "Go forth, little book . . . if thou shalt succor one perishing soul, if thou shalt lighten one heavy burden, if thou shalt bring hope to one despairing heart, or transform hate into love—thou shalt have *gloriously* performed thy mission." Her belief in the transformative capacity of literature would become her weapon in the fight for black women's equality. *Sowing for Others to Reap* set a template for her future work: it addressed the problem of white supremacy by chronicling and preserving black women's history. She also used it to raise funds, selling copies at the NACW's annual meeting and donating the proceeds to its work.[24]

In her early activist years, Clifford tended to be conservative. She looked to Booker T. Washington's advice and advocated hard work. Like many clubwomen, she encouraged poor women to live up to her own middle-class standards. As she wrote in one of her presidential reports, the activities of the OFCWC had "the purpose of educating and directing the tastes of our people for worthier things by members of our own race." She also discouraged activities she saw as vices, becoming an active member of the Woman's Christian Temperance Union.[25]

Clifford's initially cautious approach to the race question was shaken by the unmistakable rise of white violence against black people. In 1906 her anger at racism, which she usually held in check, burst forth after a speaking tour through "the southland" earlier that spring and summer heightened her awareness. In Atlanta she was welcomed into the vibrant black intellectual community, attending a debate judged by "prominent gentlemen of Atlanta" and Mary Church Terrell. She also met J. Max Barber, the young editor of the *Voice of the Negro*. At the same time, Atlanta gave her firsthand experience with southern segregation as she witnessed gubernatorial candidates trying to outdo each other in blaming African Americans for Georgia's woes. As her later writings suggest, she did not enjoy her visit.[26]

Clifford's trip to Atlanta was still fresh in her mind that September when news of the Atlanta riot broke. On a Saturday morning, thousands of white men attacked African Americans in downtown Atlanta. A pause in the violence revealed that twenty black men were dead and hundreds of others injured. The next day, "what began as a massacre escalated into a racial war." Whites moved to attack black neighborhoods. African Americans successfully defended themselves and their homes until three state militia companies arrived and whites entered the neighborhood of Brownsville, beating and arresting many of its male residents.[27]

The world looked on at "the terrible outburst of race hatred," and indeed, international condemnation persuaded white leaders to call for negotiations.[28] Clifford described herself as "stirred to the depths" by reports of the violence. The reason given was the old libel that Ida B. Wells had been debunking for years: that black men had sexually assaulted white women.[29]

Clifford's new friend Max Barber denied that charge. In a telegram to the *New York World*, he wrote that the cause had instead been "sensational newspapers and unscrupulous politicians" who had stoked white fears. The real crime of black Atlantans, he charged, was that they were too successful: "'Humiliate the progressive Negro,'" he wrote, "was the command to the mob." Barber signed his letter anonymously as "A Colored Citizen," but the powerful white men of Atlanta found out it was his work and gave him a choice: leave town or be arrested and sent to work on a Georgia chain gang.[30]

Barber reestablished the *Voice of the Negro* in Chicago, and in November he published an issue on "the Atlanta tragedy." It included two pieces by Clifford: a passionate letter to the editor and her poem "Atlanta's Shame."[31] The usually reserved Clifford vented her rage in the letter, confessing, "I hate the South with all the fury of my being." In her eyes, the region was "a relentless monster, continually grinding, mangling, crushing the blacks. I know nothing of its goodness, but much of its awful, unreasonable hate."[32]

Clifford used her poem to castigate white Atlantans, something she believed could be "done more impressively through rhyme than in an elegant prose dissertation."[33] Like Barber she dismissed white Atlanta's rationale for the riots: "Her cry of 'Rape,' no more the world deceived!" Instead, the true crime of black Atlantans, whom "she [Atlanta] hates with bitter hate," was that they reminded the city "of her shames," and their "noble striving . . . the more her wrath inflames." As much as they tried to deny the past, white Atlantans were unable "the foul blot to wipe from off fair history's scroll." Clearly Clifford articulated the thoughts of many readers since Barber reprinted the poem "by request."[34]

In her outrage Clifford also turned to address a wider audience—a new departure, since she had previously published only in the black press, whether by choice or because of the notorious gatekeeping by white editors.[35] She wrote a long letter to the editor of *The Outlook* that he published as part of a special issue containing three views on the Atlanta riot. Clifford's was labeled "A Northern Black Point of View." She had sought out all she could read on the riots, she wrote. While she appreciated *The Outlook*'s initial coverage, she took umbrage at a second piece titled "Racial Self-Restraint," whose author echoed assertions that upper-class African Americans needed to police their own, especially the "vicious and lawless elements of that race," who were truly to blame for the "race war."[36]

Clifford could not let such aspersions stand. Drawing upon her Christian faith, she offered her solution: "The way to a remedy is self-evident, and I am astonished that you do not seem to know it! It consists in living up to the Golden Rule," she admonished. She queried why the author had so quickly dismissed the idea of assimilation. There were not two distinct races, she argued. Moreover, white southern men had already proved that assimilation was possible. She used family history and the history of white men's sexual assaults on black women under slavery to make her point: "My ancestors were as much white as black, and family tradition says there were the Governors of two States among the number." She disavowed any desire for intermarriage but held to the freedom of choice. "I recognize the right of any man, black or white, to make his own choice in matters of the marital relationship." Although a short paragraph in her larger article, this assertion caught her audience's attention.[37]

Clifford was most surprised by the African American community's reaction: "The blacks were as vehement in arguing for race purity as were the whites. To say the least, this rather took me off my feet! I was assaulted in the house of my friends, so to speak." She responded in the *Colored American Magazine* with a piece titled "Which Shall It Be?" She enumerated the various strategies often suggested for solving "the Negro problem," including segregation, emigration, assimilation, elimination, and the Golden Rule. Again, she advocated for the last. She also took her community to task for its colorism. "The idea of race purity gets from me no toleration whatever. The Bible says, 'God made of one blood all men,' &c. Human blood is the same wherever found and color is but skin deep, so the scientists tell us.... I contend the Negro is a man, and as such is entitled to all the rights and privileges of other men."[38]

White men also responded with letters to the editor, and author Thomas Nelson Page offered his rejoinder, "The Great American Question: The Special Plea of a Southerner," in *McClure's Magazine*. He described a white community determined to "preserve itself as a white race unadulterated and unmongrelized. We do not mean that this country, which is the hope and bulwark of civilization, shall ever become a negroid nation, with all that this implies of debasement and degradation."[39] It was a zero-sum game: "The white race is going to dominate in this country so long as it is strong enough, and when it is not strong enough, the negro race is going to dominate. They will never rule together." The violent attacks and lynchings the North decried were merely white southern self-protection (and protection of white northerners as well). "For the new negroes' aspiration is to mix with the whites. It means miscegenation—the mongrelizing and, at last, destruction of the American people," Page ranted, pointing to Clifford's article as evidence.

By 1907 Page had been a fixture on the literary circuit for three decades. He had pioneered writing that romanticized antebellum southern plantations. Page worked hard to spread that mythology through the novels and stories he published in the national magazines of the day. In his first short story, "Marse Chan," in 1884, he hit upon a particularly insidious strategy of conjuring former slaves who remained loyal to their white masters to narrate nostalgic stories of the old South. In Page's stories, enslaved men and women had been "civilized" by bondage, but emancipation had been a disaster: with freedom they were "resembling a reversion to barbarism."[40] In contrast, loyal ex-slaves remained with their former owners and supported their hopes and dreams without a thought of their own wants. Page wrote his politics into the words of these black characters. His nonfiction articles reinforced those ideas. White audiences were entranced.[41]

Incensed, Clifford could not ignore his rewriting of history. In another article in the *Colored American Magazine* she responded by criticizing "the low moral tone taken by Mr. Page throughout the article" and his hypocrisy. "Is the South now so appalled at the prospect of increase among Negroes?" she asked sarcastically. "The time was when every effort was put forth to bring this natural increase up to its highest limit," invoking the long history of the rape of black women by white men. Although social standards often kept women from discussing such topics, Clifford bravely followed the example of Ida B. Wells, writing, "It is best that facts be plainly stated, no matter how distasteful they may be either to myself or others."[42] Rejecting white men's belief that race riots were a just defense of white womanhood, she echoed Wells's observation that there were plenty of northern white women who pursued intimacy with black men, pointedly suggesting that some southern white women could be doing so, too. Clifford also rejected Page's solution of states' rights, countering that the federal government had a responsibility to intervene when people's rights were being violated. She appealed to the "fundamental law of the land which guarantees to all its people the right to life, liberty and the pursuit of happiness without regard to race or color." She offered the North as a preferable alternative to the Jim Crow South. "Even if the North does not love the Negro ... at least it lets him alone."[43]

Clifford's own family experiences suggested to her that when African American people were let alone, they could thrive. In 1905 her husband William had been rewarded for his party loyalty with a position in the Treasury Department in Washington, D.C.[44] While working in Washington he continued to return to Ohio to participate in the state's politics, to vote (which he could not do in the District), and to see his family.[45] She remained in Cleveland until 1907, when she and her sons moved to the capital to join her husband.[46] She already had a national reputation. The *Colored American Magazine* had called her "one of America's brightest women" and "a writer of note" the year before.[47]

Washington, D.C., at the turn of the century was described by European visitors as full of flowers, light, and beautiful vistas. They invariably remarked on the public buildings and often noted the public landscaping. They remembered red brick homes fronted by beautiful gardens on tree-lined avenues. They wrote of streets full of children both black and white gleefully roller-skating, well-dressed women pushing perambulators or promenading, and policemen skillfully directing traffic.[48] Longtime residents recalled that from a small, slow village, Washington had grown to a bustling capital.[49] European governments acknowledged its growing importance on the world stage as the United States advanced toward the Pacific and then beyond, expanding its imperial reach first over Native nations in the American West and then overseas to Cuba, the Philippines, and Hawaii. England and France both upgraded their diplomatic presence from legations to full embassies in 1894.[50]

Black women noticed different things. They observed that hotels in the District were closed to black patrons, a particularly galling situation, according to Mary Church Terrell, since "Indians, Chinamen, Filipinos, Japanese and representatives of any other dark race can find hotel accommodations, if they can pay for them. The colored man alone is thrust out of the hotels of the national capital like a leper." Black women were likewise aware that restaurants, theaters, churches, and colleges were segregated. Employers refused to hire them to work at the counters of department stores and shops. Only menial labor and a few teaching positions in segregated public schools were open to them. They knew that streetcars, which started "from the very heart of the city—midway between the Capitol and the White House," became Jim Crow cars upon crossing the Virginia line, and that they could be arrested for sitting in the wrong seat. They also knew that there were efforts afoot to extend those laws into the District.[51]

The year after she moved to Washington, Clifford gave a "vigorous" speech on these injustices, which she titled "Some Thoughts on the Great American Problem" (another allusion to Page's article) and in which she denounced the "Jim Crow car law, color restrictions in theaters, restaurants, etc., and the gross indifference of the colored leaders to the open violations of the Federal Constitution right here in the nation's capital."[52] Nevertheless, although it was certainly not "the Colored Man's Paradise" that some white observers derisively called it, Washington, D.C., retained a special place in African Americans' political world.[53] As Congress experimented after the Civil War with what postwar society would look like under Reconstruction, the city's African American population pushed for expansive definitions of equality. The resulting policies briefly made the city "an example for all the land." As the seat of Lincoln's government and the federal city, it was a place of promise.[54]

When Carrie Clifford arrived in the federal city, its women could not vote—but neither could its men. That had been the case for just over three decades. Since 1870 the Fifteenth Amendment had granted black men the right to vote. As long as the federal government supported fair elections in the former Confederate states, those men played a major role in politics. Not surprisingly, the vast majority, like William Clifford, affiliated with the Republican Party, the party of Lincoln. In Washington, black men (and a few women) found Republican administrations open to giving them patronage positions. During Reconstruction, the federal government also put a new system in place for governing the District: the president, Ulysses S. Grant, and a popularly elected House of Delegates would appoint a governor and council to serve the city.[55]

President Grant had appointed three black men to the council. But his administration, while admirable regarding racial inclusion—he had also appointed the first Native man, Ely S. Parker (Seneca), as commissioner of Indian Affairs—was notorious for corruption.[56] Detractors pointed to the mushrooming municipal budget and claimed that black men should not be in politics. As the governor of Washington worked to modernize a city that had grown dramatically during the war, its debt grew. The economic depression of the 1870s exacerbated the fiscal problems, but anti-black congressmen claimed it was inherent to the population and that enfranchising black men had been a mistake. In 1874 Congress reorganized the city's governing structure. In an effort to end black political power, they chose to disenfranchise all Washingtonians, black as well as white.[57]

Despite these political disappointments, Washington nourished a strong black middle class and a vibrant intellectual and activist community. Federal employment along with Howard University and the District's public schools, especially the M Street High School (later the Paul Laurence Dunbar High School), all provided good employment options compared with the jobs usually available to African Americans.[58] In 1910 African Americans made up 28.5 percent of the city's the population, and almost a quarter of them were federal employees. There was also a strong black professional class made up of clergymen, college professors, musicians, dentists, lawyers and judges, teachers, and doctors and nurses.[59] But there were few options between the professionals and the very poor. As one young man noted, "We can't all be preachers, teachers, doctors and lawyers. Besides those professions, there is almost nothing for colored people to do but engage in the most menial occupations."[60] Poor black people in D.C. lived in squalid alleys, hidden behind row houses that presented a pleasant facade to the city.

Clifford was forty-four years old when she arrived in the nation's capital, and during the next two decades she would be extremely active politically. Her husband's employment and her sons' being out of school afforded her the time and resources to engage in social and political work. She leaped into activism, initiating an extremely productive period that would last until her husband's failing health required care and she began to feel the weight of her own age.

She and her husband charmed D.C. society.[61] They were known as part of the "Ohio set" and were invited to the rounds of "receptions, card parties, dances and masquerades, banquettes and other social functions" that connected Washington's black society. Carrie held her "at homes" on Sunday evenings, with visitors who included "people prominent in educational, official, and religious and other circles in Washington."[62] She reveled in the intellectual activity, soon becoming secretary of the influential Bethel Literary and Historical Society. She was also known as a leading WCTU woman.[63]

Clifford had also become involved with a new organization, the Niagara Movement. In 1905 the male founders of the movement—one of whom was W. E. B. Du Bois—had issued a "Declaration of Principles," in which they praised black progress, insisted on manhood suffrage, and protested the curtailment of civil rights. They called for economic and educational opportunities, noted with "alarm the evident retrogression in this land of sound public opinion on the subject of manhood rights, republican government and human brotherhood," and refused "to allow the impression to remain that the Negro-American assents to inferiority." They rejected the color line and protested Jim Crow cars. They acknowledged white allies "from the Abolitionist down to those who today still stand for equal opportunity." They refused to remain silent, intending to "complain loudly and insistently," arguing that "manly agitation is the way to liberty."[64] Clifford found these declarations in keeping with her own sentiments, enthusiastically charging into the work of the organization. Although the membership was supposed to be restricted to men, she joined as a full member (paying five dollars rather than the one dollar women's associate fee) in March 1906.[65]

In August 1906 the organization held its second meeting at Harpers Ferry, West Virginia.[66] Participants debated the question of full female participation in meetings and resolved it in favor of women. Although Clifford does not appear in the few details about the program, it is likely she attended, as she was soon serving as a member of the women's committee.[67] She was also deeply influenced by the topics discussed at the meeting, especially the case of Barbara Pope. Pope was removed from a train because she refused to ride in the Jim Crow car on her way from Washington, D.C., to West Virginia. The Niagara Movement took the issue as a test case, paying Pope's legal fees and ultimately winning the case. Though it put the organization into debt, the legal triumph generated great pride. Clifford felt a deep connection to it, perhaps having experienced the humiliation of segregated streetcars during her frustrating trip to Atlanta earlier that summer. This was an experience many black feminists shared.[68] The Niagara Movement leadership asked members to help pay off the debt incurred in the case: "Don't sit down and wait on the initiative of the overworked Gen. Sect. Do something on your own initiative," they urged.[69]

Clifford, always full of ideas, responded with "Post Card[s] with a Mission." She printed quotes from Du Bois's *The Souls of Black Folk* on postcards and sold them, placing notices in Du Bois's magazine *The Horizon*. The profits went to the movement's fund for "fighting the iniquitous 'Jim Crow laws.'"[70] Her sales generated $14.10, to which she added funds she raised from churches in Washington, D.C., and Cincinnati. Out of the $98.87 solicited for the Niagara Movement's "Jim Crow Car Fund," she raised $50.50 ($1,500 dollars in present value).[71]

And she wrote. Clifford fiercely advocated self-representation for African Americans. She believed that if only white Americans, especially northerners, could see that black people were respectable, they would support their rights. She did this in the face of racist attacks by the likes of Thomas Nelson Page. "I believe that by the sheer force of our passionate longing for liberty," she asserted, "by ceaselessly contending for it, in courts, in the press, on the platform, on the stump, there will be created a sentiment in the breast of the liberty-loving Americans favorable to the Afro-Americans."[72]

She frequently addressed herself to black men. In her article "A Plea to Colored Men," she urged them "to protect colored women from the horrible 'Jim Crow' cars." They were the "most infamous" of the South's "infamous schemes" for humiliating blacks, but "the worst sufferers from them are colored women, whom white southerners have studiously and systematically degraded and insulted for nearly three centuries." The progress of a race was indicated by the way men treated women, she wrote, insisting that black men "yield to none in their determination to force a decent respect for their women." Using rhetoric similar to southern white feminists, she threatened, "If you fail to act in our behalf, you will put upon colored women the necessity of protecting themselves from this iniquity." Her poem "Shall We Fight the Jim Crow Car?," published in June 1908, carried a similar challenge: "Shall such base, unworthy treatment / Be by brave men tamely borne?" A northern black woman whose husband had influence in the Republican Party, she may not have been fully aware of the danger she was asking southern black men to put themselves in, but her notions of masculinity shaped her calls for action.[73]

In 1911, Clifford published her first book of poetry, *Race Rhymes*. The table of contents reflected her experiences of the previous few years. "Atlanta's Shame" and her Jim Crow car poems were reprinted along with verses addressing other violence done to the black community, including the Brownsville Affair ("Foraker and the Twenty-fifth") and Thomas Dixon's novel *The Clansman* ("A Reply to Thos. Dixon"). In the latter, she articulated her political strategy, rejecting his revisionist historical narrative and asserting

We hurl back the defamation.
Confound theory with fact.
Prove by thought, by word, by deed,
The falseness of the vile attack.[74]

Her insistence on proving through deed would soon result in her greater involvement in the question of suffrage. As a member of the Niagara Movement's Committee on Organization, Clifford had helped write a 1906 report that captured the urgency of the moment, announcing, "Now, if ever, is the time for the widespread and thorough organization of patriotic and liberty-loving American Negroes. The persistence and intensifying of race prejudice, and the injustice and oppression resulting therefrom, must be met by organization the more permanent and thoroughgoing."[75] The report's authors suggested founding "eminently practical" local branches to focus on fighting local wrongs. That vision was manifested in a new organization, the NAACP, founded in 1909, which Clifford also joined.[76]

She was soon helping to form a Washington branch of the NAACP. In the spring of 1912 *The Crisis* reported, "The meeting in Washington, D.C., in the interests of the NAACP was an overwhelming success, and reflects extraordinary credit on its efficient organizers, among whom that indefatigable worker, Mrs. Carrie Williams Clifford, may be specially named."[77] Clifford threw herself into NAACP work, taking on many positions, including heading an NAACP women's committee in Washington.[78]

The women of the committee were aware that at that very moment, NAWSA member Alice Paul was planning a national suffrage parade. Clifford was already a strong supporter of women's right to vote.[79] She, along with other black suffragists, would insist on taking part in the national parade.

But not everybody agreed that they should be there.

[CHAPTER 5]
The Indian Princess Who Wasn't There
The Strange Case of Dawn Mist

In February 1913, headlines exploded in paper after paper across the country: "Indian Girl in Suffragist Parade"; "Dawn Mist, Indian Girl, to Ride as Suffragist"; "Indian Maidens to Ride in Parade." Editors pounced on the story as it came across their desks on the wires. It had everything—the controversial issue of suffrage, an exotic Indian princess, a western railroad magnate, and a patriotic procession. They printed it as fast as they could.[1]

> Dawn Mist, the beautiful daughter of Chief Three Bears, of the Glacier National Park Indians, representing the wildest type of American womanhood, will ride side by side in the suffrage parade March 3 with Miss Inez Milholland, society favorite and representative of the highest type of cultured womanhood. Word came to suffrage headquarters yesterday that Dawn Mist has long been interested in woman suffrage and has persuaded Louis W. Hill, son of James J. Hill, the railroad magnate, to send a delegation of Indian women here to help their white sisters in the campaign.[2]

The articles reported that Dawn Mist and her friends would be camping in tepees in Washington, D.C., before riding in their "buckskin dresses" on "Indian ponies" in the parade. The suffragist *Woman's Journal* also reported that Dawn Mist would accompany a float portraying "the high position in which Indian women [are] held in certain parts of the country under the old tribal regime—a position relatively higher politically than the position occupied by white women in this country today."[3]

But there was no such ride, no such ponies, no retinue of pretty Indian maidens in the parade. In fact, there was no such person as Dawn Mist, only a character created by the public relations department of the Great Northern Railway. Why, then, had she so convincingly captured the nation's imagination? The answer lies in white Americans' fascination with Indians, which suffused the way they thought about suffrage.[4]

Ideas about Indians helped white Americans contemplate about what was modern in their changing society. They believed that real Indians were vanishing as modernity advanced and that Americans could measure their nation's progress against that loss. Suffrage, one of the fraught current questions, could likewise be debated in terms of its relationship to modernity and progress. Were women meant to be independent "New Women" who were equal to men? Or mothers ensconced in their homes raising children and keeping house? Which was the "uncivilized" and antimodern vision? Here again, the image of Native women gave white Americans a way to think through those possibilities of women's role in society without admitting that they were talking about themselves. Native women could be seen as "squaw drudges," overworked by their "buck" husbands, or as "princesses," independent, beautiful, and brave. Both stereotypes had long histories in American thought.[5]

The public relations machine of the Great Northern Railway drew on those ideas for its own purposes. It also took advantage of the scores of newspaper editors across the country who needed to fill their pages every day. Native feminists would additionally seek to harness these ideas as a way to reach white audiences.[6]

Dawn Mist was the figment of several people's imaginations. Earlier in the year Helen Fitzgerald Sanders, a resident of Butte, Montana, the mining capital of the world, published her novel, The White Quiver. A fictional love story fused with anthropology, it told the tale of a romance between two Piegan (Blackfeet) characters, White Quiver and Dawn Mist. Though it was fiction, Sanders tried to imbue the novel with the "memories of a time that has passed and customs that are no more," memories that she had gleaned from her "many friends among the Piegans." She dedicated the book to Helen Clarke, a woman of mixed Native and white heritage who had been particularly forthcoming with her recollections and stories. Press releases assured the public that the book was a glimpse into the distant past; it "deals with Pagan Indian life before the influence of the white man was felt."[7]

This romanticized past helped draw white tourists to the American West while erasing the Native people who lived there and had claims to the land. The Great Northern Railway was happy to contribute to Sanders's romantic story of Indian lovers who had formerly roamed the peaks and passes of the northern Rockies but disappeared when white men arrived. Louis W. Hill, chairman of the board of the Great Northern, saw an opportunity to boost publicity for the park and ridership for his line. He commissioned photographers like Roland Reed to take pictures of "Indian models posed . . . at various points described in the narrative." They wore period clothing and were surrounded by carefully positioned props such as tepees. Reed made sure to capture the sublime scenery in the photos as well. In one, Dawn Mist and White Quiver meet at the edge of a mountain stream; in another, "Dawn Mist, Queen of the Blackfeet," kneels in a wildflower-strewn prairie with an exquisitely beaded cradleboard on her back (though the cradleboard was not Blackfoot but Dakota).[8] The photographs were sent to Helen Sanders, who included many of them in her novel. In turn, the railroad sold the book in its concessions and printed reproductions of the photos as postcards.[9] The black-and-white images were tinted with color, accentuating the red and white quillwork on the Indian woman's buckskin dress and the brilliant beading on her moccasins.

Dawn Mist was becoming a celebrity.

It was Hoke Smith, storyteller and trickster, who really made it happen. "I always loved a good story so much that I never could become mercenary minded in the weaving of it," the publicist for the Great Northern Railway once said.[10] In Dawn Mist he found a muse, and the March 1913 suffrage parade was the perfect canvas. He cultivated a tale so compelling and sowed it so broadly that a hundred years later it still lives in the archive to mislead historians. But that was Smith's genius and the reason the Great Northern hired him away from the *Minneapolis Tribune* to work in its publicity department. His job was to sell the railway, especially by selling Glacier National Park.[11]

The Great Northern realized that Americans loved the idea of Indians, and there were plenty of Indians near Glacier Park. Created in 1910, the boundaries of the park abutted the Blackfeet Reservation. In fact, the mountains that were declared wilderness and set aside in perpetuity for the people of the United States had formerly been part of the reservation set aside for the Blackfeet. In 1895 the government coerced the tribe to cede a strip of land for mining. The agreement stated that the Blackfeet retained the right to use the area as they had before to hunt elk, gather plants, and travel to sacred sites in the peaks for ceremonies. Despite that legal agreement, however, the later officials restricted Indians using the park, arresting them if they crossed the line to hunt or gather food as they had for millennia. Those policies were upheld by the courts.[12]

Once the area was declared pristine wilderness and incorporated as a national park, the Great Northern turned to encouraging visitors, thus increasing its revenue from passenger service. Along with the natural scenery the corporation highlighted "picturesque Indians" in its publicity. Although they could no longer use park land for traditional uses, the railroad hired many local Blackfeet as entertainers to perform on the grounds of Glacier Park Hotel.[13]

While this kind of marketing had been underway before the railroad hired Hoke Smith, he was a master. He concocted stories that recreated the park's history and sent them out far and wide. Distributing pictures to newspaper bureaus, he included creative captions on the back as story suggestions for editors who gratefully ran them using his words. He repeopled the wilderness spaces with stories about fictional Indians. His audience, accustomed to the plots of dime novels, detective stories, and early film, ate these stories up. There was always room in the papers for an odd tale of the Glacier Park Indians, as Smith insisted on calling them for greater affiliation with the park. In place of sacred Blackfeet stories and histories in the mountains, he planted romance and thrills.

The juxtaposition of Indians and modern amenities was Smith's favorite theme. It was also compelling to his audience because this was a standard story most Americans told themselves. They marinated in an infusion of Wild West shows, films, dime novels, tourist pamphlets, paintings, history books, war memorials, museums, and newspaper articles that insisted that real Indians wore feathers, hunted buffalo, and lived in tepees. These sources also lamented that there were fewer and fewer of those real Indians left; they were quietly disappearing in the sunset of the century, overwhelmed by a modern nation that had no place for them.

The long and the short of it was that when white Americans saw someone in buckskin and feathers, they thought they saw a throwback to an earlier age, a figure out of place in the whirl of their modern moment, an unchanging relic under the dazzle and wonder of electricity, speed, and technology. Indians remained in only a few final western spaces and would soon disappear forever, observers presumed.

Hoke Smith used this contrast between the modern and the primitive to great effect. In particular, he liked to put Indian women in his stories and pictures. Hiring Blackfeet women, he outfitted them in beaded buckskin dresses and had them fix their hair into long plaits that hung straight down their chests. Then he positioned them for their shots—in a chic beauty parlor under a new modern electric hairdryer or with the tips of their fingers in a cut glass bowl, delicately waiting for their manicure. He arranged them at lunch counters with ice cream sundaes and at typewriters, pensively pulling strands of bubble gum from their mouths. Viewers got the punchline: Indians were stuck in the past and no Indian could ever really be one of the New Women populating the modern cities.[14]

Suffragists, the ultimate modern women, were often present in these depictions. The success of the Dawn Mist suffrage parade story encouraged Smith to continue to exploit both story lines. One photograph echoes many anti-suffrage depictions of white men who would be emasculated by women voting. Chief Fish Wolf Robe, another well-known Glacier Park Indian, holds a child and an armful of firewood while "Mrs. Chief Fish Wolf Robe" calls him over, crooking her eyebrow and finger at him. He "is not only a proud advocate of squaw suffrage, but is willing to be photographed as a 'brave of deeds' to prove he lives up to what he preaches," the caption reads.[15]

Blending fact with fiction, Smith also continued to run stories about Dawn Mist that were really about the park. The railroad often sent Princess Dawn Mist and a troop of Blackfeet actors around the country to conventions, fairs, and other events. They traveled to a powwow in Spokane, met with the mayor of Minneapolis, and attended a Shriners' convention in Atlanta. Newspapers covered all of these journeys, and Smith supplemented them with further news items about Dawn Mist's escapades at home in Glacier. He anchored his stories in just enough truth to sell them. Unaware that they were reading fiction, Americans

White Americans often used ideas about women of color to debate suffrage through popular culture. This photograph, part of a series created to publicize Glacier National Park, draws on familiar tropes that suggested suffragists' demands would emasculate American men by forcing them into domestic work. It evoked further humor for its white audience, many of whom believed the stereotypes of Native men as "savages" and Indian women as "drudges," by portraying the Native couple as a modern suffragist and a chivalrous "brave of deeds." (Fish Wolf Robe, ca. 1900, Elmo Scott Watson Photographs, ca 1860–1936, box 87, Ayer Photograph Collection, courtesy Newberry Library, Chicago, Ill.)

learned that "pretty Dawn Mist" would be taking a job as chief telephone operator at the Many Glaciers Hotel. Hoke Smith thus gave her a story that resonated with every country girl who moved to the big city looking for adventure: "Ardent suffragist that she is, Dawn Mist thinks that girls should do their share of the world's work, and besides, she finds it very exciting and great fun to be an important personage in a big hotel. How different from the dull camp life." A few months later, readers learned that Dawn Mist was engaged to White Quiver. Touted as a real-life romance, it was another fiction that returned to Helen Fitzgerald Sanders's novel.[16]

But it wasn't completely fictional, since Daisy Norris, the Blackfeet actress who played the character of Dawn Mist, lived a very modern life. She did also get engaged and quit her job. But Dawn Mist lived on. "The name always belonged to the leading lady at Glacier Park," remembers one descendant.[17] And there were at least three leading ladies over the years. When Daisy Norris married Bill Gilham, the railway hired another tribal member, Irene Goss, to represent Glacier Park in performances. In 1927, the Great Northern brought the Blackfeet performers to Maryland for the Baltimore & Ohio Railroad Centennial Celebration. While there, the cast visited the White House, where they met President Coolidge.[18] When Irene married and became Irene Mendenhall, her sister took over as Dawn Mist. For Daisy and the Goss sisters, playing Dawn Mist was a job and maybe a good one. It was not hard work like cleaning houses, picking sugar beets, or working for the Bureau of Indian Affairs, but it did mean engaging with the public—many of whom were incredibly ignorant.

There were other things they were prouder of than having been Dawn Mist. Daisy and Bill Gilham raised five good-looking sons, all of whom served in World War II. And the Goss sisters played on a winning basketball team, something their community remembers even today.[19]

It is not surprising that Hoke Smith chose to make Dawn Mist a suffragist. White Americans had been using Indians to help them think about suffrage for a long time, but new developments in mass media, like photographs in newspapers, spurred a spate of striking images that reinforced ideas about Indians.

Suffragists themselves had contributed to this linkage in Americans' minds, often drawing their information directly from Native women themselves. Early suffragists like Matilda Joslyn Gage had admired Native women's status in their communities, emphasizing their independence and their matrilineal authority in many traditional societies. They rejected the derogatory term "squaw," however, and instead drew upon the stereotype of "the princess."[20] Seneca Falls, New York, where Elizabeth Cady Stanton and Lucretia Mott had called for women's right to vote, had been Haudenosaunee (Iroquois) land just a few decades earlier. While no Haudenosaunee women are recorded as having attended that meeting, Stanton and Gage pointed to the matrilineal traditions of the Haudenosaunee as an example of a society in which women held political power. (Notably Mott had been visiting the Haudenosaunee community at Cattaraugus just before the Seneca Falls meeting.)[21] At the turn of the century, women's rights advocates like Mabel Dodge Luhan and the anthropologist Elsie Clews Parsons added their voices, extolling the Pueblos in New Mexico for the respected place women held in their societies. Pueblo women were the original feminists, they wrote after visiting their communities.[22]

This was a powerful strand of white feminist thought that came directly from Native people and remained compelling into the early twentieth century. For example, Joseph Keppler's illustration for Puck magazine titled "Savagery to 'Civilization'" portrays a group of Haudenosaunee women on a rocky outcrop overlooking a parade of white suffragists demanding the vote. The Native women

SAVAGERY TO "CIVILIZATION"

THE INDIAN WOMEN: We whom you pity as drudges reached centuries ago the goal that you are now nearing

Many white suffragists admired the matriarchal political power traditionally held by some Native women, especially the Iroquois or Haudenosaunee, portrayed here. The Iroquois women address parading suffragists, saying: "We whom you pity as drudges reached centuries ago the goal that you are now nearing," with their traditional rights listed in the box. These ideas came directly from Native women. Although those here are portrayed as fading into the past, Native suffragists actively engaged with white activists. (From Udo Joseph Keppler, "Savagery to 'Civilization,'" Puck, May 16, 1914, 4, courtesy Library of Congress Prints and Photographs Division, Washington, D.C.)

speak: "We whom you pity as drudges reached centuries ago the goal that you are now nearing." They elaborate that Iroquois women traditionally had "own[ed] the land, the lodge, the children" and that they held political power to choose the nation's leaders, shape diplomacy, and approve treaties. "Our lives are valued again as high as man's," they asserted. Like the white suffragists in upstate New York, Keppler's deep understanding of Haudenosaunee women's power came directly from Iroquois women and men themselves. He had strong relationships with people at Tonawanda and Cattaraugus reservations, including Seneca scholar and Society of American Indians leader Arthur C. Parker, Seneca artist Jesse Cornplanter, and Mohawk poet E. Pauline Johnson, who likely educated him on these matters.[23]

White suffragists' admiration for Native women made its way into popular culture through stories like Dawn Mist, where it could also be turned into a critique of the suffrage movement. The year before headlines about Dawn Mist flew across the country, the Biograph movie studio filmed a short feature, *The Tourist* (1912), in Albuquerque. New Mexico had become the forty-seventh state that same year and was already renowned for its wide-open desert spaces and Native cultures, thanks to the efforts of Fred Harvey and the Santa Fe Railroad, which had done for the Southwest what the Great Northern had done for Glacier National Park.

Biograph picked up on those themes for *The Tourist*. The film opens as a train pauses in a Pueblo village. An attractive female tourist, Trixie, played by eighteen-year-old Mabel Normand, notices the handsome "Big Chief" and sweetly asks him for a personal tour. True to the Hollywood version of an Indian, he wears a full Plains-style headdress with feathers down his back rather than a typical Pueblo headband or hat. Trixie fawns over him as he guides her through the village until they encounter his angry and jealous wife. "Mrs. Big Chief" and her friends threaten Trixie, chasing her around the village with clubs as the film's placard reads: "Indian Suffragettes on the Warpath." Trixie barely manages to jump onto the train as it slowly pulls out of the station, heading safely back to modernity and away from the savage Indian women. *The Tourist* must have done well because two years later, the Kalem studio produced *The Indian Suffragettes*, "an Indian Farce Comedy," staring Mona Darkfeather as Dishwater, the Indian Suffragette.[24]

Such portrayals were comedic dismissals of both suffragists and Native people, groups that had legitimate criticisms of society. The merging of the two into a single image of the "Indian Suffragette" offered a quick shorthand for disdain of both. Indians were savage, antimodern, violent, and often ugly. Suffragettes were ridiculous, disruptive, and demanding. Neither were ladylike. When articles like the one in Arizona's *Coconino Sun* that noted that Hopi women "are said to be the original American suffragettes," the meaning was largely left up to the readers' ideas about Indians. Most Americans imagined them as "uncivilized" and antimodern, so the implicit meaning was that the same went for suffrage and the white suffragettes who were being compared to Native women.[25]

Like *The Tourist*, observers and critics often used the phrase "on the warpath" to describe suffrage activity, just as they did to describe the political activity of Native people.[26] The suffragette was unwomanly, uncivilized, and sexualized, the same meanings that lurked behind the derisive epithet "squaw." So the comparison was not meant to be flattering. As the lyricist of the song "Oh! You Suffragettes" wrote, "I nearly was hazed, / By Suffragettes in war paint."[27]

The idea that Native women might be modern enough to understand suffrage was an even bigger joke. Most of them were not even citizens — they were "wards of the nation" who federal policy makers determined must be protected from themselves. Native women had been vilified as mothers so backward that the federal government had built a series of boarding schools to remove their chil-

A Mexican Suffragette.

White Americans often used suffragists of color as a comedic punch line, dismissing
their legitimate political concerns (the use of "suffragette" in the United States was often
derogatory or dismissive). This postcard refers to women fighting in the Mexican Revolution
to portray suffragists as "militant" and therefore unladylike—a charge that suffragists of
color particularly tried to avoid because they faced racial prejudice that already defeminized
them. (Passing Show Printing Co., San Antonio, Tex., ca. 1915, in author's collection)

dren from their baleful influence. The thought that they would care about suf-frage was a joke that everyone from local women's clubs to New York playwrights found amusing. The Ladies Literary Club of Ogden, Utah, celebrated its seven-teenth anniversary with a "Black and White party" that opened with members putting on a minstrel show. The program included "Chief Silver Throat" singing "The Indian Suffragette" and a troop of Hawaiian hula dancers offering a per-formance.[28] Likewise, Ned Wayburn's spectacular revue *Town Topics* played at the Century Theater in New York in 1915. The "extravagant" show included a lasso demonstration by Will Rogers, lots of legs, "dancing darkies," a henpecked hus-band, and a performance of the song "The Indian Suffragette," but, according to critic Channing Pollock, no plot to speak of.[29]

Indeed, white suffragists were not immune to using racially charged imagery to make their arguments but tended to use images of nonwhite men to critique women's lack of political power. The racial prejudice and frustration of other-wise privileged white middle- and upper-class women came through strongly. In the song "American Citizens Who Cannot Vote," author Nettie Bacon Christian included the subtitle "The Indian, the Chinaman, the Idiot and the Woman"— alluding to the famous 1893 painting *American Woman and Her Political Peers*, which depicted Frances Willard, president of the Woman's Christian Temperance Union and one of the most influential women in America, surrounded by "an Indian, a convict, a hopeless idiot," and "a raving maniac," signaling white women's in-appropriate grouping with other disenfranchised people. The image was meant to shock by placing white women—the embodiment of "civilization"—on par with incompetent and mentally incapacitated men.[30] Similarly the suffrage song "Is It Right?" from 1911 asked,

Is it right for the Negro, the Jap and the Chink
The tramp and the old whiskey bloat,
to be hauled in a taxicab down to the polls
And there be told how they must vote?[31]

As those examples also suggest, it was not just ideas about Indians that white people used to discuss suffrage. Almost any racial or ethnic group could be en-listed in the cause, whether by anti-suffrage opponents or by pro-suffrage pro-ponents—or merely by entertainers who wanted to amuse audiences with timely political gibes. Minstrel shows often used exaggerated stereotypes about Afri-can Americans to entertain white audiences, and directors wedded those ideas to mockery of suffragists. Biograph followed up *The Tourist* with another comedy, *The Suffragette Minstrels* (1913), where it joined a panoply of suffrage films released in those years.[32]

Portrayals like these dismissed suffragists and women of color as caricatures, stereotypes of sexualized or unfeminine women. For example, the song "When

Woman's Journal
And Suffrage News

VOL. XLV. NO. 23   SATURDAY, JUNE 6, 1914   FIVE CENTS

EVERYBODY VOTES BUT MOTHER

White suffragists often used the rhetorical tactic of contrasting the disenfranchisement of white women — whom white Americans held up as representatives of the highest form of civilization — with the voting rights of men of color. Here "mother" lacks the right to vote enjoyed by men of all kinds. This strategy, however, erased women of color, implying that all suffragists were white. (Woman's Journal, June 6, 1914, courtesy Schlesinger Library, Radcliffe Institute, Harvard University, Cambridge, Mass.)

Old Bill Bailey Plays the Ukulele" evoked lascivious images of Hawaiian hula dancers to titillate its audience:

> Some Suffragettes went down
> to Honolulu town
> Among these gals of brown
> They tried a "Suffrage Movement"
> The meetings that they hold
> never lasted long
> Old Bill Bailey broke them up when he played a song
> For Suffrage they don't care
> There's other "movements" there.[33]

Such stereotypes about Indigenous women's lack of political engagement hid much more complicated realities. Native people were neither stuck in the past nor passively disappearing. They had been actively engaged in politics for centuries, navigating relations with other Indigenous nations and then with the different European colonizers who arrived on the continent.[34] They adopted suffrage as a strategy for protecting their sovereignty. Dawn Mist was a white fantasy that was mostly about white people, but there were actual Native women who were engaged in suffrage debates. Their lives were much more complicated than the romanticized vision created by popular culture. But those visions created expectations among white Americans about what an Indian woman should be. Native suffragists confronted the task of how to use the stereotypes and expectations of non-Native people to their own advantage.

CHAPTER 6

An Ojibwe Woman in Washington, D.C.
Marie Louise Bottineau Baldwin

Marie Louise Bottineau Baldwin, a woman of Ojibwe (Chippewa) and French descent, went to Washington, D.C., for the same reason many Native people had before her: to negotiate a treaty.[1] Her father, Jean Baptiste Bottineau, the attorney for the Turtle Mountain Chippewa nation, had been retained to litigate their recent treaty with the U.S. government. He brought his eldest daughter with him to the capital to serve as his legal clerk. In Washington, she connected with an intertribal Native community as well as with white suffragists. She grew increasingly politically active as she tried to navigate and then reshape the attitudes of a public who believed that Native people were disappearing and who had trouble understanding her mixed heritage.

Marie Bottineau had come into the world a long way from Washington, D.C. She was born on December 14, 1863, near the Pembina River on Anishinaabe (Ojibwe)[2] land, later known as the state of North Dakota. She was named after her mother, Marie Renville Bottineau, and in the tradition of her family's Catholic faith. Called "Métis" in Canada, her family had connections to both Indigenous and French cultures. White Americans derisively called them "mixed-bloods" or "half-breeds." Native people like the Ojibwe and Cree claimed them as kin but also recognized them as different. The Cree called them Otipemisiwak or "free people."[3]

As Bottineau grew up, the American understanding of who she was increasingly mattered. In the United States, the term "Métis" did not catch on because white Americans' ideas about race rarely had room for people of mixed heritage. Under U.S. law, people were black or white or Indian. When Métis were counted as white, which they often were in the Old Northwest of the early republic, they gained the ability to vote. But that right was never secure and varied over time as well as across territorial and state lines.[4] The reality for many families was much more complicated than the singular categories the U.S. could contain. Later in life, Marie would call herself French Indian or French Chippewa (white America's word for Anishinaabe or Ojibwe), and she celebrated both sides of her heritage.[5]

In the Treaty of Old Crossing negotiated the year of her birth, the federal government forced the Ojibwe at Turtle Mountain to cede eleven million acres of land to the United States, but her world was still thick with Indigenous knowledge and presence. She grew up in a strong web of kin throughout the region. They had European and Ojibwe names and spoke French, English, and Anishinaabemowin, so she learned those languages as well. She also learned the impor-

MARIE LOUISE BOTTINEAU BALDWIN, LLM.
Expert Accountant of the Education Division of the U. S.
Indian Bureau, Treasurer of the Society of American Indians.
French-Chippewa

Marie Louise Bottineau Baldwin moved to Washington, D.C., to fight for the claims of the Turtle Mountain Chippewa Nation. This infused her suffrage activity as the first Native woman to earn a law degree in the United States. (From Houghton, Our Debt to the Red Man, *173)*

tant lines of descent and belonging, the totems or clans that connected people to their kin. While the Anishinaabe had traditionally lived with their mothers' people and determined descent through their matrilineal clan, some of those traditions began to unravel as Native women moved in with their French or Métis husbands or as white women married men of Native descent. In those cases they adjusted. Marie Bottineau's paternal grandmother had moved south to live with her husband, Pierre, and thus lost her clan membership with the Lake of the

Woods people. Their son Jean Baptiste therefore claimed the reindeer clan, the clan of Pierre's mother, Marguerite Ahdick Songab, as his own.[6] Marie Bottineau followed him and claimed the reindeer and turtle clans, the latter from her mother, a member of the Turtle Mountain Ojibwe.[7]

In 1867, when Marie Bottineau was four, the family, now including her sister, Lillian, moved south near Minneapolis. There her mother had a third daughter, Alvina Clementa, who lived only a year.[8] Despite the move the family maintained ties with their kin at Turtle Mountain. Bottineau had fond memories of traveling north to see her maternal grandmother in the winter months. "We never minded the cold," she recalled. "I love the woods anyway, and in winter they are the best."[9] They had moved south to where her grandfather Pierre had homesteaded on Bottineau Prairie just outside the city. While Pierre Bottineau continued to work in the fur trade, he also looked to new opportunities. He used his knowledge of the English, French, Anishinaabemowin, Cree, and Lakota languages to translate during treaty negotiations. He scouted for the Americans during the 1862 Dakota War. He became a surveyor, helping Americans trace squares of ownership claims over Dakota territory. He harnessed this new economic system of private property, buying parcels and establishing townships. His relatives lived near him on the tracts he organized. While his choices helped his extended family, they were to the detriment of other Native people, especially the Dakota, who were pushed west out of their traditional territory.

Marie Bottineau's father, Jean Baptiste Bottineau, also navigated the massive changes underway using similar skills. He became a jack-of-all-trades in Minneapolis, speculating in real estate and apprenticing as a lawyer. Beginning in 1880 he took over as managing editor of the *Saint Paul Globe* and, like many Métis, was active in Democratic Party politics.[10]

When Minnesota became a state in 1858, it had enfranchised "persons of mixed white and Indian blood, who have adopted the customs and habits of civilization," so Bottineau was eligible to vote. If he had returned to live in Pembina, North Dakota Territory, however, he would have been disenfranchised because the territorial constitution limited the vote to white men. The first North Dakota territorial legislature had clarified who was white when it defeated a proposal to extend suffrage to English-speaking Métis. "Under this act," argued one white legislator during the debate, "the half-breeds would have outvoted all the rest of the territory."[11]

Marie Bottineau inherited the world her parents and grandparents had helped make and also learned how to be a Métis power broker. She attended public schools in Minneapolis as well as the Catholic St. Joseph's Academy in St. Paul. She later enrolled at St. John's Ladies College in Winnipeg.[12] After graduating, she worked as a clerk in a tobacco and cigar store. She practiced embroidery and knitting, arts her mother had taught her, entering pieces in the Minnesota State Fair.[13] At some point, she met a young white businessman, Fred S. Baldwin. She was twenty-four when they were joined in matrimony at St. Andrew's Catholic Church in 1887. Like many middle-class couples, they decided to try the new honeymoon fad, traveling to Minnetonka for a few days.[14] Their match was not a good one, however, and within two years they separated. Initially she returned to her maiden name, but later she went by Mrs. Marie Bottineau Baldwin and described herself as a widow.[15]

It is likely that after her marriage ended she began to clerk for her father in his law office, where she witnessed the Turtle Mountain Chippewa nation's fight for tribal rights and sovereignty.[16] In 1876, Chief Little Shell III had hired Jean Baptiste Bottineau to protect the tribe's interests. After the 1863 Treaty of Old Crossing, the federal government wanted to move the Chippewa to the White Earth Reservation in Minnesota, but they resisted, arguing that they had ceded only half of their land, and if they moved, the government would claim they had forfeited their rights to the rest. Instead, they wanted a reservation established at Turtle Mountain.[17] As their lawyer, Bottineau insisted that the federal government honor its treaty and advocated for the creation of a reservation.[18] In 1892, the federal government agreed to a second treaty that allowed for a permanent reservation at Turtle Mountain, but it was smaller than the tribal leaders had hoped for because Americans had already settled on much of the best agricultural land. Refusing to expand the land base, the government offered one million dollars for the ten million acres lost. Tribal leaders wanted a higher price, noting that ten cents an acre was insulting. Instead, the United States focused on shrinking the population, insisting that the Métis and tribal members living off the reservation be struck from the lists of tribal citizens. Tribal leaders then asked Jean Baptiste Bottineau to go to Washington, D.C., and continue to advocate for better terms for what they derisively called the "Ten-Cent Treaty." He agreed to go, and, as his clerk, Marie Bottineau Baldwin moved with him.[19]

The Bottineaus moved into a house on the 300 block of A Street in the Capitol Hill district.[20] It put them within close walking distance of the U.S. Capitol and congressional offices. Bottineau hung out his metaphorical shingle in bold font in Washington's city directory: BOTTINEAU, JOHN B., *lawyer and counselor for Turtle Mountain Chippewa Indians of North Dakota*.[21] He also had letterhead printed that announced the "Office of the Turtle Mountain Chippewa Indians of North Dakota" in the capital city. Although it was not an official embassy, the Turtle Mountain nation had a visible presence in Washington, in which Marie Bottineau Baldwin played a major role.[22]

As a lawyer's clerk, Marie Bottineau Baldwin became an expert in the case. She also did the office work, copying documents, composing or transcribing memos and letters, answering correspondence, and filing papers. Her father may also have sent her over to the Library of Congress, just two blocks away, to research the treaties and policies on which they were building their case. Their efforts were considerable. In 1893 and again in 1898 Bottineau submitted substantial reports to the secretary of the Interior outlining the complex history of the Turtle Mountain band, its territorial claims, and its assertions of who it included as members of its community. The federal government, hoping to keep its expenditures low, wanted only to recognize "full-bloods" who lived continuously on the land it had set aside. But the Ojibwe or Anishinaabe reckoned kin relationally, not by biological ideas of blood.[23] Bottineau had also witnessed the Ojibwe people's efforts to survive the loss of land and game, describing the pitiful "destitution" of the community and imploring the federal government to deal fairly with the tribe.[24]

By 1901, Marie Bottineau Baldwin was doing more than merely clerking—she was actively involved in the various meetings with the commissioner of Indian Affairs regarding the treaty. Together, the Bottineaus worked closely with Chief Little Shell and tribal delegations when they traveled to Washington, D.C.[25] Jean Baptiste Bottineau also returned to Turtle Mountain to consult with his clients. On one such trip in the summer of 1899, the federal agent had him arrested for entering the reservation. He was fined $300 for the infraction of talking to his clients.[26]

Frustrated by his lack of progress, Bottineau accepted an offer by former New York congressman James M. E. O'Grady, who convinced the attorney that he had enough influence to help push through a better deal for the tribe. O'Grady agreed to tender his services to the Turtle Mountain Chippewa in exchange for Bottineau bringing him on as an attorney and dividing any fees. Bottineau hoped that they could "arrange this matter satisfactorily . . . without sacrificing the valuable claim of my kinsfolk." But O'Grady quickly settled the case for the million dollars that the Turtle Mountain Chippewa and Bottineau had been rejecting for the previous twelve years. He collected his fees from the settlement and refused to pay any to Bottineau.[27]

Bottineau was outraged, and like any good lawyer, he sued.

The trial was one of those serendipitous convergences in American history. Bottineau hired none other than Belva Lockwood, the most famous female lawyer in America. She was a former presidential candidate and also known for being the first woman to be admitted to the bar of the Supreme Court in 1879. Being a female attorney was difficult, but Lockwood discovered a career niche in Indian claims cases.[28] In 1875 she had taken a case for Jim Taylor, a Cherokee lobbyist for the Eastern Band of Cherokee from North Carolina, and successfully argued his nation's case in the court of claims. Taylor and Lockwood made a deal in which he would bring her Native clients and she would give him a cut of the fees. Soon afterward, she represented the Eastern and Emigrant Cherokees in their lawsuit against the United States, a case that required her to do years of research into treaty rights. It was for that case that in 1906 she argued before the Supreme Court for the second time in her career.[29] Three years later, she took

Bottineau's case, using her familiarity with treaty rights and claims to her advantage. Indeed, Bottineau won his case. The sympathetic judge awarded Bottineau his compensation and cleared his name of slanderous charges that he was not working for the tribe and was a drunk. But it was the Turtle Mountain Chippewa who lost the most. Their rejection of the Ten-Cent Treaty came to naught, and they were left with less than a million dollars to compensate them for the last portion of their homeland.[30]

The case offered Marie Bottineau Baldwin a different vision of her future. When she testified at the trial, the judge and four of the five lawyers were men. But as she watched Belva Lockwood working as a peer with the two male lawyers representing her father's case, she saw something new — the possibility that a woman could be a lawyer, not just a legal clerk.[31]

After the treaty settlement and court case, Jean Baptiste Bottineau began to slow down, while Marie Bottineau Baldwin began to speed up.[32] She became increasingly active in both the suffrage and Native rights movements. There was little reason for her to return to Minneapolis, as her mother had died three years earlier.[33] She was also offered a compelling clerical position in the Office of Indian Affairs by Commissioner William A. Jones, whom she had met through her treaty work. She had duly impressed him with her language skills and knowledge of Ojibwe culture.

In the Indian Office she joined Francis La Flesche, an Omaha man who had been working there since 1883, making her the second Native employee and first Native woman in the office. Six months later, she passed her probationary period and received a raise. In this position Bottineau Baldwin was the highest-paid Native woman in the Indian Service, the workforce of the Office of Indian Affairs — but she wasn't the only one. By 1904, the Indian Office had grown to include thousands of wom[en in its work]force. A white woman, Estelle Reel, had even been appointed as [superintende]nt of Indian schools in 1898, a position second only to the [Commissioner of I]ndian Affairs, making her the highest-ranking woman in the [departme]nt. Native women, however, had fewer white-collar opportun[ities. Like Botti]neau Baldwin, they worked in the field, on reservations, and in boarding [schoo]ls across the West. While a small number received better-paying positions as clerks, nurses, and teachers, most were hired to do the grueling work required to keep the boarding schools running: sewing, cooking, and laundering for hundreds of children. The Indian Office also hired Native women at the cheaper "Indian rate" because administrators argued that their employment was a teaching tool for assimilating them into "civilized" life.[34]

In taking this new job, Bottineau Baldwin moved out of her father's shadow, quite literally moving out of his house in the East Capitol District. She found an apartment of her own roughly three blocks from her job at the Office of Indian

Affairs in the old Patent Office Building at Seventh and F Street NW (now the National Portrait Gallery). She enjoyed walking to work, and it was an exciting part of the city in which to live. Seventh Street, along the east side of the Patent Office Building, was "the principal downtown retail shopping corridor."[35]

She worked as a clerk overseeing the contracts the government made to supply food and other resources that would be used in the schools or distributed to elderly families on the reservations. This was a notorious point of corruption in the Indian Office, as suppliers bid to provide a certain quality of goods but delivered something much less expensive and more shoddy, pocketing the money that they saved.

Bottineau Baldwin spent her days poring over contracts and corresponding with the reservation superintendents to confirm that those contracts had been fairly fulfilled. It was tedious work but meant that Indians would not be cheated. She was good at her job. Her supervisor regularly gave her strong evaluations, though her efficiency did not extend to her desk, which was constantly overflowing with papers. This infuriated her supervisor and became a running theme on her annual evaluations as he docked her while urging her to keep it neater.[36]

The office was a hub for Native people in the city. Many diplomatic delegations came through Washington. Since the commissioner of Indian Affairs was the official liaison between Native nations and the federal government, delegates' agendas always included visits to the Indian Office. There was also a growing community of Native people in and around the capital. Along with tribal delegates, they included federal employees like J. N. B. Hewitt, an ethnologist at the Smithsonian. Peoria Charles Dagenett, a good friend of Bottineau Baldwin's, was employed as the supervisor of Indian Work and was based in Washington. Others, like Rosa Bourassa (later La Flesche) and Bottineau Baldwin's best friend, Angel DeCora, worked at the Carlisle Indian Industrial School, the flagship off-reservation boarding school, just a short train ride away from Washington. There were also three legislators in Congress who were members of tribal nations or who claimed Native heritage: Senator Charles Curtis (Kaw and Potawatomi), Senator Robert Owen (Cherokee), and Representative Charles Carter (Chickasaw and Cherokee).

The members of this small Native community all made their way to the Office of Indian Affairs at one point or another. When they did, Bottineau Baldwin enjoyed chatting with them, hearing gossip, noting their concerns, and sometimes alerting them to open positions in the Indian Service. These visits irritated her supervisor, who complained that they interrupted her otherwise skillful work.[37]

In Washington, D.C., Bottineau Baldwin and her friends were seen as out of place. Even the Census Bureau did not believe that there were actual Indians living in the city. When a census taker arrived at her door in 1920, Bottineau Baldwin reported that she was "Indian" and her parents had spoken the Ojibwe language. Somewhere along the line in the census office, however, someone had crossed out these answers and penciled in "W" for white. Everyone knew Indians did not live in cities. They were either noble and dignified people whose time was past, or poor, dirty, and drunk. Bottineau Baldwin and her friends confronted these ideas frequently.[38]

For example, Isabel Anderson, a wealthy socialite and the wife of a diplomat, wrote a breezy memoir about the period called *Presidents and Pies: Life in Washington*. Along with details of the many diplomatic banquets and their exotic guests and decorations, she described a gathering Marie Bottineau Baldwin may well have attended. It was a costume party at a country place outside the city; the theme was "American Indian party." Anderson was delighted by the opportunity to wear her "corn-maiden's dress of white with black and red" that Matilda Coxe Stevenson, an amateur anthropologist in New Mexico, had brought her from "Zuni Land." She accessorized to add to the wild and exotic effect she sought, piling on "moccasins, beads and bracelets." She took down her hair and shook it out, decorating it with feathers and letting it fly around her head (no self-respecting Zuni woman would have worn it this way). Her husband, Larz, played to a much darker stereotype, the drunken Indian: "clad in a mask and a blanket, with a bottle of whiskey and a sign, 'Lo, the poor Indian.'" His costume, she delightedly declared, was "one of the best" of the bunch. Emboldened by their get-ups, the guests threw off their respectable demeanors and played "Indian" with gusto. They spent the night dancing madly around a great bonfire to "plaintive Indian music" while costumed cowboys shot off their pistols. Anderson saw a few "honest and true" Native people among the guests who lent "a touch of realism" to the party. She briefly "wondered what they thought of it all."[39]

The Native people in the city had many thoughts—and a plan.

When they met, Bottineau Baldwin and her friends shook their heads over such portrayals of Indians as drunk and wild savages. They found great comfort in each other's company, but how could they explain to white Americans how wrong this was? It was unfortunate that "part of the white race" believed "that it has inherently superior rights and was morally justified in oppressing" Native people. How could they educate them about what an actual Native person living in the twentieth century might look like? How could they convince them that in spite of all that the government was doing to wipe out Native cultures, there was value in them and they could contribute to the nation's future as it stood on the cusp of modernity? That not only did Indian people deserve a seat at the table, but it was to the nation's detriment not to let them sit there?[40]

Their solution, a classic Progressive Era one, came in the form of an organization that would educate the public: the Society of American Indians (SAI). Bottineau Baldwin joined the executive committee, and the group began to discuss what the organization might look like and what its mission should be.

In June 1911, Laura Cornelius Kellogg, an Oneida woman, invited members of the SAI executive committee to her home in Seymour, Wisconsin, to finalize their mission statement and plan the first annual conference of the new organization. Kellogg was from a long line of political leaders. The Oneida, part of the Haudenosaunee (or Iroquois) Confederacy, had been removed from upstate New York to the area just south of Green Bay in the early nineteenth century. Kellogg's maternal grandfather, Daniel Bread, was an important civil leader who had helped the nation during their relocation.[41]

Like many other members of the executive committee, Kellogg was exceptional. Her graduation with honors from the girls' school Grafton Hall in Fond du Lac, Wisconsin, in 1898 had received national newspaper coverage. She had hopes of a literary career, but like many other educated Native women, she found jobs were scarce, so she joined the Indian Service. She was appointed as a teacher at the Sherman Institute, a federal boarding school in Riverside, California, where she served from 1902 to 1904. During that time, she witnessed the eviction of the Cupeño, Indigenous Californians, from their land at Warner's Ranch in northern San Diego County. Though they had never ceded their land rights, the U.S. Supreme Court ruled that they had waited too long to assert them and therefore lost title to the land, and that the non-Native owner could have them removed. Kellogg again made national headlines, this time as "the Indian Joan of Arc" when she made a speech to the Cupeño sympathizing with them and emphasizing Indigenous resilience. In an interview from that year she announced that she wanted to work "for the uplifting of her race" and to advocate "for the Indian point of view." She soon quit her position at Riverside to study law at Stanford University. Though she remained at Stanford only briefly, she never stopped being an advocate for Native rights. She also continued to work on a degree, enrolling at Barnard College in 1908 and later the University of Wisconsin at Madison, though she did not finish. She turned to writing and giving speeches, traveling through Europe lecturing on Native issues for several years. The Society of American Indians was an extension of that work.[42]

Although Bottineau Baldwin and several others were unable to attend the executive committee meeting with Kellogg, they sent letters that were read aloud and discussed. The members who were able to travel to Wisconsin included Charles Dagenett, Emma Johnson, and Rosa La Flesche, who was the organization's treasurer. Kellogg served as secretary, keeping a precise record of the discussions. A non-Native member, Fayette McKenzie, was also there. That the majority of the group to do the organizing work were women was a pattern that would be repeated over the course of the SAI's lifetime. Gertrude Simmons Bonnin, who was briefly engaged to Dr. Carlos Montezuma (Yavapai), both later members of the SAI, had wrangled with her fiancé over what a national Indian organization might look like. He argued that it should be exclusively male. She responded, "I do not understand *why* your organization does not include Indian women. Am I not an Indian woman as capable to think on serious matters and as thoroughly interested in the race—as any one or two of your men put together? Why do you dare to leave us out? Why?"[43]

The organization that Bottineau Baldwin and her friends envisioned was mixed sex, but they decided that it would be for and by Indians. Only Native people could be voting members, though non-Natives could participate as associate members. It was necessary, they agreed, to show that Native people could run an organization without help from white people, which would be the aspersion thrown at them by doubters if there were white leaders.

In Wisconsin, executive committee members worked on the draft of a pamphlet that they had previously begun in Washington. Their frustration at the stereotypes they confronted echoes through the final draft: "To-day the white man does not believe in Indian capacity—does not believe that he has either the intelligence or the dignity to hold such a Conference as is here proposed." By successfully organizing it, they were emphatically demonstrating their ability. "The Association seeks to bring about a condition whereby the white race and all races may have a better and broader knowledge of the red race," not just its claims and needs, but also "its ability to contribute materially and spiritually to modern civilization."

"One of its high aims," they stated, "is to see the development of conditions whereby the Indian as an individual and as a race may take his place as a man among men, as an active member of the great commonwealth." Initially, the group felt that they needed to distance themselves from the past, stating that while they appreciated "the splendid elements and achievements of the old-time Indian culture," they believed that new methods were necessary to meet the "conditions of modern times." Help must come from and through themselves, they insisted, and so they hoped to come together with other Native people to discuss solutions and develop race leaders.

They then issued invitations to the first annual meeting of their new intertribal organization—the Society of American Indians. They counted at least 4,000 "progressive Indians" who would be recipients, most of them former students from the boarding schools, which had been educating Indian children for the previous three decades. Marie Bottineau Baldwin received one of these invitations. "Dear Fellow Indian," it began, "What is to be the future of the American Indian?"[44]

Bottineau Baldwin traveled to join fifty other members of the new Society of American Indians in Columbus, Ohio, on Columbus Day 1911. There were both men and women in attendance, hailing from the Sioux, Arapahoe, Peoria, Oneida, Omaha, Ojibwe, Winnebago, and Seneca tribes. They had attended Dartmouth and Yale as well as the government Indian boarding schools of Carlisle and Hampton. They were doctors, lawyers, ministers, anthropologists, authors, and Office of Indian Affairs employees. Most had spent their childhoods in their tribal communities but also had strong connections to the white world through kin, education, or employment. None was typical, but they all agreed that something needed to be done to counter the negative ideas of Indians. Moreover, most of them believed that Native people needed U.S. citizenship and all of the rights that came with it in order to fully participate and make lives for themselves as equals. They would present themselves to the nation and the world as modern Indians worthy of citizenship.

As a member of the executive board, Bottineau Baldwin had been invited to pick a topic on which she wished to speak. She chose "Modern Home-Making and the Indian Woman." It is somewhat ironic that the divorced, childless career woman chose to speak on this subject, but it seemed to reflect her own ambivalence about the path she was on. In fact, her whole speech was drenched in ambivalence and nostalgia.

The woman who gave this speech had not yet been radicalized. While there were glimpses of her future political arguments, she ultimately presented a conservative vision that was in line with federal assimilation policy. Bottineau Baldwin began by "reversing the order of the subjects of the title" to "ask, first, what was the Indian woman of the North American continent?" In answering her own question, Bottineau Baldwin lauded the traditional position of Native women in their societies. She emphasized their equal political position, a theme she would return to in future conversations: "In a large number of tribes she was on an absolute equality with her sons and brothers," Bottineau Baldwin asserted. She also described the equitable division of labor and rejected the stereotype of the "squaw drudge" that many non-Natives held.

In the second half of her talk, however, Bottineau Baldwin struggled to fit this vision of equality into the non-Native, middle-class standards of the day. "The environments of the primitive life of the American Indian woman have in large measure changed," she noted. Though these changes had, "unsolicited, [been] brought to her door . . . her outlook upon life must now be in large measure from new viewpoints." In "modern life," Bottineau Baldwin argued, Native women must fit themselves for modern housekeeping. Since the vast majority of her address emphasized the high status of women in Indigenous societies (and since it came from a modern career woman), this argument seemed a bit forced but was certainly in line with the federal Indian Office's official policies. Over the next few years, however, the sentiments of the second half—her emphasis on homemaking—would disappear from Bottineau Baldwin's thinking.[45]

After the excitement of the conference, Bottineau Baldwin returned home to Washington and to her concerns about her father's health. Just over a month later, on December 1, Jean Baptiste Bottineau passed away. He had died strong in his Catholic faith, and Bottineau Baldwin arranged to ship his body back to the family plot in St. Vincent Cemetery in Osseo, Minnesota, the town his father had founded on Bottineau Prairie. He was laid to rest next to his wife, Marie Renville, and their baby daughter, Alvina.[46]

After her father's death, Bottineau Baldwin blossomed. She was forty-eight years old and about to come into her own. In the fall of 1912, she enrolled at the Washington College of Law. Becoming a lawyer was a radical proposition for a woman, let alone a Native woman. If successful, she would be the first Native female lawyer in the United States. The Washington College of Law was itself radical—it was the first law school established by and for women in the nation. It was founded in 1896 when two female lawyers, Ellen Spencer Mussey and Emma Gillett, began to teach a class on law to several interested women. Mussey had trained in the old style of law education, as had Jean Baptiste Bottineau and Belva Lockwood. She had apprenticed with her husband, reading law under his direction and taking over the practice as his partner when he became seriously ill. The field of law was professionalizing, however, and a degree from an accredited law school was becoming more and more important. The problem was that these new law schools denied entry to women on the basis of their sex and sometimes to men on the basis of race.

The all-male schools and their supporters pointed to Harvard professor Dr. Edward Clarke's 1873 study, *Sex in Education; or, A Fair Chance for Girls*. Clarke denounced coeducation because it was modeled on education for boys. As such, he argued, it strained women's sex organs and endangered not only their own health but also the health of any children they might bear in the future. Young women working in factories did not work with their brains, he argued, and, following the eugenic thought of Herbert Spencer, "belong to a class" that had stronger bodies, thus allowing their reproductive systems to develop normally. It was brainwork that he worried about, and thus their "student sisters" who "were trained to push their brain activity to extreme" were the ones in danger. "Undue and disproportionate brain activity," he warned, "exerts a sterilizing influence," especially upon young girls. Moreover, because those being educated were often members of the "cultivated classes," any threat to their reproductive capacity threatened the health of the entire society. His work promoted the fear of "race suicide," that if white American women had fewer children, "real Americans" soon would be overwhelmed by the immigrant hordes from southern and eastern Europe.[47]

Mussey and Gillett found this argument ridiculous. In fact, Gillett insisted that working stimulated women and enhanced their health rather than degraded it. They deliberately created a coed institution, proudly pointing out that men were welcome at their school. Allowing male students made a very good point about sex equality, but it also ensured that they would be able to fill their class rosters at a time when few women were pursuing law degrees. Mussey, having administered a stenography school earlier in her career, knew that the practical considerations of filling classes were important for success. Indeed, the school prospered and continues to exist today as American University's Washington College of Law.

But their school was not the only institution in Washington where women could study law. Howard University, the historically black school founded during Reconstruction, also admitted women into its law classes. Gillett herself had received her law degree at Howard. But her and Mussey's complaint was that "none of the white law schools admitted women."[48] They ensured that their school would be one of those white schools, barring African Americans, women or men, from enrolling, a ban that remained in effect until 1950. Bottineau Baldwin's enrollment suggests that the founders did not think about Native women in the same way. She was an exotic addition but not one that threatened the carefully drawn racial lines between black and white.[49] Indeed, most of white Washington found the Indians in their midst to be interesting, and something of a curiosity to be invited into their circles rather than to be scared of and segregated.

The Washington College of Law was located at 1317 New York Avenue, a short streetcar ride from Bottineau Baldwin's apartment. That part of the city was home to hotels, churches, and a number of educational institutions, including Ralston University, the Drillery Business College, and the National Law School.[50] The Washington College of Law catered to the city's clerical workers who hoped a degree would aid them in passing a civil service exam or gaining a promotion. For Bottineau Baldwin, this would also be the case. While she never chose to practice law after earning her degree, she did rise through the ranks of the Indian Office to a position in which she was supervising three white men.[51] A number of her colleagues in the Indian Office also applied to the college, and Bottineau Baldwin acted as a mentor and served as a reference for some, including an Eastern Shawnee woman from Oklahoma, Ida Prophet Riley, who later withdrew her application due to financial constraints.[52]

Given the school's mission to train female lawyers, it is not surprising that it also became a center of the city's white suffragist movement. Howard University, where many of the city's well-educated black women worked or had matriculated, was also a hub of feminist activity for African Americans. These orbits rarely overlapped, even though they had much in common.[53] The women of the Washington College of Law saw many of their alumnae hit the glass ceilings of civil service positions. Some did well after earning their degrees, but there were still limits to how far up the ladder they could climb. They turned to suffrage. Bottineau Baldwin was with them. She listened to suffrage speakers at their banquets and even served as the class of 1914's representative at the Susan B. Anthony Pageant in 1915. Her white colleague in the Indian Office and fellow Washington College of Law student Florence Etheridge represented the class of 1911.[54]

Like Bottineau Baldwin, Etheridge was a civil servant. She had moved from Massachusetts to Washington and had taken a position in the Pension Bureau. She enrolled at the Washington College of Law and finished her three-year course in 1912, graduating with a bachelor of laws degree. When the position of law clerk opened up in the Indian Office, she requested and received a transfer.[55] (It is possible that she heard about the opening from Bottineau Baldwin.) Etheridge was put to work on Indian heirship cases and received high praise on her efficiency reports.[56]

Etheridge was an ardent suffragist. She was vice president of the Stanton Suffrage Club, a group of about fifty District women. She also served as recording secretary and chair of the legislative committee of the Federation of Equal Suffrage Clubs of Washington, which was an umbrella organization of four different clubs that she estimated to have 250 members. In 1912, she was described as president of the D.C. state suffrage association.[57]

Etheridge and Bottineau Baldwin had many things in common—including their experiences at the Washington College of Law, their employment in the Indian Office, and their suffrage activism—but they diverged, too.[58] Their identities shaped the emphasis of their activism. Florence Etheridge was more heavily involved in the suffrage movement's political organizations and later the Federal Employees Union, while Bottineau Baldwin focused her attention and energies on the work of the SAI. Bottineau Baldwin's experience as a Native woman made her aware of the specific issues faced by Indigenous people in the United States. Her kinship ties and her treaty work led her to privilege the issue of Native people's relationship to U.S. citizenship, which included suffrage but also sovereignty and land rights. Etheridge, like other white women, could focus more specifically on voting because her relationship to U.S. citizenship was much less fraught.

CHAPTER 7

Come, All Ye Women, Come!

The parade had been Florence Etheridge's idea. The energetic president of the Washington, D.C., suffrage branch set out in the summer of 1912 to propose "a National Inaugural Suffrage Procession" to the convention of the National American Woman Suffrage Association in Philadelphia.[1] A civil servant in the District, she understood politics and symbolism. But she received little support from the gathered activists at the NAWSA conference because, as she put it, "we had nobody to get it up and no money with which to get it up."[2] Her suggestion did catch the attention of another young woman at the conference, Alice Paul.

Paul, who had spent time in England with radical followers of Emmeline Pankhurst, was impatient with American suffrage leaders. In London, suffragettes were not afraid to march through the streets, disrupting routine, even smashing windows and getting arrested. Paul returned to America convinced that the suffrage leadership in her country was too timid; she wanted to demand the vote loudly and vehemently. She believed that a constitutional amendment was the only way to secure full rights for the nation's women. As she asserted to the NAWSA convention, even if women won suffrage in many states, to get Congress to pass it at the federal level would require that pro-suffrage congressional representatives be elected from all of those states. She was also tired of playing party politics. The party in power should be held responsible for women's lack of rights, she insisted.

The NAWSA leadership was unmoved. Jane Addams, however, saw potential in Paul and perhaps a bit of her own stubborn spirit. She let her know that the congressional chair for NAWSA, Elizabeth Thatcher Kent, was looking to step down and encouraged Paul to volunteer for the position. The leadership grudgingly accepted. "Ever since the death of Miss Anthony [in 1906] the national board had put all its efforts in state referendum campaigns," Paul remembered, and the national movement "had regarded the Washington work as something that had to be continued to the extent of having a speech made in Congress or something like that and having the *Congressional Record* containing the speech sent all over the country; but it was all secondary to the state campaign." She was ready to get it going again, and she liked Florence Etheridge's idea of an inaugural procession. It would dramatically announce suffragists' new and invigorated presence in the capital.

They talked, and Alice Paul remembered her a bit dismissively; she was "the president of the little group in Washington, which was very tiny." But they discussed "the possibility of having a procession the day before [Woodrow] Wilson came in, and she wanted very much to do it." Etheridge worried about the scale; she confided to Paul, "I think it would be a good idea. I don't know whether it is possible." Paul was interested and Etheridge had connections, so when the leadership appointed her to the Congressional Committee, Paul asked permission to coordinate the parade. They approved the idea but informed her that they absolutely refused to offer any monetary support.

Alice Paul moved to the capital a few months later. Other than Florence Etheridge, she knew few people there. The NAWSA headquarters had given her a list of suffrage supporters in the District, but it was woefully out of date. "I found one person after another after another had died, and then I found one after another after another after another had moved away and nobody knew their present address," she remembered, "so it narrowed down to not having so many left to see." But she hit a jackpot with the women from the Washington College of Law. She found Emma Gillett, one of the school's founders, in her office, where she practiced both law and real estate in the basement of a building on F Street, near the Willard Hotel. Gillett, Paul remembered, "was the first person I met who was friendly and interested and," more importantly, "still living." Paul liked her so much that she later returned to the Washington College of Law for her own law degree, but "I didn't dream of taking a law degree then, in 1912," she recalled, for she was far too busy.

Florence Etheridge also took Alice Paul to meet Elizabeth Thatcher Kent, the former chair of the NAWSA Congressional Committee, Paul's predecessor. She was married to California congressman William Kent. Now it was Paul who was hesitant. She had put off Etheridge's offer of an introduction "because I wanted to get a little foothold before I went to her because she would be the most important." But her concerns were unfounded. "I found such a *wonderful* welcome and such a marvelous woman. . . . Beyond words, a wonderful person." These women got Paul settled in Washington. Gillett told her about an available office space in the building next to hers, and Kent gave Paul her first donation, a reoccurring five dollars per month toward the office's rent of sixty dollars.[3]

They also agreed to help with the procession. In January 1913, when Paul held the first meeting in her new Washington headquarters to discuss it, they came with other interested women, including Belva Lockwood. Paul was awestruck by the presence of such an important "pioneer" of the previous generation who "sort of gave us her blessing." Everyone agreed to hold the procession the day before the inauguration—but that meant they had only two months in which to plan and organize it. They got to work quickly, dividing the tasks among themselves. Gillett volunteered to serve as treasurer and Etheridge was established as chair of the Committee on Finance and Organization of the Suffrage Clubs of the District of Columbia. Kent offered to secure the services of bands that would play in the parade and coordinate the use of the Daughters of the American Revolution's Memorial Continental Hall, where the procession would conclude with speeches. Other women were put in charge of organizing the different groups of women in the parade: "one was to get the nurses, one the doctors, one the lawyers, one the college graduates, and so on," Paul remembered.[4]

Somewhere along the way, Paul downplayed Etheridge's input in the parade. Paul liked to be in charge and had strong opinions on how things should be done. As it became clear that the parade would be a larger event than the leadership had realized, Paul took greater ownership of it; indeed, today it is uniformly described as her idea. This version was encouraged by the official program. A beautiful booklet, it has a striking cover portraying a female herald astride a white horse and sounding a long horn announcing the goal of "votes for women." Her purple cape swirls out around her golden brocaded dress, matching the livery of her steed. Regal and righteous, she heads toward the Capitol with marching women in her wake. Inside the cover, flanked by photographs of Alice Paul and her close coworker Lucy Burns, is an introduction proclaiming the purpose of the procession: to give expression to the nationwide demand for an amendment to the U.S. Constitution enfranchising women. "We march today to give evidence to the world of our determination that this simple act of justice shall be done. We march that the world may realize that, save in six states, the newly-elected President has been chosen by only one-half of the people. We march in a spirit of protest against the present political organization of society, from which women are excluded."

Also included were a variety of advertisers and sponsors, the program of the procession, and acknowledgments. The opening pages had pictures of the many women (all of whom were white) who had been instrumental in planning the parade. Short captions described each woman and credited her with the various tasks she had performed to bring the whole spectacle together. Etheridge was included but was almost a footnote. Removed from the photograph, her description was squeezed onto the bottom of the page with the brief final notation, "It was she who presented the idea of a National Inaugural Suffrage Procession to the convention of the NAWSA which met in Philadelphia last fall."[5]

Alice Paul did do the coordinating and cajoling necessary to carry off the massive procession. She set about getting the permit to march down Pennsylvania Avenue between the Capitol and the White House. The suffragists, however, met resistance from the city's police chief when they applied for a permit. "It is totally unsuitable for women to be marching down Pennsylvania Avenue," he told them, suggesting a residential street lined with foreign embassies would be more appropriate for a women's procession. Paul vehemently disagreed.[6] She turned to Elsie Hill, the daughter of a Connecticut congressman, who used her connections; the police soon grudgingly issued the permit.[7]

As they organized the parade, the white planners had very distinct ideas about which women should be included, calculating whether the presence of nonwhite or foreign women would help or hurt their cause. Inclusion turned on the question of symbolism and the message that would resonate with white audiences. They made a place for Native women and Chinese women, but many of them balked at black women's participation.

Women of color had their own ideas about participating in the parade. They understood that it would be a highly visible event and thus wanted to be involved but were determined to join on their own terms. They would demonstrate a great deal of tenacity in their negotiations with parade organizers, leading to a last-minute standoff over who would be included.

Planners asked Marie Bottineau Baldwin to organize a float featuring Indian women for the procession. This request likely came through her colleague at the Indian Office and classmate at the Washington College of Law, Florence Etheridge. Reports stated that the float would carry "real Indian women in genuine ancient Indian costumes, loaned by the Smithsonian Institution." They would represent the influential positions that Native women held in traditional societies in contrast to white women's relative lack of political power. Bottineau Baldwin did not disagree with this message, and in fact she often emphasized it in her speeches and interviews. As she considered the request the press got wind of it and asked her whether she had decided. She replied that she was not sure but took the opportunity to educate reporters about Native women's history, reminding them that in Indigenous societies, women often had a say in political issues.[8]

Bottineau Baldwin had a crowded schedule. She worked full-time in the Indian Office, was taking accelerated classes at the Washington College of Law, and had recently been elected treasurer of the Society of American Indians. But her hesitance may also have come from the message such a float would send to the audience. In the SAI, Bottineau Baldwin and her colleagues were frustrated by white Americans' inability to see Native people as participants in the modern world. They insisted that they were not static but people capable of maintaining traditions while also moving into the future. As Laura Cornelius Kellogg, an SAI founder, insisted, "I am not the new Indian, I am the old adjusted to the new conditions."[9]

Although Kellogg refused to divide the "old" and the "new," as did many of her SAI colleagues, Native people knew they could use these ideas to get the attention of white Americans. Bottineau Baldwin adeptly used photographs of herself to play with those ideas. She had pictures that she distributed to the press that mirrored the dichotomized ideas of "civilized" and "uncivilized" or "progressive" and "traditional" that white Americans used to categorize Native people.

For one photograph, Bottineau Baldwin dressed in the highest turn-of-the-century fashion, wearing a silk dress with her hair swooped up and fastened with a stylish feather clip. In a second, she wore a fringed shawl and her hair hung in two long braids over her shoulders. Beaded cuffs were at her wrists, and she sat in front of blankets beaded or embroidered with Anishinaabe flower pat-

Equal Suffrage Among Indians.

Mrs. Marie L. Baldwin,

Who declares that squaws have always exercised the right of suffrage and of the recall. She has been asked to prepare a float for the suffrage parade at Washington to emphasize the Indian woman's attitude toward suffrage. She, herself, is a Chippewa, employed in the Indian Bureau.

When organizers asked Marie Bottineau Baldwin to create a float for the 1913 suffrage parade, they hoped she would represent "traditional" Native women, who, the Los Angeles Times suggests, "have always exercised the right of suffrage and of recall." As her press photo indicates, Bottineau Baldwin was often willing to do so, but, in this case, she chose to march in the parade as a modern Native woman in law school regalia. (Los Angeles Times, January 31, 1913) terns. The sitting for Bottineau Baldwin's "traditional" photo seems to have taken place in the Smithsonian's Bureau of Ethnology, where her friend J. N. B. Hewitt, a man of mixed Anglo and Tuscarora heritage, worked. Perhaps the beadwork was from the Smithsonian or from Bottineau Baldwin's own extensive collection of Native art. At that same session, Bottineau Baldwin and Hewitt also playfully took a series of photos showing that they understood those ideas of the old and new Indian: Bottineau Baldwin, her plaited hair hanging loosely over her shoulders, sat wrapped in a blanket, while Hewitt stood next to her in a suit and vest, his hair cut short in a "civilized" manner, glasses on his face. Those photos do not seem to have been used for anything other than their own amusement but emphasize how well they understood the power of photography and white people's expectations about Indians.[10]

So when white feminists asked Marie Bottineau Baldwin to create a float for the suffrage parade, she knew they wanted something along the lines of old Indians, like Joseph Keppler's vision in his cartoon "Savagery to 'Civilization,'" in which traditionally dressed Iroquois women faded into the background after passing their knowledge along to the white suffragists who were moving forward into the future. That was not Bottineau Baldwin's plan. She was a modern Native woman, and she meant to emphasize that in the parade. And so she chose not to organize a float but to march as a new woman with her fellow lawyers from the Washington College of Law.[11]

White feminists similarly admired the women who had fought in the Chinese Revolution, and it is very likely that Abby Scott Baker, the woman in charge of the "foreign countries" section, extended an invitation to Mrs. Wu to join the parade.[12] Newspapers suggested that there may have been several Chinese women who intended to march, students in American colleges and universities like Georgetown or, as one report suggested, Columbia, reminiscent of Mabel Lee's appearance in the New York City parade the year before.[13] Indeed, organizers welcomed Mrs. Wu, who was very visible on the float waving the flag of the Chinese republic. If there were other women, they likely marched as a way to draw attention to China's new status as a modern republic, which was an effort to combat American notions about "benighted" Chinese. Like Native women, the Chinese women attempted to use white expectations to undermine stereotypes and challenge the racial prejudices their communities faced.

Similar invitations were not proffered to the African American women who planned to participate. They had to insist on their right to march at all. In February, Nellie Quander, president of Howard University's Alpha Kappa Alpha sorority, wrote to Alice Paul. The sorority sisters wanted to be included in the parade, she informed Paul, though they did "not wish to enter if we must meet with discrimination on account of race affiliation." Could Alice Paul assign them "to a desirable place in the college women's section?" It was the second letter that Quander had sent. She politely but pointedly suggested that the first letter must have gone astray and called Paul's attention to her repeated request.[14] Despite the fact that Washington, D.C., had both a morning and an evening post, Quander did not receive a response from Paul for twelve days. And when it did come, it was not much of one. Paul merely asked that Quander come to her office "to decide on the best place for your section."[15] For Paul the issue of black women participating in the procession was a thorny one that she hoped to avoid. For Quander and the Alpha Kappa Alphas, the parade was an opportunity to demonstrate their pride and to remind Americans that not all suffragists were white. The black women who arrived at Paul's parade headquarters were received coolly and told they needed to register for an appointment, but every time they tried, they found that the registry clerks happened to be out of the office. There were conflicting rumors about whether they would be allowed to march or would have to march in a segregated section. One rumor said that an order had gone out to segregate the parade, but a flurry of telegrams and protests poured in, and so it was rescinded. Indeed, at one point NAWSA headquarters sent a telegram explicitly denouncing the confusion. In it President Anna Howard Shaw wrote, "Am informed that Parade committee has so strongly urged Colored women not to march that it amounts to official discrimination which is distinctly contrary to instruction from National Headquarters. Please instruct all marshals to see that all colored women who wish to march shall be accorded every service given to other marchers."[16] But not everyone had received the message, and many black women were discouraged from marching by the uncertainty of it all.[17]

The women were becoming impatient as the shadows grew longer on the afternoon of March 3, 1913.[18] Thousands of them stood with their banners, sashes, and flags making a bright mosaic over the streets and lawns surrounding the U.S. Capitol, its dome shining white above them. Those on the floats and on horseback strained to look ahead over the crowd to see what was holding up the line.[19]

And the crowd was large. There were the marchers, of course, but also throngs of visitors who had poured into the nation's capital for Woodrow Wilson's inaugural parade the following day. They crowded into the hotel bars and taverns, imbibing while waiting for the festivities to begin. The procession of women offered an entertaining way to pass the time, so they had come out to see the spectacle. That was precisely what the parade's organizer, Alice Paul, had calculated they would do.

Paul was quite talented at drawing the spotlight to the suffrage cause. Interrupting President Wilson's inaugural weekend with a massive suffrage parade and announcing plans to work for a constitutional amendment seemed to her to be the perfect shot across the bow of American politics.

Like the New York City suffragists the year before, Paul had planned the parade down to the last detail. Disorganization, after all, would be cited as evidence that women were not suited to the vote. Paul charted a route that would start at the

Peace Monument in front of the Capitol, whose female allegorical figures in Grecian robes served as a reminder that women would bring a different perspective to politics. The marchers would proceed down Pennsylvania Avenue, drawing the nation's eyes from the two so-called representative branches of government and the seat of the national legislature on Capitol Hill to the home of the executive at the White House. From there the suffragists would make their way to the Daughters of the American Revolution's Memorial Continental Hall, just completed in 1905 and described as "the costliest and most impressive monument of its kind ever built by women in this country or any other."[20] There, in a building that symbolized women's patriotism, having demonstrated their organizing capacity and asserted their proud presence in the country since its genesis, they would conclude their day.

The sixty-two delegates from Illinois stood on New Jersey Avenue and wondered where their three missing members were. They were uniformly arrayed with white scarves[21] emblazoned with the word "Illinois" around their necks. On their heads sat jaunty white turbans encircled with blue stars—representing states with full suffrage.[22] Their state was not represented by one of those stars. Two of the three missing members, Virginia Brooks and Belle Squire, finally arrived, hustling up to the group. Had anyone seen Mrs. Wells-Barnett, they asked? Ida B. Wells (who had married and went by Wells-Barnett) was a staunch Illinois suffragist and the president of the Alpha Suffrage Club of Chicago. She was also the only African American delegate from their state. Unable to find her, they were alarmed and worried that she was refusing to march. Such a choice would not surprise them, considering what had happened the previous day.[23]

The Illinois delegation's trip had started out well. Most of the women, including Wells-Barnett, had traveled in style from Chicago to the capital. As they left the Windy City, hundreds of well-wishers braved freezing rain to see them off at the station. They stood waving flags and heartily singing patriotic songs as the delegates prepared to depart. In their white stoles and hats, the women bustled about the platform exuding excitement and confidence as they looked after their baggage, said their goodbyes, and posed for pictures. They teased the conductor, pinning suffrage badges to his vest until it was covered. They finally boarded "the Woman's Special," an evening train on the Baltimore & Ohio Railroad line whose cars were festooned with banners and flags of yellow, the suffrage color. Window shades of the same hue had "Votes for Women" printed on them, and yellow daffodils adorned the tables of the dining car. The *Chicago Tribune* had sent along a special reporter to cover the journey, and the railroad had hired female porters for the trip.[24]

As the delegates made their way southeast to Washington, they made several whistle-stops for speeches. The reporter observed a distinct lack of respect for the women, describing booing crowds and small boys pelting the speaker with snowballs in West Virginia. Undaunted, the women cut the speeches short and went on. They soon arrived in the vast hall of Union Station. Disembarking, they joined the throngs of visitors stepping from other trains. In the chaos, they were pleased to see the Boy Scouts who had volunteered for the suffrage parade committee. The eager boys greeted the Illinois contingent and escorted them to their boardinghouse on Delaware Avenue.[25]

In Washington, they got down to business. Their leader, Mrs. Welles, called a rehearsal at the suffrage parade headquarters. While she ran them through the drills, Mrs. Trout, another of their number, hurried into the room. She spoke quietly but urgently with Mrs. Welles as the rest of the women looked on curiously. Mrs. Welles turned to them and announced that the question had been raised as to whether Mrs. Wells-Barnett would march with the delegation. A murmur rose from the room, while the women closest to Ida Wells-Barnett stood in an embarrassed silence. A reporter from the *Chicago Daily Tribune* recorded what happened next.[26]

Mrs. Trout turned to the rest of the women and spoke. "Many of the eastern and southern women have greatly resented the fact that there are to be colored women in the delegations. Some have even gone so far as to say they will not march if [N]egro women are allowed to take part," she explained. The women in charge of the parade would "prefer for us to keep our delegation entirely white," she claimed, though this was not official policy. "So far as Illinois is concerned, we should like to have Mrs. Barnett march in the delegation, but if the national association has decided it is unwise to include the colored women, I think we should abide by its decision." She looked around for approval and got it from Mrs. Schuyler Coe Brandt, a suffragist living in Oak Park, Illinois, who originally hailed from Georgia.

"You are right; it will prejudice southern people against suffrage if we take the colored women into our ranks," she confirmed.

"But it is entirely undemocratic," interrupted Miss Virginia Brooks. "We have come down here to march for equal rights. It would be autocratic to exclude men or women of any color. I think that we should allow Mrs. Barnett to walk in our delegation. If the women of other states lack moral courage, we should show them that we are not afraid of public opinion. We should stand by our principles. If we do not the parade will be a farce."

Ida Wells-Barnett was outraged—two tears escaped her eyes before she could dash them away—and her voice trembled with emotion, but she defended herself and demanded better of her fellow Illinoisans: "The southern women have tried to evade the question time and again by giving some excuse or another every time it has been brought up. If the Illinois women do not take a stand now in this great democratic parade then the colored women are lost."

Mrs. Welles was moved by this argument and announced, "It is time for Illinois to recognize the colored woman as a political equal, and you shall march with the delegation."

But Mrs. Trout insisted that they had to confirm this with the national leaders before making any final decision. The two white women left the room to do so.

As they walked out the door, the room exploded, everyone talking at once, each expressing her opinion on the matter. A deeply disappointed Wells-Barnett sat next to her friend Belle Squire, who patted her hand and reassured her, "It will be all right, I'm sure."

She was wrong: Mrs. Trout soon returned, followed by Mrs. Welles, and spoke directly to Ida Wells-Barnett. "Personally I should like nothing more than to have you represent our Illinois suffrage association. But I feel that we are responsible to the national association and cannot do as we choose. After talking again with Mrs. Stone,[27] I shall have to ask you to march with the colored delegation. I am sorry, but I feel that it is the right thing to do," she concluded, satisfied that she had done what she could.

Wells-Barnett was not about to let this be the last word, however. "I shall not march at all unless I can march under the Illinois banner," she replied indignantly. "When I was asked to come down here I was asked to march with the other women of our state and I intend to do so or not take part in the parade at all."

"If I were a colored woman, I should be willing to march with the other women of my race," retorted Mrs. Welles, demonstrating a blithe ignorance of the capitulation to bigotry she had affirmed.

Wells-Barnett looked at her with grim determination, frustrated that she was forced to explain this to her supposed allies, women who should have understood what it meant to be excluded from their rights. Her voice trembled just a bit but she spoke forcefully: "There is a difference, Mrs. Welles, which you probably do not see. I shall not march with the colored women. Either I go with you or not at all. I am not taking this stand because I personally wish for recognition. I am doing it for the future benefit of my whole race."

Mrs. Belle Squire and Miss Virginia Brooks had stood with her and announced that if Mrs. Wells-Barnett was forced to march at the end of the parade, they would accompany her. Miss Brooks was outraged. "I think it would be a disgrace for Illinois women to let Mrs. Barnett march alone [if] the parade is intended to show women's demand for the great principles of Democracy." Some of the women seemed swayed by this argument, but Mrs. Trout quickly announced the meeting was adjourned, ending the conversation.

And so the next day the Illinois delegation stood waiting on New Jersey Avenue when Belle Squire and Virginia Brooks arrived after unsuccessfully looking for Mrs. Wells-Barnett.

As the parade began and the women from Illinois set out down the avenue, Ida B. Wells-Barnett stepped out of the crowd and into her rightful place. She was determined to march where she belonged and it was too late to turn her away without a scene.

White organizers discouraged African American suffragists from marching in the 1913 national
suffrage parade in Washington, D.C., and when that failed, they tried to segregate them.
Black women, however, insisted on marching where they chose. Ida B. Wells-Barnett
(at center) famously claimed her rightful place with her state delegation for what she called
"the future benefit of my whole race." (Chicago Daily Tribune, March 5, 1913)

Wells-Barnett was not the only black woman who took her place in the parade. Although most accounts of the event describe black women as having been segregated and forced to march at the back, that was not the case, and black women had worked hard to achieve that. They consciously fought to be included, deliberately took their places in sections throughout the parade, and, once they had marched, recorded their presence for posterity.

The sisters of the Alpha Kappa Alphas, whose president, Nellie Quander, had corresponded with Alice Paul before the parade, also insisted on participating, living out Quander's motto: to "create a memorable presence." A second Howard University sorority, Delta Sigma Theta, decided to use the procession as its first public act for the organization its members had founded at the school earlier that year. It was a bold declaration of their pride as black women and as political actors and of their solidarity with each other. The twenty-two Deltas had arrived at Howard from all across the country: Colorado, Missouri, Nebraska, Texas, South Carolina, Georgia, Delaware, New Jersey, and Washington, D.C. Some were the children and grandchildren of enslaved people, while others were the progeny of elite black families, the daughters of teachers, ministers, doctors, and bankers.[28] They were joined by honorary members, including Mary Church Terrell, the president of the National Association of Colored Women's Clubs and former teacher at the M Street (later Paul Laurence Dunbar) High School. Both sororities insisted on being in the formation with the other college women.[29] This refusal to accept segregation was a powerful statement. The editors of the Chicago Broad Ax were especially thinking of Ida B. Wells-Barnett and the Howard students when they composed the secondary headline for their article about the parade. It triumphantly asserted, "No Color Line Existed in Any Part of It. Afro-American Women Proudly Marched Right by the Side of the White Sisters." As the first part of the headline made clear—"The Equal Suffrage Parade Was Viewed by Many Thousand People from All Parts of the United States"—their actions sent a strong message about racial equality as well as gender equality to Americans throughout the nation.[30]

The women of Howard were making a bold statement. Marching in public was scandalous enough for white women, but for black women it threatened to reinforce every negative stereotype about them as promiscuous and unladylike. The black women who chose to march, therefore, had to ensure that they were on their most ladylike, respectable behavior; they could not afford to be seen as radical or militant feminists. Sensible dresses, respectable hairstyles, and digni-fied demeanors were a must. Their radicalism consisted in insisting that as black women, they were also worthy of respect as ladies (and as voters), something middle- and upper-class white women like Alice Paul could take for granted.[31]

A number of other accomplished black women joined the sorority sisters in the parade, many of whom were also affiliated with Howard or the M Street High School. Several were married to men who held federal positions, placing them in the black elite of the city, including Carrie Williams Clifford. Clifford's insistence that black women's history mattered extended to her participation in the suffrage parade in 1913. She was well aware that black women's respectability was tenuous and that despite her graceful comportment, fashionable clothes, and the great mass of dark hair piled stylishly on the back of her head, being there made her vulnerable. Clifford also understood that white Americans did not generally care about black women. National newspapers rarely published information about the black suffragists, but she made sure to record their participation, writing an article for The Crisis that put them on the record.[32]

According to Clifford, there were six other black women marching in the college section with the sorority sisters, including Mary Church Terrell, Charlotte Steward, and Bertha McNeil. McNeil had graduated with her education degree from Howard in 1908 and was teaching in the District's schools.[33] Clifford also reported that Mrs. May Howard Jackson, a Washington resident whose husband taught mathematics at the M Street school, marched with the artists. Jackson was a sculptor who had been rejected because of her race from studying art at the school connected with the Corcoran Gallery. She had a private studio in Washington and was beginning to be known as a sculptor of busts. In the months before the parade, she had exhibited her sculptures of famous black men—W. E. B. Du Bois, the Reverend F. J. Grimké, and Assistant Attorney General William H. Lewis—at the Veerhoff Gallery in the city.[34]

A number of educators marched as well. Anna Evans Murray, an activist for childhood education whose husband, Daniel, worked at the Library of Congress, was in the parade, as was Miss Georgia Simpson. Simpson had recently returned to the city after earning her bachelor's degree in German at the University of Chicago and was employed at the M Street school. Her fellow teacher Miss Harriet Shadd (later Butcher) had graduated from Smith College in 1905 and been a student at the Harvard Graduate School of Education before returning to Washington to teach. Another educator, Miss Caddie Park, chose to march in the teachers section. Canadian-born Mrs. Harriet G. Marshall had founded the Washington Conservatory of Music in 1903 and marched with the musicians. Clifford and Marion Butler marched with the homemakers. Two other black women were in the professional women section: Dr. Amanda V. Gray, originally from Kansas, whose husband worked in the Department of Commerce, and Dr. Eva Ross.[35]

Several African American women, Clifford noted, marched with the state delegations, including Mary Eleanora Delaney McCoy, a social worker from Detroit who carried the banner for the Michigan delegation; Mrs. Duffield had that honor for New York. Clifford praised the women for marching despite white suffragists' ambivalence. She congratulated their bravery in representing their communities at this historic event. She knew it required courage because many of the women had seen firsthand the potential violence African Americans faced in America.[36]

Mrs. Marion Butler, Clifford's fellow marcher in the homemakers section, certainly knew this. Like other black women, she believed suffrage could be a powerful weapon against prejudice but also against the violence facing black communities.[37] She had grown up in South Carolina and was skeptical that state governments would do anything to help make the lives of black people in the United States safer, sweeter, or better. Having witnessed the horrors of lynching as a young girl, she knew the violent tactics southern whites used to repress their communities. Eight black men in her hometown had been killed in one day, an event that terrorized the whole community. The pain remained alive in her own family as her sister later married the son of one of the victims. If black women had the vote, they could help pressure the federal government to help stop lynchings. She believed that black people could be better citizens if they did not have to live in fear and that the whole country, black and white alike, would be a better place for it.[38] Even northern black women like Clifford bore the weight of violence against the black community in their hearts as each newspaper article or shared story led them to fear for a friend or member of their family. As Clifford asked in "My Baby," a poem about her fears for her sons, "Where in this land of the brave and the free / Shall baby and I find of terror surcease?"[39]

Clifford understood the power of history and knew how important it was for black women to represent their communities in this historic parade. Her article in *The Crisis* began triumphantly, "The first parade of the National American

Woman Suffrage Association, held in the capital, is now a matter of history"—and, she added proudly, "the colored women were represented." Her decision to name each woman and describe where they marched reflects what Brittney Cooper has called the act of "listing" or naming black women, and thus contributed to the production of black women's history.[40]

May Martel, the author of the "Women's Department" column in the New York Age, also proudly reported on black women's participation in the parade. Under the headline "Colored Women in Demonstration," she indicated her pleasure in hearing reports that thirty-two black women had represented the race. She contrasted the visibility of black women in Washington to that of black women in Manhattan. She lamented the collapse of the black suffrage organization that had been funded by Alva Belmont and the fact that it meant black women had not participated in the most recent New York suffrage parade. She had "anxiously looked for women of my own race" in the line of the march but did not see them. She pressed black women to be more involved: "Colored women can't afford to be indifferent to any move which means progress." She urged them not to "allow themselves to be pushed aside, if there is any disposition of that kind by white suffragette leaders." But she also scolded black women for their seeming indifference to the cause and black men for ridiculing it. History would look unkindly on them, she warned. In fifty years, she wrote, "we shall be as incredulous when we hear how Negros in these times were violently opposed to a movement in a way quite as morally right, and with probabilities that it will be as beneficial to mankind as the emancipation of the slaves."[41]

While both Clifford and Martel wrote their articles so other black women and girls could see themselves in the movement, Clifford also wanted to provide evidence of black women's participation to a white audience. She believed that if white Americans could be shown that black Americans had made positive contributions to the nation's history, in contrast to the lies perpetrated by men like Thomas Nelson Page, then they would be moved to work for racial justice. Representation mattered for Clifford. She was also willing to try anything to reach a sympathetic audience. As she wrote in her book of poetry Race Rhymes published just a few years earlier, she was "seeking to call attention to a condition which she, at least, considers serious," and if her writing would bring that attention then she sent her "lines forth with a prayer that they may change some evil heart, right some wrong and raise some arm strong to deliver."[42]

Black women joined with the other women of the nation and insisted on their rights in an effort to change hearts. By representing their community, Clifford and the other black marchers forced Americans to acknowledge black suffragists' presence. She also knew that they were representing their race to an audience that believed that black women were inferior because of their sex and their race. In marching with dignity, order, and beauty she rejected those ideas and offered a different vision of her community. This was something she believed that black women were uniquely poised to do. As she had written in her poem "Duty's Call," "Come, all ye women, come! / Help 'till the work is done."[43]

It seemed that all of Washington, Baltimore, and northern Virginia, along with thousands of visitor from farther afield, had gathered on Pennsylvania Avenue. The street was packed from the grandstand at Seventh Avenue across from the Treasury Building up to the Capitol. Men and women surged over the sidewalks, failing to leave any room for marchers. Some men climbed to the roofs of street-cars that had been surrounded by the crowd. Patriotic bunting festooned the buildings along the route.[44]

Police officers in cars started down the crowded thoroughfare, trying to clear a path for the marchers. Honking filled the air accompanied by yells and curses from the officers as well as by squeals from spectators who did not clear their toes from the path of the tires in time. The crowd parted just enough for the cars to pass through before "ooz[ing] in again, whites and blacks, like chocolate va-nilla ice cream, melting rapidly together and drowning out the suffragists' loveli-est platoons of loveliness," one reporter from Chicago quipped.[45] He continued, mocking D.C.'s efforts: "The police foozled and delayed things even at the start-ing hour by trying to clear away people by the tens of thousands that any inspec-tor of Chicago or New York would have had off the avenue fully an hour before the parade was supposed to start at all."[46]

The men of Washington had been disinclined to help the suffragists from the beginning. They had tried to refuse them a parade permit, and the secretary of war declined to release any men to help with crowd control. The police force had begrudgingly hired temporary officers for the day, men off the street with no training. Despite the women's careful planning, the reluctance of the police and the enormity of the crowd led to chaos.

Near the Peace Memorial, the leaders of the parade were ready. The grand marshal, Mary Jane Walker Burleson, a cavalry officer's wife, sat on her husband's handsome horse. Inez Milholland in her white finery was next. Directly behind them came the amendment float, a flatbed wagon with a banner declaring: We Demand An Amendment to the Constitution of the United States Enfranchising the Women of This Country.[47] They could see nothing but a sea of hats all the way down Pennsylvania Avenue, blocking their path.

Abby Scott Baker was the leader of the first section of the parade, with the floats representing the women of foreign countries, which she had organized. She had been worried she would to be late.[48] She had started to the Peace Monu-ment from her house just after two o'clock on a streetcar, but it was slow going and the parade was scheduled to start at three sharp. She admonished herself for not leaving earlier. At Seventh Street, in a split-second decision, she stepped from the car and flagged down a passing automobile. The switch did not help. As they turned onto Pennsylvania Avenue, she saw that the way was crowded with automobiles and wagons. The sidewalks were full and people were walking in the street. "I believe I would have done better to have stayed in the car," she told the driver. The crowds on the avenue made her uneasy as well. Shouldn't the route have been cleared by now, she wondered?

She breathlessly arrived and got into her position at the beginning of the parade, just past the heralds, the amendment float, and the national officers of NAWSA. There were four more floats in her division, then a section of marchers, followed by two more floats, including the float upon which Mrs. Wu stood representing China. At a quarter to three, Baker sent word to the marshal that her section was ready, but at three no one moved.

Finally they began. As they started up and moved past the Peace Monument, she felt they were walking into a funnel, and soon they were surrounded by the crowd. On each side men and boys framed a solid mass of humanity about twenty to thirty feet wide. Behind them, she could see a wide space where the crowd could have been pushed back.[49] Hemmed in, the marchers resorted to walking between the streetcar tracks. They would move ahead a little and then be forced to stop. Small boys ran around them.[50] At Ninth Street a crowd of drunken men staggered out onto the tracks in front of them. Baker thought they seemed good-natured but immobile. She looked to the police officers to clear the way, but they stood with their arms folded, looking, she thought, rather indifferent to the whole thing. Some of the officers were joking with the crowd, laughing as people called out what she thought were rather stupid things. With the men unmoving on the tracks she approached a policeman with folded arms. He was not in uniform but had a badge pinned to his chest, one of the temporary officers hired for the day. "The crowd is doing very well," he said to her. "Can you not keep them off the car tracks?" she asked. He looked at her, keeping his arms folded, and responded, "Oh, no. I can not do anything with them." She took a few steps forward and stopped. The block seemed interminable. She heard the crowds yelling uncomplimentary and foolish things at the marchers. At one point they chanted "rats, rats, rats, rats, rats" for half a block.[51] She tried not to listen, setting her jaw and looking straight ahead, determined to abstract her mind and remain dignified, as the organizers had urged.[52] She looked up and saw the clock on the Post Office Building ahead. It read 4:20. They had traveled only a few blocks. She fastened her eyes on the Treasury Building, wondering what day and what month they would reach it.

She saw a group of Boy Scouts in their khaki uniforms carrying long staffs. Holding them parallel to the ground, they attempted to push the drunken crowd out of the street and onto the sidewalk. Their faces were flushed from the exertion.[53] The policemen looked on, amused, a few half-heartedly waving their billy clubs. She saw one exception. He was on a horse, so she thought he must be an officer, and he was harried. "Trouble has come from the Avenue not being cleared in time," he said to her. Yes, she agreed. They crawled past the Post Office

Building and then, as she approached the Treasury Building, the crowd opened up, creating a wide space. A great feeling of relief washed over her; it had been so suffocating. She could see the large grandstand on the right, and across the street to her left were the steps of the Treasury Building, where the suffragists had organized a tableau. She also saw what had cleared the way—the mounted cavalry troops who had finally been sent out from Fort Myer across the Potomac to control the crowd.[54] After that it was smooth. They proceeded across the White House grounds and over to the Daughters of the American Revolution hall without trouble.[55]

Baker had been near the beginning of the parade; the rest of the women took much longer to move down the avenue. Those who did not split off from the procession trickled into Memorial Continental Hall. They talked excitedly about their experiences. "It was the worst-handled crowd I have ever seen, and I have seen crowds in foreign cities," remarked one woman.[56] A young seventeen-year-old was appalled by her experience as she was riding on the Pennsylvania float with the state delegates. I was "sitting sideways on the float. I was on one end and my sister the other, and a man grabbed hold of my foot and pulled me, and I kicked him. So he let go." He wasn't the only one, either. "All the way up men would pass their hands down my arm. One man took me by the hand and another man grabbed my sister by the hand." Luckily one of the marshals came up and walked alongside of her, as she used the little cane in her hand to hit the men making trouble.[57] One woman recounted her shock at an African American bystander who had jeered at Harriet Stanton Blatch. "That n—— insulted us," she complained, indignantly. She was from Kentucky and they knew how to respond to that kind of behavior in her state, she said ominously.[58]

As suffrage leaders rose to give their speeches, they echoed the outrage at the "idiotic incompetency of the police arrangements" and the "disgraceful insults heaped on American womanhood." "I have marched in London; I have marched in New York; I have marched in Chicago; I have marched in Philadelphia, and never," Dr. Anna Howard Shaw thundered to her audience, "never have I received such insults, never have I seen such incompetency on the part of the police as today."[59] She added that she "was never so proud of suffragists and never so ashamed of the National Capital." Shaw was echoed by the other speakers. Alice Paul emphasized that they had pleaded for better protection but been ignored. Carrie Chapman Catt declared that many of the men in the crowd "were drunk enough for the lock-up." To bring home her point she asserted that in no other nation except Switzerland would women be forced to appeal to "the rabble" for their right to vote.[60] Shaw also used the opportunity to remind women that "the terrible treatment we have received shows how badly we need the ballot." Harriet Laidlaw later agreed, noting that the difference between the police protection during the inaugural parade and that during the suffrage procession "proves the inadequacy of the 'indirect influence,' which the anti-suffragists say women should wield." It proves, she concluded, that "women must have the ballot." If they had, the women would have been protected. They called on the new president and Congress to do something and defiantly pledged to hold another parade in the District.[61]

A number of senators and representatives had also marched in the parade, and they expressed their anger on the floor of Congress at the lack of police support. Senator Miles Poindexter, a member of the Progressive Party from Washington State, had been in the section with some twenty other congressmen. He angrily told his colleagues that there "might as well have been a lot of wooden, painted policemen so far as their control over the crowd." In the House, Representative Richmond Hobson, a Democrat from Alabama, confirmed that the crowd had overwhelmed the parade to the point where they had to walk single-file and force their way through the crowds while the police did nothing but jeer. He told his colleagues of the call he received from a constituent who told him of a "ruffian" who climbed onto one of the floats and "insulted" her daughter. Minority leader James Mann, Republican from Illinois, growled, "Her daughter ought to have been at home," expressing the opinion of a number of men who believed suffragists were asking for trouble by acting unladylike. Representative Hobson and others pushed back, responding that such behavior was "disgraceful," and they held the superintendent of police accountable. Major Richard Sylvester had "made it apparent that he was opposed to the parade" from the start. He had no right to let his personal feelings in regard to woman suffrage interfere with performance of his duties, Hobson railed. The House and the Senate called for investigations.[62]

Newspapers across the country echoed those sentiments, focusing on the chaos along the suffrage parade route, especially in contrast with the orderly inaugural parade that followed on March 4. They called out the police as ineffective and praised the cavalry for coming to save the day. In San Francisco, the *Examiner* lauded the women and excoriated the men: "Five Thousand Women March at Capital / Glorious Pageant Strong Appeal for Ballot / Jeers and Insults Greet Suffrage Marchers." Their subheadline elaborated: "Great Parade of Suffrage Hosts in Washington, Saved from Disruption by U.S. Cavalry, Ends in Indignation Mass Meeting." The local *Evening Star* pointedly critiqued the police force's behavior. "Score the Police for Inefficiency," it blasted. The specter of a constabulary unwilling to do their duty to protect the public—especially when that public included some of the country's most famous women in the nation's capital—generated extensive newspaper coverage nationwide.[63]

The Senate committee interviewed many witnesses, marchers, spectators, and police officers, all of whom seem to have been white.[64] Many spectators felt the police had done a good job and emphasized that they saw them working hard.[65] The marchers' testimony suggested that the crowd had been extremely disrespectful. Parade participants called attention to obscene shouts from the onlookers. Several witnesses pointed out that the example had come from Congressman James Heflin, Democrat from Alabama, who had made a speech on the floor of the House the day before the parade comparing the suffragists to barn animals.[66] Suffragists were also shocked by strange men laying their hands on them, pinching their arms, touching their legs, tearing their coats, and pulling at banners and flags. The women called attention to the disdain shown them by the majority of the policemen who refused to make an effort to control the crowd, even when asked directly. Witnesses often contrasted the actions of the Boy Scouts or "colored" policemen with those of the white officers, implying that those least likely to be considered gentlemen had risen to the occasion, unlike the white men who were assumed to be manly.[67] Major Sylvester defensively responded that his force had done what had been requested of it by the district commissioner but that budget cuts and the need to hire temporary untrained officers had caused the problem.[68]

Although none of the official witnesses were people of color, Carrie Williams Clifford briefly addressed the issue in her article on the parade. The black women reported "no worse treatment from bystanders than was accorded white women," she wrote. Readers who had seen newspaper reports of the parade knew what she meant.[69] A male correspondent for the Chicago Broad Ax went further, asserting that black women "were accorded every courtesy," and the Howard girls were "greeted with hearty applause all along the line."[70]

The investigating senators kept the witnesses closely reined in and often cut them off when they began to offer hearsay or move beyond the specific questions. When witnesses accused policemen of behaving badly, the committee asked if they had taken their badge numbers. Most of the women responded that they had been too flustered, frustrated, or embarrassed to notice badge numbers, which gave the committee an excuse for not disciplining anyone. In the end, the hearings left historians with a trove of information about the parade, but no one was punished. Taking place over two weeks in March and an additional two days in April, the hearings did, however, generate a great deal of publicity and kept the parade in the public's eye longer than it would have had there been no scandal. For Alice Paul, this was good news.[71]

The 1913 suffrage parade energized white suffragists but also led to another split in their movement. Alice Paul came out of it intent on a national amendment, believing that she could rally her followers around that goal. It was a clear and obvious target and one around which many women who disagreed on other issues could coalesce. It also seemed the most economical. She worried it would take another generation of struggle at the state level, while Congress's recent passage of the Sixteenth (1909) and Seventeenth (1912) Amendments suggested a national amendment was entirely possible.

She kept up the pressure. As chair of NAWSA's Congressional Committee, she immediately made an appointment with newly inaugurated President Wilson to put him on notice. Although it was up to both houses of Congress to pass a constitutional amendment and the executive branch played no official part, Paul knew the president had a national voice and could sway public policy. She had also learned from Emmeline Pankhurst the important strategy of keeping suffrage always before the public. When Congress took up its annual vote on the amendment, she organized another march. This time Major Sylvester was ready and allocated three hundred men to the duty.[72]

NAWSA leadership was split on whether the organization could focus on both a national amendment and state-by-state legislation. Some believed that finite resources would be stretched too thin and that women would elect to focus on their state if forced to choose.

Alice Paul and her partner Lucy Burns, seeking a way around this concern, formed a separate organization, the Congressional Union (CU, later known as the National Woman's Party, NWP), that would be affiliated with NAWSA's Congressional Committee but separate from it. By creating a national network, Paul and Burns could use the CU to fund-raise for the amendment fight. Paul began to build it, looking into starting a magazine that would eventually become the weekly Suffragist and hiring paid organizers in the states. She simultaneously kept up the pressure on Congress.[73]

NAWSA leadership was wary of the growing power of Alice Paul's Congressional Union. Even though it was part of an official committee within NAWSA, some were beginning to suspect that was in name only and that NAWSA funding was being used to support Alice Paul's agenda. Many were also wary of the CU's young women open admiration for the militant tactics of British suffragists— the Pankhursts, as they were called. This was reinforced when Emmeline Pankhurst toured the United States in the fall of 1913 and Alice Paul and the Suffragist praised her work. NAWSA leadership had labored hard to give their organization and suffrage itself a respectable sheen, and any hint of militancy threatened to undo that hard-earned reputation.

At the NAWSA annual meeting in late 1913, this growing unease burst into the open. Carrie Chapman Catt, who had served as NAWSA president from 1900 to 1904 (and would later serve again) raised the question: Why was NAWSA funding the CU when its own committee, the Congressional Committee, was doing the same work? She articulated concerns over the financial entanglements of the two and suggested that women would be forced to choose. In the months after the convention, NAWSA president Anna Howard Shaw urged suffragists to stay away from the CU and avoid Alice Paul. Paul felt unappreciated for the hard work she had been doing for the cause. Many of the women supporting her believed that the problem was generational. Doris Stevens, who became a CU organizer, was twenty-one at the time and wrote to Lucy Burns, Alice Paul's right-hand woman, "I dare say you and Miss Paul even now have a most level-headed and far-reaching scheme to outwit the Dear Ladies." NAWSA supporters, on the other hand, rebuked the "hot-headed young people" of the CU.[74]

Ultimately, despite efforts at compromise, the two organizations split. Alice Paul was concerned that she would become irrelevant and quickly decided that gathering a number of socially influential supporters and raising a large sum would signal that her organization had staying power. At the CU's first annual meeting in January 1914, she announced that her plan had succeeded. She then laid out their strategy going forward: they would to attack the Democrats running in the midterm, her famous strategy of holding the party in power responsible.[75]

Anna Howard Shaw was outraged. She dismissed these tactics as "militant" and "un-American." NAWSA, she declared, was "nonpartisan," and "we shall always help our friends." Ruth McCormick, whom Shaw had appointed to replace Paul as the chair of the Congressional Committee, went even further, writing an open letter of support to the Democratic president Woodrow Wilson. NAWSA would "oppose no party as a whole," she assured him, "fearing lest this small group of suffragists acting under un-American and militant methods prejudice our cause." Many of the members of NAWSA were confused and distressed by the break. A number felt that President Shaw was to blame. Most did not drop their membership in NAWSA but continued to belong to both, including Alice Paul. But the CU struck out on its own as an independent organization.[76]

Paul began to put her political plans in motion for the election of 1914. That year the Democrats held the presidency and controlled both houses of Congress, giving them full control of the government, a rare occurrence. If the Democrats wished to pass the suffrage amendment out of Congress, they could, and President Wilson, as leader of his party, could encourage that action. But he refused, arguing that he had not run on a suffrage plank and therefore could not speak for his party. At the CU meeting in January, Paul put the Democrats on notice that unless they passed the amendment before election season, the CU would campaign against them, all of them, despite individual support of suffrage. The press immediately ran articles under headlines about the plan, using familiar metaphors. The *New York Times* led with "Suffragists on Warpath," and reporters repeated that trope throughout the 1914 Congressional Union campaigns against the Democrats.[77]

PART II

At the Crossroads of Suffrage and Citizenship

1913–1917

CHAPTER 8

The Problem of the Color Line
Carrie Williams Clifford

The Washington suffrage parade symbolized the possibility of unified woman-hood despite the best efforts of white suffragists to segregate it. This vision was entirely the result of women of color insisting on inclusion in the parade on their own terms. Most clearly represented by Ida B. Wells-Barnett taking her place with the Illinois contingent, it was also visible in the work of other black women like Nellie Quander, who urged Alice Paul to include them in meetings before the parade, and Carrie Williams Clifford, who insisted that their participation be remembered after it. Marie Bottineau Baldwin also appeared in the procession the way she wanted to be seen: as a modern lawyer, not as a buckskin-clad vanishing Indian. Mrs. Wu with her flag invoked the successes and potentials of the new Chinese republic, offering a truer vision of Chinese women to Americans steeped in stereotype.

The moment was fleeting. After the parade, growing racial tensions and divisions over suffrage strategy meant that women of color faced difficult choices regarding the paths they would take forward. Those paths were increasingly constrained by a rising tide of white supremacy. This was not new: many of the women had already been challenging white supremacists on multiple fronts. The prejudices they faced, however, were not the same for all of them. The suffrage activism of women of color was shaped by their particular relationships to U.S. citizenship. The Fourteenth Amendment's establishment of birthright citizenship was intended to overturn the antebellum version of citizenship as white-only, which had been specified in the 1790 Naturalization Act and upheld by the Dred Scott decision (1857). The authors of the amendment were thinking of people of European and African descent, and the Fourteenth Amendment explicitly excluded "Indians not taxed"—in other words, citizens of Indigenous nations—from its stipulations. Possibly worried that birthright citizenship would apply to other groups of nonwhite people, like Asians, Americans sought to limit their access to the country by passing the Page Act in 1875 and the Chinese Exclusion Act in 1882.

Women's suffrage activism varied depending on both race and citizenship status. Black women's suffrage activism was infused with antiracist work. In particular, black women drew specific parallels between race prejudice and sex prejudice to make the case for enfranchising women.

The day after the suffrage parade, Woodrow Wilson was inaugurated the twenty-eighth president of the United States. There was uncertainty about his support of suffrage. His position in regard to the race question seemed more obvious. He had been president of Princeton University and governor of New Jersey but had been born a Virginian and raised in the South. He was only the second Democrat elected president since 1897 and the first southerner since 1848.

Wilson immediately signaled his intentions. He named Thomas Nelson Page, the man whom Clifford had battled in print a few years earlier, to head his inaugural reception committee. As Clifford and the other suffragists were marching down Pennsylvania Avenue, Page was meeting Wilson's train at Union Station. It was likely to Page that the president-elect directed his famous question, "Where are all the people?" as they drove from the station to his hotel. And it was probably Page who answered, "On the Avenue, watching the suffrage parade."[1] A few months later, Wilson would announce that he had appointed Page to the plum position of U.S. ambassador to Italy.[2]

For Carrie Clifford the struggle for citizenship was a cultural battle as well as a political one. If black Americans were going to be full citizens, they needed to counter the false images white culture makers were creating. Moreover, she, like other black women, recognized that the suffrage struggle faced by her community was not only about woman's suffrage but also about black men's right to vote. Indeed, Page had strong opinions about black men voting and serving in politics, views that went along with his abhorrence of the "amalgamation" of the races and his belief that black people had been better off under slavery. His 1898 Reconstruction novel Red Rock imagined a savage black leader who attacks a white woman. The man is ultimately lynched, but the lesson of the dangers posed by black men in politics was clear.[3]

Many white southerners stoked just this kind of racial fear to justify Jim Crow laws, disenfranchisement, and lynchings. These ideas were also shared by many of the men whom Woodrow Wilson appointed to his cabinet and who urged him to segregate the nation's civil service. They stirred up public anxiety about black men and white women working together in government offices. Wilson cloaked his actions in the language of efficiency, but this, too, resonated with portraits Page and others had painted of black politicians as greedy and incompetent, stereotypes that had led Congress to disenfranchise the voters of Washington, D.C., several decades earlier. It was also quite partisan. Under Republican administrations since the Civil War, African Americans had gained a foothold in federal civil service jobs, making up 5 percent of the nation's employees.[4]

Black federal employees had long worked side by side with their white colleagues in federal offices. These jobs gave them economic security and helped build a strong black community in Washington. President Wilson's administration changed that dramatically. He discouraged their hiring, and his cabinet officers refused to promote them and in some cases even demoted them. Carrie Clifford's husband, William Clifford, felt this change immediately. In July 1913 his salary was reduced from $1,600 to $1,400.[5] The space of the capital also began to change as departments separated black and white clerks with curtains, created segregated cafeterias, and put up signs labeling bathrooms as "White" and "Colored." The "Colored" bathrooms were inevitably in basements. In 1914, the federal Civil Service Commission began to require that job seekers submit photographs with their applications, further ensuring that black applicants could be identified and rejected. These limited opportunities for D.C.'s black families to join the middle class were abruptly cut off.[6]

The situation was more difficult still for black women. Years later, Mary Church Terrell remembered that even before President Wilson's administration segregated the civil service, black women were excluded from good federal jobs. Other than teaching positions in the District's segregated public schools, the positions open to African American women were low-paying menial jobs such as charwomen (cleaners) or bathroom attendants in federal buildings. Under Wilson their exclusion was even more pronounced. Terrell, who was light-skinned enough to pass as white, remembered that despite her excellent credentials—she had graduated with a classics degree from Oberlin College—supervisors refused to hire her upon learning she was African American. Even during the wartime emergency, with labor shortages and a desperate need of German speakers like Terrell, she was turned away because of her race.[7]

When it came to weaving white supremacist fantasies, Thomas Nelson Page was not unique. He may have been first to develop stories about happy slaves who transformed into dangerous black politicians after emancipation, but it was Thomas Dixon who succeeded in lodging this story more deeply in American popular culture. For both authors, the specter of black men with political power drove their imaginations. As Dixon related it, he never forgot the day his uncle took him to see the debates in the South Carolina state legislature.[8] He remembered the representatives in great detail; there were "ninety-four Negros, seven native scalawags (white South Carolina Republicans), and twenty-three white men (presumably carpetbaggers from the North)." Ashamed of his state, he vowed to spend the rest of his life fighting against the racial equality represented by that assembly. At first he thought that he could make a difference through politics. He ran for and won the office of state representative in 1884. By that time, almost all of the African Americans who had been in the legislature were gone due to voter disenfranchisement and violent intimidation, but Dixon was still disillusioned by politicians, whom he deemed "as bad as prostitutes." The young man tried his hand at a number of other jobs—actor, lawyer, clergyman, essayist, and lecturer—but none of them satisfied his crusading spirit to "set the record straight."

He picked up his pen and wrote *The Leopard's Spots: A Romance of the White Man's*

Burden (1902), the first of a influential trilogy of books. He was thrilled with his creation and sent it off to a friend of his at the Doubleday, Page and Company publishing house. Feeling confident in the story, the publisher ordered an initial run of 15,000 books. They sold out immediately. Page thereupon set to work on the sequel. It took him only a month to write *The Clansman: A Historical Romance of the Ku Klux Klan*. Picking up the same themes, it told the story of how the Ku Klux Klan had saved white southerners from the horrors of Reconstruction, especially the threat of interracial relationships and miscegenation. The novel was another success, and Dixon built on that by rewriting it as a play that also proved incredibly popular, especially in the South. It deftly rolled all of the themes of that contrived history into a powerful story. A vicious black Union soldier pursues a beautiful white woman who beats back his advances and finds the only refuge for her honor in suicide. Her death is avenged by the honorable white men of the Ku Klux Klan. Although it was a figment of his imagination, Dixon insisted that the story was a true history of the South.

Dixon was not done. He brought his ideas to a young man from Tennessee who was a pioneer in the new industry of filmmaking—David Wark, or D. W., Griffith. Up to this point, most films were shorts: the excitement was in the moving image, not the storyline. Nor was it a medium that was taken seriously as real art. Dixon, however, saw the potential for his story to reach a vast audience with this new technology, and Griffith had the skills to make that happen. Dixon brought the director a script and numerous suggestions about the story. Griffith used his exceptional eye and understanding of film technology to make Dixon's vision come alive on the screen. The result was a twelve-reel drama much longer than anything that had come before and much more visually sophisticated. It animated Dixon's message in an astonishing way. Even Dixon was amazed. After the first screening, Griffith told him that *The Clansman* was too tame a name for the film and suggested the more grandiose title *The Birth of a Nation*.

Not everyone saw the film the same way. Many people, black and white, were shocked and horrified by the story it told. In Chicago, Jane Addams summed up by saying, "It is claimed that the film is historical; but history is easy to misuse."[9] The white actors in blackface portraying brutish black men chasing ethereal white women and lording their power over manly white Confederates made a mockery of the actual events of Reconstruction. In reality, southerners had unrepentantly reelected all but the highest former Confederate politicians after the war and passed draconian laws intended to completely subordinate the newly freed black people. The film inverted the violence of the citizens' brigades who had lynched Republican politicians, both black and white; raped and assaulted the wives, daughters, and mothers of black men who dared to assert their new rights; and rejected the Reconstruction governments that had spread public education across the South.[10]

Educators, from Booker T. Washington to the president of Harvard University, denounced the film, though critics generally praised it. The NAACP protested it at theaters across the nation and seemed to have made some headway. One member, Oswald Garrison Villard, editor of the New York *Evening Post* and grandson of the great abolitionist William Lloyd Garrison, found the film "improper, immoral and unjust." In New York, the film was held up by the film board, but Thomas Dixon was not cowed.[11]

He called on an old friend from his college days, Woodrow Wilson, and asked him to lend credibility to the film by attending a showing. Still in mourning over the death of his first wife, President Wilson did not think it would be seemly to attend the theater. Dixon offered a private screening at the White House. After seeing the film, the president, a historian himself, was said to have turned to his friend and commented, "It is like writing history with lightning." Encouraged, Dixon approached the chief justice of the Supreme Court and offered him a viewing. Edward D. White scoffed that he was not interested in motion pictures, but Dixon persisted: the film, he explained, was a telling of how the Ku Klux Klan had saved southern honor during Reconstruction. The chief justice's manner changed. "I was a member of the Klan, sir," he asserted proudly and agreed to attend the screening. And so the entire Supreme Court of the United States, along with a number of congressmen who came as guests, watched *The Birth of a Nation*. It was an extraordinary endorsement, and Dixon made a point to tell the New York film commission that the president, Supreme Court, and members of Congress of the United States had all viewed and enjoyed the film. The film board reversed its decision to censor the film.

Carrie Clifford recognized the importance of opposing a cultural politics that insisted that black people were ill-suited for political participation. For the past two decades she had watched as white Americans rewrote the history of the Civil War and Reconstruction. She saw how men like Page, Dixon, and Griffith created art that propagated lies against black America. They denigrated former slaves as ignorant and vicious dupes who allied with greedy northern politicians to oppress white southerners. In their narrative, both northern and southern troops were honorable and slavery was a benevolent system that had safely contained "savage" black people. The experiment of black political participation during Reconstruction, they asserted, had gone horribly wrong. They wrote this idea into books and songs. They built it into the very landscape, raising monuments to Confederate generals and renaming parks and prominent streets for them. From the halls of academia to parlor meetings of the Daughters of the Confederacy, white men and women worked hard to enshrine this new story about the righteousness of the southern "Lost Cause." Woodrow Wilson's ascension to the White House and his embrace of the men responsible for these lies put the power of the federal government behind them.

Even before D. W. Griffith splashed Dixon's version of history onto screens throughout the nation, Carrie Clifford responded. She had battled Page in the pages of national magazines in 1907 and now took on Dixon as well. She minced no words in her poem "A Reply to Thos. Dixon" in *Race Rhymes*. "We are rising, we are coming," she wrote, proclaiming that black women would confront these lies. Dixon's fear of African American progress led him to spread "abroad this scandalous tale" that "Black men are not white men's equal," that they are "savage, soulless, scarcely human / Doomed forever to servile place." Instead she insisted "we hurl back the defamation" and would prove it wrong "by thought, by word, by deed." This was a righteous struggle and would be hard fought. There were "giants to o'ercome," she warned, and "Satan's angels to be vanquished," but she was confident that they were on the side of "Justice, God and human right."[12]

Clifford had continued to work with the NAACP to defend her community against these assaults. In June 1911, the national NAACP had selected a committee to present an anti-lynching petition to President Taft. Clifford and Mary Church Terrell were the only two women on the committee. Their meeting with the president had been made possible by Senator Charles Curtis of Kansas. Their petition highlighted the "alarming increase of lynchings in our country," and they implored President Taft, as the chief executive "into whose hands have been committed the enforcement of the laws and the preservations of the rights of all the people," to call on Congress to address the scourge of "lawlessness and murder" in the United States. He was their last hope, as appeals to governors, state legislators, and sheriffs had been ignored. Moreover, the lawlessness was spreading. The murders were encouraged by mobs including "many of 'the leading' white men and women (and even children)" who made "a sport of murder and laugh at the cries of anguish and pain of those whom they hang, shoot to pieces or burn." Despite their appeal, Taft refused.[13]

Disappointed but undeterred, Clifford moved to establish a local branch of the NAACP in Washington, D.C. *The Crisis* reported more than a thousand attendees at an informational meeting she organized, many of whom signed up for membership. A year later in June 1913, Clifford was serving as the branch's interim president.[14] Clifford also used art to counter the degrading images generated by white supremacists. The women's committee she led for the Washington NAACP raised $1,000 to provide artwork for *The Crisis* covers as well as its Christmas card and calendar. The committee's goal was "to encourage young artists and make the colored people realize how beautiful their own rich, soft coloring is." The "spiritual influence" of this project was tremendous, editor W. E. B. Du Bois concluded.[15]

Clifford's own art helped her as well. She continued to write poetry but also threw herself into work with children, seeking to instill pride in black youth through educational games, stories, and magazines. She became chair of the Education Committee of the National Association of Colored Women's Clubs and also headed its Department of Literature.[16] She was caught up in a creative outpouring by the African American community. When W. E. B. Du Bois staged

A Woman's Suffrage Symposium

Communities of color often discussed woman's suffrage in their own publications and organizations. The Crisis, the journal of the NAACP, published articles and special forums on the topic, highlighting the work of African American suffragists and focusing on the political issues their community found most pressing. The image used to illustrate the 1912 suffrage forum evoked arguments that women would use their votes to help children. (Crisis, September 1912, 240)

his massive pageant, *The Star of Ethiopia*, in Washington in 1915, Clifford was one of the three women on the local pageant committee.[17] She had always loved recitation; she had even won contests in school. Du Bois's pageant inspired her to try her hand at writing drama. She later debuted a "playlet" called *Tradition* at a benefit for Dunbar High School.[18]

In the summer of 1914, a trip to France had helped revive her spirit. She traveled to visit African American diplomat William Henry Hunt and his wife, Ida, whom she had met in Washington. In a Catholic church in the Pyrenees she saw a black Madonna, an encounter that she found especially restorative. The idea of Europeans venerating a black woman and caring for her history filled Clifford with awe, and she shared this vision of black women's potential place in society, so different as it was from her experience in the United States. "Dear Negro-America, can you believe it!" she asked readers of *The Crisis*.[19] All of this creative work celebrated the history, beauty, and vibrancy of black Americans and sustained her in the face of white supremacist efforts to rewrite the nation's history and to cast African Americans in humiliating or villainous roles.

Clifford and other black suffragists framed their arguments in the longer struggle against racism. In August 1915 *The Crisis* appeared in mailboxes across the country. The cover of the special issue sported a composite image of Sojourner Truth with Abraham Lincoln and declared "Votes for Women." This was the second women's suffrage symposium that *The Crisis* had hosted in five years, indicating the matter's importance to the editor.[20] Du Bois, who was Clifford's friend, had solicited pro-suffrage opinions from a variety of black public figures, both female and male. Twenty-five of them, including Clifford, responded in time to make the print run. Ten were written by men, religious and political figures in the African American community. The remaining fifteen came from women, the majority of them involved in the National Association of Colored Women. Clifford, for example, was listed with her title, Honorary President of the Federation of Colored Women's Clubs of Ohio.[21]

The writers offered a wide range of supportive arguments. Some proffered a human rights approach, asserting that women deserved the vote because they, like men, were human beings worthy of dignity.[22] Others pointed to the New Women, or as one put it, "the New citizen," who actively engaged in the workforce and reform movements and so deserved the ability to participate in political life.[23] Several drew on women's experience with limited woman suffrage to demonstrate its benefits. Mrs. Josephine St. Pierre Ruffin proudly told her readers that she had voted forty-one times in Massachusetts under school suffrage laws, while Miss Maria L. Baldwin, a school principal from Massachusetts, declared that female teachers in states with school suffrage had "found out that even so meagre a share of voting power has given them a definite influence."[24] Hon. Oscar De Priest, a black alderman in Chicago, argued that enfranchising women helped black candidates: when women were granted the right to vote in local Chicago elections, black women, including Ida B. Wells-Barnett and her Alpha Suffrage Club, "rolled up a very large and significant vote for the colored candidates." Hon. Robert H. Terrell, in "Our Debt to Suffragists," generously emphasized the historical role some white suffrage leaders had played in supporting suffrage for black men while likewise noting that great abolitionist men like Frederick Douglass, William Lloyd Garrison, and Robert Purvis had supported woman suffrage.[25]

In line with one ideological strand of the day, Clifford pointed to women's innate differences from men as giving them special insight that would be valuable in the political realm.[26] In her piece, "Votes for Children," Clifford expanded on her well-established maternalist stance, that women deserved the vote because they were mothers. The family was a miniature version of the state, she asserted, and women were responsible for creating the next generation of citizens. As such, "the wonder grows that [woman's] voice is not the *first* heard in planning for the ideal State in which her child, as future citizen, is to play his part." Women had advocated for many of the progressive reforms in the world, she and others noted, including temperance, kindergartens, playgrounds, and City Beautiful architecture. They had done all of it without the ballot. She then asked her readers to consider how much more efficient women could be with suffrage. "The ballot!" she mused, "the sign of power, the means by which things are brought to pass, the talisman that makes our dreams come true!" With that power women could fulfill their dream of creating a state "where peace and unity [can] be established and where love shall reign."[27]

Several authors analogized sex discrimination and racial discrimination to advocate for women suffrage. They were writing for *The Crisis* audience, most of them black, and to many black male voters. The essays reveal the historical relationship of African Americans to disfranchisement, something many black men as well as black women experienced. They asserted that black men should be sympathetic because of their own familiarity with racism. "Disfranchisement because of sex is curiously like disfranchisement because of color," wrote Mrs. Coralie Franklin Cook. "It cripples the individual, it handicaps progress, it sets a limitation upon mental and spiritual development." Mrs. Mary B. Talbert, vice president of the NACW, emphasized the intersectionality of black women's experiences. "With us as colored women, this struggle becomes two-fold, first, because we are women and second, because we are colored women," she explained. Suggesting that those resisting suffrage for black women also supported racial prejudice, she challenged black men to support the cause. "Although some resistance is experienced in portions of our country against the ballot for women, because colored women will be included, I firmly believe that enlightened men are now numerous enough everywhere to encourage this just privilege of the ballot for women, ignoring prejudice of all kinds." In reminding black men that much of the resistance to women voting in the South came from white supremacists afraid that black women might vote, she urged her audience to put themselves in the category of "enlightened men."[28]

Other authors were more pointed. They asserted that the arguments against women's suffrage drew upon the logic of "states' rights"[29] or "the old pro-slavery arguments."[30] Mary Church Terrell made this case most vociferously. "Even if I believed that women should be denied the right of suffrage," she wrote, "wild horses could not drag such an admission from my pen or my lips, for this reason: precisely the same arguments used to prove that the ballot be withheld from women are advanced to prove that colored men should not be allowed to vote. The reasons for repealing the Fifteenth Amendment differ but little from the arguments advanced by those who oppose the enfranchisement of women."[31] Indeed, many white southerners feared that discussions about a constitutional amendment for women's suffrage would reopen national conversations over the Fifteenth Amendment and the Jim Crow laws that southern states had used to disenfranchise black men.[32]

The racism that Clifford and other black women fought was not new, but its form was specific to that particular moment. As the Wilson administration came to power and brought with it a cabinet staffed with white supremacists, the consequences of disenfranchisement for black men in the South became starkly clear.

The nation's top leaders embraced a fantastical history of Reconstruction that romanticized the antebellum world of white slaveholders woven by white authors like Thomas Nelson Page and Thomas Dixon.

It was in black communities that the true history of Reconstruction—the great experiment in democracy that led to the nation's first black U.S. senators and representatives and the visions of equality that were then violently suppressed by the white leagues and the first Klan—remained alive. Carrie Clifford wrote it into her poetry, and black women's arguments for suffrage were suffused with the memory of the Fifteenth Amendment.

Black women derived their suffrage strategies from their particular experiences and historical memories. As we have seen, however, women from other racialized groups encountered different kinds of prejudice and faced alternative obstacles to full citizenship. As those women formulated their responses, they redeployed ideas about race in new and often unexpected ways.

CHAPTER 9

The Indians of Today
Marie Louise Bottineau Baldwin

Marie Bottineau Baldwin saw the segregation of the federal civil service under the Wilson administration firsthand from her position in the Interior Department, where she had been working for almost a decade. As she observed the new political landscape, she considered her own place in it.

Hers was a complicated position. African Americans were U.S. citizens, while a large number of Native people were not. Most Indians did not reckon their identity with such stark distinction, though they considered themselves members of Indigenous nations. They held a multilayered sense of belonging that could incorporate many relationships.[1] White Americans believed, and federal policy dictated, that Native people could become "civilized" and therefore eligible for citizenship only if they chose to give up their connections to their Indigenous nations. This view had a long history. Before the Civil War, people of African descent were declared ineligible for citizenship. Native people's eligibility for U.S. citizenship was more flexible. Recognized as members of sovereign nations, U.S. officials allowed that they could become citizens if they severed those ties and lived like white Americans. In his majority opinion in *Dred Scott v. Sanford* (1857), Justice Roger Taney ruled that people of African descent could never become citizens but that if a Native person "should leave his nation or tribe and take up his abode among the white population, he would be entitled to all the rights and privileges which would belong to an emigrant from any other foreign people." These ideas continued to shape Americans' ideas about Native citizenship after the war, when "Indians not taxed" had been excluded from the birthright citizenship clause of the Fourteenth Amendment. The payment of taxes indicated that a Native person had left his or her nation and begun to live as a "civilized" American. Increasingly, Indigenous people recognized that the United States used citizenship to attack their sovereignty. As racial lines hardened in the decades after the Civil War, the Supreme Court ruled in *Elk v. Wilkins* (1884) that only an act of Congress could endow U.S. citizenship on Indians.[2]

In this increasingly rigid racial regime, white Americans had trouble classifying Métis people like Bottineau Baldwin who were of mixed Native and French descent and generally decided that if they kept ties to their Native kin, they remained Indians.[3] As the Wilson administration built racial inequality into the civil service, it raised a number of very personal and immediate questions for Bottineau Baldwin. Would she be considered nonwhite and therefore categorized with African Americans? If that happened, would she be demoted or lose her job in the Indian Office? Which bathroom should she use? Would she be forced out of her law school? These were dire possibilities and required a forceful response.

She went on the offensive. If Americans thought of her as an Indian, she would prove that Indians were different from African Americans. Eight months into the Wilson administration, she pulled out a sheet of Society of American Indians letterhead, which listed her as a member of the board of advisors, and dashed off a letter to Arthur C. Parker of New York, her friend and the society's secretary. Her arguments drew directly from those put forth by white supremacists. "My dear Mr. Parker," she wrote, "there is one subject that needs stirring up and I believe the Society of American Indians should do the stirring: that is the subject of negro employees in the Indian Service." There were many reasons they should not be employed on reservations and at Indian schools, she explained. Blacks took positions from Native applicants who needed jobs. Moreover, Indians were not used to black people and therefore did not know, as she put it, "how to treat and act with the negro in order that the negro can be kept in his place." Even if they did, their jobs in the Indian Service meant that black employees were in superior positions to the Indians they oversaw—and in many cases to white and Native employees as well. As a result, she wrote, "the Indian begins to feel that Uncle Sam must consider the negro equal to the Indian and the white."

Then Bottineau Baldwin, a woman of French and Native heritage, got to the heart of her concern. Echoing the language of the Wilson administration, she raised the specter of interracial relations. "I know what the negro gets to be" under such circumstances, she cautioned. "There are enough Indians with negro blood in their veins now" as a result of the federal government forcing nations like the Seminole to make their former slaves citizens of their tribe. She began to write more insistently. "Then, too, the negro is immoral—dangerous! Pages might be written on the subject and prove that the negro should not be sent out in the Indian Service." She warned of the consequences. "Think of this and grind your teeth! A negro *physician* is employed at one Indian reservation and at a *number* of places are negro bosses over boys and girls." She signed off by asking Parker to forward her letter to the president of the organization and to respond with his thoughts. If he did respond, though, his letter has been lost.[4]

The doctor whose reputation Bottineau Baldwin attacked was Edward J. Davis, a remarkable man. He had been born into slavery in South Carolina during the chaos of the Civil War.[5] After the war, he took advantage of the Freedmen's Bureau schools, then worked his way to Fisk University, which was founded by former abolitionists. He excelled at Fisk and then, following in the footsteps of another Fisk graduate, W. E. B. Du Bois, he applied to Harvard University. He became one of the first black men to attend Harvard's medical school, graduating in 1896. After a residency in St. Louis he took a position as a doctor in the Indian

Service and was stationed far from home at Zuni Pueblo in the New Mexico Territory.

At Zuni, Davis was also thinking about how he fit into the racial categories that Americans were debating. In April 1910 he took a temporary position as census enumerator for McKinley County, New Mexico, which encompassed the Zuni Reservation. Along with completing the "Indian Census Schedule," which required that he record members of the tribe separately as befitted their status as wards of the nation, he also counted the employees at the Zuni agency. He resisted the blanket categories of black or white, instead carefully designated the African American employees at Zuni in more nuanced (but still hierarchical) terms. For Willis Williams, the Texan working as the agency sheepherder, he penned "Bl" for "black." Next to his own name as well as that of his wife, Mary, and their daughter, Pauline, he inscribed "MU" for "mulatto." He indicated that the agency cook, James Taylor from Louisiana, was mulatto as well. In other censuses white enumerators recorded Davis as "Black" or "Negro," but he insisted on a term that offered a full account of his ancestry and that also carried prestige and class status within the African American community.[6]

Initially the Zuni people expressed some ambivalence about Davis. In their histories, people of African descent were linked with Spanish conquest, beginning with Esteban the slave who had come through their pueblo with Cabeza de Vaca in the sixteenth century. But Davis learned to speak the Zuni language and became accepted as one of the more sympathetic federal employees. He had been working at Zuni for six years when Marie Bottineau Baldwin made her complaint to Arthur Parker. Davis's superiors might have been surprised by her accusations. They had read nothing but praise for him in his evaluations. In 1918 he left his Indian Service position for a job as a physician in the St. Louis public school system. Over a decade later, John Collier, President Franklin Roosevelt's commissioner of Indian Affairs, asked him if he would like to rejoin the service, an offer Davis declined.[7]

Bottineau Baldwin does not appear to have ever met Davis, though as part of her work she may have run across his reports or the careful accounts he kept of the medical supplies.[8] Luckily for him, her accusations did not go anywhere. If they had, he could have lost his job.

Bottineau Baldwin was not simply trying to be white, however. Her attack seems not to have been about Davis personally; rather, she was trying to navigate the line between whites and blacks by putting Indian people firmly on the same side as whites. She was proud of her Native heritage and made that clear as well. When required to submit a picture for her civil service file, she did not choose one of the photographs she had of herself dressed in the highest turn-of-the-century fashion. Instead, she sent in one of herself in Native dress with her plaited hair over her shoulders. It was a profile portrait, echoing those taken by anthropologists to show the supposed inherent characteristics of different races, but in this case the angle emphasized the artistry of her outfit—her beautiful dentalium earrings, the intricately beaded front of her dress, and the patterned quilt wrapped around her shoulders.[9]

She likely calculated that white Americans felt differently about Indians than they did about African Americans. After all, she had watched as President Wilson replaced James Carroll Napier, an African American registrar of the Treasury who had resigned in protest over the administration's segregation orders, with Gabriel Parker, a Choctaw man.[10] When Parker stepped down to become superintendent of the "Five Civilized Tribes" in Oklahoma, Wilson appointed Teehee Houston Benge, a Cherokee lawyer also from Oklahoma. The position was primarily a symbolic appointment—the registrar's signature appeared on U.S. currency—but it had been used since the Civil War by Republican administrations to fulfill patronage promises to the African American community.

Bottineau Baldwin also read articles celebrating people's Native heritage like the 1911 feature in the Washington Times titled "Members of Congress of American Indian Lineage." A similar piece in the "Feature Section" of the Washington Herald ran under the headline "'First Families' in the Social Register Now Proud to Trace Descent from Pocahontas and the Other Real First Families." The occasion was the upcoming nuptials of President Wilson to Edith Galt, a Virginian whom the reporter described as having descended from the "princess" Pocahontas. Indeed, finding an Indian ancestor was the latest fashion. "Everybody is searching round the roots of family trees for traces of Lo [the poor Indian] or his squaw or his papoose," the reporter wrote breezily, deploying derogatory terms that Bottineau Baldwin and her friends bristled at.[11] But, compared with the utter horror with which whites in the city, and some Natives, regarded interracial relationships with African Americans, the column signaled that Indians fit into a different category. The author introduced her readers to members of the "First Families" in the city who hailed from Native nations around the country.[13] "Besides congressional and official," the author informed them, "Washington has all at once found itself well supplied with Indian blood." She listed them in a way that would have reflected well on any white socialite:

> Miss Dorothy Owen, daughter of Senator Owen, is granddaughter of the late Narcissa Chisholm Owen, a Cherokee accomplished in art. Mrs. J. S. Davenport, wife of the representative from Oklahoma, belongs to the Shawnee tribe, and is the great-great-great-granddaughter of Tecumseh. Mrs. William H. Murray is a Chickasaw; her uncle was one of the last tribal chiefs. Misses Stella, Italy and Julia Carter, daughters of Representative Charles D. Carter, inherit Chickasaw and Cherokee blood from their father. Misses Lucille and Georgia Parker and their brother, Gabe E. Parker registrar of the treasury, are Choctaws. Mrs. Marie L. Baldwin, a Winnebago, is connected with the legal division of the Indian bureau.[12]

While the reporter had ensconced her in the wrong nation, Bottineau Baldwin must have been thrilled by the article. Amid the viciousness and violence surrounding race in Washington, D.C., Indians had come out decidedly differently from black people. Relations between certain Natives and whites were publicly sanctioned and perhaps even desired, while their offspring could aspire to be senators of the United States or registrars of the Treasury. It was not so for African Americans. Mary Church Terrell recognized this difference, too, writing about an incident in which she was harassed on a District streetcar. "I am sure that if an Indian woman, or a Japanese woman or a woman of any other dark race had been bullied in that way by two men, some gentleman in the car would have come to her defense," she reflected.[14]

All of this took place in the context of a declining Native population. At the turn of the century, there were only approximately 300,000 Indigenous people in the United States. The federal government continued to classify at least a third of all adult Indians as wards, unable to make decisions about their own lands or moneys and kept from the rights of U.S. citizenship, including suffrage. Bottineau Baldwin and her colleagues in the SAI thought that perhaps the Wilson administration, which seemed so friendly to Native people, could address this.

Indeed, the question of Native people's relationship to U.S. citizenship had been one that the SAI had pondered and debated for some time. During their previous annual meetings, members had developed a platform of suggested policies that the federal government should follow in order to address the "Indian Problem." For white Americans, the "Indian Problem" was the existence of sovereign Native nations with communally held land in the midst of what was now the United States. The government attempted to redress this problem by trying to eliminate tribal sovereignty. In 1871 Congress ended the practice of treaty-making with Native nations and began to develop a series of assimilation policies to forcibly transform individual Native people from members of Indigenous nations into U.S. citizens through allotment policies that divided tribally held land, boarding schools that removed Native children from their communities and cultures, and laws that outlawed Indigenous cultural traditions.

For Native people, however, the so-called "Indian Problem" was Indigenous people's lack of political voice—through either the recognition of their tribal governments or U.S. citizenship—and their resulting inability to fully address the dispossession, disease, and poverty that had arisen from federal policies. SAI secretary Arthur C. Parker explained how in the context of assimilation policy, individual citizenship seemed to offer the best way forward. With allotment, he wrote, "a new era had dawned," and the "Indian Problem" went from being one of Native governments to individuals. The federal government refused to acknowledge the sovereignty of Native nations and was unwilling "to admit the right of any ward-nations or circumscribed treaty-nation, to dwell independent within its borders." In these circumstances, Parker concluded, the "only Indians who really succeed are those who as voters or potential citizens compete in civilization as *producers*." The SAI endorsed this as well.[15]

At their fourth annual conference, held at the University of Wisconsin in Madison in October 1914, members resolved to present "a petition and memorial to the President and Congress of the United States and to the Bureau of Indian affairs."[16] They hoped Congress would take up legislation to improve the condition of Native people. After the conference, members of the advisory board, the memorial committee, and the executive council met in the Washington office of Registrar of the Treasury Gabe Parker and after "careful debate" formulated the memorial they would present to the president. Their number also included Marie Bottineau Baldwin, who served as both chair of the executive committee and treasurer of the organization. She influenced the language of the memorial, and as we will see, the conversations about "the historic document" also influenced her.[17]

The group was thrilled that President Wilson had agreed to meet with them. Although he had given the SAI only seven days' notice, members were determined to make a good showing. They contacted by mail all of their members who lived east of Ohio asking them to come to the capital for the event. On the appointed day, more than forty delegates from the SAI's active officers, associate officers, board, and members, including Marie Bottineau Baldwin, arrived at the White House just before noon. As she entered the Oval Office, she saw that Robert L. Owen, the Oklahoma senator who claimed Cherokee descent, and Gabe Parker were waiting with the president. Parker introduced each member of the SAI delegation to Wilson, who "shook hands cordially as each member was presented." The president remained standing next to his desk as Dennison Wheelock (Wisconsin Oneida), chairman of the memorial committee, gave a short explanation and then read the memorial aloud.[18]

Frustrated by Native people's lack of political voice, the SAI focused on individual Indians' relationship (rather than Native nations' relationships) to the United States. The memorial contained points that the SAI believed must be addressed in order for Native people to have a "chance for individual efficiency and competency." First, it asserted that federal wardship of Native people was "anomalous." It permanently "conserve[d] within the nation groups of people whose civic condition by legislation is different from the normal standard of American life." Wardship had resulted in "confusion and chaos" because it left those Native people without "standing in court or nation." Moreover, as legal wards, Native people did not control their economic lives. They could not access their bank accounts or make decisions about their property unless a federal agent approved the transaction. This lack of standing left Native people trapped in legal limbo and was a barrier to their ability to thrive. The SAI suggested a commission of "the best, the most competent and the kindliest men to be found" to recommend the passage of a code of Indian law that would address the question of Natives' legal status. The group also requested that the U.S. Court of Claims be given jurisdiction over all Indian claims against the United States, a reminder of the broken treaty promises of the United States.[19]

When the SAI members exited the White House, they "faced a battery of cameras and moving pictures," an encounter that surely pleased them. They were particularly aware of their self-presentation and appearance at the event. "Every man and woman of Indian blood," Arthur Parker wrote, "was conscious of his responsibilities and eager to meet his obligations to his race and to his country. Proud of the ability of [the] race to advance, as they were, their clothing was that of citizenship of the great nation. There were no blankets, no feathers, no relics of the past, for these men and women were the Indians of today pleading for the future." They went to the aptly named Hotel Powhatan for lunch and speeches. There, Marie Bottineau Baldwin, the lone female speaker, rose and delivered her address, "What an Indian Woman Has to Say for Her Race."[20]

Bottineau Baldwin had graduated with her law degree in the spring of 1914, completing the three-year course of study at the Washington College of Law in just two years. The journal of the SAI celebrated her success but also revealed the pressure on Native people to represent their communities: "Indian capacity was on trial, and Mrs. Baldwin as a loyal Chippewa, a loyal Indian, finished her course with honors, outstripping her class-mates," it reported.[21] She then enrolled in the school's master's program for the 1914–15 school year. Influenced by the conversations in the SAI around the question of Indian citizenship, she developed arguments for that cause in her thesis, "The Need of a Change in the Legal Status of the North American Indian in the United States."[22] She was particularly concerned with the rights of Native nations and individuals. Tracing the Western ideas that had determined the legal status of Native nations from papal bulls through the Articles of Confederation, the Constitution, the Cherokee Cases, legislation ending treaty-making in 1871, the Dawes Act of 1887, and the Curtis Act of 1898, she took her reader on a tour of the legal relationship the federal government had tried to construct among itself, the states, and Native nations. This was not law that was usually taught at the Washington College of Law, where the classes focused on the basics of legal knowledge such as torts, contracts, and constitutional law.[23]

Her conclusions reflected her engagement with the SAI and suggest her influence on the petition to President Wilson. She, too, wrote that the current legal status of Native people consisted of "confusion and chaos." Instead of a clear relationship to the United States, "no man can tell what is his exact legal or political status." Anyone trying to describe the legal status of Native people, she explained, "very soon finds that he is dealing chiefly with his political condition, so little, if any, legal status have Indians." Indeed, that status was also frustratingly flexible depending on where one was. She added that "the citizenship and rights of an Indian may be altered completely by the crossing of an imaginary geographic line," as they travel across state or even reservation boundaries. "In short, there are Indians taxed and non-taxed, citizen Indians and non-citizen, independent Indians and Indian wards, and every complicated combination of all these classes, which may be changed at any time by a very slight change of residence."[24] This confusion, she insisted, was "a barrier to the progress of the Indian race."

She urged that Native people be granted U.S. citizenship, which would "render needless all the various _____ compacts, and regulations dependent on the present subordinate _____ ians." She argued that changing times called for changing law _____ ity in governing them." She suggested a legislative remedy: "U _____ of the U.S. and of the several states so provide, and not until t _____ of Indians in this country be protected in their Constitutional _____

But Indigenous citizenship could be layered. Treaties, Bottineau Baldwin insisted, remained important. Native peoples' "political relation to white people" and their land rights "rested on the peculiarly solemn guarantees with which this government accompanied its settlement of them on their lands—by treaty, by law, or by an Executive Order."[26] She traced the legal changes through which white Americans came to believe tribes were not sovereign but "wards."[27] Treaties, she asserted, "play a very important part in regulating the relation between the Indian tribes and individual Indians on the one hand and the government on the other."[28] Indeed, she linked land loss to a failure of the government to uphold treaties, even as Native people demonstrated their loyalty to the United States. For example, she recited the contributions of Native peoples, especially the Haudenosaunee (or Six Nations), to the United States in the War of 1812, noting that their warriors were not listed on the muster rolls despite their important part in the conflict. This made it difficult for them to gain land warrants for their service while white settlers received many tracts of Indigenous land (much of it Six Nations lan _____ for their participation.[29] In fact, she noted, after the war, the Ur _____ ut commissioners to remove Native people even though "in its _____ tribes, [it had] guaranteed to each of them FOREVER a portior _____ n which they resided."[30]

When Bottineau _____ ited, newspapers touted her accomplishments as the first N _____ rn her law degree. For reporters she was an exotic anomaly, but Bottineau Baldwin had a message for young women, especially young Native women. In one interview, she asserted that every woman should study law, especially Indians, because "to a race whose lands and property of other kinds are so valuable, it is all-important."[31] Indeed, she was invested in helping young Native women. She worked with several in the SAI office, which was just across the street from the Department of the Interior in the Barrister Building. A modern office building, it towered above its neighbors. Its suites were furnished with solid oak furniture. The SAI also had a small selection of Native art that it sold, sending the proceeds back to artists on reservations. Later the centerpiece became a large painting featuring a young, well-dressed Native man sitting over a desk, perhaps in a dorm room, studying his books and smoking. In the cloud of smoke over his head forms a scene of the "old days" on the prairie, where men ride on horseback dressed in buckskin. In its journal, the SAI described it: "There is a perplexity in the Indian's face—shall he go forward to a professorship and into a profession and win a banker's daughter, or shall he fly back to the plains and become the warrior-horseman, the wise man of the tribe, the free wanderer of wide stretching prairies?" For the urban Indian community in Washington, it seemed to have captured the tensions they felt as they worked to demonstrate to the world the modern capacity of Native people.[32]

Bottineau Baldwin enjoyed spending time at the office. Several young Ojibwe (Chippewa) women, including Alice H. Denomie, Dora B. McCauley, and Rosa Bourassa (later La Flesche), worked as assistant secretaries, and she became their mentor.[33] But many of the young women in the office did not stay long in the low-wage position of assistant secretary. In fact, sometimes they were not paid at all. A number of them left for paying positions in the Indian Office. A few stayed in Washington at the main office, but most sought employment across the country on reservations or in boarding schools.[34]

Arthur Parker praised them in one issue of the SAI's journal, writing, "There are many lady members of our society who have done much to contribute to its success." In particular, he noted, "few women in any organization have been more willing to work than Mrs. Marie L. Baldwin."[35] As treasurer, she wrote incessantly to members reminding them to renew their memberships and pay their dues. Because Parker, the organization's secretary, lived in Albany, New York, Bottineau Baldwin also helped to take care of various tasks in the city, such as coordinating the mailing of the society's journal. Sometimes she wrote articles for the journal, which Parker edited.

Her mentoring extended to Indian Service employees as well. Bottineau Baldwin became especially close with Rilla Meek and Ida Prophet Riley, young Native women from Oklahoma. "She is the mother to all Indians here," Rilla Meek wrote back to friends at the Haskell Indian School in Kansas. They appreciated her community-building efforts as well as her guidance in the new and overwhelming city and her example as a professional Native woman. Their friendships also sustained Baldwin. The women enjoyed spending time together at work and additionally fraternized after hours with other close friends who were also federal employees, such as Gabe Parker and Charles Dagenett.[36]

Bottineau Baldwin's networks of female friendship stretched beyond the city and to nearby federal boarding schools, especially the Carlisle Indian Industrial School in Pennsylvania, where her best friend, Angel DeCora, a Winnebago (Ho-Chunk) woman, taught art and where several of her relatives attended as students. Although Carlisle was the federal government's flagship boarding school, DeCora did not agree with its agenda of total assimilation. When she had arrived to teach at Carlisle, she offered a radical suggestion: some aspects of Indian culture deserved to be spared and not destroyed. In particular, she pointed to the artistic traditions of Native peoples as valuable. The moment was ripe for her ideas. Well-off Americans, who had been caught up in an enthusiasm for Japanese art and interior design, had just begun to shift into an "Indian craze"; lacquer screens and jade vases gave way to Navajo rugs and Pomo baskets. DeCora began to teach the students to appreciate their own and other cultures' arts and traditions. For example, she installed looms in the Carlisle art classroom and introduced Navajo weaving designs.[37]

Administrators believed that Bottineau Baldwin would set an example for Indian students of the kind of "civilized" behavior they should aim for while studying at the school and often detailed her to attend a graduation or other events. But she also went out of friendship as well as kinship. While at the school, Bottineau Baldwin always took time to visit relatives. She had several nieces at Carlisle, daughters of her extended kin across the upper Midwest. With her frequent travels, she helped maintain the very kinship ties and family support that the government's boarding school policies were meant to destroy.[38]

Bottineau Baldwin's nieces and their young friends must have been awed by this nationally famous and fashionable Washingtonian who sometimes arrived in an automobile. Indeed, just as Bottineau Baldwin was marching in the suffrage parade, the students at Carlisle were debating women's voting rights along with the rest of the nation. The girls were all members of the school's "Susan Longstreth Literary Society," or "the Susans," which held debates on pressing social questions. In October 1912, Rose Lyons argued the affirmative to the statement "That woman suffrage is desirable in all the States." We have to wonder if she was influenced by Bottineau Baldwin, whom she had visited in Washington. Two years later, the Susans again debated the question. They also debated other issues of equality, such as the resolution "That women should receive the same amount of wages as men for the same amount of labor." The male students also got into the discussion when the boys' "Standards Club" debated the statement "That women who pay taxes should be allowed to vote."[39]

The issue was even an inside joke for the graduating class. In his "Prophecy of the Class of '14" Edward Bracklin, a young Ojibwe student, imagined a future for his classmates in which Anna Roulette, Marie's niece, had been recognized and praised by the government for her domestic work, while her friend Rose Lyons was "languishing" with the radical British suffragist Emmeline Pankhurst "in Sing Sing prison, condemned to a long imprisonment for disturbing the peace by lectures on the then unpopular suffrage movement." Whether this was an accurate representation of the girls' political stances or a joke that inverted them, it is clear that like Bottineau Baldwin and others in the U.S. capital, they were also debating women's place in the American citizenry as well as roles for Native women.[40]

Many of the active members and leaders of the Society of American Indians lived in or spent time in Washington, D.C., where they formed an intertribal community that supported its members and was politically engaged. Their experiences as Western-educated, urban Indians also shaped their approach to citizenship and suffrage. Although they often advocated for U.S. citizenship for individual Native people, this stance did not imply that they sought to abandon their heritage or their belonging in Native polities. They remained Indian, and proudly so. Nor did they intend to relinquish the claims of Native nations. Bottineau Baldwin, like many of her peers, imagined a "layered" Indigenous citizenships that could include U.S. citizenship for individuals without abandoning the rights that accrued to members of Native nations through treaties and other legal relationships with the United States. Because at this moment the federal government was not willing to acknowledge tribal governments as legitimate, these Native intellectuals saw U.S. citizenship and the political power of the vote as one way to ensure that the government upheld its obligations to Native communities.[41]

Not all Indigenous people wanted U.S. citizenship and the rights of suffrage. Moreover, those who lived in reservation communities were also very aware that they had a relationship not only with the federal government but also with the governments of the states that surrounded their communities. In New Mexico, for instance, Pueblo leaders disagreed with the call for U.S. citizenship. They believed—as did many non-Native New Mexicans—that if they voted, it signaled their assent to be ruled as individual citizens by the United States with a consequent forfeiture of their rights as independent republics, especially their land rights. While some had voted in the past, they came to believe, and were informed by U.S. officials, that the best way to protect "their existence as distinct communities, with ancient (and some not so ancient) customs and practices, rested in becoming wards of the federal government." Without that status, they were at the mercy of state officials who often ruled against them in court cases, especially those regarding conflicting land titles.[42] Thus when New Mexicans were writing the state constitution in 1910, Native people had not sought the right to vote under its provisions. The Pueblos remained under the oversight and putative protection of the federal government; state politics, therefore, was the domain of Anglos and Hispanos.

[CHAPTER 10]
To Speak for the Spanish American Women
Nina Otero-Warren

In 1912 New Mexico entered the union as the forty-seventh state. The census for that decade placed the population of the state at 327,301 and revealed a diverse population of Anglos, Hispanics, and Natives predominating. Like many other state constitutions, New Mexico's denied voting rights to "Indians not taxed," which disenfranchised Native people residing in the nineteen Pueblos, the Jicarilla Apache reservation, and the Navajo reservation—that is, a vast majority of the Native population. Moreover, many Indigenous people in the state were ambivalent or resistant to participating in state government.[1] This left Anglo and Hispanic women to engage with the question of woman suffrage. The new constitution also set a high bar for amendments, which meant that full woman suffrage would be almost impossible without federal action.

When national suffragist leaders announced their new drive for a constitutional amendment with the 1913 Washington suffrage parade, New Mexican women took notice.[2] Supporters of women's right to vote in New Mexico understood the need to work for a federal solution, and therefore the National American Woman Suffrage Association, with its primary focus on state legislation, held much less promise than Alice Paul's new Congressional Union (CU). CU organizers first arrived in the state in 1914 and tried to tap into existing networks, including the state federation of women's clubs and the Woman's Christian Temperance Union (WCTU) branches. But those networks primarily encompassed Anglo women, and Hispanas in the northern part of the state were wary of the Protestant WCTU.

In the fall of 1915, the Congressional Union sent a second organizer, Ella St. Clair Thompson, who recognized the need to reach out to the Spanish-speaking women of New Mexico. Thompson's overtures followed the CU's strategy of organizing socially prominent women.[3] The Hispanas she encouraged to participate included women related to politically powerful men. Aurora Lucero was the daughter of the first New Mexican secretary of state, Antonio Lucero, while Ramona (Mona) Baca was the daughter of R. I. Baca, state Speaker of the House. Despite her father's death, Nina Otero-Warren's familial connections meant that she, too, along with her half sisters, remained one of the prominent Hispanas in Santa Fe.

Nina Otero-Warren exemplified the elite Hispanic women who became leaders in suffrage work in the former Mexican territories of New Mexico and Califor-

Many suffragists celebrated their cause as modern and often linked it with new technologies, such as the automobile. They could also be highly mobile. Nina Otero-Warren's suffrage campaign work as well as her position as superintendent of Santa Fe County Schools required her to travel to many communities in the state. She later drew upon these connections during her congressional campaign. (Photo ca. 1915, Bergere Family Photograph Collection, image no. 21252, courtesy State Archives of New Mexico, Santa Fe)

nia. They descended from prominent, landowning families. Although they, too, experienced violence and dispossession when Anglos arrived, their elite standing helped mitigate it. The importance of Spanish-speaking voting populations gave Hispanic men some political power as long as those populations remained significant, as they did in New Mexico far longer than in California or Colorado. Hispanic women like Otero-Warren were also able to use marriages to Anglos to maintain their social standing. But they did not hide their Hispanic heritage—they highlighted it by continuing to use both their Spanish "maiden" and married Anglo surnames. Many of these women were also well educated, bilingual, cosmopolitan, and paternalistic in their attitudes. Like the men in their families, they often thought of themselves as *patronas*, representatives of the Spanish-speaking community who spoke for their less fortunate sisters.[4]

When Ella St. Clair Thompson arrived in New Mexico, she perceived that Hispanas could be an important part of the suffrage fight in the state.[5] Thompson hit it off with the women in Santa Fe, including Otero-Warren, right away. Thompson was clearly fun and spirited, bringing a breath of fresh air to the city, as one woman put it. She enjoyed New Mexico and harbored no prejudiced against Spanish speakers. In fact, she spoke some Spanish herself: "very little—but it helps a lot," she wrote to Alice Paul. She admired the beauty of the language and lamented that "it was almost a pity that Spanish children of New Mexico have to learn English when their mother tongue is so mellifluous."[6] This endeared her to the Hispanic women, many of whom were strong advocates of the Spanish language. Aurora Lucero, for example, was now serving as head of the Department of Spanish at Tucumcari High School, and in January 1916 she traveled to Baltimore to attend the second Pan-American League Convention, where she interacted with Spanish speakers from throughout the Americas.[7]

Early CU organizers wisely incorporated Spanish speakers like Nina Otero-Warren and Aurora Lucero into the cause. Working together, they printed literature in Spanish and emphasized topics, such as child welfare, that appealed to Hispanic women. "They say it is very difficult to get the Spanish ladies out, but as I have one on the program to speak in *Spanish*, I think they will come—and their husbands as well," Thompson wrote to Alice Paul. And they did.[8]

For a large meeting at the Old Palace in Santa Fe in the fall of 1915, Thompson worked with Lucero to write a speech linking women's votes with child welfare.[9] Lucero gave her speech, "El Provenir de los Ninos" (Child welfare), in Spanish, and Thompson had it translated into English. In it they "pointed out the importance of women taking an interest in politics in an age when politics must enter into the passage of laws affecting the home." The Anglo speakers also emphasized the vote as social housekeeping. Mrs. Julia Asplund responded to the old argument that women might misuse the vote. She countered with the metaphor of not allowing a woman to tend her garden for fear she would hurt herself with the garden tools. Thompson concluded the meeting by arguing that voting was merely an extension of women's social duties. She pointed to the women of Chicago who had campaigned to end the system of contracting out the municipal garbage collection, which cut their bills in half. She also took a swipe at someone in Congress, most likely New Mexico senator Thomas Catron, who had "declared that women should stay at home at the fireside." She wittily responded that "in this day we have steam radiators, which are not particularly attractive to look at," a quip that brought "ripples of laughter" from her audience, though many in the state would certainly not have had steam radiators. At the conclusion of the meeting, Thompson reminded the crowd that they would be visiting Senator Catron at his home on Thursday afternoon to request his support.[10]

Senator Catron, who had served since statehood, was strongly anti-suffrage, but this did not stop the women of New Mexico from lobbying him. At three in the afternoon on Thursday, October 21, 150 Santa Fe women "made a public act of faith in the cause of woman suffrage" by parading through the principal streets of the city in gaily decorated automobiles. The route traced a rough figure eight that emphasized the seats of power in the city. Their path also ensured that the parade was highly visible to the hundreds of people who lined the streets. The women began at the central plaza and followed a course around the state capitol building before circling back through the center of town, then around the federal building and finally arriving at Senator Catron's house on Grant Avenue.[11] Local newspapers boosted their visibility by printing the names of many of the participants, including Hispanas such as Mrs. Lola Armijo, Mrs. Trinidad Cabeza de Baca (who lent her automobile to the cause), Mrs. James Chavez, [12] Miss Aurora Lucero, Mrs. Cleofas Romero, Mrs. Secundino Romero, and Miss Marie Romero.[13] Upon arrival at the senator's house, four of the women, two Anglos and two Hispanas—the latter Miss Aurora Lucero and Mrs. Cleofas Romero— gave brief speeches formally asking him to support the Susan B. Anthony federal amendment when he returned to Washington.[14]

In her speech, Aurora Lucero stated that she would have felt timid about approaching him, but she had heard the senator give an address in which he had "counseled the delegates to put aside all personal feelings where the good of New Mexico is concerned." She thus found that it was not a difficult task "but a real pleasure" to "speak for the Spanish American women, who while conservative, want the best possible laws when their home life is the question at issue." She expressed confidence that he would support the amendment.[15]

While Senator Catron had cordially greeted the women, he informed them that "it was his painful duty to decline" their request. "It looks to me as if you are asking me to do something not exactly right," he said, "to help pass an amendment to give the ballot to people who have stated they don't want it." As evidence, he pointed to the recent defeat of the suffrage referendum in New Jersey. Men, he explained at great length, made up the hardier sex, while women represented the delicate one. The Bible had designated women to be the child-bearers. It was his opinion, he told them, that granting the ballot to women would "tend to lower her, bringing her into contact with much which was disagreeable." He claimed that he had seen this in a recent visit to California, where "the best of the sex would not vote, but the lower element would use the ballot to the detriment of the more cultured women."[16] The women present were likely not surprised, since these assertions echoed sentiments Senator Catron had shared many times. He would continue to resist woman suffrage to the very end of his term, introducing an anti-suffrage statement into the Senate just a few weeks before leaving office as a final insult to the women of New Mexico.[17]

Thompson agreed that Catron was an "awfully cross old thing" but they found Senator Albert B. Fall more open; in fact, his wife served on the original CU committee formed in 1916. At least he was "not as dense and obdurate as Catron," one New Mexican suffragist grudgingly stated. Though Senator Fall was never an active suffragist, he was a friend to New Mexican women. The state's first congressional representative, Benigno Cárdenas Hernández, followed party leader Catron's lead, though his campaign manager's wife was a suffragist.[18]

Another CU organizer, Doris Stevens, came to New Mexico in February 1916. She spoke first in Albuquerque, where fifty women attended a meeting at the house of a prominent suffragist. They named delegates who were to attend the statewide meeting in Santa Fe the next day. The purpose of the meeting was to establish an official New Mexican branch of the CU, adopt a constitution, and elect state officers. It was expected to "fuse New Mexico women into a unit in favor of national suffrage legislation." Once that was done, the CU would "provide for a thorough organization of the state from end to end," starting with a plan to hold meetings in each county of the state.[19]

Young Hispanic women were closely involved in the conference. At the entrance Mona Baca sold CU suffrage pins while Aurora Lucero solicited subscriptions to the CU's magazine, the *Suffragist*. Dolores and Rosina Bergere, Nina Otero-Warren's half sisters, worked as ushers.[20] The four young women had all attended the Loretto Academy together and often participated in fundraisers for important causes, such as the 1906 San Francisco earthquake victims, the YWCA, and the public library.[21] Often, they celebrated their heritage by dressing as Spanish ladies, but they also partook in entertainment that drew on racial stereotypes, playing mammies and "pickaninnies" in minstrel shows and Chinese and Japanese maidens at teas.[22] Nina Otero-Warren also helped plan the Santa Fe Fiesta, a pageant reenacting the Spanish conquest of Native people.[23] These women were all proud of their Spanish heritage and touted themselves as "the descendants of conquistadors," as Aurora Lucero put it. Just as Anglo-Americans celebrated their ties to the American Revolution and to the Daughters of the Confederacy, Spanish-speaking women retorted to the claim that Anglos were the only "true Americans" by insisting that their ancestors had also come from Europe and helped to settle the continent, a vision that rested on the dispossession of Native peoples.

For the CU organizational meeting, the convention hall was "beautifully decorated with flags and bunting in the colors of the union—white, gold and purple." Fresh-cut flowers and ferns added to the "pretty scene." The young women at the table with suffrage material were wearing scarves in the union colors as they cheerfully greeted delegates. Although Hispanas were thus visible at the conference, none was a speaker. And all of the women elected officers of the CU branch were Anglo with one exception: they chose Nina Otero-Warren as vice chair.[24] The following year, when Mrs. Sarah Raynolds stepped down as chair, Alice Paul personally asked Otero-Warren to take up the position. She agreed, writing to Paul, "I will keep out of local fuss but will take a stand and a firm one whenever necessary, for I am with you now and always!"[25]

The year 1917 was a very busy one for Otero-Warren. The New Mexico Board of Education appointed her interim superintendent of schools for Santa Fe County. The next year, she ran for that position and won, defeating her male opponent handily. Superintendent of schools was one of the very few offices New Mexico women could hold or vote for under the state constitution. This was her first experience campaigning but proved to observers that she was up to the challenge. She would hold this position for the next twelve years.[26]

[CHAPTER 11]

The Application of Democracy to Women
Mabel Ping-Hua Lee

People remembered Mabel Ping-Hua Lee's captivating voice. Audiences were "simply carried" away by her charm, intelligence, and oratorical ability—and this was true whether in small intimate gatherings or large crowds. They came away "Mabelized," one listener remarked in awe.[1] Lee had been a teenager in 1912 when she gave the suffrage speech that made her nationally known. Her life stretched ahead of her, an exciting vista of possibilities. Political revolutions were happening in both China and the United States, and Lee insisted that Chinese women be involved in both.

As New Mexican women began to devote their energy into the fight for the national amendment, the women of New York continued their efforts to pass suffrage at the state level. No state east of the Mississippi had fully enfranchised women, and New York suffragists were determined that the Empire State would be the first. New York boasted the largest congressional delegation in the country, so if suffragists were successful, the cause would gain many supporters on Capitol Hill. Mabel Lee's participation in the 1912 New York City suffrage meetings and parade had connected her to a number of the city's activists. Her matriculation at Barnard College the following year further enmeshed her in those networks just as the fight for state suffrage was heating up. The two state campaigns of 1915 and 1917 coincided with her time at Barnard.

White suffragists recognized the valuable contributions Lee could bring to that fight and asked for her help. As a staunch suffragist and feminist, Lee agreed, but her true passion lay in the position of Chinese women in their new nation. As she closely followed the work of Chinese feminists, conversations with American suffragists helped shape her ideas as she brought the two strands of thought together in her advocacy for women's rights in the new China. Working with white suffragists also helped her combat the stereotypes about China that white Americans held.

But as much as Lee fought for suffrage in New York, she could not vote there. As a Chinese-born woman, she had been deemed ineligible for citizenship. As we have seen, when the Fourteenth Amendment instituted birthright citizenship, many white Americans feared it would incorporate persons who they did not believe could be good citizens of the nation. Some were especially suspicious of Asians, whom they perceived as racially incapable of democratic citizenship.[2] Congress responded with the 1882 Exclusion Act,[3] which was renewed every ten years. The result was a massive decline in the number of Chinese immigrants to the United States and the solidification of a bachelor population. It also meant that the Chinese were the only group of people in the world whom the United States restricted due to their nationality and made ineligible for naturalized citizenship. Even the citizenship of those few Chinese born in the United States remained questionable until the Supreme Court ruled in U.S. v. Wong Kim Ark (1898) that they were citizens by virtue of the Fourteenth Amendment, even if their parents had been foreign-born. This placed Chinese-born women like Mabel Lee in a position unique among all other women in the United States.

After the 1912 New York City parade, Lee returned to her focus on school. She finished her studies and graduated from Erasmus Hall High School in Brooklyn as the only Chinese student and one of only two women of color in her class. The local paper reported that she and Alberta Love, an African American woman, received the loudest applause when they stepped onto the platform to receive their diplomas. She had been admitted to Barnard College pending her fulfillment of entrance requirements, including Latin, Greek, and mathematics, and approval by the regents. She began to take classes at the University of Pennsylvania to prepare.[4] In 1913, she arrived on the Barnard campus as a freshman.

Like Howard University and the Washington College of Law in the District of Columbia, college campuses across the country introduced many young women to feminism. It was an exciting time to attend. The number of Chinese students in U.S. universities was just beginning to grow, and Barnard, along with its parent university, Columbia, hosted relatively large numbers of them. Barnard was also an epicenter for suffrage debates. In 1908, the school hosted a chapter of the new College Equal Suffrage League, founded by Radcliffe graduate Maud Wood Park, in order to draw more young women into the cause.[5] Meanwhile, both the National American Woman Suffrage Association and the New York state suffrage campaign maintained headquarters in New York City. The city was a crossroads for many of the nation's feminist thinkers, who often passed through Barnard. Lee's ideas about suffrage benefited from the vibrant speeches and debates at the school, where she consistently emphasized that Chinese women had their own feminist traditions. As Lee immersed herself in these two communities — suffragists and Chinese students — she sought to educate each. When speaking to American suffrage activists, she emphasized the positive aspects of China and news of the Chinese women's movement. In her conversations with mostly male Chinese students, many of whom were being educated as future leaders of the republic, she insisted that the new nation needed to incorporate women's rights, including suffrage, from the beginning.

Barnard College was twenty-four years old, not much older than Mabel herself. She was part of a cohort of women attending college that had been growing since just after the Civil War. It had been more than half a century since the women gathered at Seneca Falls had included in their Declaration of Sentiments the lack of "facilities for obtaining a thorough education—all colleges [were] closed against" women. Things had been improving since then. Barnard came into being thanks to the efforts of women like Lillie Devereux, Annie Nathan Meyer, and Grace Dodge who had fought for women's inclusion at Columbia University. Ultimately, that occurred through the founding of the Teachers College in 1887, a teacher training school, and Barnard College in 1889 as a sister school where women would be taught by Columbia faculty.[6]

Barnard was quite open compared with other women's colleges. For one thing, it was less expensive because many students, like Mabel Lee, could live at home. While a student at Mount Holyoke in Massachusetts needed $425 for tuition, room, and board, a student attending Barnard but living at home paid only $150 for tuition. In 1890, the president of the board of trustees proudly proclaimed "Barnard College is for women of every class . . . those who are to earn their living and those who are not can meet here, each class, nay, better, each woman, helping the other, without patronage, without condescension, without bitterness."[7] Some Barnard women were daughters of wealthy New York elites who did not want to leave the city, while trustee scholarships brought students from a variety of backgrounds. Barnard also enrolled a number of Catholic and Jewish students. Laura Cornelius Kellogg, the Wisconsin Oneida founder of the Society of American Indians, had briefly attended the school in 1908. But Barnard still was not open to everyone. For one thing, the entrance requirements included skills that students could not acquire in public schools. Families like Mabel's would have to pay for extra classes in Greek, Latin, and mathematics to prepare their daughters. Also, despite its impressive diversity, Barnard would not admit its first African American student until 1925.[8]

Mabel Lee and her generation were part of a sea change. At the turn of the century, the number of college students began to grow, making the 1920s a golden age of campus culture. College, with its school pride and youthful exuberance, became a sought-after experience. Young people everywhere, college student or not, were using slang words, and people lamented that you could not actually tell a college man from a regular joe, as so many of the latter were wearing the fashionable clothes of college students.[9] Inside jokes abounded. Often those jokes hinged on casual racism. Turning through the pages of the Barnard yearbook, Lee came across photos of fellow students in blackface and dressed as Indians. The class of 1915's mascot was "the Indian," while the classes of 1912 and 1916 were represented by "the dragon." The yearbook described the dragon, and thus the class character: "A dangerous serpent worshipped in China as an embodiment of the *evil principle*; the emblem of all that is obstructive, loathsome, and horrible in nature; the ideal of the spirit of evil which is in opposition to the order, harmony, and progress of the human race."[10] Given that the dragon figured prominently on the Chinese national flag until the establishment of the republic in 1912, Lee may not have found this to be the most flattering portrait of her people.

Chinese students were becoming a growing part of the student body at American universities. In 1909 a new exchange program, the Boxer Indemnity Scholarships, provided funding for students from China. The protocols after the Boxer Rebellion in 1889 required China to pay the Western powers, including the United States, large sums or indemnities for damages and loss of lives.[11] After American families and businesses were reimbursed, U.S.-based missionary societies argued that the remaining amount should fund a scholarship program for Chinese students, expecting that those scholars would return to China, become future leaders of the nation, and spread American ideas.[12] The number of Chinese students in the United States grew rapidly from 594 in 1915 to an estimated 1,507 seven years later.[13] Most were men; the Chinese government did not award Boxer scholarships to women until 1916, and even then the awards came with one stipulation: the women must have unbound feet. Between 1916 and 1929, fifty-three women held Boxer Indemnity Scholarships.[14] Many Boxer students came to study at Columbia. The first Chinese student had enrolled at Teachers College for the 1904–5 school year, and by 1920 Columbia had 123 students enrolled, the largest Chinese student population in the country.[15]

Mabel Lee was one of four Chinese women enrolled at Barnard in 1913.[16] They were not the first Chinese students to attend the school; that honor went to Kang Tongbi (class of 1909), also a strong advocate for women's issues.[17] Lee was good friends with other Chinese students enrolled at Barnard, including Alice Huie (class of 1917). Lee had much in common with American-born Alice and knew her and her sister, Caroline who was enrolled at Teachers College. They were all from Chinatown where their fathers were ministers while the girls and their mothers worked with the YWCA and the Daughters of China Club.[18] A third student, Anna Kong (class of 1915)[19] from China, joined Mabel and Alice at Barnard.[20] They were all active students. Lee and Anna Kong found fun and fellowship in the YWCA, with Lee attending the annual camping conference at Silver Bay on Lake George. She fondly remembered those experiences, donating to the Barnard Y's camping fund after graduation.[21] Alice Huie was known as a "brilliant" hockey player and captain of her class swim team.[22]

The Chinese students focused much of their political energy on the cause of the new Chinese nation and its people. They found many like-minded allies at Barnard, Teachers College, and Columbia College. They did their best to help educate their white allies from "the point of view of the recipients" of their help, as Mabel Lee put it. When they had opportunities to address white women, including suffragists, they emphasized the aspects of Chinese culture and history worthy of admiration. They found the YWCA to be a good place for this work, and

Lee, Alice Huie, and Anna Kong all joined the Barnard branch, believing their presence and input helped guide Y policies. Indeed, they were often called upon as experts to speak about China. Anna Kong delivered a lecture on "Oriental Girls" at a Student Forum at the YWCA. Lee spoke at another Student Forum on missionaries to China. She insisted that missionary workers should have "sympathy with the intellectual and cultural tradition of the people." For her, this meant they needed to "know the language, and the beauty of Confucian ethics." They should also know, she explained, the reasons Chinese people might be suspicious of missionaries, and she highlighted the example of Chinese Christians to educate her fellow students about China's progress.[23]

Lee used an early essay to educate her readers on Chinese history. In "China's Submerged Half," she explained that China had long had theories of women's education, but until Christian missionaries arrived those had remained more theory than fact—though she proudly pointed out that "the first book on the subject of education for women was written in China, and by a Chinese woman." Closely following news of feminists in China, she suggested that the role of women in the recent revolution as well as the storming of parliament by women demanding their suffrage rights demonstrated that the nation's "submerged half" had "emerged with a vengeance." She celebrated the fact that Chinese feminists were establishing newspapers and participating in the National Industrial Exposition. But, despite that progress, she called for "a wider sphere of usefulness for the long submerged women of China," asking "for our girls the open door to the treasury of knowledge, the same opportunities for physical development as boys and the same rights of participation in all human activities of which they are individually capable." She saw herself and the other female students as the "pioneers" on whose shoulders rested the responsibility to take a "leading part" in that effort. No less than "the welfare of China and possibly its very existence as an independent nation" depended on "rendering tardy justice to its womankind."[24]

Her years at Barnard allowed her to refine her thinking about suffrage and feminism. She came to believe that suffrage was only one part of a broader feminist movement.[25] And she defined feminism as "the application of democracy to women" and called for "equality of opportunity." She did not hesitate to use the new term "feminist" to describe herself.[26] Indeed, at Barnard the term quickly gained traction.[27] Speakers attempted to define it and students debated what it meant to them. The college was a fertile place for conversations on feminism and suffrage, and Mabel, being deeply influenced by her time there, contributed to those debates. A new student group, the Feminist Forum, sprang up in 1914. The organizers invited numerous speakers to campus to lecture on topics ranging from women taking civil service exams for government positions to the peace movement. Nationally known feminists such as historian Mary Beard (who was married to a Columbia history professor who also taught at Barnard), author

Charlotte Perkins Gilman, and Dr. Gertrude Walker of the Women's Medical College of Philadelphia filled rooms with overflowing crowds.[28] Mabel likely heard or at least read about those talks in the school paper, the *Barnard Bulletin*. She became part of those exciting discussions, as her speeches on feminism demonstrate her engagement with their ideas.[29]

Despite this vibrant program, the Feminist Forum did not initially attract as many members as its founders hoped, in part because it was affiliated with the Socialist Student Association.[30] The two organizations were dominated by "radicals," which annoyed some of the other students at Barnard who felt unwelcome. They suggested the creation of an umbrella organization, the Social Science League, that could include all students interested in "economics, politics, etc." By 1915 this became a reality and the league encompassed the Feminist Forum, the Socialist Club, and a new Debating Club. Lee joined the Debate Club. A weary Dean Virginia Gildersleeves hoped that the new organization would allow for greater "debate upon civic, social and economic questions" and that such debates would "afford a chance to learn to differ contrarily and to cease confusing freedom of speech with freedom to be boorish."[31]

Lee continued to represent Chinese women for the American suffrage movement while insisting that feminism remain part of the vision of the new Chinese nation.[32] She was influenced by the movements in both countries, which had similarities, but, as she asserted, "conditions in China are different from those of western countries and will require different solutions." Where her earlier essay had cited Chinese tracts on women's education, her time at Barnard gave her a deeper awareness of the struggles in Europe and the United States. Like the speakers she heard at Barnard and the lessons she learned in her courses, she emphasized the long history of women's changing place in society, a historical progression that drew from multiple Western philosophical roots.[33] "There are great documents giving proof of these stages in the development of democracy," she asserted. "For the spiritual, we have the Sermon on the Mount; for the legal, the Magna Charta or Bill of Rights; for the political, mainly the United States' Declaration of Independence; ... for the economic, the Communist Manifesto by Engels and Marx." And it was the economic realm that most interested her.[34]

As she put together her own philosophy about women, working, and marriage, she must have also had the women she had met at Barnard in mind. Mary Beard, feminist activist and historian, had dropped out of graduate school to care for her one-year-old daughter (though her husband finished his degree). Mary Simkhovitch had likewise encountered resistance because of her marriage to another of Lee's professors. Dr. Vladimir Simkhovitch taught at Columbia and Barnard and had spoken at the Feminist Forum that Mabel attended. The couple were strong supporters of suffrage and had both marched in the 1912 parade. Mary Simkhovitch was an activist and reformer who had previously worked at a settlement house in the city. In 1902, she became pregnant and had hoped to continue working while also raising their child in the settlement house, but the board rejected that idea and fired her. She rallied her supporters, including anthropologist Elsie Clews Parsons, who donated funds to establish another settlement house, the Greenwich House, where Simkhovitch could combine work and family. Lee certainly also heard news of the debates racking the New York City public school system over whether or not women could continue to teach once married. The school board decided that married women could teach but would have to quit upon becoming pregnant.[35]

At the same time that these discussions occurred all around her in New York, similar debates were taking place among women in China around the question of whether women could marry and have a career. Many of the women who arrived as Boxer students carried with them the ideas of the New Culture Movement in China. Unlike the previous generation of female advocates for education like Pearl Mark Loo, who had emphasized the importance of women's education for the nation, women of the New Culture Movement argued that it was important for women's fulfillment as human beings. These ideas crossed and recrossed the Pacific with Chinese students and publications. One of Mabel's close friends and a great admirer, Hu Shih, a student at Columbia, was a key thinker in the New Culture Movement and editor of one of its primary mouthpieces, the journal *New Youth*, founded in 1915. In 1918, he gave a speech at the Beijing Women's Normal School in which he famously advocated for a new outlook for women, one that moved "above the 'good mother' and virtuous wife" ideal. The most precious thing humans have, he argued, was independence. He drew upon his experiences in America and his admiration for American women to describe how women could develop their own identities.[36]

Lee also continued to work with white suffrage activists, especially during the 1915 New York state campaign. When Harriet Stanton Blatch, the leader of that campaign, had to leave for England to settle her husband's estate, Mary Beard filled in for her. Beard enlisted Lee in the cause. If Beard had not heard about her from the 1912 parade, Mabel Lee surely came to her attention when Beard lectured at Barnard in January 1915. A few weeks later, she recommended Lee to Helen Maclay, a reporter for the *Evening Journal*, who hoped to interview Lee on her interest in suffrage and the movement in China.[37] Beard seems to have also coordinated Lee's address at the Suffrage Shop at 663 Fifth Avenue. Suffrage activists ran the shop to raise visibility and funds for the cause. Although they succeeded in convincing the city's merchants to include suffrage information in their store windows, the suffragists also sold items of their own. Supporters could acquire hats, fans, postcards, stationery, drinking cups, pins, food, matchbooks, badges, suffrage literature, and more at the shop. Often these were sold or given away at events or via a traveling suffrage shop carriage, but the physical shop on Fifth Avenue anchored suffragists in the heart of the city. There the women held talks and designated specific days such as "Roman Catholic

Day" and "Artists Day." Mabel Lee was invited to speak on "Chinese Day," part of an international week Beard had organized. Standing "in a Chinese blouse and a simple skirt," she apprised the crowd on the situation of women in China. Once again, Chinese women were seen as important sisters in a worldwide movement, but not necessarily as American citizens.[38]

Indeed, white suffragists remained interested in Chinese women. Their parades continued to feature marchers who invoked Chinese suffragists, though it is unclear whether any of them were actually Chinese. At the beginning of September 1915, the state Woman Suffrage Party and the Empire State Suffrage Association held a parade in Manhattan from Sixtieth Street up First Avenue to Jefferson Park at 111th Street to drum up votes for the November referendum. Newspapers reported that suffragists carried signs in Chinese as well as in Italian, German, Yiddish, and Bohemian.[39]

Suffragists were hoping to encourage immigrant men to support the referendum, including the men in Chinatown. Lavinia Dock of the Henry Street Settlement House and her "squad" of suffragists carried banners through the neighborhoods of the Lower East Side. The messages had been "translated by cordial residents," one of whom was Lee's mother, Lia Beck who, "despite being heir to all the Chinese traditions about women," including bound feet, supported suffrage.[40]

The next month, Carrie Chapman Catt's Empire State Campaign Committee held another parade that incorporated all five of the boroughs for "one immense demonstration." A special feature of that march was the "International Division" that was headed by Catt, founder and president of the International Woman Suffrage Alliance. Behind Catt, marchers carried a large banner that read "Woman Suffrage Is a World Movement." This group was followed by a "proxy procession" of women in white representing the twenty-six nations of the alliance "led by America and Uncle Sam." Newspaper articles suggested that "whenever possible women native to the countries will be chosen to serve as standard bearers," but the marchers would not carry the "national colors" of their nations—instead, they would hold aloft banners with "little known facts connected with the history of the International Alliance." There was no mention of whether a Chinese woman marched. A photograph from this parade does show a white woman carrying a sign that invoked the sight Catt had witnessed in 1912: "Nine Women Served in Canton Assembly under the Republic," it read. Another apparently white woman held the sign "National Chinese Woman Suffrage Association."[41] Mabel Lee may have marched with the 150 Barnard women organized by the Feminist Forum and the Socialist Club. In their caps and gowns they followed their sky-blue banner declaring them "Barnard Suffragists."[42] But neither Lee nor any of the other women from Chinatown seem to have participated in the international division, perhaps because they could not carry the Chinese national flag as they had in other parades. Indeed, this parade reversed the message of the 1912 parade where Anna Howard Shaw had marched behind the Chinese women and emphasized the United States' need to catch up. In this case, the white women of the United States were shown as leading the suffragists of the world.

Mabel Lee was not interested in being led by white suffragists; she wanted to ensure that women's rights, including suffrage, would be built into the new republic in China from the beginning. Like other Chinese-born people in the United States, Lee had no prospects for U.S. citizenship and therefore planned to return to China in the future. She was beginning to put most of her energy into the Chinese Students Club at Columbia. The club affiliated with the Chinese Students' Alliance (CSA), a nationwide organization that sought to unite all Chinese students in the United States. Most of the members in the club were men, but female members were quite visible. At Columbia, Mabel Lee and her friends were vital additions. In 1913, the club secretary reported "the representatives of the fair sex form a good percentage of the Chinese colony about the Morningside Heights."[43] The addition of the "fair sex" seemed to breathe "new life" into the club, which just two years later had forty-five members, making it one of the largest in the Eastern Section of the CSA.[44]

Mabel Lee and Alice Huie found fun and fellowship in the Columbia Chinese Students Club. The meetings often included "merry making and eating." With Lee on piano, they practiced songs, including the Columbia fight song.[45] The students also used the club to educate fellow American students about their nation and heard updates about their new national government. They put on performances, listened to Chinese opera, and showed stereoscope slides of China. They welcomed traveling dignitaries, missionaries, and alumni for talks about developments in China.[46]

The newly energized Columbia club became a powerhouse of the Eastern Section of the national CSA, and for Mabel Lee, the CSA became the key vehicle for her women's rights advocacy and suffrage activism. Lee jumped right into governance of the organization at the national level. In the fall of 1913, during her second semester at Barnard, she took the first of her many positions in the organization, joining the membership committee of the Eastern Section of the CSA.[47]

Lee worked hard to keep the issue of women's equality squarely in front of Alliance members. In June 1914 she must have been thrilled to see the cover of the *Chinese Students' Monthly* (CSM), the national magazine of the Alliance. There in black ink on a jade background was her name and the title of her first article, "The Meaning of Woman Suffrage." The article echoed the many speeches on suffrage that she gave on campus and to white women's groups. It also reflected her time at Barnard and the feminists she encountered there. But she explicitly published it in the CSM because Chinese students were the audience she hoped to reach. A copy of the CSM was delivered to every Chinese student in the United

States as well as to interested businessmen, government officials, and others, Chinese and American. Lee insisted that they remember the ladies in the new nation. As we are building our new republic, she argued, we should look to the West and learn not only from their example but also from their mistakes. The current suffrage movement in Britain and the United States indicated a weakness in Western models of equality. "The building up of western civilization has, as it were, left every other beam loose in its construction by leaving out its women, and now there naturally has to be a time of difficult and careful readjustment before the structure can be made solid." She called on her colleagues, as students and patriots of China, to consider this problem. "With the introduction of machinery and Western methods in our country, we cannot keep the women ignorant. Are we going to build a solid structure," she asked them, "or are we going to leave every other beam loose for the later readjustment in spite of the lesson herein presented?" For Lee the answer was clear. "I cannot too strongly impress upon the reader the importance of this consideration," she urged, "for the feministic movement is not one of privileges to women, but one for the requirement of women to be worthy citizens and contribute their share of the steady progress of our country towards prosperity and national greatness."[48]

In August 1914, as war broke out in Europe and Asia, Mabel Lee and her colleagues traveled north to the cool Berkshire Mountains around Amherst, Massachusetts. They were Columbia's representatives to the weeklong tenth anniversary CSA Eastern Conference being held on the campus of the Massachusetts Agricultural College. The chairman of the Eastern Section opened the conference with a speech that was both optimistic and focused. Enjoy the athletic events and the competitions, he urged, but remember that our primary purpose is "to bring before our attention the many perplexing problems which we are or soon will be called upon to solve."[49]

Mabel Lee arrived at the conference as a known quantity and popular CSA member. She was scheduled to compete in the English oratorical contest, an event that "had always excited great interest in former years." Lee's competition was Z. T. Nyi. Both speakers took as their topic their duty to their home country. Nyi put up a gallant fight in his speech, but it was Lee's oration that the crowd was waiting for: "High was the expectation of what Miss Lee could do," reported the CSM.[50] Titled "Chinese Patriotism," her speech emphasized filial piety and focused on the students' duties to China. She drew upon Chinese history and current events to demonstrate how Chinese overseas students could be patriotic. Like many supporters of the Chinese Revolution, she saw their struggle as akin to that of the American Revolution. She compared Yuan Shikai, the president of the new republic, to George Washington, but with a twist. Where Washington was a great leader for refusing to remain as president and setting the precedent of serving only two terms, she argued that Yuan was great for remaining in power at a time when China needed a strong leader. Her support for Yuan Shikai seems puzzling in hindsight as he later usurped power and sought to have himself made emperor. But during the summer of 1914 he may have seemed to be a great leader who could unite a vulnerable new nation. Columbia students had been enthusiastic about his leadership when he first became president in 1912.[51]

Her speech was the talk of the conference. (The CSM published it as well, expanding its audience.)[52] Riding the wave of acclamation, Mabel Lee was elected as English secretary of the section. She joined Miss Fung Hing Liu of Wellesley and later Teachers College, who was elected vice president of the section.[53] As English secretary, Lee became chair of the membership committee and was pleased to report that as a result of her labors and the collaboration of the campaign workers on individual eastern campuses, the Eastern Section had ninety-eight new members. Fourteen of the twenty clubs she was responsible for reported as "100% Clubs," having enrolled all of the Chinese students at their institutions. Surely she was proud when her numbers were reported in the CSM next to the other sections. The Eastern Section's new members were more than double the Midwest Section's forty-five new members; those in the West Coast Section shamefacedly reported only seventeen but assured their colleagues that they were starting a recruitment campaign sure to "sweep the West as far as [they] could reach." Such sectional rivalry among college students mirrored the school spirit of sports teams.[54]

Lee's work in the CSA gave her experience in elections and organizational management. Her colleagues clearly found her to be efficient and exuberant. They confidently continued to elect and appoint her to positions. At the 1915 Eastern Section Conference she served on the resolution committee. In 1916 she was nominated and then elected as a member of the National Alliance Council. This put her in charge of membership for the entire organization. She took on the job of redoing the directory.[55] Columbia dominated the National Alliance Council that year. Lee served with two New York colleagues, H. K. Kwong as president and T. C. Hsi as treasurer.[56] For her part Alice Huie helped steer the Columbia club, having been elected as its vice president for 1916.[57]

Feeling confident, Lee published her third article in the CSM in June 1916. Although she gave it the title "Moral Training in Chinese Schools," she primarily used the piece to ruminate on democracy in the new Chinese republic rather than explore specific points of pedagogical theory. She demonstrated not only her engagement with the new educational and democratic theories coming out of Barnard, Columbia, and Teachers College but also her knowledge of Chinese classical works and history. The traditional Chinese educational system of the past, with its focus on the classics and its exam system, she argued, was elaborate and efficient. As a result, China, with its large population and territory, had been held together for many centuries by its bureaucratic exam system and "became a 'people of the book' so to speak." However, circumstances had drastically changed and required new methods. The old morality "was adapted to an entirely different form of society," and to attempt to reassert it "in an age of democracy and progress is to court ultimate extinction as a nation." The new form of democratic government ushered in by the revolution required a new educational system.[58]

Mabel Lee of 1916 was less naive than Mabel Lee of 1914. The "uprisings and bloodshed" of the civil war that had followed the revolution had made her well aware of the "maladjustment" of her nation to democracy.[59] Here Lee was surely influenced by the conversations in New York as Americans, especially social theorists at her university, looked out at the new immigrants in their cities and asked how democracy could continue to function with the large influx of new cultures and peoples. The classes she had taken in history, philosophy, politics, economics, and education taught by scholars who used New York City and its immigrant neighborhoods as their laboratory addressed the same questions. She drew upon them to offer answers for her nation. Arguing that both individual and environmental solutions were necessary, she urged a change to the system. "Democracy is more than a form of government," she asserted; it was a whole system of social interaction, "primarily a mode of associated living, of conjoint experience." This was much harder than what had come before in China. In the past, the hierarchical system in which tradition was represented by the classics meant that individuals adjusted to the system by following precedent. In the modern period, individuals must learn how to adjust to the situation but also learn how to adjust the situation to the individual. "It is true that it means the breaking down of sectional, racial and caste barriers and the giving of expression and participation to the people," she wrote. Addressing society as a group of individuals instead of classes meant "the whole system of society has become so much more complex, and hence so much the harder to find expression. It is not easy to know how to co-operate with our fellows, to be able to keep our individuality and at the same time have equal respect for that of others." Perhaps Lee was reflecting on her calls for equality between men and women or her experiences with the CSA as she urged Chinese people to come together to govern democratically.[60] She did not seem to see parallels between the struggles the Chinese faced in the United States and African Americans' struggles to exercise their citizenship rights. She had briefly, and somewhat dismissively, acknowledged their difficulties in her 1914 suffrage article, noting that the idea of political equality as found in the Declaration of Independence "is being worked out in this country in spite of the interruptions of the negro question."[61]

By October 1916, when the CSA was holding its annual elections, Lee was at the top of her game. Her peers nominated her to run for national president of the organization for 1917. A confident leader, she accepted and believed she could win. But despite her strong national reputation and experience corresponding with many of the members in her position as secretary, she lost by a single vote to the incumbent, T. V. Soong of Harvard. Stung, Lee demanded a recount; Soong responded by accusing her of impropriety. The back and forth went on all summer. In the end, Soong was declared the winner.[62]

In this campaign, Lee got her first real taste of politics, and it was disappointing. While the election was definitely a power struggle between two high achievers, it is also worth noting that although many women served in lesser administrative positions and on the executive board, they had a fraught relationship with the CSA presidency. Two women had served as president, but neither had been elected, and one quit early under mysterious circumstances. Like Lee, they, too, turned to the less prestigious but more labor intensive positions on the CSM editorial board.

This reflected the wider pattern of post-college life for most of the Chinese students. The men who returned to China took influential positions in the government or business, which was the goal of the Boxer program. The winner of the election, T. V. Soong, returned to China a few years later and became a notoriously corrupt politician. His sisters, also educated in the United States, became famous for their marriages to powerful men. For example, Soong Ching-ling married Sun Yat-sen. Her sister, Mei-ling Soong, who had attended Wellesley College, was better known as Madame Chiang Kai-shek, wife of the politician who became the republic's president in 1928. She was known for her diplomacy and skill at public relations as a politician's wife but was not a government official herself.[63]

Despite her defeat in the CSA election, Lee continued to serve the organization as a member of the executive board and the education board. She also doubled down on her insistence on living her feminism. As she had asserted in her 1914 article, feminism was equality of opportunity, and women were showing that they were equal to all kinds of things that had been denied to them for years, particularly access to education. As they gained that access, women demonstrated their intellectual abilities. "At present there is still the cry that though woman has gone so far, she can go no further, that she cannot succeed in the professions," Lee had written. "But this again is being refuted by the success of pioneers of today." In 1916 she decided to become one of those feminist pioneers herself.[64]

PART III

The War Comes

1917–1920

[CHAPTER 12]
Mr. President, Why Not Make America Safe for Democracy?

Carrie Williams Clifford

During the fall of 1916 speakers and organizers from the Congressional Union and the National Woman's Party—who merged into one organization called the National Woman's Party in 1917—fanned out across the western states where women could vote.[1] They stumped hard against Democrats, though they did not officially endorse a party. It was a tough job. National American Woman Suffrage Association leaders were outraged and denounced their tactics as harmful, noting that most of the Democrats they were stumping against supported suffrage. The public often ridiculed them on the campaign trail, and several were attacked by a mob in Chicago. Inez Milholland campaigned so hard she collapsed onstage in Los Angeles and died from pernicious anemia a month later. She was only thirty years old. Many regarded her as a martyr for the cause. Despite their efforts, President Wilson was reelected. There was one bright spot for women, however; Montanans elected Jeannette Rankin, a Republican, to the House of Representatives, making her the first woman to serve in Congress.[2]

Another new arrival in Washington was Democratic senator Andrieus Aristieus Jones, elected by the men of the state of New Mexico. Jones had served as assistant secretary of the Interior for three years, and many New Mexicans hoped he would chair the important Public Land Committee, where he could focus on developing irrigation in the state.[3] Instead, he found himself in the crosshairs of the suffragists as the new chairman of the Senate Committee on Woman Suffrage. Until that committee voted on the language of the proposed constitutional amendment and passed it out of committee, it was going nowhere.[4] The *Albuquerque Journal* found the assignment amusing, with the subheadline "New Senator to Become Most Popular Gentleman in Washington with Workers for the Anthony Amendment." It concluded that Jones's assignments, including seats on committees charged with education and labor, expenditures in the Interior Department, Senate contingent expenses, finance, geological survey, Indian affairs, manufacturers, mines and mining, and public lands, were on the whole a "good showing" and enviable for a new senator, reflecting his experiences with "the working of Washington machinery." That said, the paper's editors chuckled that the Committee on Woman Suffrage was sure to keep him busy, "for the suffs and the anti-suffs are both very much in earnest over this question." Describing him as an "out-and-out advocate of suffrage," they concluded that Jones would be "apt to 'get by' where a more wobbly statesman would be up to his ears in trouble."[5]

Having failed to keep President Wilson out of office, Alice Paul and her colleagues in the NWP turned to publicly shaming him. At the beginning of 1917 Paul organized women to keep a vigil in front of the White House. Every day, several women stood as sentinels outside the gates, holding signs and banners and wearing suffrage ribbons, mutely testifying to their disenfranchisement. President Wilson was initially amused. He invited the picketers in for tea on a rainy day; they declined. He cajoled, but they refused to leave their posts. On the March day of his second inauguration, they again tried to steal his thunder. That evening, more than a thousand women braved icy rain to march seven times around the White House, echoing Joshua's march that brought the walls of Jericho tumbling down. Wilson remain unmoved.[6]

But soon the nation as a whole seemed on the march, the foot soldiers armed with far more than trumpets. There had been anticipation for months, ever since the German government had announced that it would resume unrestricted submarine warfare in the Atlantic in February 1917. Although President Wilson had cut off diplomatic relations with Germany, he had gone no further. In March, however, German submarines torpedoed three unarmed American merchant ships, and the nation buzzed with anger and expectation. Former president Theodore Roosevelt summoned memories of the Rough Riders with his calls for volunteer military regiments, which he would, of course, lead. Peace activists, many of whom were women, were dismayed.[7] In Washington, young men rushed to enlistment stations. The Board of Trade members, each waving small American flags, insisted "there is no hyphen in the citizenship of Washington" and condemned "German militarism." Bellhops at the Willard Hotel began to drill daily on the rooftop, and 2,000 Boy Scouts practiced mobilizing themselves for "first aid work, police and detective duty." Pacifists like David Starr Jordan, the president of Stanford University, hurried to the city to plead with the president and Congress to avoid war, but the mood they found was disheartening. The District's National Guard threw yellow paint on the headquarters of the Emergency Peace Foundation and threatened to smash the building. The chief of police refused permits to either a loyalty or a peace parade.[8]

On the evening of April 2, "a soft fragrant rain of early spring" fell over the city. President Wilson entered his car at the White House and, escorted by cavalrymen in case of pacifist protesters, rode up to Capitol Hill to declare to a special joint session of Congress the U.S. entry into the war. Above Pennsylvania Avenue "the illuminated Dome of the Capitol stood in solemn splendor against the dark wet sky." The chambers of the House of Representatives were packed in anticipation of President Wilson's "communication concerning grave matters." In the first row sat the members of his cabinet and the justices of the Supreme Court. Behind them sat the diplomats, with the notable absence of German ambassador Johann von Bernstorff, whom President Wilson had dismissed two months earlier.

With the declaration of war, the city immediately changed. Thousands of people from across the nation began to arrive. Soldiers began training in the vicinity, and federal agencies desperate for office space erected temporary quarters on the mall. The Department of the Interior was uprooted from its building on F Street and sent to the far end of the mall in Foggy Bottom, just a few blocks from the NWP headquarters on Lafayette Park. Marie Bottineau Baldwin moved to a small apartment several blocks away from the new building so she could continue to walk to work. She also took in a boarder, taking advantage of the increasingly strained housing market in the city as people from around the country arrived to aid the war effort.[9]

America's entry into the Great War instantly changed suffragists' calculations as they reassessed their political strategies in light of the conflict in which their nation was now enmeshed. Suffragists held a wide variety of opinions on the war. Many of them were part of the massive women's international peace movement and abhorred the conflict. Newly elected representative Jeannette Rankin for one stood by her principles and voted against the war measure; it cost her reelection the following year. Others, like Carrie Chapman Catt, now president of NAWSA, claimed that the war was an opportunity to demonstrate how organized and resourceful women were. By supporting the war effort, she told suffragists, they would prove their worth to the nation. NAWSA leaders ensured that publicly they appeared focused on the war effort, and leading feminists accepted important and demanding wartime positions while their lobbyists continued to work behind the scenes. Those lobbyists emphasized women's war work as evidence that they deserved the vote.[10]

Anna Howard Shaw was one of those leaders. In April, while on a suffrage speaking tour in Atlanta, Georgia, she received a telegram from the director of the Council of National Defense calling her to Washington. The council, composed of the secretaries of War, the Navy, the Interior, Agriculture, Labor, and Commerce, had been created by Congress to coordinate the looming national crisis. The men asked Shaw to chair a women's committee to help orchestrate women's defense work. She agreed but with one caveat: she would not give up her suffrage work and would continue giving speeches in favor of women's enfranchisement. She added that if any of the other women on the committee, several of whom opposed suffrage, objected, she would resign immediately. None of them did.

By May the seventy-year-old Shaw had moved to the city and set up headquarters in an elegant brownstone at 1814 N. Street. There she set about coordinating the nation's women. Following now well-honed tactics, she designated a chairwoman for each state who would cooperate with women's organizations to create county and local units that could mobilize women in every community.

Schoolteachers were often elected as the chairs of those local units. Eventually, Shaw oversaw an operation that contained 18,000 units, including at least one in every state as well as in the territories of Hawaii, Alaska, and Puerto Rico.[11]

Some 82,000 women threw themselves into preparedness. In Washington, under the oversight of the Council of National Defense's newly appointed food administrator, Herbert Hoover, the city's "wives, mothers, and daughters" took food conservation classes to learn to can and dry vegetables so more resources could go toward the war effort.[12] Suffragists around the country found a variety of ways to contribute. Marie Bottineau Baldwin joined the Red Cross in the city and knitted socks and bandages for the troops.[13] In New Mexico, Nina Otero-Warren helped form the New Mexico women's auxiliary of the Council of National Defense. She was appointed chairwoman of the First Judicial District and got to work distributing Hoover Food Administration cards (in Spanish and English), placing war posters and bulletins in libraries, and selling Liberty Bonds. She also joined the Red Cross and took on the position of chair of its membership committee for Santa Fe County, while also serving as an officer with the executive bureau.[14] Aurora Lucero assisted with "Hooverite" fruit-drying demonstrations for housewives and schoolchildren on the Santa Fe Plaza. After her brother Antonio Jr. enlisted in the navy, she volunteered with the women's section of the Navy League.[15] Despite these new demands on their time and, for some, the emotional toll of having loved ones in the military, the women remained engaged in their political activism and continued to fight for suffrage and women's rights.

Carrie Williams Clifford faced the advent of wartime with what must have been great anxiety and ambivalence. At the same time that her two sons were subject to conscription into the armed forces, President Wilson was drawing some very unfortunate parallels between wars present and past. In June, headlines jovially reported "Confederate Armies March on Washington." It was the twenty-seventh reunion of the United Confederate Veterans and the first time they were meeting north of the former Confederate states.[16] When President Wilson took to the stage to address the veterans, he reflected on historic coincidence. That morning at seven sharp, hundreds of whistles, bells, and horns had "screamed a blood-tingling salute" calling the District's men to the opening of forty-one polling places, where they would register for military service. In the crowds around the precincts, gray-clad veterans of the Civil War mingled with the young men waiting to register and offered them words of encouragement. To President Wilson, this serendipitous concurrence was inspiring. As he looked out over the crowd of Confederate veterans and their families, he did not see traitors who had fought to destroy the Union but saw the "spirit of chivalric gallantry," a testament to democratic volunteerism that was reflected in the actions of the young men now registering for another war. It was, he concluded, very fine. These were days of "oblivion as well as of memory, for we are forgetting the things that once held us asunder," he told them. "Not only that, but they are days of rejoicing, because we now at last see why this great nation was kept united for we are beginning to see the great world purpose which it was meant to serve." He was glad that "the passion of difference of principle is gone—gone out of our minds, gone out of our hearts." General George P. Harrison, the head of the United Confederate Veterans organization, agreed. His evidence was before him on the stage: "When I contemplate the fact that Woodrow Wilson, a southern man, has twice been elected and is today President of the United States, and as such the commander-in-chief of its army and navy; that southern men constitute a part of the cabinet; that my old comrade, Chief Justice White, has with him on the Supreme bench other representative southerners," well, it was clear: "I know that the war of sections is over."[17]

Carrie Clifford understood better than most that this represented another capitulation to racism by Wilson, who had already segregated the capital's buildings and workspaces. The president's forgetting of the "things that once held us asunder" erased the conflict over slavery and the contributions of the 200,000 black Union soldiers during the war. The national passion for liberty and equality for all had been abandoned, and the reunion the president celebrated was based on embracing white supremacy and Jim Crow.[18]

This was especially injurious to Clifford because the horror of racial violence in the United States had by no means abated since 1906, when she had pleaded with white Americans to follow the Golden Rule. If anything, it had gotten worse. It exploded in the modern cities of the New South and appeared to be spreading as the wartime migration of African Americans to northern cities revealed strong currents of racism and violence against blacks in that region as well. The list of attacks was long, and Clifford, loyal supporter of The Crisis, read about and contemplated all of them. The assaults against their communities drove Clifford and other black women in their suffrage work as they desperately sought means to stem the violence.

Lynchings rose in the first decades of the twentieth century. News of searing violence against blacks came again and again through newspapers, inflicting a secondary violence on African American readers throughout the country. In May 1916 the nation was shocked when news spread of a grisly lynching that had taken place in the modern city of Waco, Texas. Jesse Washington, a black farmhand, was accused of assaulting and killing the wife of his employer. The white population of the city and surrounding county, some 10,000 people, participated in the hideous murder by dragging Washington from court into the town square. Men, women, and children cheered as Washington's body, chained around the neck, was lowered into a bonfire and raised back up over and over again as he was tortured for two hours. Someone, possibly the mayor, who watched the event from a nearby rooftop, had informed a local photographer where the lynching would take place. He set up his camera and documented the entire killing (a new departure from the usual lynching pictures, which tended to immortalize the dead and tortured bodies of lynching victims but not the act). The pictures, which capture a gleeful crowd around the crisped body, were sold as souvenirs.[19]

The Crisis dubbed it the "Waco Horror," and the NAACP hired white suffragist Elizabeth Freeman to investigate. Freeman, a New Yorker, was already in Texas for a statewide suffrage convention in Dallas. With grim determination she took on the task, posing as a reporter sympathetic to white Waco. The mayor happily gave her the full set of the photographs. W. E. B. Du Bois published her report and the pictures in July 1916 edition of The Crisis. Some members of his board were reluctant to include the photos, but he insisted that the world see the kind of evil the self-professed modern community had perpetrated.[20]

In May 1916, Memphis, Tennessee, became the site of another horrific lynching when Ell Persons was dragged off a train heading to his trial and decapitated. White southern leaders often dismissed lynchings as the work of a few backward rural whites, exceptions rather than the rule. The lynchings in Waco and Memphis, however, could not be dismissed so easily, as they were perpetrated by thousands of urban citizens in the cities of the "New South." They gave the lie to apologists and demonstrated that racial violence was rife throughout the region.

Despite the violence aimed at African Americans and the racism of the nation's political leadership, both of Carrie Clifford's sons heeded the whistles and bells of Washington on the morning of June 5. They made their way to Precinct 8A and registered for the draft. Maurice, the younger at twenty-nine years old, was there early, number 419 at the precinct, while Joshua, one year older, registered as #1582.[21]

As their sons, husbands, fathers, and brothers answered their nation's call, African Americans women like Clifford continued to urge the federal government to do something to address the violence that white supremacists visited on their communities across the country. Indeed, as the nation rallied for war, many wondered how they could fight for democracy abroad when they were so oppressed at home. The NAACP had hoped that the principles for which the United States fought would lead the federal government to take a stand against lynching. Instead, President Wilson insisted that the army remain segregated, and that black units be led by white officers. Through lobbying and pressure, the NAACP managed to convince the army to train black officers. It opened a segregated training school for them in Iowa. Yet they still faced prejudice within the armed forces as many white commanding officers believed black troops were unfit for combat and refused to send them to the front, instead ordering them to work in support positions.

The assaults on African Americans at home continued even as black men— eventually 350,000 of them—risked death on the battlefield in defense of their country. Nor was the racial terror limited to the South. In July 1917, racist attacks on the black community in East St. Louis, Illinois, killed almost two hundred

African Americans and left thousands displaced by fire. East St. Louis, directly across the Mississippi River from St. Louis, Missouri, was an industrializing city whose politically active black population had been shaped by its position in a free state but bordering one with slavery. The city's African American population had grown dramatically due to the Great Migration as war industries drew poor black sharecroppers north with the offer of better jobs and relief from the cycles of crushing debt and the brutalities of the Jim Crow South.[22] In Illinois, African American men could vote, and their growing population meant increasing black political power in the city.[23] The changes also exacerbated white concerns about housing shortages and job competition. When a carful of white men drove through East St. Louis indiscriminately firing a gun out the window, they set off the events that led to the destruction of the city. When a similar make of car returned several hours later, residents mistook it for the same group and returned fire. This time, however, it was an unmarked police car, and one of the occupants was killed. Whites in St. Louis responded with fury, descending on East St. Louis and attacking its African American residents.

Property damage to the community was massive, and the terror of attacks went on for weeks.[24] Photographs show the blackened shells of homes, the painful burns on the bodies of survivors, and the destruction wrought by white men and women who stormed the neighborhood. Du Bois published these images in The Crisis as well. Clifford, an avid reader of the journal, witnessed what she called the "bestial revelries" of "race-hate" in its pages.[25]

The NAACP organized a silent anti-lynching parade in New York City soon after the East St. Louis riot. The silence of the marchers pointedly highlighted and condemned the silence of white Americans, including the president, in the face of ongoing racial terror. "We March because we deem it a crime to be silent in the face of such barbaric acts," one sign read.[26] Between 8,000 and 10,000 African Americans turned out for the procession down Fifth Avenue, from Fifty-Ninth Street to Madison Square at Twenty-Third Street. They silently walked the length of the route with muffled drums keeping time. Black marchers filled the streets for blocks, passing under the flags many New Yorkers had prominently displayed on their buildings when the nation had entered the war just three months earlier.[27] The parade was led by three hundred children followed by nearly 5,000 women, all wearing white. They may have been deliberately echoing suffrage tactics, and indeed observers linked the silent parade to the suffragists' "silent sentinel" protests in front of the White House. The silent marchers also carried provocative signs. Like the suffrage protesters, they alluded to President Wilson's words about why the nation had recently gone to war: "Mr. President, why not make America safe for democracy?" Other signs appealed to the nation's professed Christianity and sympathy of other mothers: "Thou shalt not kill"; "Mother, do lynchers go to Heaven?"; "Give us a chance to live."[28]

After the women and children came the men, many in their military uniforms, underscoring their service to the nation, and others in their Sunday best. Their signs also emphasized their patriotism and claims to citizenship: "We helped to plant the flag in every American dominion" and "We have fought for the liberty of white Americans in 6 wars; our reward is East St. Louis." Other signs emphasized how the disenfranchisement of black men in the South gave white supremacists more political power than northerners: "Each white man in the South by disfranchising the black working man casts from 3 to 13 times as many ballots as YOU." Uniformed black Boy Scouts handed out leaflets explaining their protest. "Why Do We March?" Because of "Segregation, Discrimination, Disenfranchisement, and LYNCHING." The leaflets detailed the horrific civil rights violations of the previous few months in Waco, Memphis, and East St. Louis.[29]

Clifford likely attended the protest, and it would later influence her own political strategies. She wrote her poem "Silent Protest Parade," about the march, in the first person: "Were you there? Did you see? Gods! Wasn't it fine! / Did you notice how straight we kept the line." This powerful communal response gave her courage, and she believed change was in the air. "I was so happy I wanted to cry," she wrote.

> Youth and maid
> Father, mother — not one afraid
> Or ashamed to let the whole world know
> What he thought of the hellish East St. Louis "show."[30]

Her feelings of empowerment were short-lived, however. While the parade successfully garnered attention from the national press, it did not stop the violence. In 1918, Mary Turner, a pregnant black woman in Georgia protesting the murder of her husband, was herself lynched. She was shot, hung upside down, and set on fire. Her tormentors cut the baby from her belly and stomped it beneath their feet. Clifford felt this deeply. Her poetry, including a poem for Mary Turner, helped her work through her anguish and despair over the race hate in her nation.[31]

Meanwhile, both of her sons were fighting in France to protect that nation. Maurice served for a year, from July 18, 1918, to July 12, 1919, before being honorably discharged at the end of his service. He was a sergeant-major with the 808th Pioneer Infantry.[32] Like most of the black troops, the Pioneers were assigned to labor detail rather than combat. They helped the 12th Engineers construct a narrow gauge railway at the front that ran supplies along the lines. Although the American leadership refused to allow most black troops to fight, they continued to do their part for the war effort, winning praise along the way. The 808th sang as they worked while shot and shell rained over them. Like the other troops in the trenches, they lived in small dugouts where rats and "cooties" were legion.[33]

Joshua Clifford attended the officer training school in Iowa and then served as a first lieutenant in the 367th Infantry, formed at Camp Upton in New York.

The regiment was christened "the Buffaloes" by its white commanding officer, Colonel Moss, in honor of the African American "Buffalo Soldiers" who fought in the Indian Wars of the late nineteenth century. They embarked for France on June 10, 1918, landing at Brest nine days later. Upon arrival they received seven weeks' intensive training in trench warfare and gas instruction with several other regiments of the 92nd Division. They were then sent to the front to take their place in the trenches in the Vosges sector.[34]

The Germans sought to take advantage of the divides between American ideals and the day-to-day racism within U.S. society. One morning terror struck in the Vosges sector as the troops of Joshua Clifford's 367th Infantry Regiment were bombarded with what they assumed were gas bombs. The terror turned to amazement as they realized the Germans were lobbing propaganda at their line. Written in English, the pamphlet addressed black soldiers directly: "Hello, boys, what are you doing over here? Fighting the Germans? Why? Have they ever done you any harm?" Reminding them of their second-class citizenship, it asked, "Do you enjoy the same rights as the white people do in America, the land of freedom and Democracy, or are you not rather treated over there as second-class citizens?" It urged them to "come to Germany" and not allow war profiteers to "use you as cannon fodder." Although black soldiers were frustrated to the point of despair by their treatment at home and in the army, they remained loyal and rejected the invitation.[35]

Some leaders in the War Department were concerned that German propaganda and the violence that African Americans faced on the home front would affect the morale of black troops. Two members of the Army General Staff and Military Intelligence drafted legislation to protect "potential soldiers and their relatives" from the crime of lynching during the war. What became known as the Hornblower-Spingarn Bill was proposed by Representative Warren Gard, a Democrat from Ohio's Third District, though nothing came of it.[36]

With both her boys overseas, Carrie Clifford could only wait and hope. Men could die in so many ways: ships were sunk on their way to Europe, the flu struck down thousands more, and of course the ravages of war itself killed and maimed many.[37] Again, her poetry helped her through the dark times. She empathized with other mothers, black and white, the "Queens, who bear the birth-pangs of a world," whose "fondled darlings, combed and curled, / Are in the shell-torn, shamble-trenches hurled." She believed that her sons and theirs were fighting "to save / The world from horrors darker than the grave." Like other women, she feared that she might be called on to make the greatest sacrifice to the war: her precious children.[38]

Perhaps wishing she could be there too, Clifford wrote another poem in praise of the black women working overseas with the troops, "Our Women of the Canteen." Only nineteen black women were sent with the YMCA, sixteen of them not until the end of the conflict. Her friend and fellow suffragist Addie Hunton along with Kathryn Johnson were two of the first three to arrive in France. They later wrote about their experiences in *Two Colored Women with the American Expeditionary Forces*. They lauded the bravery and patriotism of the men they worked with, including Clifford's sons, but also recorded the cruel insults and frustrating persistence of racism in the midst of the struggle for democracy. These came from American military officers as well as YMCA workers. They were deeply disappointed, though not surprised.[39]

As the war dragged on in Europe, the politics of suffrage seemed to have stalled out in the United States. The proposed suffrage amendment had been introduced in the Senate with the help of Senator A. A. Jones of New Mexico, but it was caught in a series of parliamentary maneuvers that saw it going back and forth between Senate committees and close defeats in floor votes. As Clifford worried about her sons and prayed for them to stay safe and whole in the bogged-down trench warfare of France, it must have felt to her as if everything she cared about most was continually in suspense.

CHAPTER 13

Pacific Currents

The women Carrie Chapman Catt chose to work on Capitol Hill, Helen Hamilton Gardener and Maud Wood Park, were savvy and observant politicians. They managed to convince congressmen to create a Committee on Woman Suffrage in the House of Representatives early in the summer of 1917.[1] They worked slowly and steadily throughout the war years to convince Congress that women deserved enfranchisement through a national amendment. And they often pointed to the extensive work the nation's women were doing in the war effort.

Maud Wood Park detailed the amendment's tortuous winding through the labyrinthian process of being voted on in Congress. Park, Gardener, and other members of the National American Woman Suffrage Association's Congressional Committee carefully shepherded the amendment through the process. Park noted that "'watchful waiting' and 'Marking time' were two phrases that we learned the full meaning of."[2] As the women coordinated the suffragists' agenda, lining up votes, strategizing with congressional allies, and timing the move of the amendment from committee to the floor of the House, Park acknowledged that it was essentially a full-time job done by volunteers. That made it the province of women who could afford to do such work. The lobbying network also extended to women on the state and local level. But even there, Park emphasized, it was often well-connected women who contacted their representatives. "Care should be taken in forming delegations to choose, if possible[,] women whose families have political influence in the man's own party. . . . It is well to have a small group of persons of real importance in the district rather than a large group of less prominent people," she advised her state workers at the opening of the Sixty-Fifth Congress in 1917. On the whole that meant well-to-do white women.[3]

But that did not mean people of color were absent from the congressional process. Park made very clear which congressmen had been allies and which had not. Among the men she listed as strong supporters were Senator A. A. Jones of New Mexico; Kansas senator Charles Curtis, a Native man; and Delegate Kalaniana'ole, the congressional representative from the territory of Hawaii. The latter two were men of color, as were many of Jones's constituents in New Mexico. While by no means the only men she conferenced with, they each played important roles in supporting the suffragists' cause.

In the Senate, Park worked most closely with Senator Andrieus Aristieus Jones, chair of the Senate Woman Suffrage Committee. Initially, she was unsure about him and his lack of political savvy, though she was amused by his grandiose name—she could not believe that the Senate had not only an Andrieus Aristieus in Jones but also a Marcus Aurelius in Senator Smith of Arizona.[4] As a freshman senator, Jones was inexperienced, though he had been President Wilson's assistant secretary of the Interior for the past three years. "We were fearful," she wrote, "that our resolution would be handicapped in the hands of an inexperienced member. Then, too, as far as we could find out, he had not taken any stand on the suffrage question." Jones may have been placed on the Woman's Suffrage Committee precisely because of his inexperience and the fact that he represented a somewhat small and remote state, but he rose to the occasion.[5]

Women of color were consistently part of these congressional discussions— sometimes directly, as when Senator Jones heard from constituents like Nina Otero-Warren, and sometimes obliquely, as when southern anti-suffragists warned that enfranchising women meant black women would vote and argued against the amendment in the name of states' rights. During one period of "watchful waiting," as the amendment stalled in the House Rules Committee, Park and other suffrage lobbyists turned to the question of women's votes in the territory of Hawaii to keep up momentum. The question of suffrage in Hawaii had a long history. When Congress was preparing to admit the islands as a territory in 1898, the commission overseeing the process ignored the precedent of earlier Organic Acts (the laws creating new territories) that empowered the territorial legislature to determine the qualifications of voters after the formation of the territory. Similar clauses in their Organic Acts had allowed the territories of Wyoming, Utah, and Washington to grant women suffrage. Susan B. Anthony, president of NAWSA at the time, vigorously complained about this breaking of tradition in the case of Hawaii and organized a petition campaign from suffragists across the country, to no avail.[6]

Since Carrie Chapman Catt's visit to Hawaii in 1912, suffragists and their male allies continued to petition Congress to give the Hawaiian legislature the authority to vote to enfranchise women. By 1915 both the Democratic and the Republican Parties in the islands had pledged to support the issue. The territorial legislature did also, assigning the territory's delegate to Congress, Jonah Kūhiō Kalanianaʻole (Prince Kūhiō), with presenting it to Congress. The story of Prince Kūhiō, the only member of royalty to serve in the U.S. Congress to this date, suggests the extremely complicated relationship Indigenous people had to suffrage.[7] Thirty years earlier he had been imprisoned for his part in a "rebellion" against the Republic of Hawaii as he resisted the overthrow of the sovereign Hawaiian Kingdom. His aunt, the deposed Queen Liliʻuokalani, who was under house arrest at Iolani Palace in Honolulu, wrote four national songs, or mele lāhui, that signified a "desire for the nation to be restored." They were smuggled out of her prison and published in Hawaiian-language newspapers. Thematically, they indicated that that she continued to support her people and her nation, despite contrary stories run in pro-republic newspapers. She addressed the third mele specifically to Prince Kūhiō signaling her approval of her nephew's actions. She also reminded him of their genealogy and links to the shared ancestors who gave them membership in the royal line. Once released from prison and after time abroad, he returned to Hawaii, where he continued his political work, which remained influenced by his loyalty to the Hawaiian nation. He aligned himself with Republican planters and missionaries who controlled Hawaii's politics, and he was elected as the second Hawaiian territorial delegate to the U.S. Congress in 1902 and held the position until his untimely death in 1922.[8]

Prince Kūhiō's wife, Elizabeth Kahanu Kalaniana'ole, was a staunch suffragist. During the war, she headed the Red Cross unit of Native Hawaiian (Kanaka Maoli) knitters, known as the Iolani Unit, which along with other Kanaka Maoli war efforts received positive attention on the mainland. Although Indigenous women had long favored suffrage, during the war white women in the islands became more supportive as they involved themselves in war efforts and sought to prove their loyalty to the nation. It seemed to many that woman suffrage was a foregone conclusion in Hawaii, but Congress needed to be convinced.[9]

As congressional delegate, Prince Kūhiō worked for suffrage for many years. He was doing the bidding of the territorial convention, but many also noted that "the native women particularly are agitating in behalf of suffrage."[10] He had twice attempted to bring the territorial resolution before Congress in 1915 and 1916, but both attempts were ignored. Native Hawaiian women then used their networks to mobilize mainland suffragists on their behalf. They worked through Bostonian suffragist Almira Hollander Pitman, the wife of Benjamin Pitman, whose mother was a Native Hawaiian. Almira Pitman been visiting Hawaii and interacting with women "from the highest social circles in the islands," including Wilhelmine Dowsett, the Kanaka Maoli suffrage leader who had invited Catt to speak in Honolulu in 1912. They charged Pitman with using her connections to help Delegate Kūhiō. Upon her return to the mainland, Pitman contacted Carrie Chapman Catt, who connected her with Maud Wood Park, who joined forces with Kūhiō.[11]

To Park's and perhaps Kūhiō's surprise, things now moved fairly quickly, at least in the Senate. There Senator John Shafroth introduced Kūhiō's resolution at the beginning of the summer, and it was favorably passed out of the Committee on Territories for an uncontested vote in September 1917. The House, which had referred it to the Committee on Woman Suffrage in May, came back to it in April 1918 and held a hearing at which Park, Pitman, and Anna Howard Shaw were present. Pitman spoke for the Hawaiian women who had assigned her with this work. The committee questioned the women before giving the bill a favorable report, and in June it passed without roll call in the House. Park recorded her surprise at the speed with which Congress had dealt with the resolution. There was the tinge of frustration that often accompanied white suffragists' commentary on the extension of the vote to other groups. In this case, she even rhetorically excluded Hawaii from the United States: "It gave us a striking opportunity to contrast our own difficulty in getting action from the Senate with the ease of enfranchisement in the case of the Hawaiian women."[12] It did not enfranchise Hawaiian women, however; it merely empowered the territorial legislature to do so. The fight moved back to the islands. Despite Hawaiian suffragists' continued efforts—this time including their "Oriental sisters" as well—they did not convince the legislature before 1920 but were enfranchised by the Nineteenth Amendment.[13]

Alice Paul and Lucy Burns, leaders of the National Woman's Party, disagreed with Carrie Catt and NAWSA. For one thing, Alice Paul's Quaker background led her to take a strong antiwar stance against entering the conflict. They also saw no reason to let up on President Wilson and began to use the war to shame him and the nation. How could the United States claim to be fighting for freedom overseas, they asked, when American women lacked suffrage and full citizenship at home? They accused the United States of only pretending to be a democracy. Soon the women outside the White House were holding aloft banners that taunted the president, calling him "Kaiser Wilson." "Have you forgotten your sympathy with the poor Germans because they were not self-governed?" one boldly printed banner read; "20,000,000 American women are not self-governed. Take the beam out of your own eye," read another.[14]

All summer long the women of the NWP picketed. Large crowds gathered around them, jeering and frequently tearing their banners out of their hands. Sometimes they attacked the women while the capital police stood by. Often times the police arrested the suffragists (though never the men harassing them) on charges of obstructing the sidewalk. While some people deplored the mobs who attacked the suffragists for their peaceful protests, many claimed they had brought it upon themselves with their unladylike behavior. One anti-suffrage congressman suggested "these poor, bewildered, deluded creatures, after their disgusting exhibition can thank their stars that because they wear skirts they are now incarcerated for misdemeanors of a minor character." He denounced them as women of "a certain class," a code for prostitutes, who "posing with their short skirts and their short hair within the view of this 'very capitol and our office buildings'" did not deserve sympathy.[15] Congressmen also often conflated the picketers with all suffragists, which infuriated NAWSA leaders, who believed it hurt their lobbying efforts. They worked hard to educate the public and politicians that there were important distinctions among suffragists and insisted that NAWSA also found the protests problematic.[16]

At first the arrested picketers were released without sentencing, but as they persisted and the violence against them continued, district courts began to give them jail time. Initially the sentences were for a few days, then they grew to six weeks and eventually six months. Some 218 women were arrested from twenty-six different states, many of them several times; 97 of those women served time. At first they were sent to the District jail, but soon they were being sentenced to time in the Occoquan Workhouse in Virginia. At Occoquan, the jailers attempted to shame them in multiple ways. They fed them rancid and wormy food, gave them only buckets in which to relieve themselves, and dressed them in the coarse uniforms of the prison. They also used white Americans' racial hierarchies to humiliate them. They did this by placing them in cellblocks with black prostitutes, considered the lowest of low women by virtue of both their race and their profession, thus demonstrating to the white suffragists that their actions cost them their respectability. According to Doris Stevens, who wrote about her experiences in the memoir *Jailed for Freedom*, jailers also encouraged "race hatred" by summoning "black girls to attack white women." Although the "negresses were reluctant to do so," Stevens wrote, "they were goaded to deliver blows upon the women by the warden's threat of punishment." She also remembered that former inmates sometimes came by the NWP headquarters after their release, hoping the women with whom they had shared the cells might help them. She did not comment on whether or not the suffragists offered any assistance.[17]

In October, Alice Paul was arrested and sentenced to seven months in the Occoquan Workhouse. Drawing on her experiences with British suffragists, Paul and another fighter, Rose Winslow, began a hunger strike to bring further attention to their cause. Jailers had Paul transferred to a psychiatric ward to discredit her as a madwoman. Her hunger strike stretched out to ten days, when officials made the decision to force-feed Paul and the other hunger strikers in what became known as the "Night of Terror." The public was horrified, and under political pressure, authorities unconditionally released Paul, Lucy Burns, and twenty other suffrage prisoners.[18]

Stevens and the NWP argued that this harsh treatment gained them sympathy. They noted that in September, the chair of the Senate Women Suffrage Committee, Senator Jones of New Mexico, visited the jail and was moved by their plight. The following day, he allowed the suffrage bill to be reported out of his committee, after having refused to do so for six months. It would still take a year and a half of politicking by NAWSA to pass it.[19]

Not all women had their lives significantly disrupted by the war. Two weeks after the United States declared war on Germany, Mabel Lee found out she had been accepted into the Ph.D. program in the Department of Political Science, Science, and Philosophy at Columbia University. Along with three other women, she was awarded the Curtis University Scholarship, the first Chinese woman to receive the honor.[20] Columbia College remained an all-male school until 1983, but the Columbia graduate school had begun to admit a small number of women into their doctoral programs. Anthropologist Franz Boas was especially helpful in pressing for change, arguing that female students were essential because male anthropologists were often unable to access women's knowledge in other cultures. He began to admit women like Margaret Mead, Elsie Clews Parsons, and Ella Deloria (Dakota) to his anthropology program. Indeed, female doctoral candidates in the humanities were on the rise, but an intrepid few like Lee ventured into the fields such as economics, politics, and law.[21]

Within her new department, women like Lee with bachelor's degrees could study history, economics, and social science. The men who taught there included racist historian William Archibald Dunning, who influenced and trained a generation of scholars with his argument that Reconstruction had failed because white northerners were corrupt and blacks were inferior. But the department also included progressive historian Charles Beard, whose scholarship emphasized the economic disparities at the founding of the nation.[22]

While a Ph.D. student, Lee remained closely involved in the Chinese Students' Alliance. She helped coordinate celebrations of the seventh anniversary of the founding of the Chinese Republic. She was also involved in the opening of China House, a four-story building close to campus intended as a boardinghouse and rendezvous point for Chinese students. It contained a library with Chinese books, newspapers, and periodicals. The Columbia branch of the alliance began to hold its meetings there. It also determined that there would be a publicity committee to "correct or defend" any negative press against the Chinese in the American news media. Sometimes the battles hit close to home; one wonders if the Chinese Students' Alliance responded to the *Barnard Bulletin* article under the headline "Ching Ching Chinatown," which luridly described a Barnard student tour of Chinatown that used imagery of tongs, opium dens, and the rescue mission to turn poverty, violence, and addiction into a sort of fun house scare.[23]

Lee chaired the social committee in these years, teaching the members to sing national, college, and patriotic songs.[24] The CSA, like many groups, emphasized its support for the Allies in World War I, especially after the United States had entered the war in 1917. Its members' patriotism, however, was also focused on China. They had been following events there closely since the war broke out in 1914. Japan had pointed to its formal alliance with Great Britain to declare war on Germany. It then used this as an excuse to attack German concessions at Shandong Province in China.[25] In 1915 the Chinese Students Club of Columbia sent a telegram to President Yuan as well as to newspapers in Peking and Shanghai urging him "to use all his influence to resist the Japanese."[26] After the United States entered the war, the students created a "Chinese Patriotic Committee" that coordinated with students on other campuses and leading businessmen of New York. They knew that China had been contributing to the war effort by sending thousands of laborers to England and France. They surely mourned the more than five hundred Chinese workers who died when German submarines sunk the French ship *Athos* in February 1917. And they likely celebrated when China officially declared war on Germany in August of that year.[27]

In 1918, Zhang Mojun, the feminist revolutionary and founder of Shenchou Girls' School whom Carrie Chapman Catt had visited in Shanghai in 1912, enrolled at Columbia Teachers College. She chose an "American name" for her time there and was known as Sophia Chang.[28] Like other Chinese students, she found a welcome home in the CSA. The members recognized her organizational talent and quickly elected her to the officer corps. At the November 1918 meeting, Chang was elected chair of the social committee to replace Mabel Lee, who was taking time off for an unstated reason.[29] The following spring, Chang was elected president. The club proudly reported this event as historic: "For the first time in its history, the Chinese Students' Club of Columbia University has as its president for the current semester a lady educationist." It touted her feminist work in China, noting that "for years she has been a motive force in the movement for better education of Chinese girls." Her election "does not only bring with it a certain degree of feminine atmosphere which is generally lacking in a bachelor organization, but also indicates that the day has gone when the club politics used to be a masculine diversion." Though this was perhaps a bit of an overstatement as both Mabel Lee and Alice Huie had been officers, it was nonetheless exciting.[30]

A major figure in China at the time, Chang seems to have been mostly unrecognized outside of the Chinese community in the United States. Perhaps she reconnected with Catt, but no record has surfaced. The Chinese community, however, invited her to speak on a number of occasions. For example, in December she was invited to Harvard for the first annual conference of the Kuo Fong Hui. The conference-goers discussed the responsibility of returned students to the regeneration of China and the educational needs back home. She was an honored guest, sharing the stage with Mr. Chengting T. Wang, the vice speaker of the Chinese Senate. They lauded her for her work at the Shenchou Girls' School.[31] She gave a speech at the banquet and was asked to serve as a judge for the debate on a resolution that "China should adopt the American federal form of government."[32]

If they did not remember Chang herself, American suffragists kept alive memories of the Chinese suffrage movement. The year Chang arrived at Columbia, Ida Bell Lewis issued *The Education of Girls in China* as Teachers College publication #104. While the book does not mention her or her school by name, it did refer to Chang and her sister suffragists in Shanghai: "Women leaders have also a claim on the progress in China. During the Revolution equal suffrage was urged with much vigor and earnestness upon the new republic. . . . Many of the Chinese private schools are managed entirely by women. . . . Women in institutions of learning in every province of China and in many colleges of America will carry on the movement which is bringing a new era for the women of their nation." Like Mabel Lee, Bell asserted that the challenge that educators in China faced was mediating between the old and the new, tradition and the modern.[33] Chang entered into these conversations at Columbia, bringing her enormous experience in women's education as well as in the development of the new republic. She took charge of an exhibit for the Educational Museum at Teachers College on the topic of education in China, calling on the members of the CSA to help her collect "the most representative articles made by the school-boys and girls in China."[34]

Chang left the country after her one-year program ended. She traveled east to Europe, joining the Chinese delegation at the Peace Conference. There they hoped that China's provision of thousands of laborers in the war effort would help them in their attempts to dislodge the Japanese from mainland China. They were disappointed to have received only two seats at the table to Japan's five.[35] By 1921 she had returned to China and to a position as president of the Nanking High Normal School for Girls.[36] Certainly her degree from Teachers College was helpful to her as she began to train the next generation of Chinese women.

In the meantime, Mabel Lee flourished in her Ph.D. program. She found support in economist Dr. Vladimir Simkhovitch, who was part of a group of Columbia's faculty who were pushing the boundaries of scholarship by crossing disciplinary lines. They all also chose to teach classes at either Barnard or Teachers College, something few of their colleagues were willing to do. The group included Franz Boas in anthropology, Frank Giddings in sociology, John Dewey in philosophy, and Charles Beard in history. They supported social reform and were involved in the settlement movement. Not surprisingly, many of them were also feminists.[37] Simkhovitch taught on Marxist socialism and advocated for the history of the everyday, something that put him at odds with many in the department who argued scholarship should be focused on the political and economic elite.[38]

Although Lee took classes from other faculty members, Simkhovitch became her mentor and dissertation advisor. He did not steer her to write on a "woman's topic" but encouraged her to use her language skills to explore the neglected subject of historical Chinese agricultural policy. She rose to the challenge. Her dissertation, "The Economic History of China: With Special Reference to Agriculture," was sweeping and ambitious in its scope. It covered hundreds of years and multiple dynasties. In the large appendix she included numerous documents that she had translated from Chinese into English for the first time. Indeed, scholars still draw upon her arguments and cite her findings today.[39]

For Lee, graduate work also provided an opportunity to help guide the development of her nation. She believed that her work could help the Chinese government with its modern agricultural politics. She pointed out that revolutionaries had little interest in history; indeed, their project had been to overthrow tradition and form a new China based on Western ideas. But, she countered, rather than be a dead weight on innovation, the past could offer a guide as they began to develop their new economic policies. She argued, "We can neither afford to be dominated by the authority of the old just because it is old, nor by that of the new just because it is new." Instead, she advocated for searching the old records for data that could be interpreted "in the light of modern science."

When the time came to file her dissertation, she dedicated the work "in appreciation of my American friends, to friendship and better understanding between the American and Chinese peoples." She also carefully chose how her name would be entered into the scholarly record. She accentuated her "Chinese name," proudly insisting that "Mabel Ping-Hua Lee" appear on the title page. Ping-Hua was a name the Immigration Service would later call her "alias," and it was "foreign" to most Americans. Perhaps she was responding to the great American wag H. L. Mencken, who several years earlier in his book *The American Language* had held up her name along with those of many of her colleagues in the CSA as examples of the "bizarre combinations" found in the "Americanized" names of immigrants. But Lee was undeterred. In 1921, she became the first Chinese woman to receive a Ph.D. from Columbia and perhaps the first in the nation.[40]

As a Chinese woman with a doctoral degree in the United States, Lee was unique, but she was not the only woman in that position. The choices of other women Ph.D.s suggest some of the possibilities and some of the limitations of her position. Harriet Bradley, a friend in the doctoral program, had also written a dissertation under Dr. Simkhovitch with a focus on the enclosure movement in England. Mabel Lee saw their two projects as addressing "similar problems in economic history," and the women worked through their ideas together. Upon her graduation, Bradley, who was white, received a job offer at Vassar College, which she took.[41] Women's colleges like Vassar were important sources of employment for women with advanced degrees. It was much harder to get a position at a coed school and nearly impossible at an all-male institution. In fact, women with Ph.D.s found landing a job harder than completing their dissertations, itself a rigorous and multiyear process. Male and female graduates had very different experiences on the job market, even with the same advisor. At Columbia, Franz Boas, the famous father of modern anthropology, struggled to place his female students, while his male students easily landed plum positions at Berkeley and even Harvard. Between 1900 and 1930, women flocked to Ph.D. programs, and the percentage of Ph.D.s awarded to women doubled but then fell for the next three decades. The problem was structural; no one would hire them. Emilie Hutchinson, an economist from Barnard who had also received her doctorate from Columbia, studied the question in 1929. In her book *Women and the PhD*, she quoted one professor resignedly stating, "Every president and head of department insists on having only men in higher positions; it seems to me idiotic to encourage women to take the higher degrees with the thought of getting anything like a fair deal."[42] This did not bode well for Mabel Lee's academic future.

In 1921 no Chinese or Chinese American woman taught at a college or uni-

DR. MABEL P. LEE

Mabel Lee's feminism was capacious. Unable to vote when New York State enfranchised women in 1917, she found other ways to be a feminist "pioneer." She became the first Chinese women in the United States to earn a Ph.D., graduating with a degree in economics from Columbia University. Jobs for women with higher degrees were hard to come by, however. She is pictured here in 1923 departing for a trip to postwar Europe and China to study economic systems. (*Courtesy George Grantham Bain Collection, Library of Congress Prints and Photographs Division, Washington, D.C.*)

versity. A very small number of Chinese men held positions as lecturers and tutors but not as professors in U.S. institutions. Opportunities for educated Chinese women were much more readily available in China. Lee's friends Alice Huie and her sister Caroline had also enrolled at Teachers College after graduating from Barnard. Then, even though they had been born in New York, they went to China.[43] They both took jobs with the YWCA in Shanghai. Alice Huie, ever the athlete, taught physical education and hygiene, while Caroline Huie quickly rose through the ranks and eventually became chair of the National Board from 1938 to 1939. She also served as dean of women at St. John's University in Shanghai in 1935.[44]

New York State had enfranchised women in 1917, but for Mabel Lee, who could not vote, the way forward as a feminist was to build a career. But there, too, she was stymied. Even Chinese American women faced very limited job options in the United States, and a number of them went to China where there were opportunities, especially in church- and mission-related positions.[45] Mabel Lee faced the question of what to do and where to do it.

[CHAPTER 14]

Americanize the First American

Gertrude Simmons Bonnin

A few months after the United States declared war on Germany in the summer of 1917, Gertrude Bonnin moved to Washington, D.C.[1] The Society of American Indians had elected her secretary, and the move placed her closer to the organization's headquarters, but it was also a relief to leave the Uintah and Ouray reservation at Fort Duchesne, Utah. She had made the best of her time there but was not interested in keeping house while her husband, Raymond, served as the reservation superintendent. Several times she had sent in applications for a teaching position at the reservation school, but each time administrators turned her down. It was not due to lack of qualification. Her degree from Earlham College and her previous experience teaching at the Carlisle Indian Industrial School made her more qualified than most Bureau of Indian Affairs employees. Bored and frustrated, she began to do unpaid community service among the women of the reservation. She enjoyed the work. The women were good company. They often told funny stories during sewing classes, and the gatherings were full of laughter. But they were also serious, soberly considering the poverty and isolation their people faced on the reservation. They formed a reading group, meeting for conversations about children's health and education, local conditions, and the tribe's economy. Bonnin also tried to visit other women who lived farther from the agency headquarters, but the land was rough and "much time and energy [were] lost on the road."[2]

Bonnin felt isolated from the vibrant literary scene of the East Coast that had feted her a decade earlier. Her work with the woman at Uintah had been important and living on the reservation eye-opening, but she missed city life.[3] She did not write for the first ten years she spent in Utah. Then, in 1913, she joined the SAI, and the inspiration began to flow again. It flourished in the form of an opera about her people's sacred celebration, the Sun Dance, that she cowrote with Brigham Young University professor William Hanson. Soon she was writing columns for the SAI's journal. But she missed the fellowship of other writers. When the opportunity to move to Washington presented itself, she jumped at the chance.

Marie Bottineau Baldwin warmly welcomed her as she had other Native women who had come to the city. She sent Bonnin a package of maple candy, a playful allusion to Bottineau Baldwin's Ojibwe heritage from the north woods. But if Bottineau Baldwin thought that she and Bonnin were going to be friends, she was mistaken. Although they shared much in common as modern Indian women, a friendship was not to be.[4]

184]

Things between the two women got off to a bad start. Bonnin immediately began to order things to suit her. She abruptly closed the SAI office in the Barrister Building and moved the headquarters into her own house at 707 Twentieth Street NW. She left Marie Bottineau Baldwin's law library in the old office, sending her a brief note to let her know the lease was expiring at the end of the day. Bottineau Baldwin was furious at the slight. She complained to her friend in Albany, Arthur C. Parker, the former SAI secretary. It was a "high-handed" move, she fumed. Bonnin had made the decision "without an even 'by your leave.'" And what was more, as the organization's treasurer she felt bound to point out that Bonnin "intends to charge the SAI office rent" and thus "intends the SAI to pay part of her home's rent." The society would certainly not be getting its money's worth, she huffed, as she would now be doing the work of treasurer from her own home. Parker was disappointingly unsympathetic.[5]

Others were charmed by Bonnin's "cozy flat." On the walls of the neat living room, which doubled as the society's offices, "hung gayly-beaded moccasins and other souvenirs of the reservation." She also cultivated an air of middle-class domesticity, with "a fine photo of her husband, who is an officer in the army," decorating the piano.[6] Indeed, soon after they arrived, Raymond had been commissioned as second lieutenant.[7] He went to work for the quartermaster's department in the city.

Gertrude Bonnin also managed to juggle war work with advocacy for other causes, which quickly brought her into the orbit of politically active white women in the District. She displayed a masterful political sense, gaining white allies by deploying her identity as a Native woman. She would use a similar strategy in her suffrage work. With her home unpacked and arranged, she quickly turned her energy to a ban on peyote use.[8] Peyote, a hallucinogen made from the buttons of a cactus plant, was used in ceremonies of the Native American Church, a syncretic religion that had become popular on western reservations, including on the Uintah and Ouray Reservation. The religion offered solace to people who had experienced the dramatic disruption of their lives and cultures and also allowed them to hide some of their traditions in plain sight. In their churches they blended Christianity with Native culture, using peyote buttons in their sacramental ceremonies.

Bonnin saw it differently. Peyote was an "alarming menace," she argued, and one that was misunderstood. "Peyote has been represented as a sacrament in an Indian religion," she acknowledged, but "it is not Indian." Instead, "the Rituals of the church have been borrowed as a cloak to hide under, and to evade the laws of morals and decency," she charged. Somewhat ironically, for a woman who had written an article titled "Why I Am a Pagan" and an opera about the Sun Dance, she insisted that "religion is the adoration of the Maker with a rational mind. No one in the state of drunkenness, by whatsoever cause, can be in his rational mind; and he cannot practice religion." Perhaps her adamant stance was a strategy for finding allies, but her experiences with a peyote roadman in Utah had soured her on the religion.[9]

By December, she was speaking in front of the Woman's Christian Temperance Union national convention, urging the temperance women to support antipeyote legislation. Peyote was "dry whiskey," she informed them. It was "the twin brother of alcoholic beverages and first cousin to habit forming drugs." And it was being used indiscriminately by men, women, and children. The peyote buttons were grown in the Southwest and smuggled north on railroads. She had seen its effects in Utah, she explained. There Native people were told that eating them would give them supernatural powers, prevent disease, and negate the need for education.[10] The WCTU women were sympathetic. After all, the accusations Bonnin made against peyote mirrored their concerns about alcohol.[11]

At the national convention she shared the stage with newly elected congresswoman Jeannette Rankin and, in most reports, overshadowed her. Many newspapers published articles that included Bonnin's plea to the temperance women. They highlighted the fact that she wore "full Indian costume" for the speech. It was exactly the reaction she had hoped for.[12]

Bonnin had trained as a violinist at the Boston Conservatory. She had performed at Philadelphia's Association Hall, at New York City's Carnegie Hall, and at the Paris Exposition.[13] She knew about staging. She also knew Americans were fascinated by all things Indian and hoped to use that to her advantage. She anticipated that the exotic clothing would serve as a "drawing card,"[14] opening many doors to her. She began to hand out pictures of herself to reporters to accompany their articles. She was carefully portrayed in her "costume," a buckskin dress with fringe at the wrists and ankles and beadwork at the shoulders. Her long black hair hung in braids over her chest, and a silver belt held a small bag at her waist.[15]

The pictures soon began to appear, most of them next to articles about Bonnin's testimony before Congress in early 1918. As they considered that year's Indian Appropriation Bill, legislators debated adding a rider to outlaw the importation of peyote. The hearings in the Senate Committee on Indian Affairs, chaired by Senator Charles Curtis, drew a number of "Indians from the far west, clad in their native costumes." Most of them were advocating for peyote use. But Bonnin eloquently urged the congressmen to include the rider. After all, they had already outlawed alcohol on Indian reservations. Linking peyote to alcohol was a good strategy. That very same Congress had passed the language of the Eighteenth Amendment, Prohibition, a month earlier in December 1917. Five states (Mississippi, Virginia, Kentucky, North Dakota, and South Carolina) had ratified it by the end of January, just as the peyote hearings began.[16]

Most of the other Native witnesses, however, disagreed with Bonnin and testified to the sacred nature of the peyote ceremony. Even the Society of American Indians, which Bonnin was said to represent in the hearings, was divided on the issue. But reporters were sold on the negative effects of peyote. One melodra-

MRS. GERTRUDE BONNIN
Social Worker among Indians, Lecturer and Writer, Secretary
of the Society of American Indians
French-Sioux

Like other Native suffragists, Gertrude Simmons Bonnin (Zitkala-Ša) knew that
white audiences often had specific ideas of what an "Indian" should look like. She
used this strategically, referring to the outfit she is wearing here as a "drawing card"
that gave her access to audiences. Once in front of those audiences, however, she
undermined their ideas about Indians being stuck in the past by advocating for
"the Indian woman of today." (From Houghton, Our Debt to the Red Man, 206)

matically opened his article, "While bullet and bomb are destroying the white man on the battlefields of the world, the American Indian is called upon to fight an enemy which is rapidly undermining his race."[17] What they did not mention was that thousands of Native men were also in the U.S. military, including Gertrude's Bonnin's husband, Raymond.[18]

The publicity from Bonnin's congressional testimony soon brought her a number of speaking invitations from organizations in the city. As she suspected, most wanted her to talk about Indian culture, to weave the legends and sing the songs of her "primitive people," but she primarily used these platforms to educate her audience on "the Indian women of today" and to advocate for Native rights to citizenship and suffrage. This sometimes startled her audience. Her talk to the Improved Order of Red Men, a fraternal organization for white men, was more along the lines of "a lecture on the present life of the Indians" than on traditions, one observer noted in a somewhat disappointed tone. She addressed the "trials, dangers, schooling, [and] farming" issues faced by Native people on reservations. With her husband in the audience, she also proudly noted that "out of the 9,000 [Native] eligibles for service in the army 5,000 had volunteered."[19] And yet, she concluded, many did not have citizenship in the nation. She also gave an "address and appeal for citizenship" to the women of the Anthony League, a suffrage club that was doing the work of selling war bonds and knitting garments for the Army Emergency Department.[20] Soon after, she spoke on the "Indian Past and Present" to the Congressional Club, an eager audience of the wives of congressmen. She gave the same speech to the WCTU.[21] Later that summer she again extolled the patriotism and sacrifices of Indian men to the YMCA at Camp Meigs. Proudly "clad in the native costume of her race," she informed the crowd that thousands of Native men were fighting on the Western Front and thousands more were in training camps across the country. Surely the men giving such loyal service deserved full citizenship in the nation.[22]

Gertrude Bonnin was usually introduced as a "Sioux Indian" whose "tribal name is Zitkala-Ša wife of Lt. Bonnin, USA, and graduate of Carlisle Indian school" (though she had not graduated from Carlisle, she had taught there). She was immensely proud of all those things: her Native culture, her marriage to a military man, and her education. Sometimes papers claimed she was the granddaughter of Sitting Bull, which she was not. But she was happy to let Americans be mistaken, as she certainly claimed the legacy of warrior for her people.[23]

As she moved throughout the city lecturing that year, Bonnin witnessed the growing radicalism of Alice Paul's National Woman's Party. Walking three blocks east from her flat brought her to the White House, where suffragists had been picketing every day since January 1917. Walking just half a block farther north brought her to the NWP's headquarters on the east side of Layfette Park, where she had given a lecture in early June 1918. Two months later, in August the NWP began to hold open-air meetings in the park, hoping to attract the attention of the clerks leaving their offices. With tricolored purple, yellow, and gold banners held high, one hundred women joined Alice Paul there for the first meeting on August 6, and forty-eight of them were arrested. They were released on bail. Six days later, they held another meeting; thirty-eight were arrested that day. Two days later, they returned for yet another demonstration. Thirty women were arrested and released on bail only to return that evening for another demonstration. The next day, the first group had their trial and were sentenced to ten to fifteen days in the Old District workhouse. Their request to be treated as political prisoners denied, twenty-four of them began a hunger strike. It was a battle of the wills that Bonnin witnessed.[24]

She and her SAI colleagues were talking about the NWP pickets but also thinking about their own position relative to U.S. citizenship and suffrage. The Winter 1917 issue of the *American Indian Magazine* had several articles making the case for Native citizenship. Bonnin, whose short story "A Sioux Woman's Love for Her Grandchild," was also published in the issue, certainly read them. In "The Fighting Sioux," her fellow tribesman Chauncey Yellow Robe asserted Native claims using martial citizenship, an argument Bonnin often used. American Indian men were proving their patriotism on the battlefields of Europe, he argued. Then he took a swipe at the NWP: "The Sioux are not picketing the White House in a heckling campaign for rights and votes," he wrote; "their battle is broader. Their finest men are picketing on the war front in France and asking the world court if the defender of liberty is not entitled to its privileges." He also differentiated Sioux women from the NWP picketers. Instead of protesting, they invested in Liberty Bonds and volunteered for the Red Cross and YMCA. His article suggested that their loyalty deserved recognition through citizenship. In the same issue Charles Eastman addressed the question of "Sioux as Officeholders" in his article, "The Sioux Past and Present." In it he mused on the growing number of Sioux voters in South Dakota as people were allotted land and granted citizenship. "They are not ignorant or indifferent voters, either," he noted. "The Indian is a clear thinker, a good talker and really a natural politician." Editor Arthur Parker articulated the SAI's goals: "Make the Indian a citizen, eliminate the Bureau, demonstrate that America is a safe place for every American citizen." But he cautioned, in calling for the end of the bureau, "We are not advocating for the abandonment of the legal and moral obligations of the Government to the Indians, but a recognition of these obligations in such a manner that the first Americans shall become, indeed, real Americans in every sense, and that they may become the good citizens they ought and would like to be." Bonnin, too, held similar opinions about the necessity of citizenship for Native people and the potential power of Native voters and self-governance. But these Indigenous intellectuals also emphasized that even if it granted all Native people U.S. citizenship, the federal government would still need to honor its ongoing obligations to Native nations.[25]

In September 1918, as NWP protesters continued their vigils at the White House, Gertrude Bonnin boarded a train from Washington to Pierre, South Dakota, for the Society of American Indians' annual conference. The conference was her triumph. She had managed to steer the organization to the Sioux. The meeting was being held in the heart of their territory, and she had been elected secretary-treasurer of the organization and editor of its journal. Their new president-elect, Charles Eastman, was Santee Dakota, another branch of the Sioux. Marie Bottineau Baldwin refused to attend. It was the first conference she had missed, but the Ojibwe woman was angry at the takeover and at attacks on members like her who worked for the Indian Bureau. She had tried to warn Arthur Parker, but he dismissed her concerns. "I am not afraid of what the Sioux may do or what the Chippewas may do, providing the conference places are shifted from time to time out of reach of tribal influences," he wrote back. But he would not be attending either due to his wartime obligations.[26]

As the train rushed along, Bonnin was keenly aware of the baskets of letters sitting at home, waiting to be answered. Being secretary of the SAI was a labor of love. She was not paid in currency, but she was happy with the work the organization was doing to help her people. She had only so much time, however, and only two hands. Her mind buzzed with a long to-do list as she contemplated the annual report she would give at the conference: thousands of letters to be sent out and responded to, dues collected, and membership lists to be updated. People wrote for help and information on legislation moving through Congress. The letters sat there waiting for an answer, but there were also trips to the commissioner of Indian Affairs' office to make and congressional committee meetings to attend. The war made it so hard to get clerical help. How could the SAI compete with the high salaries of government wartime jobs?[27]

She noticed a fellow passenger eying her service pin. Clearing his throat, he asked, "You have a relative in the war?" She answered quickly and proudly, "Yes, indeed. I have many cousins and nephews, somewhere in France. This star I am wearing is for my husband, a member of the great Sioux nation, who is a volunteer in Uncle Sam's Army." His face registered his understanding of the dark-haired woman in front of him. "Oh! Yes! You are an Indian! Well, I knew when I first saw you that you must be a foreigner."[28] Foreigner? She stared at him in disbelief. Her mind flashed to the 10,000 Native soldiers on Europe's battlefields, many of them volunteers who were "mingling their precious blood with the blood of all other peoples of the earth" for the cause of democracy. She thought of their mothers, grandmothers, and sisters buying Liberty Bonds, working for the Red Cross, and conserving food for a country that within their lifetimes had confined their people to reservations, converted their sacred places into national parks, and sent their children away to boarding schools.[29] Many of them mourned a dead loved one in the war. Didn't he know geography?, she blurted out. Native people were the original inhabitants of the country; America was their home.

She suggested some articles he could read to educate himself. Had he seen the June issue of *Designer* about the Native children doing Red Cross work? There were others she could offer as well. His eyes glazed over with disinterest. Shaking his head, he moved on down the train car leaving her with her thoughts about the sacrifices Native people were making in a country that did not appreciate them. And what did they want in return, she pondered, but "a very simple thing—citizenship in the land that was once his own—America."[30] Sometimes, she thought, "it takes courage to live." "Every Indian, who stands firmly on his own feet, for the cause of right justice and freedom, is indeed a hero—a living hero in the skirmishes of daily life!"[31]

Two months after the conference, when the armistice was signed, Bonnin was optimistic. Surely the sacrifices Native people made during the war would convince white Americans that they deserved to be part of the citizenry, able to control their own destinies. "The eyes of the world are upon the Peace Conference sitting at Paris. Under the sun a new epoch is being staged," she wrote. The unprecedented talks offered her hope for her people. "Small nations and remnants of nations are to sit beside their great allies at the Peace Table; and their just claims are to be duly incorporated in the terms of a righteous peace." She excitedly wrote that "little peoples are to be granted the right of self determination!" The opportunity for Indigenous people to press their claims seemed ripe, and she hoped that the world was "to be made better as a result of these stirring times."[32]

She observed that many "classes of men and women were clamoring for a hearing" in Europe, including labor organizations, women of the world, and Japanese representatives. From the United States, she saw that President Wilson had sent Dr. W. E. B. Du Bois and Dr. Robert Moton of the Tuskegee Institute to represent "the Black man of America." A group of New Yorkers also appealed to the president for his "aid on behalf of self-government for the Irish people." Where, however, were Indians? Bonnin wondered. "The Red man asked for a very simple thing—citizenship in the land that was once his own," she asserted. "Who shall represent his cause at the World's Peace Conference?" Once again she reminded Americans of the sacrifices Native soldiers had made for the country. They shared the same values as white Americans and deserved equal treatment. "He loves democratic ideals. What shall world democracy mean to his race? There never was a time more opportune than now for America to enfranchise the Red man!" She wrote to President Wilson, hoping he would appoint a Native representative, but he ignored the request.[33]

But the argument Bonnin and other SAI members had been making about the irony of Native men fighting for a nation that refused many of them citizenship was powerful, and Congress was swayed. Martial citizenship claims, the claims of people who fought (and in some cases died) to defend a nation, often have great resonance. Because men made up (and continue to constitute) the bulk of the armed forces, martial citizenship tends to be an argument most effective for men. Precisely a year after the war ended, on November 6, 1919, Congress passed legislation granting Native veterans of the Great War the right to petition for U.S. citizenship. Two months later, the commissioner of Indian Affairs sent a circular to reservation agents instructing them to inform "the Indians of your jurisdiction" about the provisions of the act. It stated that "every American Indian who served in the Military or Naval Establishment of the United States during the war against the Imperial German Government" and who had (or would) receive an honorable discharge "shall, on proof of such discharge before a court ... and without other examination except as prescribed by said court, be granted full citizenship with all the privileges pertaining thereto, without in any manner impairing or otherwise affecting the property rights, individual or tribal, of any such Indian or his interest in tribal or other Indian property."[34]

While this may have seemed straightforward, the question of Native citizenship remained opaque. For one thing, the act required veterans to initiate the petition. Joseph Dixon, a researcher interested in Native soldiers, sent questionnaires to many Native veterans in early 1920, soon after the passage of the Veterans Citizenship Act. He received 2,846 responses from Native soldiers and sailors, but none of the men indicated that they had petitioned the courts for citizenship following their military service. Moreover, many seemed not even to have known of the legislation. As Marie Bottineau Baldwin observed, Native citizenship status was extremely confusing. Dixon's questionnaires had two questions on one line, suggesting that they were opposites: "Are you a citizen?" "Are you a ward of the Government?" Of the 904 Native veterans who answered affirmatively that they were U.S. citizens, 325 of them (more than a third) also checked that they were wards of the government without full rights, especially over their allotments. The confusion had extended to the draft. Noncitizen Indians had been exempt from mandatory service but were still required to register. They were also allowed to enlist. Of the 374 men identified as noncitizen Indians, 217 enlisted, but 151 were drafted. Twenty-six-year-old Private Ambrose Gabe (Sioux) from Wakpala, on the Standing Rock Reservation in South Dakota, wrote on his questionnaire, "About the question in the enclosed blank, it says Are you a Citizen? ... That is a hard question to answer although I am natural born. ... I don't know whether I am a ward of the Government or a citizen." He had served in Troop B, 314th Military Police, 89th Division.[35]

The arguments that Bonnin and other Native advocates of U.S. citizenship made about martial citizenry had worked. But the question of Indian citizenship remained unresolved. Few veterans applied for it due to the complex nature of the bureaucratic structures and the ongoing confusion about the status of Native people. Further, that legislation applied only to veterans of the Great War. Many other Native people remained under federal wardship. Bonnin would continue to advocate for their citizenship in the coming years.

CHAPTER 15

Courting Political Ruin
Nina Otero-Warren

Throughout the war, suffragists in individual states closely followed the federal amendment's progress through Congress. Journals of national organizations, newspapers, and visiting speakers kept them abreast of the struggle. Sometimes the women themselves traveled to the capital and came back with updates. This was the case with Nina Otero-Warren, who made at least two trips to Washington. She met with other New Mexicans, including the politicians, in the city. She lobbied for the amendment and connected with her fellow National Woman's Party activists, and her visits were reported in the *Suffragist*.[1]

In the early spring of 1918, for example, Otero-Warren traveled to the capital with friend and fellow educational leader Isabel Eckles. While in the city, the NWP feted Otero-Warren for her suffrage work in the Southwest. Elizabeth Thatcher Kent, former NAWSA Congressional Committee chair and wife of a former California congressman, hosted a tea in her honor. Alice Paul herself assisted Kent, and the party's organizer, Anne Martin, presided over the table. Guests included officers and members of the NWP.[2] At this meeting Otero-Warren may have learned that Anne Martin was planning to run for the Senate seat in Nevada, making her the first woman in the United States to run for that office. Back in New Mexico, *La Voz del Pueblo* reported the news, calling Martin the "íntima amiga" (intimate friend) of Otero-Warren and reminding readers that she had been one of the "centinelas callados" or silent sentinels who had picketed the White House.[3]

When Otero-Warren returned to Santa Fe, she was recognized as an expert on the federal situation by the members of the Santa Fe Suffrage League. The first lady of the state, Deane Lindsey, was a "staunch friend" of suffrage as was her husband, New Mexico's third governor, Washington E. Lindsey. Mrs. Lindsey invited the Suffrage League to meet at the executive mansion, where Otero-Warren often gave presentations. The war infused the tone of the meetings, which were described as "deeply patriotic," with Mrs. Lindsey serving "wartime refreshments." In September, after one such reception, which included a number of prominent Albuquerque suffrage leaders, a general meeting was called to strategize for the upcoming convention and legislative session. The women were confident that the federal amendment would soon be passed by Congress, so they focused on the problem of putting "machinery" into place that would ensure that their state would ratify it. They named a committee of five women representing different parts of the state who would chair subcommittees in charge of various aspects of the work. Otero-Warren was chosen as chairman of the political parties and platforms.[4]

Otero-Warren was incredibly busy in the fall of 1918 as she balanced her leadership in suffrage activism with her educational and war work. She had been serving as appointed superintendent of Santa Fe County schools but was now seeking to win the office in an open election. She was the only woman but not the only Hispanic Republican candidate for county office. The party's advertisement touted "this splendid lady" who through "her educational qualifications, her firmness, and magnificent tact" benefited the children of the county.[5] When she won in November, papers across the state and into California noted that she had beaten a man for the office.[6]

In October, Otero-Warren learned that the National Catholic War Council, headquartered in New York, had approved the archbishop of Santa Fe's recommendation that she be appointed vice chairman of the Victory Boys and Victory Girls of the Archdiocese of Santa Fe. At the same time, she was selected to go overseas with the Red Cross and began training with that organization.[7] She hoped to see her brother Luna Bergere, who was deployed in France as commanding officer of the 143rd Machine Gun Battalion of the 40th Division. Her stepfather, Alfred, was also overseas, serving as head secretary of the Knights of Columbus establishing recreation centers for soldiers in France and Belgium. But in November 1918 the war ended and the armistice was signed before she was deployed.[8]

There was plenty of fighting for her to do at home. As 1919 dawned, she joined the executive board of the New Mexico Federation of Women's Clubs to map out its legislative program. Many of the women had also been at the meeting of the Suffrage League earlier in the fall. The topics they discussed ranged widely from a state home for delinquent girls, the creation of a state department of health, a proposed child welfare department, the teaching of art in schools, scholarships for domestic science courses, a declaration of New Mexico Day to commemorate the reconquest of the region by Diego de Vargas, higher salaries and free textbooks for indigent students, and the censorship of motion pictures. Otero-Warren, as chair of the legislative committee, presided over part of the meeting. She then presented their decision to focus on two issues in the upcoming legislative session: the care of delinquent girls and the child conservation commission bill.

Suffrage was also in their sights. The federation had previously gone on record as supporting the Susan B. Anthony amendment, and there was great applause when Mrs. R. P. Barnes, the chair of the suffrage committee, reported that the House of Representatives had approved the suffrage amendment. They voted to thank the House and to urge the Senate to do the same.[9]

The newly elected governor, O. A. Larrazolo, and his wife invited the clubwomen to a reception at the executive mansion. Governor Larrazolo had been born in Mexico and became a naturalized citizen. Like his predecessor Governor Lindsey, he supported women's suffrage. It was an exciting reception crowded with legislators in town for the session; the executive board of the New Mexico Federation of Women's Clubs (many of whom were suffragists); and a number of "war heroes" just returned from overseas. Many of the young women from Santa Fe assisted at the party, including Nina Otero-Warren's sisters Dolores and Rosina Bergere and Ramona Baca. Indeed, a large number of the guests were Hispanic. The executive mansion was aglow "from the basement to the flagstaff," and the first lady had decorated it with fragrant snapdragon blossoms of pink and white accented with green foliage. She served ice cream and cake in harmony with the color scheme.[10]

Otero-Warren, anticipating that women would soon be enfranchised, moved to ensconce herself in party politics. The men in her family were powerful Republican leaders in the state. Her cousin Miguel Otero served as territorial governor, her maternal uncle Solomon Luna had led the state constitutional convention, and her brother Eduardo Otero was a current Republican Party leader. Otero-Warren planned to join them in the top ranks of the party. She stepped down as state chair of the National Woman's Party and accepted the position of chair for the New Mexico GOP State Women's Committee. The committee was formed to work with the party's national committee and "take an active part in forming the politics of the Republican Party."[11] Otero-Warren was a seasoned lobbyist, a well-known figure in the state, and a Hispana, and the party knew she was a valuable asset. When she agreed to serve, her busy schedule got busier. She had her job as county superintendent of schools, and in April, Governor Larrazolo appointed her to the state health board, making her the first woman in the nation to be appointed to such a position. The board promptly elected her chair. She did care about public health and had actively lobbied the state legislature for the health bill during the recent session, but she later stepped down due to lack of time.[12] She was also traveling widely. Newspapers reported that she returned to Washington, D.C., in May for the Republican Women's Committee meeting, that she was delegated to go to the National Conference of Social Work in Atlantic City in June, and that she went to the National Education Association meeting that same month in Chicago.[13]

On June 4, 1919, the Senate finally passed the amendment sending woman suffrage to the states for ratification. New Mexico's suffragists could be proud of their congressional delegation, who had all voted for the amendment. Otero-Warren had charge of planning a "suffrage jubilee" in Santa Fe to celebrate its passage and rally the forces for the ratification fight. Scheduled for Flag Day, June 14, it would coincide with the visit of Mary Winsor, a national suffrage speaker. The participants would "discuss the tremendous advancement that the granting of suffrage to women means." Because both parties had endorsed suffrage, the event was to be nonpartisan.[14]

At a similar meeting in Albuquerque the day before, however, Otero-Warren gave full rein to her Republican partisanship. She claimed that the amendment had passed the U.S. Senate by a Republican vote and challenged the men in her party to "make every effort to see that this amendment is ratified."[15] Because New Mexico's legislature met only in January, she also called on the governor to summon a special legislative session for ratification. He hesitated; like many governors, he was worried about the extra cost of a special session.[16]

As states began to take up the issue of ratification, Carrie Chapman Catt of the National American Woman Suffrage Association took a western tour in support of the amendment. Although concerned about western governors who were reluctant to call special ratification sessions and growing charges of bolshevism aimed at suffrage activists, Catt exuded optimism by traveling with three women from the League of Women Voters who were organizing new branches.[17] Their itinerary brought them to New Mexico in December. Catt and her companions spent their two-day visit in Albuquerque addressing a statewide suffrage conference.[18] The Rotary Club hosted Catt at a luncheon where she spoke on the question "What Is the League of Women Voters and Why?" The league had begun as a new NAWSA committee at its annual meeting that past March. Its objective was to "improve the American electorate and the entire political system of government." She noted that preparation for the war had revealed a number of weaknesses among American voters, especially a "large ignorant vote," which she suggested was due to immigration. As a result, one of the league's committees would focus on citizenship education.

Catt also tailored her address to the Spanish-speaking women of New Mexico. She noted that in the postwar world, their understanding of Spanish would be essential to the nation's influence in the Western Hemisphere, as well as in the fight for women's rights in Latin America. That evening she delivered her keynote address, "Wake Up America," a history of the right to vote, to an audience of 150 women and men at a suffrage dinner at the YMCA. The following day, Ida Baca, wife of a local lawyer, organized and served as toastmaster for a luncheon and musical program at the Women's Club where Catt regaled a packed house with another talk. The women she traveled with also gave a series of speeches addressing morals, children, the nation's food supply, and the need to standardize the law code for women. Catt left the state with a newly established branch of the League of Women Voters and suffragists determined that the special ratification session the governor had called for early February would be successful.[19]

A few weeks later, Otero-Warren and the five Anglo women who made up the "state committee for ratification of the amendment" sent a letter to each member of the state legislature. They were sure the men were going to do the right thing, the letter stated, but they nonetheless urged legislators to take action at

the special session. They cited the taxpaying women of the state who had no political representation on the expenditure of public moneys. They also reminded
the lawmakers that New Mexican women had done their share of war work and
insisted that their contributions continued into the reconstruction period, which
they characterized as "fraught with the gravest dangers," especially "the advancing wave of bolshevism and radicalism in this country." New Mexico women
deserved the opportunity to address these issues with the vote they asserted.[20]

February 15, 1919, was Susan B. Anthony's birthday and the day before the
New Mexican legislature's special session. Otero-Warren and other Republican
women opened their new headquarters in Santa Fe's Griffin Building on Washington Street, just a block from the Palace of the Governors and the plaza.[21]
Reporters noted that unlike male campaign headquarters, which were often
bare rooms littered with cigar stubs and burned matches, the women had furnished theirs with cozy chairs and a rug. But the pictures of party leaders General
Leonard Wood and Theodore Roosevelt on the walls and the piles of campaign
literature on the table signaled the room's purpose. Otero-Warren anticipated
that ratification would happen in time for women to register to vote in 1920,
noting that headquarters would soon be "buzzing" as women set out to organize
the state's twenty-three counties.[22]

However, as the special session opened, it became clear that ratification
was not a sure thing. At the last minute, several legislators suggested that the
amendment should be put to the voters as a referendum. "Suffrage Totters on
Edge of Defeat by Pledge-Breakers," blared headlines. Otero-Warren and the
suffragists in Santa Fe redoubled their efforts. They urged women to attend
the legislative session. The sudden resistance was rumored to be the fault of
the Democratic Party. Someone paid for an ad in the *Santa Fe New Mexican* reminding the Republican legislators of their pledges and their party. Frustration
seethed through the text, which asked if the New Mexican Republicans were
going to line up with southern states, including Mississippi and Alabama, in refusing to enfranchise women. If so, the ad warned, the state's Republicans would
become "a howling joke" nationally. The opposition of southerners to woman
suffrage was based on their desire to deny black women the vote, it asserted. Although the author vaguely acknowledged the backwardness of this opposition,
it urged New Mexican men to protect the state's women (presumably Anglo and
Hispanic) from being treated like African American women. "Is the opposition
[in New Mexico] afraid to give the ballot to the hundred or two negro women
resident in New Mexico? Or does it class all the womanhood of New Mexico on
a par with the negro women of the south?" The ad played on Hispanic fears of
white southern migrants, especially from Texas, bringing Jim Crow policies into
New Mexico and deploying them against Nuevomexicanos. In fact, the advertisement was headlined "Is New Mexico Going to Line Up with Texas?," even though
Texas had already ratified the amendment in June; but the Lone Star State stood

for southern white supremacy in New Mexico. The author concluded by chastising wavering Republicans, warning them that in violating their pledges they were "making a political bonehead play and courting political ruin" as well as "slapping in the face the splendid women of New Mexico."[23]

Otero-Warren and Republican male allies like Governor Larrazolo and state party chairman George Craig hurriedly wrangled their straying members. Her brother Eduardo Otero and Holm Bursum, the Republican national committeeman, were called to Santa Fe to help discipline the pledge breakers. One paper described the rebellion as coming from the "rank and file," as Republican leaders were "almost to a man" for ratification. As head of the recently formed Women's Division of the Republican Party, Otero-Warren caucused with the legislators of her party in their closed-door session and fiercely urged them to support ratification. Indeed, much of this fight took place off the floor, but in the corridors and offices of the politicians suffragists doggedly fought to the very end, cajoling and urging the men to vote for ratification.[24]

Their battle was hard-fought, but in the end they were successful, and New Mexico became the thirty-second state to ratify. Otero-Warren, grateful for the support of party leaders and politically savvy, wrote an open letter thanking the governor and celebrating the pledges of support from both parties. Already looking ahead, she was confident that full ratification was just weeks away and that women would be able to vote that fall. "We believe that the women will use their ballots and will take great interest in the important issues which are before this country," she wrote. She closed by inviting the women of the state to visit the Republican women's headquarters to begin campaign work.[25]

Back in Washington, D.C., news of the ratifications rolled into NWP headquarters, a four-story brick building with striped awnings shading the windows and neatly planted window boxes at 14 Jackson Place. An American flag always waved over the entrance, which was flanked by white columns under a sign that boldly proclaimed the National Woman's Party's presence in the city. A circular brick driveway wrapped around a garden island in which stood two announcement boards with figures of nymphs draped over their corners. These held the "women's suffrage bulletin." Alice Paul and her helpers constantly updated them with photos and news of recent events.[26] But for ratification, Paul wanted something even more dramatic.

The states of the upper Midwest were the first to ratify. With legislatures in session, Wisconsin, Illinois, and Michigan all concurred on the same day in early June 1919. They were followed by Kansas, New York, Ohio, Pennsylvania, Massachusetts, and Texas by the end of the month. Alice Paul procured a long banner in suffrage colors. As each state ratified the amendment, she sewed a victory star onto the banner, counting down to full ratification. She sewed ten more stars on by the end of the autumn.[27] By the turn of the New Year, Paul had sewn on eight

THE WAR COMES, 1917–1920

more.[28] Nevada, New Jersey, Idaho, Arizona, New Mexico, and Oklahoma joined in February, and West Virginia and Washington ratified it in March, but then the momentum stalled, one state short of the thirty-six necessary for ratification.

Nothing moved forward as spring 1920 turned to summer. Instead, there was a series of disappointing setbacks. In February, Maryland and Virginia rejected the amendment. In March, Mississippi followed suit. In June, Delaware said no, and in July, Louisiana and Georgia followed. Southern Democrats fiercely resisted legislation that might add black voters to the electorate; but the legislation also disrupted their ideas of how women should behave. As August loomed, Tennessee's governor called a special session to deliberate.

PART IV

Our Women Take Part
1920–1928

CHAPTER 16

Everyone Who Had Labored in the Cause

It was the height of a humid southern summer when the suffragists arrived in Nashville, Tennessee, for what seemed destined to be the final battle for ratification of the Nineteenth Amendment. Victory was achingly close but remained uncertain: as of March 1920, thirty-five state legislatures had voted to ratify the woman suffrage amendment, just one short of the "perfect thirty-six" needed for it to take effect.[1] But throughout the first half of the year disappointment had followed on disappointment as state legislatures across the South rejected the amendment and others refused to vote on it. Finally, in July the governor of Tennessee convened a special session.

The Volunteer State's capital city was instantly transformed into a hotbed of political intrigue as pro- and anti-forces rushed in and began lobbying legislators with fierce energy. Carrie Chapman Catt, the veteran president of the National American Woman Suffrage Association, arrived after a statewide tour of stump speeches urging ratification. Catt's presence inspired local suffrage leaders, but she left the face-to-face lobbying to her lieutenants, directing the campaign from her suite at the Hermitage Hotel.

Catt found the weather "hot, muggy, nasty," but not nearly as nasty as the politics. Anti-suffragists were pulling out all the stops in their effort to keep the ballot out of women's hands. Catt was called vulgar names, received threatening letters, and had her telegrams stolen. She accused antis of attempting to defeat the amendment through deception and fraud. Some were trying to buy votes, she believed, noting that despite Prohibition, bourbon and moonshine flowed freely to legislators from a room on the eighth floor of the hotel.[2]

Although the Tennessee state senate had overwhelmingly approved the ratification, Catt called the fight for the house "desperate." It had come down to this, she recalled: after a nationwide campaign that had lasted decades, the "political fate of the nation's women now rested in the hands of a minority of a single legislative chamber."[3] The suffragists redoubled their efforts. Despite the heat, they lobbied unceasingly, visiting every legislator; in order to bend their ears, they followed home "by train, by motor, by wagons, and on foot" those who ducked out at the statehouse. Each day Catt scrutinized her list of house members, marking down and updating who had pledged to vote for ratification, who needed to be convinced, and who might be slipping away due to the persuasions coming from the eighth floor. The list changed daily. Privately, she admitted to feeling low but kept up a courageous public face.[4]

The morning of the vote, Catt resolved not to go to the statehouse. Instead she sat nervously in her room listening to the noise of the crowd through her open window. She later heard the dramatic recounting of events. The legislative hall fairly glowed with the golden yellow of suffrage. Women wearing the color packed the chamber's balcony gallery to sit in vigil over the proceedings. They carried golden banners and wore sashes across their chests demanding "votes for women." On the house floor, young girls "bedecked with sunflowers" had placed bouquets of golden glow, with its long yellow petals, on every representative's desk.[5] Having brought the light into the chamber, the women could do no more than watch and hope as the ninety-six men on the floor decided their fate.

As the session began, the tension in the hall was so great that legislators abandoned their usual banter for silence. They soberly called out their vote in conventional tones without additional discourse. With each aye vote, the suffragists in the gallery burst into loud cheers; some stifled sobs at the nos.[6] But the voting ended with a tie of forty-eight for and forty-eight against. Someone called for another vote. This time things began to move: slowly, like the almost imperceptible shift in a patch of snow before an avalanche, the vote turned. When the last legislator, young Harry Burn, a first-termer from the southeastern part of the state, stood to cast his vote, it seemed the ballot would be tied again. He was on Catt's list as undecided, as his constituents opposed woman suffrage. Instead, his voice rang out in the affirmative, placing the count at forty-nine for and forty-seven against. To bring it to the constitutionally required fifty, another legislator stood and changed his vote so that the final tally stood fifty to forty-six. Cheers of wild enthusiasm "rang through the legislative chamber and were heard far down the street."[7] Women clapped so hard they split their gloves.

Representative Burn later revealed the letter his mother had written to him to encourage his vote. "Don't forget to be a good boy and help Mrs. Catt with her 'Rats,'" she had written. "Is she the one that put rat in ratification, Ha! No more from mama this time. With lots of love, Mama."[8]

Across the state, mayors ordered "the ringing of bells and the blowing of whistles." Around the nation women gathered to celebrate with meetings, processions, and flag raisings. In Washington, D.C., the more radical Alice Paul sewed the last white star on her purple and gold ratification banner and flung it over the second-story balcony of the National Woman's Party headquarters, where it was met with cheers and waved in glory. Over the next few weeks, organizations transformed themselves from suffrage associations into the League of Women Voters.[9]

Catt and her officers traveled triumphantly back to their headquarters in New York City. Representatives of the Democratic and Republican National Committees along with the old-guard suffrage supporters met them at the train station. They pushed a huge bouquet of flowers into Catt's arms, and she climbed into an open-topped automobile. Following her, they marched through the city streets as a group for the last time, played on by the 71st Regiment Band made up of veterans from the Civil and Spanish-American Wars. Many marchers held high the "old familiar banners" from their years of battle. At the Waldorf Astoria Hotel they made rousing speeches, congratulating and praising one another. Both the Democratic and Republican Parties, hoping to win the new voters to their side, claimed that their organizations had carried the amendment to victory. Everyone praised the Tennessee suffrage activists and the "faithful 49," the legislators who had cast their votes in favor.

They celebrated their achievement of full citizenship, announcing, "Now that we have the vote let us remember we are no longer petitioners. We are not wards of the nation but free and equal citizens. Let us do our part to keep it a true and triumphant democracy."[10] Catt concluded, "The victory was everybody's victory who had labored in the cause."[11]

But not everyone was able to enjoy the fruits of victory.

The new amendment changed the political playing field of the nation. In the fall of 1920, many women of color saw the real potential of the women's vote to address the struggles in which they were already engaged. Their responses to the post-amendment world varied because they held distinct political priorities based on their communities' histories. The women considered here seized the moment to further their causes. They also faced different challenges and, for some, unique opportunities, depending on where they lived, who they were, and the particular ways white Americans had racialized them. The suffrage histories of women of color bridge 1920, so to see that year as an end point leads us to tell a story that inevitably ignores them and truncates our understanding.

In Wisconsin, Laura Cornelius Kellogg, a citizen of the Oneida nation, sprang into action for the election of 1920. Her activities are an excellent example of the intersection between suffrage politics and identity. Kellogg understood that the post-amendment status of full suffrage for Wisconsin women offered her a new opportunity to gain support from white women for tribal sovereignty. As she had written earlier that year, "So far as the Indian is concerned, it matters very little whether the name is Democrat or Republican, politics is everlastingly one and the same thing. I see no hope in the party politics of the United States until the women of the land get the suffrage and form a no-party organization."[12]

Little more than two weeks after ratification, she was working under the auspices of the Wisconsin Constitutional Defense League, organizing its auxiliary, the Wisconsin Women's Defense League, headquartered in Wausau, a short distance from her home in Seymour.[13] As head of the league's speakers bureau, Kellogg was responsible for recruiting a series of female lecturers to canvass the state. She herself traveled to at least twelve cities in the northeastern part of Wisconsin, lecturing and organizing local leagues. Her objective was to "line up the women, the great body of newly enfranchised voters, in defense of the American Constitution." Touted as an "Oneida Indian Woman," she gave speeches like

"The Americanization of the Woman's Vote."[14] By all accounts, she was a dynamic speaker; one scholar calls her one of the best Haudenosaunee orators of her generation, in both English and Oneida.[15] She directed her audience's attention to the "national problems that confront women."[16]

Her speeches were part of a wider effort to educate female voters about their new responsibilities. Newspapers announced that members of women's organizations who were studying political science would receive credit for attending.[17] Wisconsin had been one of the first states to ratify the amendment, but woman suffrage in the Badger State had followed a tortuous path. Women had demanded suffrage in school elections in the decade after the Civil War and had successfully lobbied for legislation that passed in 1884. In 1887, however, courts nullified the law, and the battle began again. School elections were reinstated in 1901 only to have the legislature take that voting privilege away again in 1913.[18]

It was more complicated for Kellogg as a Native woman. In 1920 almost a third of Native people, female and male, were categorized as wards of the nation, not U.S. citizens, and therefore could not vote. The status of many others remained uncertain. Even within Wisconsin the Indigenous people of many different nations had different statuses.[19] The Oneida who had moved to the state early in the nineteenth century were viewed as further along the path to civilization than some of the other nations, like the Ho-Chunk, and most Oneida had been granted U.S. citizenship and potentially the right to vote.[20] Under "special inquiries related to Indians," for example, the federal census of 1900 listed Kellogg as a citizen.[21] As a woman, Kellogg's right to vote in Wisconsin would have been limited to school-related elections; however, her educational concerns focused on the federal Indian school at Oneida, which did not fall under the state public school system, so it is unlikely that she participated in local educational elections.[22]

Other Native women had very different opinions on suffrage, often depending on their relationship to U.S. citizenship. As Esther Deer, a Mohawk actress who went by the stage name Princess White Deer, pointed out in an interview that got national attention, Native people worried that voting in U.S. elections could cost them their land and communities. Deer explained that citizenship came with owing property taxes, which often resulted in massive land loss for Native people. She was not alone in this—many believed that if they exchanged their status as wards for citizenship, it would mean relinquishing their claims to being sovereign nations, especially their land claims.[23] This had, in fact, happened to the Oneida who remained in New York State. In *United States v. Elm* (1877), a judge ruled that when Abraham Elm attempted to vote, he had "abandoned his tribal relations" and therefore forfeited his claims to tribal affiliation. The judge's ruling "applied a principle that U.S. citizenship was inimical to the existence of a viable tribal relationship."[24]

Some Native feminists prioritized participation in tribal governance over U.S.

institutions. After ratification, newspapers carried intermittent flurries of coverage about Native women from different nations demanding enfranchisement in their tribal elections. The *Daily Ardmoreite* of Oklahoma reported that women of the Osage nation demanded the right to participate in the annual tribal election, though they were denied. According to the paper, "The women then caucused and announced they would urge the tribal council to amend the tribal laws so that women may vote." It is quite possible that these newspapers were continuing the non-Native tradition of using images of Indian suffragettes to mock women's political participation. But the stories may have held an element of truth.[25]

In Maine, for example, Mrs. Peter Nicolar, wife of the former leader of the Penobscot nation, wrote to the governor, stating, "Now that the women of Maine have full suffrage, we, the . . . members of the Penobscot tribe, believe that we should have the right to vote in all tribal meetings." At the time, the Penobscot nation was not a federally recognized tribe and instead members were wards of the state government. Local attorneys had advised that "we always had the right to vote [in tribal elections] and that the agent cannot refuse to accept our votes at election time." Mrs. Nicolar asked him to confirm this with the state attorney general, who concurred.[26]

The story was picked up by newspapers throughout the nation, including in places with large Native populations like Ardmore, Oklahoma, and Albuquerque, New Mexico. Published under the headline "Woman Suffrage Fight Isn't Won Yet: Maine Indians Won't Let Squaws Vote," the *Boston Globe* reported that for the Penobscot nation "neither the men nor women enjoy State or National suffrage" and that "the question of woman suffrage within the tribe was left to their own decision." Blaming the men of the Penobscot nation was rich indeed when the tribe's members were considered legal wards of the state. The paper's condescending reportage suggested that the tribe was fairly evenly split on the issue and that it may have been bound up in a larger question of legislation that would change the relationship between the tribe and the state of Maine.[27] In the years to come Native women remained engaged with the question of voting rights, which for Indigenous people were complicated by issues of gender, sovereignty, and citizenship. They would devise multiple strategies for addressing those issues and achieving their goals.

Black women also moved quickly to exercise their right to vote under the Nineteenth Amendment. Ida B. Wells-Barnett returned to Memphis in the fall of 1920 for the first time since being run out of that city in 1892. She gave two speeches to newly enfranchised black women. Mary Church Terrell's father, Robert, a founding member of the Memphis NAACP and the Lincoln League, an organization that encouraged black voter participation, invited her to return a few months later as one of the female delegates for the league's conference.[28]

Thousands of southern black women shared their optimism and moved quickly to register for the 1920 election. One of them was Anna Clemons, a nurse from Southport, North Carolina. That October Clemons had gone to the county registrar's office and presented herself. The registrar had administered a literacy test to the well-educated Clemons, claimed she had failed it, and refused to add her to the voter rolls. This scene had repeated itself countless times across the South as local officials disenfranchised black people while following the letter though not the spirit of first the Fifteenth Amendment and now the Nineteenth. White county registrars and sheriffs held enormous power, administering literacy and understanding tests, collecting poll taxes, and recording the local voter registrations. Many were the front line of campaigns by white supremacists bent on keeping African Americans like Anna Clemons from voting.[29]

Having been turned away from registering, Clemons wrote to the NWP for assistance before the election. She asked the organization to help her figure out how to vote by mail since "a colored person in my county is unable to vote, because they are colored," she wrote.[30] Seemingly unaware of the Jim Crow conditions in North Carolina, the NWP secretary blithely wrote back that women had to register in person in North Carolina, and so Clemons should try to do that and get back to them.[31] Clemons responded immediately, explaining that she had indeed tried to register, but the county registrar had refused to accommodate her. As she patiently explained, the county board "requires all colored to be able to read and write to 'suit' the registrar and all persons of colored origin in this whole county have been unable to suit the registrar." Since this was obviously fraudulent, she asked the NWP to investigate.

Clemons assured the NWP that she was not an "agitator" but a respected property-owning professional who had nursed people in most of the homes in her town and worked with "one of the South's best surgeons." She had even been given a certificate from the state for her heroic work during the 1918 Spanish flu epidemic. She belonged to the Methodist Church and "attend[ed] to [her] own business" as a law-abiding citizen. Nonetheless, she was still terrified of what might happen if word got out that she was looking for outside help in this matter. She hastened to add, "Please do not let my name be brought into this matter there is so much prejudice existing [that] I am most assured I will be a victim of lawless mob."[32] Although the NWP secretary assured her the organization would not mention her name, Clemons must have been disappointed in her overall reply. There was nothing the NWP could do for her for this election, the secretary wrote, but the organization would encourage Congress to pass an Enabling Act that would make interference in election laws a federal offense. But Clemons, like so many other southern black women, was kept from voting in 1920.[33]

While black women in the South found their access to the vote limited by Jim Crow laws and racist county registrars, in the North black women determinedly turned out for the elections of 1920. The African American populations of northern cities had grown dramatically during the war years as a result of the Great Migration. These changes sparked a series of violent responses from northern whites. Indeed, large-scale urban riots against African Americans seemed to come at regular intervals. The summer of 1919, for example, became known as "Red Summer" for the deadly violence whites launched against African American neighborhoods in Chicago and Washington, D.C.

But the same shifts also empowered northern black communities. In urban wards with large black populations, politicians recognized their indebtedness to black voters and the need to act on their behalf to address the violence aimed at their constituents.

This was the case for Congressman Leonidas Dyer of the Twelfth District in St Louis, Missouri. He sponsored the Dyer Anti-Lynching Bill in the wake of the East St. Louis riots. Representing a majority black district, he listened to his constituents who demanded that the federal government address the issue. His bill was "an act to assure to persons within the jurisdiction of every State the equal protection of the laws, and to punish the crime of lynching." It defined lynching as a mob of three or more persons acting in concert to deprive a person of life without authority of law and held states accountable for denying equal protection of laws to people in their jurisdiction. State officials who failed to protect citizens in their care were personally liable, as were counties themselves. Moreover, instead of requiring proof of guilt beyond a reasonable doubt, the bill specified that a conviction required only a preponderance of the evidence. The act could even be construed as addressing violence against Chinese, Mexicans, and potentially Native people as well, as it also included "the rights of a citizen or subject of a foreign country secured to such citizen or subject by treaty between the United States and such foreign country."[34]

The 1920 election gave Congressman Dyer help. Thanks in part to the votes of newly enfranchised black women in the North, the Republican Party made significant gains in the Sixty-Seventh Congress. It won majorities in both the House (229 members) and the Senate (59 members).[35] In the coming years, the question would be whether its representatives would recognize that African American votes mattered.

In New Mexico, Anglo women and Hispanas won full suffrage with the passage of the Nineteenth Amendment. The day that U.S. secretary of state Bainbridge Colby signed the proclamation announcing that the Susan B. Anthony Amendment had been added to the Constitution, New Mexican women celebrated with their sisters around the country. Whistles and bells sounded while women affixed flag pins to their dresses and hung larger flags in front of their houses.[36]

They also immediately turned to preparing women for the upcoming election in November, a mere two months away. In Albuquerque, Mrs. A. B. Stroup, Bernalillo County chair of the Republican Women's Committee, was happy with ratification but felt "a sense of responsibility rather than a feeling of exultation." The women realized, she stated, "how complex the situation becomes with the ratification coming just when it does, so near election time." Luckily, she knew that the state Republican Women's Committee, led by Nina Otero-Warren, already had "plans for the work among the counties and precincts which will enable us to organize rapidly."[37]

The issue that remained was whether women in New Mexico would be able to hold office. Even before the amendment was officially ratified, people were questioning whether this was legal in the state. After all, the state constitution explicitly stated that only male citizens could hold office. Consensus quickly emerged that the state constitution should be amended (only amendments changing franchise rights required the steep electoral majorities to pass). Both Democrats and Republicans in New Mexico endorsed the idea of the amendment, likely because each was courting new female voters. The Democrats got a jump on things by opening their primaries to female delegates, and the Republicans soon followed suit. They also both incorporated women into the state party central committees and as delegates to their conventions.[38]

Otero-Warren, already a major player in state politics, was determined that women would make a strong showing at the upcoming Republican convention in September 1920. She called on every county chair of Republican women's organizations to attend if possible. It was the first convention where the women attending would be "actual voters" and that would involve "the enthusiastic and actual participation of ALL Republican voters on a basis of absolute equality."[39]

The first order of business was to disband the state Republican Women's Committee and merge female members into the state party central committee. This followed the precedent of the national Republican committee. Some two hundred women from across the state were at the convention, including Otero-Warren's sister-in-law Josefita (Mrs. Eduardo) Otero. Republicans moved quickly, putting women in three of eleven positions on the state executive committee. Fifty-seven women, including eighteen Hispanic women and eight former suffragists, landed on state committees.[40]

Otero-Warren addressed the women at a luncheon: "A tremendous task confronts the women of New Mexico," she cautioned. Believing that women could reach women more easily than men could, she asserted that they would "naturally shoulder the organization of the women and their registration." She particularly addressed the question of "Spanish-American" women and the ballot, assuring her audience that she found them "exceedingly interested and receptive in anything which touched the home and their children." She added that many women had been in attendance at the primaries in Santa Fe earlier that year. What was needed was "sympathetic and able [Spanish] speakers to explain the platforms to them," as they would be more interested in the positions than in the candidates. Otero-Warren was optimistic about Hispanas' participation. She was sure that they would exercise their new right to vote and would do so primarily as Republicans. According to a report, she added that this would be to the party's benefit as "there are unusually large families with a majority of women members among the native Spanish-Americans."[41]

At the convention Otero-Warren was elected state vice chair of the Republican Party. Indeed, a number of Hispanic women held positions in the party, often as delegates to state and national conventions.[42] She was confident that Republicans would reap the benefits of enfranchising women, arguing that the majority of states that ratified the amendment had been held by Republican majorities. She also maintained that in New Mexico, Hispanic women, who outnumbered the men, would augment the Republican Party, which already counted 75 percent of Hispanic men as partisans.[43]

Otero-Warren also joined her fellow attendees in designing the GOP platform. They insisted that it should include an endorsement of the proposed amendment to the state constitution allowing women to hold office. They also recommended a series of laws that she had presented as especially appealing to Hispanas, including those regulating women's work hours and working conditions, giving women equal rights in child guardianship cases, creating adequate child labor laws, and raising teacher salaries.[44]

The Republicans had a good year in 1920, and when Republican governor Merritt Mechem took office he got right to work. In his address to the joint session of the legislature he urged the lawmakers to fulfill their campaign promises by passing the policies promised in their platform, what the *Santa Fe New Mexican* called "the most drastically progressive program . . . since statehood." This included the amendment permitting women to hold state office.[45]

The legislature quickly passed the proposed amendment to the state constitution "permitting women to hold public office but releasing them from payment of poll taxes or from jury duty." It would then go to the voters in a special election that fall. Most observers were optimistic. "We'll have the ladies here on the floor with us next season," one legislator was said to have remarked. Some people wished the amendment had gone further in securing women equal rights with men in all areas but were willing to be expedient. In hindsight it is worth noting that New Mexican women did not gain the right to serve on juries until 1954.[46]

The special election was scheduled for the following September 20, 1921. The voters of New Mexico were considering ten amendments to the state constitution as well as senatorial candidates to replace Albert Fall, who had resigned to become secretary of the Interior for President Harding. Newspapers across the state endorsed the women's office-holding amendment, and both parties included supportive language in their platforms. The Democrats pledged to support legislation calculated to wipe out arbitrary discrimination against women, while the Republicans more pointedly recommended its ratification explicitly.[47] While women do not seem to have specifically campaigned for the amendment outside their party influences, a number of Republican women, including Otero-Warren, took out a full-page ad in support of senatorial candidate Holm Bursum in response to an attack ad that had been aimed at female voters. They also directed their appeal at the "Women Voters of New Mexico," especially mothers, and enumerated the policies Bursum had supported that contributed to the "material and moral welfare" of the state.[48]

Holm Bursum won the election, and the voters of New Mexico agreed to amend their constitution to allow women to hold public office. A few other amendments also passed, including one preventing "aliens who are ineligible to citizenship from owning land or leases." This meant "Asiatic land ownership," and the amendment was intended, the *Albuquerque Morning Journal* wrote in its endorsement, to "anticipate and prevent an oriental invasion."[49]

In the wake of the election, a writer for the *Alamogordo News* imagined the press releases from the capital in the not-so-distant future. A woman governor would "pour the hot shot at times into her political enemies," while her husband sat beaming in the gallery. The legislature, with its many women members, would pass a series of laws that fined men for not marrying and women for making "goo goo eyes" at other women's husbands. The female state game warden, with "blood in her eyes," would track down poachers shooting deer out of season. Finally, the writer imagined a Mrs. Octaviana Guerra, warden of the penitentiary, who had introduced "radical innovations" of allowing convicts out on parole to visit their families for three days every month. Although the reporter's tone was tongue-in-cheek, his vision of the future imagined both Anglo and Hispanic women in a range of state offices.[50]

The experiences of women of color in the aftermath of the ratification of the Nineteenth Amendment varied widely. It was both a moment of possibility and a recognition of the many battles still to be fought and the many inequalities that remained. But women's votes helped change the calculus.

[CHAPTER 17]
The Value of the Ballot

White feminists were not done reenvisioning society, either. Six months after Alice Paul's star-spangled banner had triumphantly waved from the National Woman's Party balcony, the organization held an open meeting to celebrate the winning of the vote and to decide what it should do next. Alice Paul convened the conference—ostensibly to generate ideas, although she had already made up her mind. Still, she invited the leading women of the nation as well as the leaders of the national political parties to make their pitch to her organization. The political machine she had built stretched into every state. The women of the NWP knew how to organize, how to make compelling political arguments, and how to lobby, and now they had the vote. What should they fight for next?

Once again, the NWP organizers mobilized symbolism. The business of the conference looked largely to the party's future, but the organizers also honored the struggles of the past. The conference began on February 15, 1921, on what would have been Susan B. Anthony's 101st birthday. On the first day, participants gathered at the Capitol Rotunda to unveil a memorial to "suffrage pioneers" in the form of a statue featuring the busts of Susan B. Anthony, Elizabeth Cady Stanton, and Lucretia Mott. It had been carved out of Italian marble by feminist sculptor Adelaide Johnson. Articles noted that the Congress that would accept the statue was the first to be "elected by the women of the country as a whole."[1]

The presentation was accompanied by a procession and pageant featuring 250 women representing the forty-eight states, multiple women's organizations, and foreign countries who laid wreaths at the statue's base. They wore Grecian robes of different colors and carried banners announcing their affiliations, including the Army Nurses Corps, National Council of Jewish Women, Catholic Women's Service Club, Washington College of Law, National Council of Women Voters, and National Federation of Federal Employees.[2] African American women insisted on taking part as well. Hallie Quinn Brown, president of the National Association of Colored Women, and her "flower girl," Miss Josephine Hamilton, a teacher in the District's public schools, joined Mrs. Monen L. Gray, who held aloft their royal purple banner announcing in white lettering that the association was present. Also participating were representatives of foreign countries, with "young women of the Embassy staffs in national costume" as well as "prominent women" from the diplomatic corps.[3]

The ceremony embodied the potential and the limitations of that moment. The procession indicated a capacious vision of a broad women's movement that

African American women, like other women of color, were proud of their participation in historic moments and chronicled it in their publications. Here President Hallie Quinn Brown and her attendants represent NACW at the dedication of the "Suffrage Pioneers" statue in the capitol rotunda in 1921. (Competitor [Pittsburgh, Pa.], April 1921, 30)

included women of multiple races, religions, and classes. Leaders of the NWP, however, continued to see the suffrage struggle as fundamentally a movement of white women. In memorializing the history of the suffrage struggle, they literally carved that version in stone.

Black women had vehemently insisted on attending the conference and hoped to convince white feminists to continue to fight for all women's right to vote, especially southern black women. In reality the leadership of the NWP was not very interested in helping them. As the organization prepared for its conference, the NAACP was determined to put the protection of the franchise for all women on its agenda. Throughout December, Mary White Ovington of the NAACP sought help from members of the NWP advisory board in New York to get Mary B. Talbert, former president of the National Association of Colored Women, on the program. The members agreed and several, including Florence Kelley and Harriet Stanton Blatch, contacted Alice Paul to encourage it. Paul objected that the anti-lynching legislation on which black women were focused was not a feminist issue, and only women's measures were going to be included on the program. She also assured them that the NWP would push for an enforcement act that would address black women's disenfranchisement, but to have a black woman on the program would "enflame the Southerners" and hurt the bill's chances. Talbert was skeptical. "I do not believe that Alice Paul is at all sincere. I doubt her very much on the color line," she wrote. Ovington disappointedly concluded that "Miss Paul unquestionably is more influenced by her southern white constituency than those northerners who believe in working for the colored woman."[4]

But the NAACP had not given up. The association's field organizer, Addie Hunton, had returned from her war work in France ready to take up another battle, that against race prejudice. She traveled to Washington, D.C., and began to coordinate with Carrie Williams Clifford and other members of the Washington African American community to get their message to Alice Paul.[5]

Hunton arrived early and "labored very earnestly" to get the NWP to appoint a committee for its conference that would urge Congress to investigate the violations of the Nineteenth Amendment in the 1920 elections. But, despite her efforts, "we have met with denial," she reported. She turned to another strategy: if Paul would not listen to her, perhaps a large group of black women could persuade the NWP's leader. Hunton called on local black women and sent a flood of letters and telegrams to women from Virginia, New York, Pennsylvania, Ohio, Indiana, and New Jersey to come "swell this delegation." For $1.50 per night they could stay at the newly opened Phyllis Wheatley YWCA, where the Washington NAACP was headquartered. It was, she believed, "a wonderful opportunity to push the Woman's Party to protect the Amendment which they fought so hard to have passed. We must make them recognize that it included the five million colored women in this country."[6]

Hunton received immediate responses. Alice Dunbar-Nelson wired from Wilmington, Deleware, that six women representing the League of Colored Republican Women would attend. Ora B. Stokes, president of the Negro Women Voters League of Virginia, also wrote of her intent to join the delegation. In Washington, Hunton and local NAACP members planned the meeting. She requested 2,000 pamphlets from the national NAACP office, assuring leaders there that "I think we are very well ready now to meet Miss Paul." If Paul refused to listen, the prevailing opinion of their group was for picketing the conference. The national office endorsed this plan, writing, "The prospect of the Woman's Party being picketed will get you all the reporters that you want." Hunton wrote to the members of the Washington NAACP urging strong local turnout: "We feel it fitting to call the attention of this Party to the flagrant violations of this Amendment in the elections of 1920, and to ask them to make some effort to have Congressional investigation of these violations." She encouraged members to come see Miss Paul and make the "deputation as strong as possible." We believe, she added, that "you will give an hour for the cause of justice to five million colored women in the United States." Carrie Clifford, who was at that time serving as the Washington NAACP's chair of propaganda, received the letter from Hunton and likely attended the meeting. She certainly followed the proceedings closely.[7]

Along with women from Washington, D.C., sixty black women from across fourteen states arrived in the capital a few days before the convention. They went to the National Woman's Party headquarters and requested a meeting with Alice Paul "so that they might take up with her the question of the disfranchisement of the women of their race." In an echo of their 1913 parade experience, they were told she was too busy to meet with them. They replied firmly that they would wait. They outlasted her. When she finally agreed to see them, they presented her with their memorial:

> We have come here as members of various organizations and from different sections representing the five million colored women of this country. We are deeply appreciative of the heroic devotion of the National Woman's Party to the women's suffrage movement and of the tremendous sacrifices made under your leadership in securing the passage of the Nineteenth Amendment. . . . The colored women of this country . . . know the value of the ballot, if honestly used, to right the wrongs of any class. Knowing this, they have also come today to call your attention to the flagrant violations of the intent and purposes of the Susan B. Anthony Amendment in the elections of 1920. These violations occurred in the Southern States, where is to be found the great mass of colored women. . . . Complete evidence of violations of the Nineteenth Amendment could be obtained only by Federal investigation. There is, however, sufficient evidence available to justify a demand for such an inquiry. We are handing you herewith a pamphlet with verified cases of the disfranchisement of our women. . . . Five million women in the United States can not be denied their rights without all the women of the United States feeling the effect of that denial. No women are free until all are free.[8]

They asked that the NWP appoint a special committee to request a congressional investigation into the violations of the amendment during the recent election.[9]

Alice Paul was unmoved and, according to Hunton, "thoroughly hostile." Despite their disenfranchisement, she continued to see race as an issue that would keep southern white women from supporting her agenda rather than as something that was already dividing women. It was only after they threatened to cause a scene by picketing the conference—or as one reporter put it, to give the NWP a taste of their own medicine—that Mary Church Terrell, a leader in the National Association of Colored Women, was given a moment to present their statement to the Resolution Committee.[10]

As with the 1913 parade, white organizers welcomed women of color who were not black, including the Society of American Indians' representative, Gertrude Simmons Bonnin, and Wai Ling Sze, the niece of the Chinese minister in Washington.[11] These women were joined by powerful activists from throughout the nation. Representatives of the five major political parties in the country—Democrats, Republicans, the Socialist Party, the Farmer-Labor Party, and the Committee of 48—were in attendance. A number of other organizations also sent representatives to solicit the NWP's endorsement. The list was a who's who of the period's famous activists, including Julia Lathrop, head of the U.S. Children's Bureau; Ada Gertrude Little Merriam (publicly known as Mrs. J. C. Merriam) of the National Consumers League; Lida Hafford of the General Federation of Women's Clubs; Mabel Kittredge of the Women's International League of Peace and Freedom; and Fanny Garrison Villard, daughter of the famous abolitionist William Lloyd Garrison, who represented the National Women's Peace Society. Mrs. Maud Wood Park of the League of Women Voters (formerly the National American Woman Suffrage Association) and Miss Ethel Smith of the Women's Trade Union League also traveled to the conference, despite the league's growing disagreements with Alice Paul.[12]

This distinguished crowed gathered at the Hotel Washington,[13] a grand new edifice built by the renowned New York Beaux Arts architectural firm of Carrere and Hastings. The firm had also designed the New York Public Library, Washington's House and Senate buildings, and most recently the Arlington Memorial Amphitheater at Arlington National Cemetery across the Potomac. The buff-colored limestone and brick Italian Renaissance building embodied the American belief that the United States was heir to the intellectual glory of the European Renaissance. Adding to its symbolic weight, this "palace of the public" was situated at the prominent intersection of Fifteenth and F Streets and Pennsylvania Avenue, NW. It sat one block east of the White House, faced the U.S. Treasury Building, and fronted Pennsylvania Avenue, the ceremonial way to the Capitol. In choosing this hotel for their conference, the leaders of the National Woman's Party projected a statement about their new political power.

Entering under the ornate iron marquee on Fifteenth Street, participants found themselves in an elegant lobby with a formidable marble and brass registration desk. The high curves of the windows were reiterated by the arches of an interior arcade running the length of the lobby.[14] At the center of that space stood a bank of elevators whose cars were segregated into black and white. Did Gertrude Bonnin hesitate before choosing an elevator? Not likely. Washingtonians viewed Indians differently from black citizens. Afterall, their current first lady, Edith Galt Wilson, proudly claimed direct descent from Pocahontas.[15]

Organizers scheduled Gertrude Bonnin during the session on "Legislative Programs, Affecting Women's Interests in the United States." When she took the stage at the Washington Hotel to address the audience, she wore her usual lecture outfit: buckskin dress and headband atop her braids.[16] She chose as her title "America's Indian Problem." She greeted the women as "sister Americans" and celebrated their recent victory: "The Indian woman rejoices with you" in "this dawn of the enfranchisement of her white sister." But, in their "moment of triumph," she hoped that they would "remember the Indian woman and her keeper," the BIA. Ruminating on "the principles of democracy," she reminded them that what "is beneficial to a group of humanity is beneficial to the whole" and that "the American Indian is part of the whole human family." She urged them to support two legislative measures in front of Congress: an anti-peyote bill as well as "a bill to grant American citizenship" to their "little sister" and "her household including the men heroes in our late war." Her speech was met with "great applause" from her audience.[17]

At the conference, the women of the Chinese Revolution remained a powerful symbol for American suffragists. Maud Wood Park of the League of Women Voters even referenced Anna Howard Shaw's "Catching Up with China" banner in her talk. But they still positioned Chinese women as a foreign population rather than part of the American citizenry. Conference organizers invited Wai Ling Sze,[18] niece of the Chinese minister to the United States, to speak during the "Programs of Women in Foreign Countries" session. Sze used her time to tell the audience about "the great awakening of the young women of China." She briefly discussed the suffragists of the 1911 revolution who had urged the inclusion of women's rights in the new republic and whose goals had been stymied by President Yuan Shikai. But she primarily focused on the more recent 1919 student movement, the New Culture Movement in which Mabel Lee's friend Hu Shih was closely involved. Sze described youth strikes in Peking and Shanghai protesting government policies. She herself had taken part, proudly recounting the fundraising work she and her fellow students had done with "sympathy and help from our American teachers." Young women in China were insisting on their right to an education and were "a great tide" that could not be held back. Sze was heartened by the suffrage victory in the United States and hoped that American women would "stretch out their generous hands to help these sisters who are seeking the same thing."[19]

Mary Church Terrell's turn to speak came at the Resolutions Committee meeting. Black women "appreciate the effort of their sisters of the dominant race to secure the suffrage and their success," she began. "Unfortunately, however, colored women in a large section of this country are deprived of their right of citizenship." Millions of black women, she stated, had been disenfranchised in the 1920 presidential election. "No woman in this country needs the ballot more than the colored women of the south. There they are the victims of lynching, the convict Lease System, the Jim Crow Lines and of unjust discriminations in the various pursuits and trades," she pleaded. Like Anna Julia Cooper and others, she insisted that race mattered as well as sex. "They are handicapped not only because they are women but because they are colored women," she explained. "They bear the burden of color as well as of sex. They are doubled cross so to speak."[20]

Terrell urged the members of the NWP to do everything in their power to help black women secure their right of citizenship as conferred by the Nineteenth Amendment "but which was openly and flagrantly violated with impunity during the recent presidential election in some of the southern states." Then she publically presented their resolution, asking for a special committee to pressure Congress to investigate.[21]

The NWP stenographer's report of the conference did not include Terrell's statement but did record the words of the black women's white ally Mrs. William Murray of New York. At the business meeting, Murray gave the minority report of the organization's advisory council from a meeting they had held a month earlier on January 28. She told the audience that she had brought the resolution from black women to that earlier advisory council meeting, where she had asked for the council's endorsement and had been voted down. She also stated that the organization had "forgotten" to include the black women's resolution in the meeting notes, which were then published in the NWP's journal, the *Suffragist*. Those notes were meant to inform the membership of things to be discussed at the February conference, so this omission was frustrating.[22] Murray wanted to be sure that this time, it was on the record.

She went on to insist that the disenfranchisement of black women in the South was not a mere race issue but a broadly feminist one. If the vote is withheld from one group, she argued, it could be taken from other groups: "It is not a question of race, my friends, because what is being done in one portion of the country now, namely, in the Southern states ... sometimes affects both," she said, alluding to race and sex. "In the effort being brought about to keep one race out, they are willing that white women shouldn't vote in order to keep out the colored. Can't you see that they are keeping us out?" Although she couched her plea in terms of benefit for white women, Murray was cognizant of black women's concerns and had been part of the NAACP conversation before the conference. A white delegate from Massachusetts also supported Murray's specific point, describing it as a "vital matter." There were other white allies at the conference as well. Florence Kelley, for example, pointedly described the work of the National Consumers League among black and white communities as well as among women and men.[23]

The next day the conference took up the question when voting on the resolutions. Murray again made a motion that should the NWP be reorganized, the new party would "appoint a special committee to bring pressure to bear upon Congress for the appointment of a special Congressional committee to investigate the violations of the intent and purpose of the 19th amendment, through perversion or evasion of the State election laws." The chairman allowed for brief discussion in which delegates from Louisiana and South Carolina voiced their displeasure.[24]

The NWP ultimately did not accept the resolution to address the disenfranchisement of black women, but Addie Hunton, who had coordinated black women's strategy, still found reason to be happy with the outcome.[25] She had forced the NWP to go on record against the resolution that Alice Paul had hoped to avoid altogether and would have preferred to keep off the floor entirely. She was also thrilled with the large number of black women who "proved that they were alert to the situation" by coming to help. And she had been pleasantly surprised by the number of white women who had supported it, even if it did not pass.[26]

Alice Paul insisted that women needed to focus on a single issue, not split again over what she saw as "diversions." She dismissed black women's concerns as "racial," not "purely feminist," a judgment that very narrowly defined what "feminist" was. She was, however, correct in her assessment that white southern women would balk at the participation of black women. The delegation from North Carolina initially refused to register for the conference in protest against black women's presence, though they were eventually persuaded to attend.[27]

And yet, even the National Woman's Party had to recognize the part that black women had played in the fight to pass the amendment. A month before the conference the NWP had sent a letter to Mary Church Terrell and her daughter Phyllis inviting them to attend and informing them that they would be receiving a picket pin on the last day of the event. The pins were "to show appreciation of the militant workers in our campaign of whom we are all proud." Wearing a white dress with white shoes and stockings, as instructed, the two women returned to the Washington Hotel to receive their honor. One of the white North Carolina delegates refused to accept hers because of Terrell's presence at the ceremony. She would not eat as an equal with a black woman.[28]

Years later, in her memoir, Terrell described attending the conference but did not mention the mistreatment black women had received. Instead, she insisted on writing herself into the history of the suffrage movement even as so many white women had worked hard to erase her and the other black feminists. Proud of her time on the picket line, she concluded, "There is no doubt that this gesture on the part of determined women called attention to the injustice perpetrated upon them by denying them the suffrage and hastened the passage of the nineteenth amendment the year before."[29]

Carrie Clifford was proud of the black women who had taken on the NWP as well. She wrote to the NAACP headquarters in praise of Addie Hunton's efforts. She wanted to let the organization know, she wrote, "what a splendid piece of work Mrs. A. W. Hunton accomplished in Washington." Perhaps remembering her own difficulties with the politics of the 1913 women's march as well as of the local NAACP several years earlier, she mused on Hunton's political savvy. "When one considers the currents, cross-currents, counter-currents and under-currents that obtain in a great Capital like this what was achieved was," she concluded, "nothing short of marvelous."[30]

Black women, disappointed in Alice Paul's NWP, also turned to other women's organizations. NAWSA, having transformed into the League of Women Voters (LWV), also held a conference in 1921, two months after the NWP's event. It took place in Carrie Clifford's hometown of Cleveland, Ohio. In April, Addie Hunton, who had led the charge at the NWP conference,[31] wrote to Maud Wood Park, first president of the LWV, encouraging her to include black women on the conference program. "I am sure that you are cognizant of the present need of colored women to have sympathetic cooperation of the white women of this country," she noted. If white women would listen to black women, they would form "a definite understanding of our situation" and could make an "honest effort to cooperate for the securing of justice and right for all American citizens."[32] Unlike Alice Paul, Maud Wood Park quickly responded by telegram stating that the LWV would be happy to listen and that a representative of the NAACP would be given fifteen minutes at the executive council meeting to make the group's appeal.[33] Hunton was thrilled with the "hearty and kind manner" of Park's reply, which was refreshingly different from Alice Paul's response to the black women's requests.[34] Hunton's secured a local woman, Mrs. Thomas Fleming, to make the presentation, and all agreed that she did an excellent job. White southern delegates, however, were once again aroused and unified by the fact that the executive council had given a black woman a hearing. Frustrated, Hunton recognized their typical tactics. "As usual, they threatened to leave the convention if the question came to the floor or was given newspaper publicity by the leaders of the convention." They were "organized closely and systematically worked the whole convention for sympathy," arguing that southern men opposed suffrage because it "would make keener the agitation on the whole subject of Negro franchise." If the LWV brought the question up again before it was established in the South, it would be to their detriment, they warned. Many of the white delegates found this to be a persuasive argument.

The local black community telegraphed Hunton to come quickly to fight back against southern white women. She arrived in a hurry, losing her suitcase in the process.[35] She rushed to the convention to join the few other black delegates to lobby for the cause of black voters. Florence Kelley helped them by offering useful advice, which Hunton appreciated during the next two "feverish days."

She had frequent conferences with allies like Kelley as well as a two-hour meeting with Maud Wood Park and Mrs. Slade, where she was pleased to find that despite white southern efforts, the leaders still agreed that the black women should be heard.

On the last day of the conference at the final meeting of the board and state officers, Park presented an address on the whole matter. Her arguments swayed the board, which passed a resolution empowering the chair to appoint a commission "to study and help remedy as far as possible the violations of the Nineteenth Amendment and the other wrongs to which colored [people] are subjected." Hunton was anxious that the right people be appointed, as she knew that such a commission would be for naught if the members were not sympathetic. But she was also elated that the LWV was on record as recognizing the violations of the Nineteenth Amendment and compared that action with her treatment by Alice Paul: "The real difference between the Woman's Party and the LWV," she noted, was "the difference in the attitude of the leaders of the two groups. The Woman's party chairman was first evasive, then discourteous and finally hostile, while from the first we met kind courtesy and a willingness to cooperate as we dealt with the chairman and her associates in the LWV. What was done at Washington was done in spite of the Woman's Party while at Cleveland it was accomplished by reasoning together." She felt heartened by the fact that in both instances it was clear that there were a large number of white women who were "open-minded on the whole problem of the colored race" and "that we have a strong force ready to fight for justice."[36]

In 1922, the National Woman's Party was ready to announce its post-amendment strategy. Once again members chose to do so with a large symbolic event, and once again women of color insisted on being there to represent their communities. NWP leaders wanted to make their new political power clear by moving their headquarters to Capitol Hill. New York feminist Alva Belmont had donated the funds, and they had chosen a building that had served as the nation's capitol from 1815 to 1819 and was the site of President Monroe's inauguration in 1817. It was located on the corner of First and A Streets Northeast (where the Supreme Court Building now stands). This placed it just half a block from the home in which Marie Bottineau Baldwin and her father had lived and which she still owned and leased.[37]

In May, the NWP held a large celebration to dedicate its new headquarters and to symbolically plant its presence on Capitol Hill.[38] Hundreds of women arrived from across the country to represent their states. Thousands of others tuned in for a radio broadcast, the first ever for a national women's gathering. A platform for speakers had been constructed in front of the building, and many distinguished people sat upon it: "officials and friends of the organization as well as members of the national community." Both major political parties sent representatives. President Harding was scheduled to give an address but had to drop out at the last minute, sending instead written congratulations.

A procession of women clad in white dresses opened the ceremony by striding up the street to the music of a band. They carried the NWP standards of purple, gold, and white as well as the banners that had been borne during the party's picketing of the Wilson White House just a few years earlier. Many of the women carrying them had been imprisoned for their part in the protests and proudly wore their prison pins—a silver cell door crossed with a chain—given to all who had "'suffered' imprisonment for the ideals of the party." They were followed by women representing individual states, many of them the wives of congressmen and senators, waving their state flags. The spouses of diplomats from Bolivia, the Dominican Republic, Great Britain, Guatemala, Serbia and Slovenia, Czechoslovakia, Honduras, and Germany were also there. Wai Ling Sze and Betty Sze, the niece and daughter of the Chinese minister, marched with them.[39] They, too, carried flags, and many wore their national clothing. The governments of forty nations sent their congratulations. The procession also included women representing particular occupations, including Emma Gillett and Ellen Spencer Mussey of the Washington College of Law. Representatives of the National Association of Colored Women's Clubs also marched; they were led by Carrie Williams Clifford, once again proudly taking part in a historic event.[40]

The women assembled on chairs set up in front of the speakers' platform, adding to the large audience of men and women who spilled over onto the lawn of the Hill. Everyone was able to hear as the speakers' voices were directed through modern "amplifiers" protruding from the building's second-story windows. A Marine Corps band played as the District police skillfully directed the crowd. They had even stopped the streetcars from running past the buildings for the duration the event. The respect shown to the newly enfranchised women was a far cry from the chaos of the 1913 parade just a decade earlier.[41]

Speakers reflected on the historic nature of the occasion. Some remembered the party's humble beginnings in the one-room basement office that Alice Paul had rented when she first arrived in Washington, the disrespect shown to the women in the parade of 1913, and the violence aimed at the White House picketers. The distance women had traveled from those years to this day, when they were celebrating their new "shrine to women," was vast and purchased by their struggle. They were proud of the history they had made. The speakers acknowledged that.

What they did not acknowledge were the limits of their victory: the black women disenfranchised in the South, Native women still considered wards of the government, Chinese immigrants barred from citizenship, and even the residents of Washington, D.C., who could not vote in federal elections.

After an invocation and introductory remarks, Gail Laughlin of California praised the willing sacrifice the women in front of her had made for suffrage.

Now, the NWP was pledged to remove the discriminations against women civilly and politically. "What we are asking for is equality," she announced, "a square deal, and women will be satisfied with nothing else." Sex prejudice was "a heritage of an age when women were the chattels of men" and had no place in the present. But she was confident that "a fire has been kindled that shall burn out discriminations against women." As she sat, Alva Belmont rose to a loud ovation. The sixty-nine-year-old wore a youthful white shift dress overlaid by a crocheted tunic with long fringes falling from the sash cinched at her waist and ending a few inches below her knee. Her hair was still dark beneath her hat, but she did don round framed glasses to read her speech. She praised the women for their struggles that had led to their acceptance into the nation's political life. Next, she laid out their plan for the future. They were forming a new party, the Woman's Political Party, to serve as a party for women. She was dismissive of "the current political parties" that "cater to and accept the woman's ballot, but in no way is her influence or her point of view considered." Instead, this new party would "set higher standards in the body politic." Women would not just work to "patch up evils. It will be our will that evils will [not be] born." She gestured to the building behind her; within its walls "we shall handle questions long neglected by those in power, and from the neglect of which humanity is greatly suffering." This would be a difficult struggle and they had placed the bar high, but she concluded, "With God's grace we shall attain it."

Next the legislative chairwoman of the NWP, Maud Younger, stood and "predicted that the twentieth century would be noted in history for the total emancipation of women." Then she outlined for the audience the NWP's practical strategy, specifically its decision to focus on the fight for equal rights legislation. With its battle plans laid out, the formal dedication of the NWP headquarters took place. A clear bugle song rang out, and a silk banner in the party's colors was run smoothly up the flagpole.

The few men on the platform wore dark suits, their presence a small island surrounded by the sea of bright white worn by the women who flanked them on both sides. Representatives of the two major parties that Alva Belmont had just dismissed finally had their chance to speak. The legislative branch of the government was represented by two Republicans, Representative Simeon Fess of Ohio and Senator Charles Curtis of Kansas. They congratulated the women for their work and wished them success in their new undertaking. "We in Congress will be privileged in our lifetime to further such work for women," Representative Fess proclaimed. Senator Curtis, a longtime friend of the NWP, was relaxed and jovial. The round-faced man with a bushy mustache stood with his hands loosely held behind his back on the stage surrounded by his new female constituents. When he spoke, however, he addressed the men of the nation, reassuring them they had no reason to fear female voters. He was sure to point out that he himself had voted for suffrage, and he knew that women were going to vote in the inter-

Senator Charles Curtis's presence at the dedication ceremony for the National Woman's Party headquarters on May 21, 1922, foregrounds men of color who supported woman suffrage. Curtis, who was an enrolled member of the Kaw nation, was a supporter of the NWP. He introduced the Equal Rights Amendment in the Senate for the first time in 1923. (Courtesy Harris & Ewing Photograph Collection, Library of Congress Prints and Photographs Division, Washington, D.C.)

ests of all people. Laughing, he concluded that the women had already begun to exercise their power over the Senate as they had limited his remarks to a mere two minutes, a rule he wished the Senate itself would adopt.

The congressmen each placed a formal greeting from their house of Congress in a box that was to be placed in the cornerstone. Alice Paul then placed a scroll containing the names of the founders of the party as well as those of the 629 women who picketed during the campaign. The two youngest participants in the ceremony, a small boy and girl, walked forward hand in hand, "in token of the future equal partnership of men and women," to present her with a large bouquet of purple, white, and yellow irises. The cornerstone was then sealed with a silver trowel by Mrs. Charlotte Pierce of Philadelphia, the sole remaining participant in the 1848 Seneca Falls women's rights convention. The dedication ceremony closed with the military band striking up the national anthem.[42]

Black women who sat in the audience, like Carrie Clifford, knew that some members of the NWP were sympathetic about the disenfranchisement of African American women. But the party as a whole had demonstrated that its grand statements about the total emancipation of women did not include black women. This lack of action led black women to acknowledge "the vital importance of our getting together and taking control of our own destinies in place of leaving them in the hands of white friends."[43]

[CHAPTER 18]
A Terrible Blot on Civilization
Carrie Williams Clifford

Black women were disappointed that white-led women's organizations seemed uninterested in the fact that a large group of American women were being kept from their right to vote, but they did not have time to stop fighting. For them, it was a matter of life and death. They were terrified and outraged by rising numbers of lynchings in the American South. This trend preceded 1920, but the newly ratified amendment seemed to offer them a new strategy, at least to black women who could vote. Those living in northern states without laws disenfranchising them could become active in party organizations and work alongside black men to pressure politicians, especially Republicans, to support anti-lynching legislation at the federal level.

Carrie Williams Clifford and other black women following the lead of Ida B. Wells-Barnett had been fighting for years against the lynching and the mob violence that periodically swept over black communities. They knew that it was one of the many ways whites sought to intimidate black people to keep them from voting and to keep them in second-class citizenship. Many black feminists had firsthand experience with the violence of white supremacy. Clifford continued to use her pen, her presence, and her organizational skills to demand that America protect its black citizens. After 1920 she worked to encourage white women to support legislation, influence politicians, and turn out black voters.

Black women like Clifford understood their campaign for the vote within this ongoing struggle against white supremacists. It would give them some power to fight back against the violence of lynching and Jim Crow. White racists knew this, too, which is why they had so vehemently resisted including black women in the suffrage movement or fought woman suffrage altogether. In the South, whites turned to the tried-and-true methods of disenfranchisement they had been deploying against black men for decades: intimidation, poll taxes, literacy tests, and everyday corruption. In response to black women's organizing they also began to devise new strategies of voter repression, like the all-white primary.[1]

The NAACP as a political organization was also growing and learning effective strategies. Amid the massacres and murders of recent decades, black communities channeled their outrage and sorrow into organizing. After Ell Persons's lynching in Memphis in 1917, African Americans in that city founded an NAACP branch that quickly became the largest one in the South. The year before that, the national organization had 9,000 members; in response to the spikes in racial violence against their communities, the membership increased tenfold by 1920.

One of the NAACP's efforts was to reveal to Americans the extent of the violence they faced. W. E. B. Du Bois's dedication to publishing articles and photographs from the lynchings and riots in *The Crisis* was followed by the first NAACP book, *Thirty Years of Lynching in the United States, 1889–1918*, published in 1919. And indeed, lynchings and white supremacy were on the rise. Lynch mobs murdered thirty-six people in 1917, sixty people in 1918, and seventy-six in 1919 with white rioters killing hundreds more. Membership in the Ku Klux Klan also grew massively in these same years. By 1920 the terrorist organization had a membership of 4 million and had spread across the North and West.[2]

The NAACP increased its efforts to educate Americans while reminding politicians of the black voters in the North. For example, during the 1920 campaigns, *The Crisis* sent questionnaires to candidates asking them what they planned to do for African American communities. The Republican Party, which had gradually abandoned black voters after Reconstruction, began to selectively listen. In 1919 the NAACP held an anti-lynching conference at Carnegie Hall attended by 2,500 men and women. Charles Evans Hughes, the 1916 GOP nominee for president, gave the keynote address. The conference produced a report titled "An Address to the Nation on Lynching," which was signed by former president Taft. This endorsement was a reversal from Taft's 1911 refusal to sign the NAACP's anti-lynching petition.[3] Black clubwomen supported this most recent resolution as well. Mary Talbert, president of the National Association of Colored Women, pledged members' support to fight for the NAACP's recommendations: anti-lynching legislation, the organization of state committees to address public opinion, and fundraising work.[4]

These tactics worked, and in the 1920 presidential campaign, as many newly enfranchised women geared up to vote, the Republican Party included an anti-lynching plank in its platform. After the election, the NAACP's executive secretary, James Weldon Johnson, who was also on the GOP's National Advisory Committee, pressed President Harding to keep the party's promise. He did, urging Congress in his first annual message in 1921 "to wipe the stain of barbaric lynching from the banners of a free and orderly, representative democracy." Three Republicans in the House immediately introduced new bills, with St. Louis representative Leonidas Dyer's gaining the most momentum.[5] It remained a slow process, however, due to fierce resistance from white southerners, and much depended on pressure from constituents. In the Judiciary Committee, Republicans now held the upper hand, but two of its members, C. Frank Reavis of Nebraska and Ira Hersey from Maine, refused to support the bill. "We as a party owe the colored people nothing, and for one I refuse to be politically blackmailed," Hersey stated. Black Americans kept up the pressure. Twenty-seven state branches of the NAACP sent letters to eighty-seven representatives demanding action on the Dyer Bill. The national office issued a statement that "a vote against the Dyer Bill is a vote for lynching." *The Crisis* urged its readers, "If your Congressman votes against the Dyer Bill mark him down as your betrayer in the hour of trial and defeat him by every legitimate means when he asks your suffrage next fall." The press in other states such as Ohio, Missouri, and Michigan also reported on black Republicans threatening to vote for Democrats in the midterms if the party did not come through with the Dyer Bill.

In June 1921, the bill finally passed out of committee, and the House took it up for consideration. A number of southerners attempted to leave the chambers, a tactic known as "disappearing quorum" to keep it from being considered, but the Speaker ordered the chamber locked and dispatched the sergeant at arms to locate and return the missing members. On January 26, 1922, with a crowd of several hundred African American supporters in the gallery, the Dyer Bill (H.R. 13) passed with 230 members of Congress in favor and 120 opposed. The vote followed party and regional lines. Only eight Democrats, all but one from urban areas of northern states with large numbers of black voters, voted for it. Only seventeen of the 241 GOP members voted against it.[6]

Upon passage in the House, the bill moved to the Senate, where Dyer was optimistic about its chances. President Harding declared, "If the Senate of the United States passes the Dyer anti-lynching bill, it won't be in the White House three minutes before I'll sign it; and having signed it, I'll enforce it." The elections of 1920 had given the Republicans a generous twenty-two-seat margin, but many senators on key committees were from states without large black populations. Moreover, black voters had less political clout in statewide Senate races than in House districts. But African Americans kept up their efforts. They drafted a petition signed by a prominent politicians and leaders from across the country. They sent newspaper accounts and their own reports about lynching directly to the D.C. offices of senators. At the Republican Party's annual convention, they reminded members of the GOP's platform promises.[7]

In Washington, D.C., the community also mobilized. Carrie Williams Clifford was again in the thick of things. Inspired by the 1917 silent lynching parade in New York City, she helped plan a similar event to be held in Washington. Such a procession would bring attention to the Dyer Bill and encourage senators to support it. A "Committee of One Hundred" took charge of organizing. Its chair and executive committee were all men, as was the marshal of the parade, but, as usual, women did a great deal of the labor. The female members were mostly elite black women who had been on the front lines of race work in the capital. This included Clifford and Mary Church Terrell as well as Coralie Franklin Cook, a member of the board of education; Mrs. S. A. McAdoo, the head of the Phyllis Wheatley YWCA; and Mrs. Madre-Marshall, president of the Bethel Literary Society.[8] Several of them were members of the newly formed Colored Women's

Republican League, and a number, like Clifford, were also affiliated with the NACW's District Union for the Suppression of Lynching.[9]

The members of the Committee of One Hundred spent two months planning the parade, holding their meetings in the newly dedicated Phyllis Wheatley YWCA building. Like the suffragists in 1913, they carefully choreographed their plans. They chose June 14, Flag Day, as the day for the march. They mapped the route, requested permits for the parade, designed hundreds of banners for participants to carry, determined the marching sequence for the different groups who would be taking part, and selected a dress code. They also fundraised. Once again, Carrie Clifford demonstrated her financial acuity, raising $230.32 (about $3,500 in constant dollars) for the cause.[10]

The marchers followed a route that took them around the Capitol grounds, down Pennsylvania Avenue, and past the White House to Seventeenth Street, retracing the path of the suffrage parade in which Clifford and Terrell had marched a decade earlier. The procession was led by a group of motorcycle police and "colored police officers," behind whom marched the women of the Committee of One Hundred along with local clergy. After them were seven divisions of marchers, encompassing fraternal and sororal associations, civil rights organizations such as the Race Congress and the NAACP, groups of children including the Boy Scouts, mutual aid societies, and a large group of "Women in White." The parade concluded with black veterans of the Civil War, the Spanish-American War, and World War I.[11] The organizers emphasized the successes of the race, with men and women "representing every profession in which the negro has achieved success."[12]

The Washington *Evening Star* reported that the absence of music that normally accompanied processions in the capital "lent additional impressiveness to the demonstration." Mary Church Terrell reflected, "As I walked in silence up Pennsylvania Avenue, I thought of the fine boy whom I knew as a girl, who had been brutally lynched when he became a man."[13] To draw the thoughts of spectators along the route to the horrors African Americans faced, the marchers carried "scores of posters and streamers setting forth details of recent lynchings that were declared to have set a new record in May." The powerful signs included one carried by a group of young boys that stated, "We are fifteen years old; one of our age was roasted alive." Another declared, "Congress discusses constitutionality while the smoke of burning bodies darkens the heavens."[14] Women's posters focused on motherhood, which they hoped would move their audience to action. "What Would You Do if Your Sick Mother Were Hanged and Her Bones Burned?" one sign asked. "We Mourn as Mothers Whose Sons Might Be Lynched," read another. A third pointed to the violence against women as an indictment of white America's morality: "We Protest the Burning of Babies and Women . . . American Cannibalism." Similar parades took place that summer, such as the one in

Brooklyn that, although led by veterans and including a representative of all the colored fraternities in the borough, was primarily made up of women who wore white dresses and hats with Red Cross sashes.[15]

The march in Washington was not the only way in which black women advocated for the Dyer Bill. The NACW was also scheduled to meet in Virginia in August, and organizers dedicated a large portion of the meeting to the bill. Ida B. Wells-Barnett, who had not attended in a decade due to internal politics, put her hurt feelings aside to come and offer her support. African Americans, including women voters, planned to hold unsupportive Republicans responsible in the upcoming November elections. A handbill published by the Washington, D.C., anti-lynching committee of the Northeastern Federation of Colored Women's Clubs made this very clear. On the first page was a striking image of a hanged man with the large heading "A Terrible Blot on Civilization." The text emphasized the number of lynchings (which it placed at 3,424) in the previous thirty-three years. For some of the women, those years covered the entirety of their lives. The pamphlet also described the Dyer Bill's course through Congress and included a list of those representatives who voted against it, noting the Republicans with an asterisk. "Two victims always of a Lynching—a human being and a civilization," it asserted. The second page documented the action African Americans were taking through two images. The first was of the silent parade— women are prominent, marching past the Capitol Dome. A small boy, perhaps a Boy Scout, joins them. The heading reads "Exercising the Right to Petition." In the second image, an elegant black woman joins two black men marching to the voting booth and is captioned "Join This Silent Parade." The implication was clear—women and men should vote, targeting Republicans who did not support African Americans in an attempt to increase political pressure on Congress right before the midterm elections of 1922.[16]

It was a valiant and impressive effort, but the Senate failed to pass the legislation.

Looking back from 1927, Alice Dunbar-Nelson was disappointed in black women's use of the ballot. Six years was a very short time to ask for results, she wrote, but as "the question continues to be hurled at the woman, she must needs be nettled into reply." Certainly tens of millions of women, black and white, had received the vote, but for Dunbar-Nelson, the question was less what difference women had made and more had their enfranchisement "made any appreciable difference in the status of the race?" Dunbar-Nelson remembered that black suffragists had insisted that unlike black men, they would not be beholden to the Republican Party, and that their votes would be independent and not "a joke" or the result of "a deadening sense of gratitude." She was frustrated that this seemed not to be the case. She accused black women of slipping "quietly, safely, easily and conservatively into the political party of her male relatives," which was to say, Dunbar-Nelson added, "she became a Republican"—an enthusiastic one,

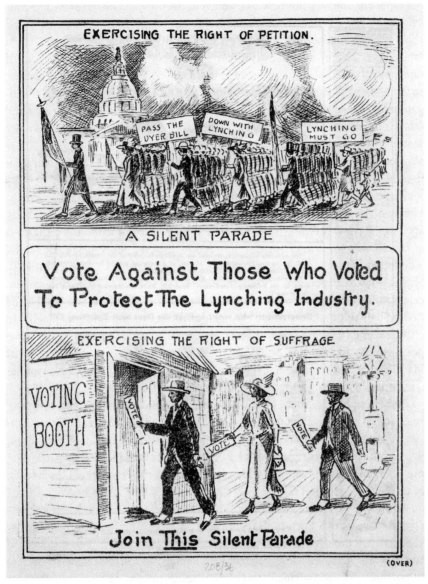

Black women who could vote used their newly won right to advocate for federal anti-lynching legislation. The women of NACW distributed this pamphlet in 1922 in their campaign to get the Senate to approve the Dyer Anti-Lynching Bill. The front of the pamphlet names each member of the House of Representatives who had voted against the bill. The back, seen here, highlights black women's political strategies, including petition, specifically the 1922 Washington, D.C., silent lynching parade, as well as wielding their vote at the ballot box. (From a pamphlet prepared by the Committee on Public Affairs, Inter-Fraternal Council, issued by District of Columbia Anti-Lynching Committee Northeastern Federation of Colored Women's Clubs, 1922, courtesy Library of Congress Prints and Photographs Division, Washington, D.C.)

perhaps, but one who nonetheless "added to the overhead charges of the political machinery, without solving racial problems."

Dunbar-Nelson pointed to one exception, however: the election of 1922, when "the Negro woman cut adrift from party allegiance and took up the cudgel (if one may mix metaphors) for the cause of the Dyer Bill." She pointed especially to the work of the anti-lynching crusaders in New Jersey, Delaware, and Michigan, where Republicans who had voted against the bill had been defeated and "the women's votes unquestionably had the deciding influence." This gave her hope. "When the Negro woman . . . will strike off the political shackles she has allowed to be hung upon her," Dunbar-Nelson concluded, "she could win freedom for her race."[17]

That year Carrie Clifford also published her second book of poetry, The Widening Light, which again chronicled many of the current events Clifford had witnessed, such as the silent lynching parade in New York, World War I, and the dedication of the Lincoln Memorial. She also lionized historical figures, black and white, who fought for equality. And, of course, she included women's history with "To Phyllis Wheatley," perhaps written upon the opening of the YWCA, and a poem celebrating black women such as Addie Hunton who helped with war work titled "Who Shall Tell the Story of Our Women of the Canteen?" But how much had changed since her first book in 1911? Arguably, things had gotten worse. One poem condemned the East St. Louis race riot, another lamented the lynching of Mary Turner, and she responded to The Birth of the Nation in a third.[18] No wonder she turned to working with children; they gave her hope.[19]

Clifford's hope for the future was not misplaced. Though it would be a long road, the efforts by this generation of activists helped pave the way for the victories of the mid-twentieth-century civil rights movement. Certainly the children, grandchildren, nieces, and nephews of these women continued to battle race prejudice and the injustices to which it gave rise. Sometimes it was the women of Clifford's generation themselves. Mary Church Terrell, for example, initiated a lawsuit at a segregated Washington, D.C., restaurant in 1950 when she was eighty-six years old. Born in 1863, the year of the Emancipation Proclamation, she died two months after seeing the Supreme Court rule in Brown v. Board of Education (1954) that racial segregation was unconstitutional.[20] Likewise, despite Alice Dunbar-Nelson's lament that black women had settled into a comfortable Republican Party rut, the coming decades would see African Americans begin a gradual party realignment toward the Democrats, part of the larger political shifts of the twentieth century. As Carrie Clifford knew, black women were central to those rights struggles and political battles. In championing the work and celebrating the lives of the black women in the early twentieth century, she left us with a genealogy of this long civil rights movement.[21]

CHAPTER 19

Candidata Republicana
Nina Otero-Warren

In New Mexico, the general election of 1922 was the first in which women could run for offices other than superintendent of schools, and they did so with gusto. Both parties nominated two women, two of whom were Hispanic. These were some of the first women to run for office after the passage of the Nineteenth Amendment, and certainly among the first women of color in the nation to do so. Moreover, because of the demographics of New Mexico, it was the first state where women of color not only voted but also became officeholders.[1]

The Republicans turned to Nina Otero-Warren, who was already a political powerhouse. Not only was she well known for her suffrage work, but she had campaign experience, having served as the point person for Alice Paul's National Woman's Party and having been elected as Santa Fe County's school superintendent. She also appealed to both Anglo and Hispanic voters. Otero-Warren was bilingual and had insisted that suffrage literature needed to be written in both English and Spanish so as to reach the majority of the population. She ran in the primary against the incumbent, Néstor Montoya, beating him handily and becoming the Republican Party's candidate for congressional representative in 1922.

When Otero-Warren made her formal announcement to run for the Republican nomination, she laid out her political platform. She stood by the Harding administration's efforts to make the United States "a factor in promoting world peace and world justice," but she primarily focused on helping the people of New Mexico. She nodded to the major developmental issues in a high desert state dependent on agriculture: reclamation, tariffs, and farm credits. Well known for her job in balancing the Santa Fe school system's budget, she endorsed a budget system for the state as a way to reduce the tax burden without reducing government efficiency. Finally, she advocated for women and children, calling for federal aid for education and child health and welfare. She also favored an amendment, if necessary, to support child labor legislation. In the English-language press she did not explicitly address the question of Spanish language or land rights, but she signaled elsewhere that she believed that Spanish-speaking women in the state cared deeply about the issues affecting their children.[2] The Spanish language paper *La Revista*, however, noted that she "habla ambos idiomas, Inglés y el Español, perfectamente" (speaks both English and Spanish perfectly) and was "competente y capaz al igual que el más educado en Estados Unidos" (as competent and capable as the most educated in the United States).[3]

Nationally, Otero-Warren was one of three women (and the only Hispana) nominated by the Republican Party to run for Congress in 1922. She was joined by Winnifred Mason Huck of Illinois, who was running to fill the seat left vacant by the death of her father, and Lindsay Patterson of North Carolina.[4] Their pictures ran in papers across the country. The New York Tribune reminded its readers that Otero-Warren had once lived in the state with the subtitle "Mrs. Adelina Otero-Warren, Former New Yorker." Many of the articles asserted that she had the best chance of success, especially because she had beaten an incumbent, Néstor Montoya, in the primary. That feat suggested the "passing of the time when women candidates were given complimentary nominations in districts where victory at the polls was highly improbable and where no male candidate was hungry for the post."[5]

New Mexicans were pleased that her campaign "para diputado al Congreso" (for congressional representative) was covered by "todos los grandes diarios de Estados Unidos de costa a costa" (all of the big newspapers from coast to coast in the United States), as La Revista proudly noted. But, it quickly added, she had not sought out the publicity, and her widely circulated photograph was the first she had ever taken for publication. Part of the nation's interest, the paper asserted, was her her noble Spanish ancestry—"la Nobleza Aragonesa de España" or "aristocracia española," as they put it—especially that of her maternal Luna family.[6]

Otero-Warren campaigned hard using the skills she had honed working for suffrage. One paper called it "one of the most remarkable campaigns ever made in New Mexico and probably in any other state." As soon as she was nominated she started out on the campaign trail, and there were "very few parts of the state that have not received a visit from her." Considering the size of the state and lack of railroads, one reporter noted, "this is a most remarkable achievement." Otero-Warren made the trips by car. She was initially accompanied by her sister and later by her friend Mrs. B. Z. McCullough. Observers often commented on her style, which one reporter described as "combining the proper amount of dignity, with a cheery and earnest frankness that people like." Another stated that the interviewer found her charmingly political.[7]

Despite her efforts, she lost the election—in part it was rumored because her cousin, the former governor Miguel Otero, revealed that she was not as respectable a widow as she often let people believe but was divorced, a much more scandalous position at the time. But it was also a difficult election year for the Republican Party more broadly, and they lost seventy-seven seats in the House of Representatives. Nevertheless, Nina Otero-Warren had achieved a great deal just by running. She would continue her career in politics, serving on Republican Party committees and eventually going on to work for the Roosevelt administration as director of the Work Conference for Adult Teachers in Puerto Rico, helping to set up bilingual education programs.

Spanish Don's Daughter Among 4 Women in Race for Congress

Mrs. Adelina Otero Warren, Former New Yorker, Wins a Hot Republican Primary Fight in New Mexico; Suffragists Here Elated Over Her Victory

Seeks Seat in House

Four Republican women have tossed their toques into the ring as candidates for Congress this fall.

Of the four the most picturesque is Mrs. Adelina Otero Warren, of Santa Fe, N. M., who represents the old Spanish tradition in the Southwest. She is the new type of woman in politics, the daughter of a Spanish don, with a background of family wealth and culture, yet herself one of the vigorous younger generation who espoused the cause of the militant suffragists of the National Woman's Party and went in for public office as soon as women won the vote.

Mrs. Warren is a daughter of Don Manuel Otero and Donna Eloisa Luna Otero, names redolent of the romantic Spanish past, and her early education was in accord with the family tradition. But ten years ago the young woman cast away the past and asserted her birthright as an American. She came to New York to carve out her career, choosing as a medium the Vacation Association, founded by Miss Anne Morgan for the benefit of working girls. Miss Otero served as instructor in dancing, singing and dramatic classes.

She then returned to Santa Fe, where she took up club work and became chairman of the legislative committee of the New Mexico State Federation of Women's Clubs. She pushed bills in the state Legislature affecting child welfare and education. In 1918 she was made county superintendent of schools, and chairman of the State Health Board. She married, in the mean time, and as Mrs. Warren became well known throughout the Southwest for her activity as chairman of the women's division of the Republican State Committee of New Mexico.

Mrs. Warren is reported to have defeated in the primary contest the pres-

Mrs. Adelina Otero Warren, who has been chosen by the Republicans of New Mexico to make the race for a seat in the House of Representatives.

In 1922 Nina Otero-Warren was one of three women nominated by the Republican Party to seek election to the House of Representatives, making her the first woman of color nominated for that seat by a major party. Her candidacy made national news both because she was one of the first women to run for Congress after the ratification of the Nineteenth Amendment and because of the nation's interest in her "noble Spanish ancestry." (New York Tribune, September 14, 1922)

Otero-Warren was not the only suffragist in New Mexico to run for office. Aurora Lucero had left New Mexico for South America in 1919 when she married the Anglo businessman Garner D. White.[8] When she returned, she, too, became involved in politics. While she was serving as school superintendent for San Miguel County, her name was put forward by the Democrats for state school superintendent. A few years later, the Democratic state chair appointed her to serve on the party's state committee.[9] Indeed the position of school superinten-

dent fit easily into notions held by many men and women that women were particularly suited to address issues that pertained to children and other women. It
was an idea many suffragists had advocated in their struggle for voting rights. In
the 1922 race for school superintendent, both parties nominated Anglo women.

The 1922 election was a good one for Democrats in New Mexico, which helped
Soledad Chávez de Chacón of Albuquerque, who represented the Democrats in
the secretary of state race. She was the first Hispanic woman to win a statewide election in the nation and the first woman in the United States elected to
that office. Like Otero-Warren, she was a member of a politically active Hispanic
family.[10] The connections between New Mexico Hispano politicos and the suffrage fight remind us of the important role of political networks and take us back
to Washington during the final years of the ratification struggle.

When Senator A. A. Jones went to Washington in 1917, he brought along Dennis
Chávez, a young Hispano who had served as his Spanish-language interpreter
during the campaign. Chávez was Soledad Chávez de Chacón's cousin. Jones
secured a position for Chávez as clerk for the Senate and may have helped get
his wife, Ymelda Espinoza Chávez, her clerical position in the Department of
Commerce. Dennis, or Dionisio, as he was formally named, was born in 1888
not far from Nina Luna-Otero at his family home, Los Chávez, about twenty
miles south of Albuquerque. But unlike her, he was born into a poor family.
His parents, David and Paz Chávez, moved the family to Albuquerque when
Dionisio was eight, enrolling him at the Presbyterian mission school, where he
learned English. But the move did not improve their financial circumstances,
and Dennis, as he was called at school, had to drop out and begin working to
help his family.

Dennis thought a great deal about politics. His father had been a loyal political lieutenant of Otero-Warren's powerful uncle Solomon Luna, but Chávez was
frustrated that it did not seem to improve his father's position in life or the living
conditions for most people in the county. He pointedly abandoned the Republican Party and even before he could vote began to support the Democrats, giving
speeches and serving as an interpreter for candidates.[11] In New Mexico almost
90 percent of the population were monolingual Spanish speakers, and politicians knew they had to appeal to them. A good interpreter could be even more
persuasive than the politician, and interpreters played a key role in helping politicians get elected.[12] Chávez's skills and his party loyalty were rewarded by the
newly elected Jones.

Washington opened up many opportunities for Chávez. He enrolled in law
school at Georgetown University, clerking during the day and taking classes at
night. In the Senate, he also had a front-row seat to the women lobbying for
the suffrage amendment. He saw his mentor consulting with Maud Wood Park,

Carrie Chapman Catt, Helen Hamilton Gardener, and other suffrage leaders. He heard speeches on the floor emphasizing that female voters were essential to the future of the major political parties. He watched Jeannette Rankin, who had arrived in Washington the same year he did, navigate the House as the first woman elected to Congress. So when he returned to New Mexico in 1920 after the amendment enfranchised most women, he understood that they were now an important political constituency.

In 1922, Chávez and the Democrats met in convention at the armory in Albuquerque. The new female voters, Anglo and Hispanic, were on their minds, and they made several gestures to women, putting forth names for different offices. Secretary of state seemed a likely good office for women, and the Democrats nominated Frances Nixon along with Chávez's cousin Soledad Chávez de Chacón. Nixon, a veteran suffrage activist and founder of the New Mexico Federation of Women's Clubs, was at the convention. When she saw that Chávez de Chacón would receive the majority of the votes, she withdrew her name and moved to make the nomination unanimous. Chávez de Chacón herself was not at the convention. As the story goes, she was baking a cake in her kitchen when her brother-in-law Felipe Chacón and cousin Dennis Chávez drove up with three other male delegates from the convention. They came into the house and told her that her name had been put forward. She was shocked. "Oh, no, not me!" she said, before adding that she would have to consult her father and her husband. That story might be true, but she was not politically naive; as she later put it, "I was raised among politicians."[13] Moreover her best friend, Ymelda Espinoza Chávez, was Dennis Chávez's wife. Ymelda Chávez had also lived and worked in Washington, D.C., during the final dramatic years of the fight for the amendment.[14] The two women were both members of the League of Women Voters[15] and of the city's Minerva Club, which had discussed the suffrage amendment at meetings and been delighted when it passed. But perhaps all of Chávez de Chacón's seemingly feigned disinterest in the office was merely to set people at ease and make a female candidate more palatable. As an article a few years later described her, "She is not a militant suffragist, but believes that women, since they have been given the ballot, should use it."[16] Her positioning worked, and she won handily.

But clearly there was some unease about female politicians, especially, it seems, among male party leaders. Soledad Chávez de Chacón and Ymelda Chávez appear to have had big plans that were immediately thwarted. The secretary of state was responsible for appointing the assistant secretary of state, and Chávez de Chacón chose Ymelda Chávez. But Dennis Chávez did not want his wife in the capital of Santa Fe while he lived in Albuquerque: at least that was the story. There may have been more to it than that because party leaders also pressured Ireneo Eduardo (Ed) Chacón, Soledad's husband, to take the position. An employee of a furniture store in Albuquerque, he had been looking forward to opening and managing a branch in Santa Fe but put aside those plans to work for his wife. Perhaps this arrangement reassured people. The Democrats renominated her by acclamation in 1924, and voters returned her to office for a second term. She beat the Republican candidate, Joaquín V. Gallegos, by 4,774 votes, making her the third-highest vote getter among the Democrats, who won ten of the twelve state and federal positions that year.[17]

Chávez de Chacón was on her way to a long political career. She gained some national attention by being the first woman elected to a secretary of state position and even more when she served as acting governor of the state in 1924—she was the second woman in the nation to do so, the first being Carolyn Shelton of Oregon in 1909. And the times were changing as both Nellie Ross of Wyoming and Miriam (Ma) Ferguson of Texas were elected to the executive position of their states in the fall of 1924. According to the New Mexican chain of command, when the governor left the state, as Governor James Hinkle did for two weeks during the summer of 1924 to attend the Democratic convention in Boston, the lieutenant governor became acting governor. The New Mexican lieutenant governor had died, however, and his seat had not been filled. Second in the line of succession was the secretary of state. On one hand, this seems like a trivial and arcane fact, but on the other, it was not merely window dressing. Chávez de Chacón was doing substantial work. She signed a requisition to the war department for funds for the New Mexico National Guard and pardoned a man on the recommendation of the trustees and superintendent of the New Mexico Industrial School. She issued several notary public certificates, appointed a doctor to the State Board of Chiropractic Examiners, and issued papers to the governor of Kansas for the extradition of a man charged with grand larceny in New Mexico. After her second term ended in 1926, the family went back to Albuquerque. Her daughter, Adelina, or Lena, and son, Santiago, or Jim, were fourteen and thirteen, respectively. Her husband went to work in real estate, but she seems to have stayed home caring for the children for several years.[18]

In 1934 she returned to politics, this time running for a two-year state legislative term as representative from Bernalillo County. The other three Bernalillo County state legislators elected with her were non-Hispanic male Democrats. She was the first Hispana elected from Bernalillo but not the first in the state legislature. That honor went to two women who had been elected the year before: Mrs. Ezequiel Gallegos of Mora County and Mrs. P. Sáiz of Socorro and Catron County were elected for two-year terms in 1931. When Chávez de Chacón arrived in Santa Fe, she was joined by the representative from San Miguel County, Mrs. Susie Chávez, who was also elected in 1932. One year later, in 1933, Concha Ortiz y Pino of Santa Fe was elected to the first of her three legislative terms. While little is known of the first two, Susie Chávez had worked as a secretary for the county. She was married to an icehouse timekeeper and had an eight-year-old son.[19] Concha Ortiz y Pino, like Otero-Warren and Chávez de Chácon, was from a deeply political family. She was the sixth generation of her family to serve in the New Mexico legislature.[20] Indeed, these family political networks were key. Dennis Chávez, who by 1934 had returned to Washington as a congressman for New Mexico, reported back on the young men and women of the state who were working in the capital for the state's delegation or the federal government. As he noted, "Most of them are taking college work after office hours," preparing for a future in which they would "prove to be of untold value to the welfare of the state." Those young people included Soledad Chávez de Chacón's son, Jim, who was enrolled in the National Law School earning his law degree, just as Dennis Chávez had been several years earlier.[21]

In fact, despite New Mexico's initial reluctance to enfranchise women, after the passage of the amendment, women swiftly moved into public service. From 1922 to 1934, seventeen women, including the five Hispanas mentioned above, were elected to the state legislature. That was not the most of any state, but it was part of a trend of a rising number of women in state legislatures directly after the passage of the amendment. Because many states had enfranchised women before 1920, 25 female state legislators from Arizona, California, Colorado, Idaho, Kansas, Montana, New York, Oregon, Utah, and Washington had voted to ratify the amendment.[22] After 1920, those 25 were joined by more women in the statehouses, and by 1930 there were 150. Other than the five Hispanas in New Mexico, however, it is likely that all of them were white.[23]

The fall after her failed congressional campaign, Otero-Warren was appointed as inspector of Indian schools in New Mexico, the first woman to hold that position. Perhaps it was orchestrated by her Republican friends in Washington like Senator Holm Bursum. Otero-Warren faced a tough job at a moment when the federal government was aggressively attacking the Pueblo people. The schools were in deplorable condition. At the Santa Fe Indian School, one of the largest in the country, she found overcrowded dormitories; filthy, fly-covered food storage and preparation areas; and children sharing towels, toothbrushes, and beds. Forty-six percent of the children at the school had trachoma (contagious conjunctivitis), which often caused blindness and spread easily in close quarters. Otero-Warren insisted that the superintendent fix as many of those problems as he could and immediately sent a report to the commissioner of Indian Affairs in Washington urging an investigation as well as an increased budget.[24]

While Otero-Warren was an effective investigator, she worked within a colonial system and supported the goal of assimilation for Native people. She believed that the schools could develop race leaders who would help their people to "become self-supporting and ready . . . to accept the responsibilities of citizenship." As with her own Hispanic heritage, she did not agree that the system should alienate Native students from their families and even argued that they "must be taught to appreciate the history and traditions of [their] own race and thus aspire to continue the native arts of [their] own people." But she also maintained that they should acquire a "new type of learning" and insisted that Christianity was a part of that.[25] She approached Native people in New Mexico with a paternalism that she also often exhibited toward poor Hispanics in the state, emphasizing their ignorance, especially women, who only needed to be shown the right way to do things for the community to prosper. She also believed that the Spanish conquest of New Mexico had been positive for Native people. "Spain's was the most comprehensive, humane, and effective 'Indian policy' ever framed," she claimed.[26]

As a member of the Republican Party, Otero-Warren had also advocated for legislation that would give the state more access to federal lands for the funding of public education.[27] For party leaders, this also meant removing federal protections from Native land in order to open it to settlers. In Washington, her colleagues Senator Bursum and former New Mexico senator and current secretary of the Interior Albert Fall moved to make this happen. Senator Bursum introduced the bill, on which he had campaigned, that would have allowed non-Native squatters—both Anglo and Hispanic—on Pueblo land to claim land and water rights if they had lived there for a period of years despite clear Pueblo claims. The bill provoked immediate resistance by the Pueblos of New Mexico who came together in the Council of All the New Mexico Pueblos (now the All Pueblo Council of Governors) to articulate a common response. They reached out to the members of the General Federation of Women's Clubs (GFWC), especially those of the California branch, who had hired John Collier as their investigator, and launched a national campaign against the Bursum Bill. Together, they successfully raised public awareness and stopped the legislation.[28]

The next year, a substitute, the Lenroot Bill, was proposed. As Otero-Warren was now the superintendent of Indian education, she found herself in the middle of this intense discussion with people looking to her as an authority. Many non-Natives in New Mexico found the bill to be a good compromise that protected some Indian lands but opened others to settlers. Otero-Warren fell into this category. When the Albuquerque Women's Club invited her to offer suggestions on Indian affairs, she "urged the support of the bill . . . which will embody justice and equality to the Indian and the not Indian settler in good faith."[29] The All Pueblo Council and the national GFWC disagreed and pushed back against this bill as well.

At the same time, the Pueblos faced a renewed assault on their cultural rights. In 1921 and again in 1923, Commissioner of Indian Affairs Charles Burke issued his infamous Circular #1665, or the Dance Circular, which severely restricted Native dances because of the supposed "elements of savagery and demoralizing practices" in them. Especially aimed at the Sun Dance of the northern plains, Pueblo dances also came under scrutiny. The All Pueblo Council, Collier, Stella Atwood of the California Federation of Women's Clubs, the GFWC, and a number of modernist reformers from New Mexico's artist colonies also fought against these orders. But some Pueblo people, often returned students, disagreed. Described by non-Natives as "progressives," they believed that the ceremonies represented "paganism," which they rejected. They turned to missionaries and federal employees to bolster their position. As such, federal policies exacerbated rifts within Pueblo communities, though these divisions were not always as clear-cut as non-Natives assumed. Pablo Abeita of Isleta Pueblo, who was sometimes referred to as a progressive, rejected the non-Natives' emphasis on political factions and refused to align himself with any one non-Native group. "I am a friend of our best cause," he told Otero-Warren, emphasizing Pueblo well-being.[30]

Again, Otero-Warren's federal position placed her at the center of these debates, which came to a head in 1924. At the beginning of the year, the All Pueblo Council invited her to a meeting where the issues were discussed. Frustrated about the land and dance issues, the Pueblos determined to send a delegation to Washington, D.C. In their resolution, they stated, "We call to the American people to pay attention to our distress, and to help us to keep these rights of life and land which were guaranteed to us by President Lincoln, as Spain had guaranteed them before." They also specifically noted that "we are voteless," a reminder that they had rejected U.S. citizenship and remained under wardship in order to maintain their land claims and sovereignty.[31]

Otero-Warren also traveled to visit with the Progressive Council of Indians later that spring. She tended to side with the "progressives" on the religious questions and with non-Native New Mexicans on the land question. When the Progressive Council sent a delegation to the GFWC meeting in Los Angeles in June, she accompanied them and served as their Spanish-language interpreter. She used her substantial political skills to orchestrate their presentation and gain support for their position as opposed to that of the All Pueblo Council. She met with GFWC members, lobbied the Bureau of Catholic Mission representatives, arranged interviews, and used her friendship with the president of the GFWC to get the progressive Pueblos' concerns on the program. She declared her understanding of "the clear-cut issue which was that of Christianity against paganism." The New Mexico Federation of Women's Clubs representatives also supported them because their cause was linked to the compromise Lenroot Bill.[32] Otero-Warren triumphantly reported that their resolution — "to the effect that individual religious liberty be guaranteed to all Indians" — had triumphed over that of the All Pueblo Council, as represented by Collier and Atwood.[33]

While Otero-Warren and the six Pueblo men she was with at the convention were successful in shaping the GFWC's resolution, the question of Pueblo land had been resolved when Congress passed the Pueblo Land Bill on June 7, in the midst of the GFWC's convention. It created a three-person Pueblo Land Board to arbitrate disputes and provided for compensation to those who lost lands. In the end, the board determined that the Pueblos had lost more than 40,000 acres of land valued at $1.9 million, but in implementation, they received only $600,000 for it.[34]

Otero-Warren's tenure as inspector did not last much longer; she was removed from the position later that year.[35] But her work in the Indian Office had given her a high-ranking position in the federal bureaucracy. She had influence on Indian policy and authority over Native people. This was a result of her political connections and the skills she had honed over many years in public service. But her position as an elite Hispanic woman also helped boost her authority. The emphasis she and others placed on their Spanish colonial past and its legacy of conquest of New Mexico's Indigenous people placed them on par with Anglos in a way that Native women could not access.

CHAPTER 20

To Help Indians Help Themselves
Gertrude Simmons Bonnin

At the very height of the struggle over the Nineteenth Amendment, leading Indigenous feminists were completing and publishing their major works of political theory. This was not a coincidence. Native women had long been engaged in the fight for political participation, citizenship rights, and women's place in the United States. They built on their previous years of activism, drawing on the lessons they learned about honing their arguments, winning allies, and navigating the particularities of state, federal, and tribal political structures. Now they surveyed a changed political landscape and deployed those skills and strategies to help their own communities.

The year 1920 fell amid what is often called the nadir of Native history, a period characterized by poverty, disease, massive land dispossession, and scant political power—all of which were the direct result of federal policies. Native feminists marshaled multiple strategies to address these problems. In some cases they loudly and directly called upon newly enfranchised white women to address what one called "the Indian situation as it is today." In others they looked to access U.S. citizenship and suffrage rights for the nearly one-third of adult Native people who were still considered wards of the federal government. Women also worked within their own communities and their own political traditions to protect their lands and cultures.

In 1920, Laura Cornelius Kellogg published her first book, *Our Democracy and the American Indian: A Comprehensive Presentation of the Indian Situation as It Is Today*. As her title suggested, it was a meditation on the United States' system of governance and the place of Indigenous people in it as well as her plan for the future.[1] Surveying the conditions of Native people in America, she emphasized that lack of control over their political affairs and consequent land loss were the biggest threats to Indigenous self-determination. Her nation, the Oneida, had been removed from New York in 1821, and the allotment of their Wisconsin reservation had begun in 1892 with disastrous results. In 1917 federal bureaucrats arrived at Oneida. They were there to determine who was "competent" enough to have their land removed from trust status. The label was liberally applied. Once lands were removed from federal trust, however, they were subject to state taxes. Many allotments were lost to unpaid assessments; others were sold by their owners to combat poverty. By the 1930s, their reservation territory had been pillaged, shrinking from 65,436 acres to less than 90 acres of tribally held lands with about 700 other acres held in individual allotments. Kellogg saw the opportunity to prevent all of their land from slipping away and with it any possibility of self-sufficiency. As she wrote, keeping reservation land intact "gives a chance for a better day to arrive, while the dismemberment of [the] Indian domain puts the Indian out into the world of the white men, landless."[2]

To address this crisis, Kellogg formulated an economic and political plan she called Lolomi, a term she drew from the Hopi word for beauty and goodness. She proposed an Indigenous alternative to complete assimilation into U.S. citizenship, with an emphasis on "layered citizenships" that moved beyond the false dichotomies of citizenship or sovereignty and indigeneity or modernity. Why couldn't Native nations coexist with the United States, she asked, while maintaining their sovereignty and land base? She advocated for tribally held property using a term familiar to Americans: the corporation, but with tribal members as investors.[3] Lolomi involved "federal incorporation of a self-governing body." Individuals would pool their allotments into shared property that would support all tribal members, each with a single vote.[4]

Incorporation also clarified the political relationship of the Oneida nation to the United States. The biggest issue was the hold the Bureau of Indian Affairs had over Native people. Currently, she argued, Indians were not free, and Indian Service agents were "absolute despots." Lolomi "is diametrically opposed to Bureaucracy in all things," she asserted. Her plan would do away with "the status of semi-citizenship (the status of wardship), which is at once unconstitutional and chaotic." It "presuppose[d] a state of self-government" for the Oneida, free from Indian Office oversight and more akin to the position of the states within the union.[5] Kellogg, whose Oneida heritage linked her to the Iroquois or Haudenosaunee Confederacy, did not fully reject participation in the U.S. system, as many other Haudenosaunee had. But she did suggest a confederated relationship between the two nations.[6]

Central to Kellogg's economic vision of sovereignty was communally held land. That, however, along with traditional modes of governance had been major targets of federal assimilation programs, since they raised the specter of communism for policy makers.[7] Despite that, Kellogg seized the opportunity to defend the ideas that underlay Lolomi in a way that might appear surprising from our vantage point. In her post-ratification speaking tour for the Wisconsin Constitutional Defense League in the fall of 1920, she took on a prominent role in the league, which had developed from the rising anti-communist agitation in the wake of the Bolshevik Revolution of 1917 and grew during the war into what became known as the first Red Scare. Feminists, especially the socialists calling for radical social change, became targets.

The National Woman's Party was often included in this group due to its militant protest style during the fight for the amendment. And many of its members were socialists (though not necessarily communists) advocating for protective labor laws, birth control, and women's rights. In the changing political climate, this became a liability. A white suffragist from Wisconsin reported to NWP headquarters that it had been difficult to recruit new members in the state because the national organizers had a reputation for being socialists. Although they had left the state after the ratification battle, the feelings lingered.[8] Through her speaking tour, Kellogg was shielding feminism from those charges by urging newly enfranchised women to defend the Constitution "against attacks of radicals who would overthrow it on the promise of building a new order of society and government on some theoretical basis," by which she meant communists.[9]

Through her Wisconsin Constitutional Defense League speeches, Kellogg may also have been protecting Lolomi from criticism by demonstrating her anticommunist stance, but she had another angle as well: her activities with the league also defended the document that signified the nation-to-nation relationship between the Oneida and the United States. Haudenosaunee claims were based on the treaties of 1784 and 1789 that gave the Iroquois "the status of an independent protectorate" with "protected autonomy, with the title of the original territory vested in them." Any scheme to overthrow the Constitution threatened that relationship and Oneida claims. Kellogg also asserted that the Constitution was itself based on the Haudenosaunee Confederacy. The ideals of "freedom and equal opportunity" within a confederate government were, she argued, Haudenosaunee ideals given to their Confederacy by Sagoyewatha, the Great Awakener. "Without the spirit which promoted the first Awakener of the People to lay the foundations of American liberty," she wrote, "democracy is dead." It was only fair that the originators of the system be allowed to participate in it. "I love my country," she insisted, "just as my fathers who first dreamed of democracy on this continent."[10] If this were the case, to defend the Constitution was to defend Haudenosaunee principles. From this perspective, the Oneida could both be part of the American union of states and maintain their sovereignty. As Kellogg strategically embraced anti-bolshevism and woman suffrage to defend Oneida self-determination, she was not the only Native feminist to see white women as potential allies.

In 1921, just a few months after her speech at the National Woman's Party conference, Gertrude Simmons Bonnin released her second book, *American Indian Stories*. It had been two decades since she had published *Old Indian Legends*. She pulled together several magazine stories that had brought her to the literary world's attention and added some new pieces. She organized the stories so that they walked her reader through the life experiences of an Indian child, student, teacher, and finally political activist. The pieces peeled back the benevolent rhetoric of federal Indian policy to show the sorrow of reservation and boarding school experiences from an Indian girl's point of view. They powerfully personalized the damage that federal assimilation policy inflicted upon Native families and communities. Two of her new pieces emphasized that Native and white women held the power to change these conditions.[11]

The culminating chapter was not a story, however, but a further elaboration on her speech before the NWP, "America's Indian Problem." The title was the same, as were the themes, but her call to action for the women of America was more direct. The essay opened with a challenge: Do you know what your Bureau of Indian Affairs in Washington, D.C., really is? How it is organized and how it deals with the wards of the nation? She then laid out how the inadequate administration and its "sham protection" provided cover only for the graft and appropriations of those who were supposed to be stewards of Native lands and resources. Being trapped in guardianship with a guardian that was not honest was harmful in the extreme. Native people's "lack of political rights" was at the root of their dispossession and government mismanagement. She called on the "women of America" to take up the issue: "Now the time is at hand when the American Indian shall have his day in court through the help of the women of America." Women now had a voice in the vote and needed to use it to help "a voiceless people within our midst," she argued. "We would open the door of American opportunity to the red man." This could be done by "removing the barriers that hinder his normal development." The solution was obvious. "Wardship is no substitute for American citizenship," she concluded; "therefore we seek his enfranchisement."[12]

Members of the NWP were not the only white women to whom Bonnin brought her message. She had much more success with the two million members of the General Federation of Women's Clubs (GFWC). In June 1921, Bonnin presented at the GFWC biannual convention in Salt Lake City. Again, she castigated the bureaucracy of the Indian Office, arguing that the "prolonged wardship" of people under its authority was "not compatible with the idea of American freedom and American ideals." Like Kellogg, she positioned Native people as the true representatives of democracy.[13]

Bonnin found a strong ally in California Federation of Women's Clubs worker Stella Atwood of Riverside, who had been championing Indian reform in her state. Because of their speeches, the national federation was persuaded to make the cause of the Indian a central focus of its organization, and despite ongoing discussions about cutting back on the number of departments, it created a new Department of Indian Affairs, which Atwood was elected to chair.[14] The organization's magazine, Federation News, reported, "With Women Suffrage won, following a war of fifty years, standing organized women of America will now work for the enfranchisement of 'the first Americans,' who are still denied rights of citizenship." It was said that Bonnin shed tears of gratitude at the GFWC's decision, stating, "It has begun. Nothing can stop it. We shall have help."[15]

For the next three years Bonnin traveled the country under the GFWC's auspices, appealing to white women to support Indian citizenship. She spoke to women's clubs in practically every state, "acquainting the public at large with the present condition of the Indian."[16] She used her lectures to theorize her own version of "layered citizenships," which could be a model for relations between the United States and Native nations. She used her own community of the Yankton Dakota as her example and envisioned Native leadership and communally-held land as the features necessary for self-governance. Atwood became a strong supporter, often quoting Bonnin in her own speeches and testimony to Congress.[17]

One speech Bonnin often gave, "Bureaucracy Versus Democracy," drew extensively on *Americanize the First American*, a pamphlet she published and distributed. In it, Bonnin contrasted Native wards controlled by federal agents with community self-governance. She illustrated this with a diagram bearing two circles labeled "Bureaucracy" and "Democracy." Each contained further descriptions of the elements of the two systems. "Bureaucracy" was labeled "What we have" and "Democracy," "What we want."[18] Under the latter she had outlined a detailed plan for tribal sovereignty, which she imagined as a "democracy wheel," an image possibly inflected with the Lakota philosophy of the sacred hoop.[19]

She visualized government relations between nations as concentric circles. Though encircled by the Constitution of "your American Government" at the rim, the Native community was separate from it.[20] The wheel's "hub shall be an organization of progressive Indian citizens," she asserted, driven by "community interests . . . of the Indians themselves."[21] Next, District Offices across reservations would represent their communities on a Reservation Executive Council. At the third level, an Indian Citizens' Association would liaise with the Indian Office in Washington. All levels would be filled with Native leaders educated by competent teachers with standardized courses on law, American government, and the treaties. Bonnin included women's political participation, urging them to "study the uses of the housekeeper's vote" in the multiple jurisdictions of "her home, community, state, and America." Economically, this system of self-governance would be supported by tribally controlled economies, especially communally held stock ranges and farm equipment, an argument made by many Sioux people. This vision, she believed, offered Native people "a plan of regeneration."[22]

Like Kellogg, Bonnin believed that it was possible for Native nations to coexist with the United States as separate yet related political entities. Native people in this vision remained citizens of their Indigenous nations but could also participate as citizens of the United States. Her decision to surround the "democracy wheel" with the U.S. Constitution placed Native nations within its federated states and under its protection. Moreover, she reminded listeners that "treaties with our Government made in good faith by our ancestors are still unfulfilled" and "American citizenship is withheld from some three-fourths of the Indians." Her organizational plans suggested that she, unlike many white policy makers, could imagine Native people as citizens of both the United States and

AMERICANIZE THE FIRST AMERICAN

By ZITKALA-SA (GERTRUDE BONNIN)

A

PLAN OF

REGENERATION

Gertrude Simmons Bonnin urged newly enfranchised white women to advocate for U.S. citizenship and suffrage rights for Native people after the ratification of the Nineteenth Amendment. This pamphlet, decorated with U.S. flags, contains speeches she gave in those years, which outline her vision of a "layered citizenship" in which Native people could be U.S. citizens as well as citizens of their own nations without giving up tribal sovereignty and treaty rights. ("Americanize the First American" pamphlet, National Council of American Indian Records, MSS 1704, box 1, folder 4, L. Tom Perry Special Collections, Harold B. Lee Library, Brigham Young University, Provo, Utah) their own nations. She appealed to the "Womanhood of America" to address these problems and make things right, to "extend American opportunities to the first Americans."[23]

Bonnin's and Kellogg's visions in the 1920s had a number of similarities. Each woman drew on her personal experience as an employee of the Indian Service to critique the federal bureaucracy. In its place, both suggested a relationship between Native nations and the federal government that allowed for tribal self-governance and economic self-sufficiency through communal property holding.

Along with her speeches, Bonnin was also driving GFWC policies in other ways. In 1923, the federation hired her as a research agent for its Indian Welfare Committee. (The year before, the California branch had hired John Collier as its investigator of Indian conditions and pending legislation, which led to his fight against the Bursum Bill and Dance Circular.)[24] The federation was undertaking a joint investigation with other reform groups: the long-standing Indian Rights Association and the American Indian Defense Association, a group founded by John Collier of which Bonnin later became a member. The representatives of the other two organizations were white men. Together they were investigating the situation of Oklahoma tribes who had come into substantial mineral wealth due to the oil boom. Many of the Native people in Oklahoma were legally wards rather than citizens, and their guardianship was under the oversight of the state rather than the federal government.[25] As a result, an elaborate system of corruption to swindle Native people out of millions of dollars had sprung up between local judges who determined who would serve as guardians and the local whites they appointed.[26] The three investigators spent five weeks in eastern Oklahoma during the winter of 1923 "making a first-hand study of the conditions." They came to damning conclusions about the horrible situation of the Native people there; their investigation, published in pamphlet form as *Oklahoma's Poor Rich Indians*, "discloses a situation that is almost unbelievable in a civilized country, and makes clear that radical and immediate change of the system" was necessary to save "members of the Five Civilized Tribes from pauperization and virtual extermination."[27]

Kellogg also spoke to the defrauding of the oil-rich tribes in her book. She explained to her readers that she had been part of an investigation on the Osage reservation in 1913, where "we found seventeen different kinds of offenses committed against this group." She emphasized that it was the wealth from Native people's land that enriched white Americans. Kellogg concluded her book with a harsh indictment of those who dismissed the difficulties faced by Native people as their own fault, musing that "it looks like a long way between Wall Street and the Reservations, but it is not very far."

Bonnin heartily agreed. In a chilling section of *Oklahoma's Poor Rich Indians* on kidnapping and sexual assault in connection with the fraud, Bonnin linked the plundering of Native resources to the violence perpetrated against Native women. Later investigations would uncover elaborate murder plots against Osage women as white men sought access to their wealth. Bonnin's coauthors deferred to her, writing, "There are some phases of our investigation that can be presented best by a feminine mind." She described the kidnapping of young Native girls who were taken out of state and held until they signed papers relinquishing their land and mineral rights. In the parlance of the time, Bonnin suggested that "white slavery" charges be filed on behalf of those who were raped. These were emotional meetings. Bonnin movingly described embracing one of the women she interviewed, overwhelmed by the horror of her experiences. After a visit and interview with another Native woman, she wrote, "I felt an overwhelming sense of indignation." These women had been robbed economically and of their dignity. She concluded that "legalized robbery of the rich Indian is an ugly practice and abhorred by all self-respecting Americans." Her publications, speeches, and reports also repeatedly demonstrated it was not only rich Indians who had been pillaged.[28]

The GFWC members took Bonnin and her coauthors' report seriously. The national director, Leslie S. Read, encouraged clubs to read and discuss the pamphlet. Read also touted the federation's role in stopping the Bursum Bill and linked it to the subsequent resignation of Senator Fall and the Teapot Dome Scandal. With Bonnin's report, it seemed the clubwomen would tackle corruption in Oklahoma next.[29]

Initially, reception seemed positive. Congress agreed to hold hearings, and the pamphlet was read aloud in the congressional subcommittee on Indian Affairs. A year later, hearings began. Laura Cornelius Kellogg would not have been surprised to hear that the authors of the report were attacked. After all, they were disrupting an extensive and profitable system, and powerful forces were arrayed against them. Kellogg noted that people who called out these problems in Indian country faced retaliation. "When he becomes too uncomfortable to someone, he may suddenly find his reputation gone, or he is indicted, or he is starving or destroyed." She was speaking from personal experience as it was during her 1913 investigation in Oklahoma that she had been arrested for the first time (the charges were later dismissed). "I merely mention this to show that my facts are not secondhand," she wrote.[30]

An initial subcommittee investigation in Oklahoma under Senator Homer Snyder dismissed Bonnin's report as "hearsay evidence" and suggested that it had been exaggerated. While the committee conceded that there were some corrupt attorneys and guardians, they acquitted the county court system that Bonnin and her fellow investigators had placed at the center of the corruption schemes. The committee ultimately recommended no further congressional hearings on the matter.[31]

While Kellogg and Bonnin looked to enlist newly enfranchised white women to protect Native people nationally, other Native women focused on their own communities. In 1922 the Kaw nation elected a woman as their principal chief, an action that caught the attention of U.S. citizens as they adjusted to the idea of women voting. "The Kaw Indians not only have given women the right to vote, but have elevated one of their number to the highest office in the tribe, that of elected chief," papers explained.[32] Reporters again used notions of Indian women to frame the political changes taking place, though it was true that the Kaw had elected Lucy Tayiah Eads as their leader. Reporters also noted that other tribes, including the Seminole, had recently chosen female leaders.[33] Numerous papers repeated Eads's story under slightly different headlines: they described her as a full-blood woman but an educated and pretty one who was married to a white man and was a good mother. Orphaned as a child, she had been adopted by Chief Washunga and raised by him until she left for the Haskell Indian School. There she trained as a nurse before moving to New York, where she worked in hospitals for several years. When she returned to Kansas, the Kaw, in need of a new chief who was a "full-blood," elected her.[34]

One story made the connections to the national women's movement explicit: "Red Feminist," the headline of the *La Crosse Tribune* in Wisconsin announced. Lucy Tayiah Eads "is a red—not politically but racially, since she's a Kaw Indian." She was the first woman chief, and her "principal official function will be pressing the Kaw's $15,000,000 claim against the government."[35] It is quite possible that the editor remembered Laura Cornelius Kellogg as she stumped against the Reds throughout Wisconsin just two years earlier and was referring to it.

Lucy Tayiah Eads's story reveals that reporters were somewhat aware that many Native people remained without American citizenship. Those reporters also displayed some knowledge that they had their own tribal governments, though these were not recognized by the federal government as national governments. But the non-Native reporters did not acknowledge that American citizenship was premised on people giving up (or being forced to give up) those governments as well as tribal membership and their cultural traditions.

Eads's story also suggests how one Native woman garnered political power in her own community by drawing explicitly on cultural traditions. She deftly used the symbolism of providing for her people, as Kaw women had done in the past. Upon her election, she revived the tradition of hosting a barbecue open to all tribal members. She herself made what reporters called "squaw bread," a fried dough that sounds much like today's fry bread. She gave a speech in English and it was translated into Kaw, while the response of the oldest tribal member was made in Kaw and translated into English, demonstrating her respect for elders and their wisdom.[36]

The story of the Kaws' new leader caught the nation's attention in part because of its relevance to the Nineteenth Amendment and newly enfranchised women. But it also resonated because one of their tribal members was a famous national politician: Senator Charles Curtis, who was already known as a friend of women's rights.

Charles Curtis had represented the Senate at the opening of the National Woman's Party's new headquarters on Capitol Hill in 1922, but that was neither the beginning nor the end of his relationship with the organization.[37] Although the NWP had heard pitches from many movements after ratification, members ultimately decided that the best way to "continue to be the standard bearers in the movement for the liberation of women" was to focus on the "complete emancipation of our sex." They wanted to push society further down the path of sex equality. To that end, NWP members decided to continue with their winning strategy of amending the Constitution by pushing for an amendment that would enshrine their goal of sexual equality. Between 1913 and 1919 the Constitution had been amended four times, ushering in the federal income tax, the election of senators by citizens rather than by state legislatures, the prohibition of alcohol, and removing sex as a restriction on voting. The idea that it could be amended to guarantee equality between men and women did not seem too far-fetched in this exciting moment.[38]

In 1923, Alice Paul composed the language of what would come to be known as the Equal Rights Amendment, or ERA: "Men and women shall have equal rights throughout the United States and every place subject to its jurisdiction." The second part—every place subject to its jurisdiction—meant Indian reservations, U.S. territories like Hawaii and Alaska, and the overseas colonies of Puerto Rico, Guam, and the Philippines.[39] Perhaps the women of the NWP felt that they were addressing the concerns of Gertrude Bonnin and Madame J. C. De Veyra of the Philippines, both of whom had spoken at their convention. The party members christened it the Lucretia Mott Amendment in honor of another of the founding mothers of the women's movement.

Then they looked for congressional sponsors willing to introduce it to Congress. They found Senator Charles Curtis and Representative Daniel Anthony, both of Kansas, who submitted it to their respective chambers of Congress in December. Kansas held a special place in suffragists' thinking, though perhaps ironically, as it had been at the center of a split in the movement during Reconstruction, a split Lucretia Mott had tried to repair. It was right in the center of the nation. It had a long history of reform activism, starting with the righteous antislavery struggles of Bloody Kansas. Elizabeth Cady Stanton and Susan B. Anthony's efforts in a state suffrage referendum in the election of 1867 had relied on racist rhetoric, but they had come close to winning, and it remained prominent in the imagination of white suffragists. Also, in 1912, Kansas became the eighth state to enfranchise women before the passage of the national amendment.[40]

In 1923, both Kansas politicians whom the NWP picked to introduce the ERA were champions of women's rights. Representative Anthony was also a nephew of Susan B. Anthony.[41] He had sponsored a bill to address the fact that by precedent and, after 1907, by law, American women who married foreign men lost their U.S. citizenship. The same laws did not apply to American men who married women who were foreign citizens. Indeed, those women automatically became American citizens without going through the official naturalization process. Newly enfranchised women in the League of Women Voters focused on this issue after the ratification of the Nineteenth Amendment, calling for a woman's citizenship to be separate from her husband's. In 1922, Congress passed the Cable Act or Married Women's Citizenship Act. Although a step in the right direction, it had several weaknesses. It stated that American women would not lose their citizenship upon marriage to foreigners if they remained in the United States: but those who left the country to reside with their husbands could and did lose their citizenship if they were gone for more than two years. They could regain it only by going through the naturalization process. Moreover, if American women married "people ineligible to become citizens," the Cable Act did not apply, and they still lost their citizenship. This meant that American women who married Chinese men were denationalized. This happened to Louise Van Arnam Huie, the mother of Mabel Lee's classmates Caroline and Alice Huie. Because her husband, Huie Kin, could not become an American citizen, Louise, in marrying him, lost her American citizenship. She would regain it again in 1933, but she lived for years in legal limbo. Had she left the country, she might not have been able to return. As a white woman, Louise Huie was somewhat unusual. American-born women "not identified as Caucasian or of African descent" who married aliens ineligible for naturalization were most likely to be affected, like Alice and Caroline Huie, who both married Chinese citizens. Their status could not be reversed by subsequent divorce or widowhood, because the Chinese were barred from naturalization. Having lost their birthright citizenship through marriage, they could not become American citizens again.[42]

Senator Curtis was a good friend of suffragists as well. He was a stalwart Republican who had first come to Congress as a representative in 1893. During the years of suffrage battles, he periodically stopped by the NWP headquarters. Surrounded by the large wooden filing cabinets in which the group's leadership kept the vast correspondence necessary to coordinate their campaign across the states, he would talk and joke with the women working in the office. Curtis himself was also an inveterate keeper of records. On small note cards he recorded information about each of his Kansas constituents. He noted whom they were related to and what issues they cared about. He spent much time reviewing them and thus could greet people with a strong handshake and a few personal words. Such attentive constituent services endeared him to the people of Kansas, so much so that he survived the transition wrought by the Seventeenth Amendment, which shifted the election of senators from the state legislature to a direct vote by the people. Kansans happily sent him back to the Senate in 1914, the first election after that change went into effect.[43]

The voters of Kansas liked Curtis's memory for personal details, but they also liked his story. It was a classic American tale that seemed to have been pulled straight out of a dime novel. It also had the added romance of the frontier past, a not-so-distant time when the vast plains of Kansas had belonged to Native people and the buffalo.

He had been born in 1860 alongside the Kansas River in a log cabin on a piece of land that would become North Topeka. The Kaw or Kansa nation had signed a treaty with the federal government in 1825 that had set aside 2 million acres west of Topeka for the so-called full-blooded Kaw Indians. The treaty also stipulated that twenty-three "half-breeds," in the language of the treaty, were to receive individual plots, called fee simple land grants, along the Kansas River. These one-square-mile "reservations" were all assigned to the mixed-race children of French men and Kaw women. Julie Gonville and her siblings, grandchildren of Chief White Plume, one of the signers of the treaty, all received land in this way. Julie Gonville married Louis Pappen, and they began to run a ferry across the Kansas River. Their daughter Helene was Curtis's mother.

Curtis's mother died in 1863 when he was three years old and his father, a white man named Oren Curtis, received a commission in the U.S. Army. Initially, Charley Curtis lived with his paternal grandmother, Permelia Curtis, in Topeka. She was stern and "believed that being a Methodist and a Republican were essential for anyone [who] expected to go to heaven." When he was six years old, he went to live with his maternal grandmother, Julie Pappen, a Catholic, on the Kaw reservation. He learned to speak Kaw and French. Just two years later, conflict between the Cheyenne and the Kaw sent Charley back to Topeka, and in 1873, the federal government removed the Kaw from Kansas to Indian Territory, just south of the Kansas border.

He spent the rest of his boyhood in Topeka. When he was fourteen, he started to return to the reservation with a group of Kaw who had been visiting the city, but the story he told was that his Grandmother Pappen discouraged him. She "told me what I might expect on the Indian Reservation and that I would likely . . . become a reservation man with no future." Instead, she encouraged him to return to Topeka and start school again. His Grandfather Curtis had also passed away, so to help support his grandmother and half sister, Dolly, he took odd jobs, selling newspapers, driving a hack cab, and riding as a jockey in local horse races. After high school he read law with a local attorney and passed the bar. He also became involved in Republican Party politics, winning the office of Shawnee County district attorney. It was the beginning of a long career.[44]

Curtis was a complicated figure. His political opponents often used the phrase "beat the Indian" in their campaigns (though it was rarely successful). In the press, he was regularly described as an Indian, with pictures of men in feathered headdresses often illustrating articles about him. But non-Natives also held him up as a self-made man and proof that federal assimilation policies could work.[45] Curtis himself was proud of his heritage. He was happy to regale people with stories of horse races and the Comanche raid from his time on the reservation. A consummate politician, he joked in stump speeches, "I'm one-eighth Kaw, but one hundred percent Republican."[46] In 1892 he won a congressional seat that he held until 1907, when the Kansas legislature elevated him to the Senate. In 1914, the people of Kansas sent him back to that seat, which he held until 1929. For the last four years he served as a powerful Senate majority leader. While Curtis held progressive ideas on women and African Americans,[47] he also believed that to survive and thrive, Native people needed to give up their traditional ways. As a result, in 1898 he supported and helped pass the devastating legislation that bears his name. The Curtis Act was strongly opposed by tribal leaders because it began the process of dismantling the tribal governments and tribally held lands of the Cherokee, Chickasaw, Choctaw, Creek, and Seminole nations, paving the way for their incorporation into the state of Oklahoma. Four years later, he was serving as chair of the House Committee on Indian Affairs and helped pushed through the Kaw Allotment Act. As a member of the tribe, he and his two children received an allotment of approximately six hundred acres of tribal land.[48]

In 1924 Congress passed the Indian Citizenship Act, which endowed all Native people "born within the territorial limits of the United States" with citizenship rights. The act also stipulated that citizenship did not "impair or otherwise affect the right of any Indian to tribal or other property." Although the Indian Citizenship Act had passed just a week after the National Origins Act that restricted American immigration, in neither debate did legislators make explicit links to the other.[49] The juxtaposition of their timing, however, suggests a relationship in policy makers' minds. Both pieces of legislation were part of the drawing of boundaries around citizenship and the nation's population that occurred around the turn of the century. White Americans experienced growing anxiety as the number of immigrants from southern and eastern European countries increased populations in the United States whom they believed were "different" from "real Americans," who they defined as descendants of northern Europeans.[50] The act was designed to limit this migration by using a tiered system of immigration quotas that heavily favored immigrants from northern European countries. It also reinforced that people from China did not merit citizenship, making the Exclusion Acts permanent, and expanded those restrictions to all immigrants from Asia. At the same time, the government granted citizenship to some populations under the wardship of the United States. In 1917 the government extended citizenship to Puerto Ricans with the Jones-Shafroth Act. The rhetoric of Native men's military service along with the hardening of the nation's boundaries helped convince federal officials to rectify what they saw as the anomaly of Native wards within the nation's borders.[51]

Some Indigenous people, including many Haudenosaunee, refused the offer of U.S. citizenship, but Bonnin was thrilled. She later included "Helped get Act through Congress granting citizenship to all Indians" in a list of her greatest accomplishments.[52] She believed that enfranchisement offered Native people a way to engage the system and make changes in their communities. She quickly acted to work with newly empowered Native people to use this to their advantage. Initially, she joined the advisory committee of John Collier's American Indian Defense Association, but, as her biographer states, she had always believed that women should lead the fight. Two years later, she acted on that belief.

In February 1926, Bonnin and her husband, Raymond, founded the National Council of American Indians (NCAI), giving it the motto "Help Indians Help Themselves in Protecting Their Rights and Properties." By now, she was well versed in organizing. She printed up letterhead and wrote a constitution and by-laws laying out the shape of the association. She gave herself, as president, a great deal of control. She would preside over all meetings and sign and execute any documents required and authorized by the board of directors. Moreover, all officers and committees would report to her annually. This would be her show.[53]

President Bonnin's first action was to send a petition to Congress announcing the association's intent. She modeled the statement on the Declaration of Independence and emphasized that the relationship between Native nations and the United States was based on treaties that recognized tribal sovereignty and land rights. In light of the recent citizenship legislation, the NCAI was "a constructive effort to better the Red Race and make its members better citizens of the United States." But this could not be achieved "unless the Indians are accorded the rights essential to racial self-respect and a spirit of loyalty to the United States," rights that the petition demonstrated had been repeatedly violated. If the United States would not uphold treaty promises that guaranteed the right to self-government and land, then "the citizenship that has been conferred upon them" was only "a sham" that "increased their liabilities without in fact according them the rights of human beings, much less those of citizens."[54]

The NCAI would use suffrage to pressure the United States to respect those rights. In relating the organization's origin story, Bonnin described having been attacked by South Dakota congressman William Williamson from the floor of the House during debates. The Native delegations there for the hearings were shocked and outraged, as were the Bonnins. After talking it over, they determined to form an organization for mutual support. The bill under debate, for example, would give the Bureau of Indian Affairs the power to imprison Indians under its jurisdiction for up to six months. There was a deeper motive, Bonnin stated: "*They want to take all the land away from the Indians.*" Writing to Native people in South Dakota about the new organization, she asserted that "Williamson is no friend to any Indian" and urged, "You Indians out there should see to it he does not get re-elected. You should all register and vote against him."[55]

Bonnin convinced a group of non-Native financial backers to hire Raymond Bonnin as an investigative agent for Native communities that summer. The couple took extended trips into Indian country during the summer months for the next three years. Such trips aligned with the congressional calendar and suited the Bonnins plans for the NCAI. In the post–Indian Citizenship Act world, she looked to local Native communities rather than to the Indigenous intellectuals who lived primarily in cities (like herself). Instead, she proposed that her new organization would work "to establish Local Lodges in Indian country for self-help and study." Their travels allowed them to visit reservation communities and advocate for the new organization.[56]

She and Raymond packed up and went on the road in June 1926. They put over 10,000 miles on their car that year visiting Native communities. Despite citizenship, Gertrude Bonnin observed that "the outstanding wrongs throughout the entire Indian reservations of the United States are: Starvation, imprisonment, lack of proper medical care for the sick, wasting Indian property under Bureau control, withholding Indian tribal and individual funds, misappropriation of these funds, starving school children, whipping, killing, and breaking child labor laws by placing heavy institutional work upon young boys and girls."

With their NCAI work, the Bonnins set forth an ambitious agenda: "to organize Indian voters" to change those conditions. "Only when the Indian wields his vote effectively will the system be reformed," they believed. If "their political influence [was] felt by congress," their goals could be accomplished. Bonnin also reminded the local lodges of the NCAI that voters meant both men and women. Remember, she wrote, "women are invited to join because women are voters. They must join, and try to be informed about their tribal affairs, so that every Indian man and woman will vote for the benefit of themselves as a whole."[57]

In fact, the Bonnins' work in 1926 seemed to reinforce the difference Native voters could make. The NCAI took aim at Congressman Williamson of South Dakota, distributing a pamphlet critical of his record on Indian policy titled *Representative William Williamson and the Indians*. The pamphlet concluded by asserting, "The Time for Scaring Indians Has passed." His opponent reached out to the NCAI, and the organization campaigned for him. Despite this hard work, Williamson won, but the NCAI was able to celebrate the defeat of Senator John Harreld of Oklahoma, who had served as chairman of the Senate Committee on Indian Affairs. He also represented the state whose corrupt guardianship system had so outraged Gertrude Bonnin. The group also claimed to have a hand in electing a congressman who was supported by the Native people of South Dakota. And it kept up its work; the following year, the NCAI printed another pamphlet, *Information Service for Indian Citizen Voters on Scattered Indian Reservations*, to educate Native voters.[58] As one non-Native observer concluded, "Thus did the

Indians[,] forced into politics at last, manifest the power with which the politicians unwittingly had but recently endowed them. The cry which now arose from the defeated candidates was long and loud!"[59]

Indeed, these actions did seem to cause consternation.[60] Congressman Williamson again attacked Bonnin on the floor of Congress, likely in response to her pamphlet. Describing her as one "who poses as president" of the NCAI, he dismissed her work (including her criticisms of his record) as uninformed. She was one of the "self-styled friends of the Indians [who] do them a great wrong . . . by false or misleading statements," he charged. At no point did he acknowledge that Bonnin was a Native woman from South Dakota. Reservation officials also expressed skepticism about the Bonnins' visits. On the Standing Rock Sioux Reservation, Superintendent Mossman did not believe they "were the sort of people to make research investigations" and tried to ban Gertrude Bonnin from the reservation. Concerned about the potential political ramifications of the Bonnins' visit, he sent a questionnaire to his sub-agents asking them a series of questions about the "Activities of the Princess," including, "What effect did it have on the Indians?" In a 1928 congressional hearing, in response to the question, "What is Mrs. Bonnin doing on the reservation?," one official replied, "Raising hell as usual."[61]

The outcome of the election of 1928 seemed to justify Gertrude Bonnin's optimism in participating in the electoral system, and yet it obscured a more concerning trend. That year Republicans nominated Senator Charles Curtis as Herbert Hoover's vice presidential candidate.[62] The Boston Globe announced that the candidate was "Curtis, of Kaw Indian Ancestry, Lived as a Boy in Prairie Tepee." Such a description would have sounded familiar to Indigenous public figures like Bonnin, as it represented non-Natives' difficulty in reconciling modern Native lives.[63]

Curtis appealed to many constituents. Because of his support of the ERA, the National Woman's Party endorsed the Republican ticket. The party announced that its platform "accepts wholeheartedly equality on the part of women" and pointed to its record in appointing women in "the legal, diplomatic, judicial, treasury, and other governmental departments" as well as to its own national committee. In a reminder of women's new political power, Curtis's daughter Leona Curtis Knight, a delegate from Rhode Island, seconded his nomination.[64]

Bonnin and the NCAI had also used their political connections and the Republican Party's interest in "the Indian vote" to influence the Republican platform. Written by a member and approved by the NCAI leadership, the plank went into the platform without changes (where it was followed by an anti-lynching plank).[65] It began with a reminder that with the Citizenship Act, "national citizenship was conferred upon all native-born Indians in the United States." It then called for the creation of a committee to investigate "the rights of the Indian citizens" as well as the "repeal of any law and the termination of any administrative practice which may be inconsistent with Indian citizenship." It forcefully concluded, "The treaty and property rights of the Indians of the United States must be guaranteed to them."[66]

Soon after Charles Curtis won the nomination, he visited the Kaw nation, which held a feast in his honor. One article described the visit as one in which the "primitive and the modern are strangely blended." It would be primitive because "the ancient form of Indian feast will be followed, in which the food is cooked over open air fires and men and women sit apart while they eat." And yet, it would also be modern because the chief "who will preside over the festivities, is a woman," Lucy Tayiah Eads. Americans were struck by this representation of a Native nation that could maintain its traditional culture while simultaneously adjusting to the modern world. As if to help them resolve this seeming paradox, the article concluded by stating that "nearly every member of the tribe — even those accounted 'full bloods' — has a strain of French blood." For their part, the Kaw were proud of Curtis but also hopeful that with one of their own as vice president, their land claims might be addressed. The government owed them $15,000,000 for their reservation in Kansas, from which they were removed in 1873. Like the Turtle Mountain Chippewa, the Kaw claimed their land was worth much more than the ten cents an acre the federal government had paid them for it.[67]

Other Native voters were also thrilled by the nomination. Many attended Curtis's rallies and cheered him on. Papers reported that Natives in Montana, including women, were eagerly registering to vote.[68] Other Native people worked for the campaign, including Omaha Eunice Stabler, who took a position with Nebraska's Republican State Committee as a member of its Speakers' Bureau in the "Indian Field."[69]

Curtis's place on the Republican ticket highlighted Native issues and forced the Democratic candidate Al Smith to tout his own credentials. John Collier wrote Smith's statement on Indian policy. It excoriated Republican Indian policy since 1921, pointing to the Bursum Bill, Albert Fall's corruption, and the recently released Meriam Report from the Brookings Institution. The statement promised to "stop the slow massacre" of Native people and give them a future.[70] In interviews, Smith pointed to his work with the Haudenosaunee in New York during his time as governor.[71] Laura Cornelius Kellogg supported Smith and stumped for him in Michigan, stating, "Hoover hasn't got all the Indian votes." She vehemently disagreed with the Curtis Act's attack on tribal sovereignty, but she may also have believed an endorsement from the former New York governor could help Haudenosaunee land claims.[72]

Bonnin was happy to have a Native man on the ticket and congratulated Curtis on his nomination. "Honor is reflected upon our Indian race," she wrote. Soon after, she sent letters to both presidential candidates asking for "justice for the American Indians" and policies that would give them "a voice in their own affairs." Smith responded; Hoover did not. That, along with the Republicans' grievous Indian policy record of the past decade, led the NCAI to endorse Smith. "Vote for the man who will help you," Bonnin urged her membership.[73]

The year 1928 also highlighted white fears of new Native voters. In some states, their numbers could make a difference. An article on Oklahoma observed that the "racial pride of the Indians" may be a "determining factor in the outcome." Another astutely noted that while the total number of Native voters was low overall, in states like Oklahoma, Arizona, New Mexico, Montana, and South Dakota, "practically solid voting by Indians would be influential in determining the outcome." The author also observed that "political strategy is including careful study of the Indian situation," and "the Indians will have no cause to complain about a lack of political attention."[74] And yet after 1928, that did not come to pass.

A number of states had previously excluded Indians from voting, but the Citizenship Act and the mobilizing of "the Indian vote" in the elections of the 1920s raised the question again, leading many to implement new laws. The Montana legislature moved quickly, instituting at-large elections for county commissioners. More insidiously, it passed a law stating that only qualified taxpaying residents of their respective districts could serve as deputy registrars, thus disqualifying most Native people. Then it dropped all registered voters from the state rolls and required that they re-register, a task made exceptionally difficult in Native communities by that very lack of deputy registrars.[75]

In Arizona, two men from the Gila River Reservation registered to vote but found on Election Day that their names had been dropped. The registrar, Mattie M. Hall, was a white woman who had run for the office in 1926. The men sued, but the Arizona Supreme Court ruled in *Porter v. Hall* that despite the Citizenship Act, Natives living on reservations remained under federal guardianship and were ineligible to vote under Arizona's constitution. Similar tactics were used across the country, much like the Jim Crow laws that disenfranchised African Americans. Western legislators also used the unique relationship between Native nations and the federal government to aid in that disenfranchisement.[76] Gertrude Bonnin was outraged: "If our Vice-President-elect, Hon. Charles Curtis, an Indian, had lived as a member of a tribe on a reservation in Arizona, he would be disfranchised. He could not vote, much less run for the Vice-Presidency of the United States," she argued.[77] Nonetheless, the ruling in Arizona stood until 1948, when two Yavapai Apache men successfully brought suit before the Arizona Supreme Court.[78]

The passage of the Indian Citizenship Act of 1924 brought an initial wave of excitement about "the Native vote" and how it would reshape American politics, much as the ratification of the Nineteenth Amendment raised similar questions about the women's vote. Native suffragists like Gertrude Bonnin believed they could now effect change through the ballot box. Other political observers, including party leadership, calculated how Native populations, especially those concentrated in certain states or counties, might change the balance of power, and they speculated as to what that would mean. But it turned out that the more precise analogy was with the experience of African American women in the Jim Crow South and the vigorous efforts to disenfranchise them and reinscribe existing power relations. States with large Native populations borrowed heavily from those southern examples while also using Native people's unique relationship to the federal government to keep them from voting.

We live with this legacy today. On one hand, Native women continued to engage in formal political activism over the course of the century, both in U.S. and tribal politics.[79] This work culminated in the election in 2018 of the first two Native women to the House of Representatives: Deb Haaland (Laguna Pueblo) of New Mexico and Sharice Davids (Ho-Chunk) of Kansas. But efforts to suppress Native voters also continue. The same election saw North Dakota state officials argue that street addresses were required to register to vote, effectively disenfranchising Native people on reservations, including Turtle Mountain, where the Bureau of Indian Affairs and tribal governments have not assigned street addresses. Other communities continue to face obstructions such as long distances to registration sites or polling stations and at-large voting districts that work to undermine concentrated populations of Native people. If there is one thing that was and remains clear, it is that the energy that suffragists of color have put into the right to vote matters greatly. If it did not, they would not have faced such deep resistance to their participation.

Remembering and Forgetting

The suffragists of color whose stories are told in *Recasting the Vote* waged lengthy campaigns for the ballot and advanced the cause in multiple ways: they delivered speeches, marched in parades, lobbied politicians, hoisted banners, wrote pamphlets, and convened meetings. They contributed key arguments to the suffrage movement while also encouraging new groups of women to join the ranks. Their numbers were sometimes small, but their presence in public debates was greatly amplified by their symbolic role in arguments over the vote. They leveraged white Americans' interest in their communities in order to win opportunities to address larger national audiences. They then used those platforms to educate the public and to seek allies for their causes among white women. Their struggles for equality transcended the suffrage movement as conventionally understood because they addressed issues that were vital to their communities. While they shared some experiences, women of color did not form a coherent group: the way they engaged was shaped by their position in America's racial hierarchies, their citizenship status, and their class standing.

In the years since, however, the historical literature on suffrage has remained overwhelmingly focused on white women who gained the right to vote in 1920. More recently scholars have highlighted the important work done by black women, but other women of color rarely appear.[1] Including these suffragists of color in our histories of the movement requires that we expand the geographic and temporal bounds of our usual narratives. When the struggle is seen from their perspectives, places seemingly on the periphery of the story of woman suffrage in the United States — South Dakota, New Mexico, Hawaii, Canton (Guangdong) — suddenly become closely connected. Moreover, for many of these women the struggle for voting rights spanned 1920. Ending the story of suffrage in that year truncates and obscures the full range of women's contributions.

Suffragists of color engaged in both a historic struggle and a contest over historical memory. They understood that the histories white Americans were telling themselves shaped their ideas about who belonged, who deserved citizenship, and whose rights should be upheld. This is not surprising, as the template for those histories was set in this period.

In the decades around the turn of the century, the question of who was an American took on intense meaning. A wide variety of changes drove this issue: women demanding the right to vote, the so-called closing of the frontier, demands for equal citizenship by African Americans, urban growth and industrialization, increased immigration from eastern and southern Europe, and the nation's expansion and annexation of overseas territories, which brought many people of color into the nation's citizenry.[2]

White Americans faced these challenges with nostalgia for the mythical past of their parents and grandparents. They told themselves stories about how their ancestors built the nation and thus had claim to it. The Daughters and Sons of the American Revolution traced their genealogies back to the ships sailing from England, and they lauded forefathers who fought the British. They searched their attics for their foremothers' spinning wheels and exalted women's contributions to the Revolutionary boycotts. They memorialized the ways their ancestors had tested their mettle against the "wilderness" and against the noble Indians who had lived in it, all supposedly long gone in the age of progress.[3] Historian Frederick Jackson Turner lamented the end of the frontier, while Buffalo Bill performed it.

In the American South, the sons and daughters of Confederates built an imposing historical narrative about a past in which genteel white planters and their southern belles had paternalistically watched over their simple slaves. The Civil War and Reconstruction had destroyed this idyllic way of life, they argued, and left former slaves free to follow their worst tendencies, including giving in to their violent personal and political passions. White southerners spread this gospel of the noble Lost Cause far and wide across the nation, raising statues, dedicating highways, and inscribing it in history books.[4]

White suffragists also recognized the power of history. They fought against the idea of "great man history" by insisting that there had also been great women. Those suffragists happened to be white, and they used the same tools that had been used to venerate great white men: monuments, busts, collections in libraries and museums, and historical volumes. Their insistence on placing a statue of Susan B. Anthony, Elizabeth Cady Stanton, and Lucretia Mott in the Capitol Rotunda was part of their efforts.[5]

Additionally, many of the women carefully chronicled their experiences in the suffrage fight. Carrie Chapman Catt wrote several memoirs. Doris Stevens of the National Woman's Party wrote *Jailed for Freedom*, and National American Woman Suffrage Association lobbyist Maud Wood Park published her memoir. As Lisa Tetrault has revealed, Anthony, along with Matilda Joslyn Gage, Ida Husted Harper, and others, carefully crafted the story of the movement in their magisterial six-volume *History of Woman Suffrage*. Anthony ensured that theirs would be the last word. Through her networks, she asked her fellow suffragists to send in their materials, scrapbooks, letters, and memorabilia from the fight. She kept it all in her attic, meticulously organized, as she and Harper wrote their history. When they finished, many years later, she took all the materials and documents into her backyard and burned them. She solidified the story she wanted told. That story, too, was powerful but, as we have seen, left out many people.[6]

Histories like these were everywhere and suggested that white people were the real Americans; others were too violent, too primitive, too Catholic, too brown, too new, too foreign to be true Americans. The stories were very powerful and very compelling—and, as the women of color knew, very incomplete and often false. In response, they fought back against their erasure and defamation by embedding their own histories and community stories in a variety of ways and places.

A TEPEE IN ARLINGTON NATIONAL CEMETERY: GERTRUDE SIMMONS BONNIN, ZITKALA-ŠA OF THE SIOUX

Before Gertrude Bonnin died in 1938, she chose—or perhaps Raymond, her partner in activism all those years, chose for her—to be buried across the river from the nation's capital in Arlington National Cemetery. This privilege was open to her because of her husband's service to the nation during the World War, but she and Raymond were making a significant symbolic gesture about citizenship and belonging.[7] She had always insisted on the sovereignty of the Yankton Dakota (Sioux) nation but also claimed U.S. citizenship and had been proud of her husband's service in the U.S. Army. She had also spent a large portion of her life in Washington, D.C.

Her tombstone left a final statement of identity, with a Plains-style tepee engraved on the back and the inscription "Gertrude Bonnin 'Zitkala-Ša' of the Sioux Indians" on the front. It was very theatrical, very bold, very Gertrude Bonnin. She declared herself proudly Indigenous, proudly Sioux, proudly American in the heart of U.S. military memorialization. Members of the Seventh Cavalry had been laid to rest there as well.[8] Bonnin's gesture refused the erasure of her Indigenous nation, denied the binaries of Indian or American, and claimed both.

Her tombstone endures, leaving that message to the future. At the time of her death, the New York Times, the Washington Evening Star, and the Washington Post all ran obituaries for her praising her work, especially as president of the National Council of American Indians. All also perpetuated the story that she was a granddaughter of Sitting Bull—again, symbolically if not actually true. Commissioner of Indian Affairs John Collier, speaking at Washington's Church of the Latter-day Saints at a memorial service arranged by longtime friends from Utah, acknowledged, "The Sioux and all Indians have lost a real leader."[9]

And yet, as her biographer suggests, among white Americans her legacy was already fading. Indicative of that was the description written by the doctor who performed her autopsy: "Gertrude Bonnin from South Dakota—Housewife." In the spring, just a few months after her death, a revised version of The Sun Dance Opera, which she had cowritten with William Hanson, debuted with the New York Light Opera Guild. Hanson claimed that the opera was his alone, and she received virtually no credit as a collaborator. Most notably, as a writer, she was forgotten for several decades.[10]

It was only with the rise of the Red Power movement in the 1960s and 1970s; the subsequent development of ethnic studies, especially Native American studies; and the republication of her works that a new generation was introduced to her arguments and claims. This led to a great deal of scholarship on her published works. But her most explicit writings on the vote remain unpublished, and as a result, her role in suffrage activism has rarely been emphasized in that scholarship. Her activism as a suffragist should also be part of her legacy as a Native intellectual.[11]

SOWING FOR OTHERS TO REAP: CARRIE WILLIAMS CLIFFORD

By 1927, Carrie Williams Clifford, normally a fount of energy, was tired. She confessed her frustration in a letter to her friend W. E. B. Du Bois: "If I had time to devote to it, I feel I could do a great deal; but the care of my husband, whose long continued illness has sapped me physically and mentally, prevents my doing very much."[12] When William died later that year, Carrie may have hoped for a return to her activism. But her own age became a drag on her abilities. Just a few years later, in 1932, the now seventy-year-old Carrie Clifford wrote again to Du Bois, "My interest in the NAACP is as keen as ever, but [alas] I am not physically able to work as I formally did. The weight of years sits heavily upon me."[13] Like many women, Clifford had led a remarkably active life but one that ebbed and flowed around the rhythms of her domestic responsibilities. Caretaking and aging were constant refrains in the lives of the women discussed here. On November 10, 1934, she died at her home in Washington after a short illness. Her sons, Joshua and Maurice, buried her next to William in the Woodlawn Cemetery in Cleveland, Ohio.[14]

Clifford's life of activism and her publications have formed the basis upon which she is remembered a century later. Her writings remain in the pages of journals, and her volumes of poetry are stored in libraries across the nation. She has been praised by the Ohio Federation of Colored Women's Clubs and the Washington NAACP, who continue to remember her as their founder. Her family kept her memory alive as well. In the 1970s, Carrie Clifford's granddaughter Rosemary Clifford Wilson reissued her poetry with an introduction that, like Clifford herself, insisted on the importance of black women's history. Clifford's great-granddaughter and family historian, Rosemary Clifford McDaniels, has continued to collaborate with scholars and to do family research.[15]

More recently, growing attention has resulted in Carrie Clifford being remembered in other ways as well. In 2012 the Woodland Cemetery Foundation in Cleveland received grants from the United Black Fund and the Cuyahoga Arts and Culture Agency to place a new headstone on the graves of William and Carrie

Clifford. It was installed at the cemetery on June 24, 2012, for Black History Day. The marker is engraved with the seals of the NAACP and the state of Ohio and includes mottos for both husband and wife. William's reads "Living to Serve," while Carrie's echoes the title of her first book, "Sowing for Others to Reap."[16]

We should be grateful to Carrie Clifford for the seeds of history she planted one hundred years ago, which I and other scholars have found, following her life through the pages of books, the letters of organizations, and articles in newspapers, many of which she wrote herself, always insisting that black women's history mattered and deserved to be preserved. Her granddaughter Rosemary Clifford Wilson has continued that tradition. As she said of her grandmother, "She was a black woman who lived and spoke and wrote and worked ceaselessly for the rights of all black people." Without those writings or that work, our history would be less rich.

OUR DEBT TO THE RED MAN:
MARIE LOUISE BOTTINEAU BALDWIN

By 1919, Marie Bottineau Baldwin was feeling isolated and pushed aside in the Society of American Indians, the group she had helped found. Gertrude Bonnin was both editor of the SAI's journal and had just been elected secretary, the true leadership position for the organization. Any of the work that Marie had formerly done for the SAI—writing articles for the journal, coordinating mailings through the Bureau of Indian Affairs office, giving talks at the annual meeting—had been done in cooperation with the former secretary, Arthur C. Parker. Now she would have to work with Bonnin, and the two women did not get along. She stopped going to SAI meetings and concentrated on her work in the Indian Office, disappearing from many of the usual notices in newspapers and letters in the SAI papers.

Bottineau Baldwin also may have been deeply struck by the sudden death of her best friend, Angel DeCora, in February 1919. In her will, DeCora left her beautiful wooden Winnebago (Ho-Chunk) flute to Bottineau Baldwin.[17] Perhaps that inspired Bottineau Baldwin to focus on her collecting, which she used to resist the erasure of Native women's lives. She had always been interested in women's artistic creations, likely a legacy of her mother's emphasis on embroidery. She had kept a collection of Indigenous women's work, many of the pieces purchased from her relatives at the White Earth Reservation in Minnesota. She had added to it by acquiring the collection of another Native collector, "a Miami Indian, who at the time was an agent traveling throughout the Indian reservations of the country." That purchase added "some beautiful pieces of Navajo, Hopi, Pueblo and other tribal handiwork."[18] A few years later, she mounted a display of her collection in the Indian Office's library at the Department of the Interior. Although federal policies had shifted in the 1920s to welcome greater incorporation of Native music and "crafts" into boarding school curricula, the preponderance of those

Bottineau Baldwin used her high profile to celebrate Native women's artwork and to make claims to the ongoing value of Indigenous cultures. This photograph of her with items from her art collection—including a buckskin shirt decorated with American flags—appeared in the August 22, 1925, edition of the Washington Post's *"What a Capital Camera Sees" feature. Four years later she displayed her collection in the Department of the Interior building. (Courtesy Library of Congress Prints and Photographs Division, Washington, D.C.)*

policies was still to destroy Native cultures and replace them with middle-class American values. In displaying her collection in the bureaucratic heart of the Indian Office, Bottineau Baldwin insisted that Native women's traditional skills had merit, creativity, and beauty. In the various articles that accompanied the exhibit, she also continued to emphasize that Native people could comfortably live in the modern world. She used her own experience as an example, narrating her history as a story of progress from wilderness to modernity with which Americans were quite familiar. "I have traveled in practically every conveyance known to this country. I have traveled by 'travois,' . . . I also traveled in a prairie schooner in 1874 from Minneapolis to what is now Red Lake Falls, Minn. I traveled by canoe from Pembina, N.Dak., to Winnipeg, Canada, and back to Breckenridge, Minn. And now I can say I have traveled by airplane, and I find it is wonderful." As a Native woman symbolically marching through technological advances, she undercut the narrative that it was white Americans who had history and Indians who were stuck in the past.[19]

By 1932 Bottineau Baldwin, too, was feeling the weight of her age. Chronic hip pain caused enough mobility problems that she retired that year. Perhaps her health brought her thoughts of mortality. Like her father upon his retirement, she began to focus on maintaining her family's history and their contributions to U.S. history. Her interests were further galvanized in 1933 by a threat to the Bottineau legacy. The area of Minneapolis where Pierre Bottineau had a farm had changed dramatically over the years. By the 1930s, it was a predominantly Polish neighborhood. The community there wanted to make its own claims to an American past. Citizens approached the city with the request that Bottineau Field be renamed for the famous Polish Revolutionary War hero Casimir Pulaski. There were too few monuments to the Polish contribution to American history, they argued. Latching onto the classic American story of white settlers developing civilization out of the wilderness, local Poles claimed they had created a neighborhood out of what had before been prairie.[20]

Others came to the defense of Bottineau Field. The Polish were not the only people in the neighborhood, they insisted; Germans, Scandinavians, and others were represented, too. Community organizers got a message to Marie Bottineau Baldwin in Washington, and she wrote a lengthy letter to the city's park board objecting to the change. In it she "outlined the Bottineau history in considerable detail," staking a claim to her grandfather's role in the creation of the city. Ultimately, the parks commissioner ruled against the name change, as the city had a policy of naming parks and playgrounds for "Minneapolitans."[21]

A few months later, at a meeting of the Hennepin County Territorial Pioneers Association, "sixty of the first settlers" sat in the kitchen and living room of the Godfrey house celebrating firsts. Their number included the "first white girl born in the village of St. Anthony," as Minneapolis had been called, and the house in which they met was the first frame dwelling built in the city. These events were sure markers of the transition of the space from Native territory to American "civilization." As they reminisced, the settlers passed around "bows and arrows gathered up after the Sioux massacre of 1862," today known as the Dakota War. Those talismans suggested a story of Indian aggression that had been punished and one in which the offenders had been removed. That some Native people remained was forgotten.

Indeed, at the very same meeting they passed around other "relics" and told stories about them as well. Those relics included a pair of snowshoes used by Pierre Bottineau, described as the "famous trapper and guide," seemingly having morphed into a white pioneer.[22] This was part of a larger shift in which white Minnesotans embraced him as a settler rather than as an Indigenous person. It hinged on their inability to see beyond a binary of white or Indian, which also tracked onto the present and the past. Indians had faded into the past, while whites had brought settlement to the country. In their telling, Indians had been the aggressors in the Dakota War, and Bottineau had been a pioneer. His more

EPILOGUE

complicated story as an Anishinaabe cultural broker was erased and made palatable.

How much did Marie Bottineau Baldwin contribute to this narrative whitening? In 1929 she donated portraits of her grandfather Pierre and her father, Jean Bottineau, to the Minnesota Historical Society.[23] Oil paintings of great men were a standard trope of Western historical tradition, but the society does not have a record of any other information that came with the portraits. Her letter to the park board might have offered some clue, but it was not retained in their files.[24] Certainly earlier in her life she had not shied away from insisting on an identity that was both Indigenous and European. From her work in the Society of American Indians to her contributions to the book *Our Debt to the Red Man*, a history that explicitly celebrated the French Indian or Métis contributions to American history, she never hid her Indigenous heritage. Moreover, in her obituary for her father, she referred to him as "a French-Chippewa, mixed blood."[25] She was proud of her family's role in helping to create modern Minnesota, but she was also proud of being a Native woman, and it seems unlikely that after a lifetime of celebrating that heritage she would choose to hide it in her final decades.

Details of Bottineau Baldwin's later life are elusive, and few records remain to tell us about it. The 1940 census lists her as living in Minnesota with her sister, Lillian. In 1949, her sister passed away and Bottineau Baldwin moved to California. Her nephew Earl Nichols lived in Los Angeles, but she also had connections there through Rilla Meek, a good friend from her Washington days who had married and moved to Los Angeles. There was also a large Native community in that city thanks to the film industry, and it had been a dream of hers to fly across the country to the West Coast. She lived quietly in Los Angeles for a few more years before dying in 1952 from a cerebral hemorrhage at the age of eighty-eight.[26]

Bottineau Baldwin's death was a quiet event for such a pathbreaker; a mere one-sentence funeral notice appeared in the *Los Angeles Times* stating that she was buried in Forest Lawn Cemetery. It said nothing about her important life, nor did it identify her as Ojibwe. It was likely her nephew who made the arrangements, as he signed her death certificate. It does not seem that he inherited the family interest in history, or perhaps he did not have the means to do so. The fate of her art collection is unknown.[27] Her history faded over the twentieth century, kept in small pockets here and there—in the name of a scholarship for women of color at the Washington College of Law, in the records of the Society of American Indians, and in portraits held by the Library of Congress.

OLD SPAIN IN OUR SOUTHWEST: NINA OTERO-WARREN

In New Mexico, along with their ongoing involvement in politics, Nina Otero-Warren and Aurora Lucero also turned to history. They increasingly emphasized Spanish cultural heritage as a way of laying claim to Americanness. Both had long been advocates of the Spanish language, protecting and promoting it in their role as educators in the state.

The political power of Spanish speakers in New Mexico had diminished with the influx of Anglos, as Otero-Warren knew. Her life had spanned those changes, and she had been touched by their violence. While Spanish speakers certainly remained important constituents and still advocated for the use of Spanish, as Rosina Lozano has noted, their arguments began to shift by the 1930s. They now framed their support for Spanish as a language of heritage and an instrument to help the United States develop its pan-American reach. These were arguments that women like Otero-Warren and Lucero had been making for many years. They may have reached a more receptive audience in the 1930s, however.[28]

Otero-Warren engaged in her first written history when she authored a piece for *Survey Graphic* in 1931. She had been encouraged by her friends in the flourishing art colony of Santa Fe—including feminist author Mary Austin, poet Witter Bynner, and the editor of *Poetry* magazine, Alice Corbin Henderson[29]—to capture on paper the stories and performances she had shared with them over the years. The issue of *Survey Graphic* addressed the question of the growing number of Mexican immigrants to the United States, describing both Mexicans and Mexican Americans at a time when the U.S. census had just classified both groups under the term "Mexican" as a race rather than a nationality. It included pieces by sociologist Paul Taylor, husband of Dorothea Lange and expert on migrant labor in California; the novelist D. H. Lawrence; and poet Mary Austin. The visual material in the issue included a photograph by Ansel Adams on the frontispiece, a painting by Georgia O'Keeffe, and drawings and murals by Diego Rivera.[30]

By contrast, Otero-Warren's article insisted on identifying Nuevomexicanos as Spanish-Americans. In the article, titled "My People" and published under the name Adelina Otero, she described the beauty of the northern New Mexico villages and landscapes she encountered during her work as county superintendent of schools. She called on her audience to consider a curriculum that might "preserve the arts, the customs, and the traditions of this New Spain in an effort to save its charm, which is its very life." As she walked her readers through the villages and customs of New Mexicans, she reminded them of the relationship between Hispanics and the United States and of their claims to citizenship. This was, she suggested, a two-way relationship. "The appeal which I make to my people is this: that since the American Occupation in 1846, we have been American citizens, members of *another* great nation, and it is to our best interests that we become educated according to the standards of that nation."[31] She reminded her Anglo audience that "whether it is in defense of America or war with Spain, we respond. We are avowedly citizens of the United States. There is no shirking of our suffrage responsibility. In times of national and state elections we go eagerly to the polls, for we love the political game." And yet, despite their deep claims to

Americanness, they did not want to lose their distinctive culture. "What, then, is to be the trend of education in New Mexico? Is it not a question of our gradual merging, of our assimilation, into this great nation, but at the same time of conserving our distinctive contribution through the preservation of the customs, traditions, the arts and crafts of the Spanish Southwest?" Increasing numbers of Anglos were moving into the state, she noted, but only the one who "takes this country and the people into his heart" could truly appreciate it. Without that embrace, "we still remain foreign to him."[32]

She used deliberate language to emphasize their identity. They were Spanish, people with a European heritage, but one that was unique to the Southwest. She carefully avoided the more racially ambiguous term "Mexican." "Why are we Catholics?" one of her characters asks. "Because we are Spanish," comes the answer. Throughout the article, she demonstrated that Hispanics were also patriotic Americans, from the schoolchildren who sang "My Country 'Tis of Thee" as well as "La Golondrina" to the American flag flying on a pine tree in front of the schoolhouse.

But this Americanness rested on the conquest of Indigenous peoples. The Spanish also had their history of conquest, she reminded Anglos, even earlier than their Puritan ancestors, if they did the math. "The Spaniards made their first stand against the Indian early in the 16th century" and then "reigned supreme over New Spain," she pointed out to her readers. After the annexation they became "a part of e pluribus unum!"[33] Such touchstones in American history, conquest of Native people and the incorporation of multiple groups of Europeans into the nation's citizenry, would have been very familiar to her readers and supported her community's claims to full citizenship.

At the same time, she was working on a book manuscript based on her childhood memories from Los Lunas that she ultimately published as Old Spain in Our Southwest in 1936. As the title suggests, she insisted on the importance of the Spanish experience in American history, but she also imagined the Southwest explicitly as part of the United States and herself as part of it as well with the use of the word "our." The book became an important staple in children's literature throughout the twentieth century.

When Franklin Roosevelt came into office, Otero-Warren, a former Republican, accepted a position with his administration as the state director for the Civilian Conservation Corps. In this capacity, she continued to emphasize education and bilingual literacy. The work eventually led to a position as director of the Work Conference for Adult Teachers in Puerto Rico.

Aurora Lucero also turned to writing to make claims to belonging and nation-building in the United States. In publishing Spanish literary traditions in the Southwest, she also emphasized the deep European past in that region. This included articles for New Mexico Magazine. In 1925 she published a booklet, Los Hispanos, with Sage Press out of Denver, Colorado. The raw material of the work—traditional Spanish-language stories, songs, and plays—had been gathered from their communities by her students at Pojoaque High School and later Highlands University in Las Vegas, New Mexico. She also did some collecting while working for the Works Progress Administration's Federal Writers' Project. *Los Hispanos* later became a section of her 1953 book *Literary Folklore of the Hispanic Southwest*.[34] Most of her publications came out in the 1940s and included *Folk Dances of the Spanish-Colonials of New Mexico* (1940), *Coloquios de los Pastores* (1940), and *The Folklore of New Mexico* (1941). Her bibliography indicates that she was part of a larger group of southwestern Hispanic writers trying to preserve their traditions. Her citations include Nina Otero-Warren's *Old Spain in the Southwest*, Fabiola Gilbert's (Fabiola Cabeza de Bacas) *The Good Life* (1949), and Cleofas M. Jaramillo's *Shadows of Our Past* (1941).[35]

Those same women also joined Jaramillo's Sociedad Folklórica, founded in 1935. Its aim was to "preserve folklore of New Mexico." At their meetings they shared stories and plays, including some they later included in their publications. They also cared for and displayed historical dresses from their mothers and grandmothers. They brought all of these things together in the Santa Fe Fiesta, where they participated in their historic costumes, performed dances, and reminded the public of the long Spanish tradition in the Southwest.[36] Yet as the Spanish-speaking population of New Mexico sought to claim a place in the Eurocentric history of the United States, the fiesta's celebration of the Spanish past came at the expense of Indigenous New Mexicans, who were portrayed as conquered primitive people in contrast with "civilized" Europeans from Spain.[37]

Both Otero-Warren and Lucero died in 1965. It is striking that the deaths of these members of the previous generation of feminist politicians occurred the year that Patsy Takemoto Mink, a Japanese American woman from Hawaii, took her seat in the House of Representatives as the first woman of color elected to Congress.[38] These Hispana feminists are celebrated in New Mexico through murals, entries on state historical society web pages, and historical markers, but they are now little known outside the state. During the suffrage era, however, they were part of a national feminist fight for the suffrage amendment and dialogue around women's post-enfranchisement political engagement.

THE ONEIDA NATION: LAURA CORNELIUS KELLOGG

In 1920, the same year she published *Our Democracy and the American Indian*, the federal court ruling in *United States v. Boylan* offered Laura Cornelius Kellogg another avenue for advancing tribal self-determination and protecting sovereignty. In response, Kellogg shifted her efforts from voting to litigation and focused more than ever on Oneida nationhood. In *Boylan*, the U.S. Second Circuit Court found that New York had no right to dispose of Oneida land in the state despite the tribe's removal. This, Kellogg believed, made litigation based on treaties the best means to regain that land. During the next decade she would focus on building connections between Haudenosaunee people in Wisconsin, New York, and Canada while fundraising for lawsuits. She also sought to solidify those traditional alliances by restoring Haudenosaunee forms of governance under the clan mothers at Oneida.[39]

Indeed, in 1925, she attempted to revive the traditional system of tribal governance at Oneid by organizing "the biggest Indian ceremonials of the last 100 years." At the ceremony, eighteen Oneida chiefs representing three Oneida tribes—those who had remained in New York, the Wisconsin Oneida, and a third group that had moved to Ontario, Canada, in the 1840s—were formally "installed." Kellogg was hoping to strengthen both the Oneida nation and the old alliances of the Haudenosaunee Confederacy. As she stated, "The Six Nations inaugurated a program of rehabilitation and have re-established their chiefs throughout the Six Nations groups. These ceremonies at Oneida are part of this program." Oneida historian Doug Kiel emphasizes that the event celebrated Oneida culture rather than the pan-Indian vision of the SAI. The celebration featured Haudenosaunee social dancing and a dinner of traditional Oneida corn soup.[40]

Kellogg's emphasis on sovereignty and nationhood was based on the nation's relationship to land and the Haudenosaunee Confederacy. Installing new leaders went hand in hand with Kellogg's efforts to regain land owed the confederacy under treaties. She sought to finance the lawsuit by raising funds from members of the confederacy in New York and Canada, an effort that led to her arrest by the Royal Canadian Mounted Police in 1925. She and her husband were accused of "conspiring to obtain $15,000 by false pretense from Canadian Iroquois." The Canadian jury acquitted them, but the damage to her reputation was done. Her name evokes some mistrust in Haudenosaunee communities even today.[41]

In 1927 the U.S. District Court dismissed the Oneida land-claims suit in *Deere v. St. Laurence River Power Company*, arguing lack of jurisdiction. Kellogg continued to advocate for her nation, moving to Washington, D.C., to facilitate her work. Though a local Wisconsin newspaper praised her in 1935 as "one of the outstanding Indian women in Oneida history," historian Laurence Hauptman argues that her vision of tribal self-sufficiency was less appealing during the New Deal when federal policy changed to promote cultural relativism. He asserts that "by the 1940s she was a forgotten woman who had outlived her time. According to Oneida tribal sources, she died in obscurity sometime in the late 1940s."[42]

Kellogg's complicated legacy led to her being less well known than contemporaries like Gertrude Bonnin and Charles Eastman. Their books were republished during the mid-twentieth century and became staples in American Indian studies, literature, and history courses, but Kellogg's remained out of print.

Oneida scholar Kristina Ackley and her co-editor, Cristina Stanciu, reissued the book in 2015, almost one hundred years after its first publication. A novel Kellogg wrote remains lost to posterity.[43]

21 PELL STREET: DR. MABEL LEE

Mabel Ping-Hua Lee's legacy lives on in the bricks and mortar and in the memories of New York's First Chinese Baptist Church and in memories of its congregation. She spent the second half of her life working to make and keep that space for her community. They in turn have kept her memory for history.

Lee did not choose to go to China immediately after graduating. Perhaps it was too far from her parents. As an only child, she felt responsible for them, and they were aging. She also seems to have loved research. For two years, she continued to do work at Columbia, using her alumna status to access the libraries. Then in 1923 she planned a trip around the world to study economic systems in Europe and to visit China.

Before she could leave the country, however, Lee had to ensure that she could return. Her status required navigating the complex bureaucracy of the Chinese Department of the Immigration Service. She traveled from her home in northern Manhattan to the office of the inspector in charge of the Chinese Division, at the southern tip of the island. She filled in Form 431, "Application of Lawfully Domiciled Chinese Merchant, Teacher or Student, for Preinvestigation of Status," and endured an interrogation about her life and family. Perhaps annoyed by the whole process, she submitted her scholarly credentials in the form of her two diplomas from Columbia, both signed by President Nicholas Murray Butler and carrying the seal of the university. She also included her weighty 641-page dissertation. Surely these were proof enough that she had been engaged in the occupation of "student," a group exempt from the Chinese exclusion laws. Once again, the fact that the U.S. government did not trust Chinese people was made vivid as she was asked to provide the names of "credible witnesses other than Chinese" who could testify that she was who she said she was. With their corroboration, the government was willing to let Lee leave the country with assurances that she could return.[44]

As Lee toured Europe, the ravages of war remained visible on the landscape in France, while in Germany she experienced the plummeting value of the currency.[45] She continued on to China. It was her first visit since her arrival in the United States in 1901. Much had happened in that time, and she had followed the news from a distance. She would now see for herself what republican China was like.[46] She noticed that many of her peers — the students who had studied in America, especially her male colleagues — now served in powerful positions in the new nation. She later reflected, "It seems that China is run by my personal friends. One is head of this University and another of that; one is in charge of all the railroads in China, and another of Finance or Education, etc."[47] Had she been a man, she might have joined them in government. She was offered a position as dean of women at one university but turned it down. Mabel was more ambitious and sought to enter the business world. She drew on her economics degree and her connections in China as well as on her family's connections in New York to set up an import business in that city. Printing up stationery for the Wing Co., she planned to import Chinese herbal medicine like ginseng into the country.[48]

But Mabel Lee's plans were disrupted in November 1924 when her father, Rev. Lee Towe, walked out of his home healthy and was carried back through the door having been struck down by a stroke. With Mabel and her mother at his side, he died later that evening; the course of Mabel's life was set on a new path.

In those chaotic and sorrowful days, the future of the Chinese Baptist Church was up in the air, and Mabel Lee had a choice to make: should she continue to lay the groundwork for her business or honor her father by securing his life's work? She had once written that one of the "the two things that every Chinese child has been compelled to learn" was "filial piety," so she chose to put aside her own dreams and continue her father's work for the church.[49] As one of her favorite hymns read,

> I would be faithful through each passing moment;
> I would be constantly in touch with God;
> I would be strong to follow where He leads me;
> I would have faith to keep the path Christ trod.[50]

She needed her faith in the next decades as she battled the Depression and the Baptist Missionary Board to keep her church.

Five weeks after her father's death, the American Baptist Home Mission Society and the New York City Baptist Missionary Society appointed her director of his mission. When Mabel Lee took over, the mission consisted of a rented building in the heart of Chinatown. She decided to memorialize her father by finding it a permanent home. Lee spent the next decade raising funds and building the church. While the people of Chinatown helped her raise the money, she also appealed to the wider Baptist community. She enjoyed travel, and her fundraising work took her throughout the East Coast, where she lectured at various churches and to women's groups. Unlike her work with the Chinese Students' Alliance, her audiences were not Chinese, nor were they suffragists. They were, however, invested in supporting Chinese Christians. By 1935 the Chinese Baptist Church was secure in its new five-story building at 21 Pell Street. A plaque inside the church named the Chinatown associations that had donated in Lee Towe's memory.[51] Mabel Lee's good friend from college Hu Shih, the Chinese intellectual and poet, wrote the calligraphy over the door in honor of its opening.[52]

Although Mabel Lee had believed her time with the church would be temporary, she had already been there for ten years.[53] On a 1936 visit to New York, Hu Shih pushed her to think about her future. As they strolled together before his departure, their walk took them to the top of the Empire State Building, a mere five years old and the world's tallest building. Looking out over the city he asked her if she was happy. Later, as they sat at tea together, he urged her to consider herself—to "revive your scholastic and intellectual interest by doing some research work along the lines you had once begun." Now that she had established the church, what was her vision? he asked. "Did you really mean it to be merely a small Baptist church in China Town?" She told him she was happy; he didn't believe her. He continued his travels and mulled over her answers, finally writing to her. They were friends, he wrote, so he would speak frankly: "It is strange that you should spend your life on a thing that is merely a Baptist church in China Town." Didn't she "once imagine it to be the beginning of a Hull House of a Chinese Jane Addams? Or a Henry Street Settlement of a Chinese Lillian Ward?" he asked, invoking the famous settlement house founders in Chicago and New York who helped establish social work as a profession.[54]

What did Mabel Lee think of her friend's candid advice? It is unclear, but a few months later she set into motion plans to visit China again.[55] She remained for two months that summer, during which time she witnessed the beginnings of the Second Sino-Japanese War. In July, the Japanese army occupied two northern Chinese cities, unifying the Chinese against them. Soon after she returned to the United States, the capital of Nanking (Nanjing) fell to Japanese troops. They perpetrated the infamous "Nanking Massacre," killing over 300,000 civilians and surrendered troops and raping tens of thousands of women. That violence and the coming of World War II a few years later likely convinced her that her future was in the United States.[56]

With returning to China an unlikely possibility and with limited options as a Chinese woman in the United States, Lee focused her energy more directly on the church. She wanted to make it independent of the missionary board and under the control of the Chinese community. The economic precarity of the Depression seemed to offer an opportunity when the Baptist Missionary Board decided to sell the building. Lee offered to buy the board out with the stipulation that the property's title be transferred to the church.[57] This seemed fair because it was the memorial to her father and had been purchased in part from donations from the Chinese community. Initially amenable, the missionary society later reneged on the agreement. It was one of many frustrations that Lee, as a highly educated woman, felt under the control of the missionary board.

Her struggle with the missionary board continued through the war years and into the 1950s, when she was finally successful in getting the church title vested in the congregation. During that decade and the next she had full control over the church. The size of her congregation remained quite small, however, as there were few Chinese immigrants to the city in those years. The exclusions set in place by the 1924 Immigration Act loosened just slightly during the war when China fought with the Allies. In gratitude, the United States granted China a small 105-person immigration quota in 1943. The 1952 McCarran-Walter Immigration Act did not change the quota for Chinese immigration but did formally end the racial bar to citizenship. This meant that Asians could now apply for naturalization status. Naturalization was still limited according to the quota of 105 persons. The United States also admitted a few thousand Chinese refugees in the 1950s and early 1960s, especially Chinese students stranded in the United States after the communist victory and establishment of the People's Republic of China. But because of their professional standing, many of them "disappeared" into the suburbs and did not move to the nation's Chinatowns.[58]

Mabel Lee died in 1965 just as immigration reform legislation passed that would change the face of the Chinese community in New York. The legislation eliminated quotas that had restricted immigration from the great majority of countries in the world.

The First Chinese Baptist Church congregation has remained small, though committed, in part because most new immigrants live in other parts of the city, the borough of Queens, and suburbs throughout the tristate area rather than in Manhattan's Chinatown. Nonetheless, many of today's members remember Mabel Lee and have worked hard to keep her legacy alive.[59] The upper rooms of the church building are lined with pictures of Lee Towe, Lai Beck Lee, and Mabel Lee. The church maintains a small archive of Mabel's papers, while the current pastor, Bayer Lee (no relation), and the board have invested much time and energy in preserving Mabel's history. They have also been very generous in sharing their special memories. The church often produces bilingual publications for special occasions with member reminiscences, articles about Mabel Lee, and reprints of documents about or written by her. Just this past year they worked with Congresswoman Nydia M. Velázquez to have the Chinatown post office at 6 Doyers Street named in Dr. Lee's honor. The dedication ceremony took place on December 3, 2018.[60]

This centennial of the Nineteenth Amendment is an important moment to reflect on who has been part of our suffrage stories and who has been left out.[61] Each woman in this book demonstrated how history mattered; how it could be used to include or exclude, to erase or elide; and its ramifications for the present and future shape of the nation. The histories white Americans were writing erased or denigrated their communities. They responded by making their own histories, creating their own documents, and maintaining the memories of their communities for the future. Their insistence on putting themselves on record with their publications, newspaper interviews, photographs, or correspondence with white suffragists means that our knowledge of their participation in the suffrage movement is possible. Their efforts were sometimes tinged with the racism that white Americans used to make their claims, and they sometimes used the same terms of conquest and anti-blackness to make their cases. After all, the narrative of white American history was arguably successful for decades, and these women, their communities, and their contributions rarely if ever appeared in national stories.[62] But the foundations they laid preserved their memories alive in their own communities and families.[63]

This book is only possible due to their work and those who kept their histories over the past century. I have tried to follow the lead of these women by centering their experiences and concerns. Doing so offers a different angle into American history, one that can be a better model for our future. As Carrie Williams Clifford wrote in *Sowing for Others to Reap*, her first foray into chronicling women's history, she labored so "that coming generations may herein glean something of the efforts, the hopes and fears, the work and aims" of women like her. Instead of being on the periphery, she would offer a history "of their well-being, of their progress, and of their achievement."[64]

Some scholars have taken up the projects these women began at the turn of the century, but there is still room for more histories—and a need for those stories to be in conversation with each other—just as the women themselves were. Including the history they made changes our national narrative. It also requires us to take a broader view of political activism and to confront the many racisms in American history. The lives and activisms of these women of color intersected with each other but did not always run parallel. Rewriting the story means assessing 1920 as a moment in a longer struggle for voting rights. It means looking at the relationships of women of color with other nations besides the United States. It means celebrating their historical work, which saved much of this history for our present, but also acknowledging that they sometimes wielded the power of race and citizenship to make their own claims to belonging at the expense of other groups. It additionally means asking how they were forgotten, ignored, and written out but also who remembered them and who saved their stories. And most importantly, it means acknowledging their visions of the future and what they imagined America could be: a nation dedicated to the equality of opportunity and justice for all its people, a country that honors its treaties and respects the unique relationships it has with Native nations, a nation that celebrates the contributions of all of its citizens no matter their race, gender, religion, or language and encourages them to excel to the best of their abilities.

[ACKNOWLEDGMENTS]

Writing acknowledgments is always such a humbling process. It reminds me of the sheer number of people who have generously assisted and supported me over the many years I've been working on this project. I am deeply grateful to the scholars and community members who liberally shared their time and knowledge to help guide me and for my friends and family who gave enthusiastic support and encouragement. The following is by no means a complete list of the rich communities of wonderful people whom I am honored to be connected to, but it does reflect the immense generosity of many. That being said, all mistakes and oversights here are my own.

I've been incredibly lucky to have been part of two wonderful scholarly communities. This project began to take shape at the University of New Mexico, where I benefited from the collegial support of exceptional friends and excellent scholars Durwood Ball, Judy Bieber, Melissa Bokovoy, Luis Campos, Margaret Connell-Szasz, Jon Davis-Secord, Sarah Davis-Secord, Jennifer Denetdale, Tiffany Florvil, Kimberly Gauderman, Fred Gibbs, Elizabeth Hutchison, Linda Hall, Paul Hutton, Bob Jefferson, Erika Monahan, Julie Newmark, Anna Nogar, Dave Prior, Noel Pugach, Mary Quinn, Mike Ryan, Enrique Sanabria, Virginia Scharff, Jane Slaughter, Jason Scott Smith, Taylor Spence, Charlie Steen, Sam Truett, Shannon Withycombe, and Chris Wilson. Warmest thanks to Dana Ellison, Hazel Mendoza-Jayme, Yolanda Martínez, and Barbara Wafer for all of their help as well as their friendship.

Colleagues at Penn State University warmly welcomed me and offered scholarly and social support during the final stages of this project. I'm grateful for the good food and fellowship from David Atwill, Jyoti Balachandran, Kate Baldanza, José Capriles, Amira Rose Davis, Sophie De Schaepdrijver, Martha Few, Lori Ginzberg, Amy Greenberg, Chris Heaney, Ronnie Hsia, Faisal Husain, Michael Kulikowski, Jacob Lee, Dan Letwin, Mary Mendoza, Kate Merkel-Hess, Mike Milligan, Zach Morgan, Julie Reed, Matt Restall, Kathy Salzer, Crystal Sanders, Amanda Scott, Rachel Sheldon, Christina Snyder, Ellen Stroud, Chris Tounsel, Timeka Tounsel, Cathy Wanner, and Cynthia Young. I also greatly appreciate doctoral student Steven Xu, who helped track down and translate articles in Chinese newspapers for me.

I'm extremely grateful to those friends who did heroic work of reading most or all of the manuscript when it was considerably less coherent. Many thanks are due to Lori Ginzberg for her deeply thorough read and insightful comments and to Kimberly Hamlin for her guidance in helping me rearrange the manuscript and avoid some embarrassing mistakes. Mary E. Mendoza is a fabulous friend to think with; she makes hard concepts fun, helps give them real-world applicability, and constantly astonishes me with her courage. Virginia Scharff continues to be an amazing mentor, and her admonitions to "be the boss" of my manuscript and celebrate each stage of the process are excellent words of wisdom.

I'm also grateful to those who read portions of the manuscript and helped me clarify and articulate my thoughts at key points in the process, including Erica Ball, Liette Gidlow, Steve Kantrowitz, Tatiana Sejas, and Terri Snyder. My thanks also go to all the participants of the Princeton history department reading group, the Penn State University Anthropology Colloquium, the University of New Mexico History Workshop, the UNM Feminist Research Institute Workshop, and the Vanderbilt Americanist Seminar. I am quite grateful to my fellow panelists and the audience members who offered important feedback at the Alice Paul Institute, the American Historical Association, the Berkshire Conference of Women Historians, the Organization of American Historians, the University of Oklahoma, the Western History Association, and the American Association for Ethnohistory.

Thanks also go to Kristina Ackley, Jacobo Baca, Peter Blodgett, James Brooks, Kathy Brosnan, Margot Canaday, David Chang, Maurice Crandall, Mishuana Goeman, Tiffany Gonzalez, Jim Grossman, Rosina Lozano, Ellen Levine, Tiya Miles, Mae Ngai, Erica Perez, Josh Reid, Brenden Rensick, Kim Reilly, Madeline Shu, Linda Waggoner, Kim Warren, Michael Witgen, Ellen Wu, and Judy Wu.

Over the course of this project I was lucky to be part of several incredible writing groups that provided encouragement, support, and discipline. Cristina Stanciu, Lindsey Passenger Weick, Karen Marrero, Adriana Greci Green, Claire Bourne, and Melissa Girard helped me write that thing! Amy Scott, Anja Dubinowski, and Elaine Nelson offered weekly encouragement. And Traci Bryne Voles, Mary Mendoza, Kathy Morse, Virginia Scharff, and Christina Snyder helped me to balance work, play, and scheming amid spectacular scenery. Rosina Lozano and Beth Lew Williams made me feel very welcome during a sabbatical year at Princeton.

Liza Black, Kent Blansett, Boyd Cothran, Joe Genetin-Pilawa, Frederick Goodding, Andrew Needham, Nick Rosenthal, and Eric Yellin, with whom I worked on tangential but related projects, were all extremely patient with me and supportive when the manuscript was overwhelming.

The best part about the centennial celebration of the Nineteenth Amendment has been the group of incredible scholars with whom I've been in dialogue. Their work has shaped my thoughts on this project in such important ways. I can't imagine what it would have looked like without conversations with Tom Dublin, Ellen DuBois, Crystal Feimster, Charlene Fletcher, Dee Garceau, Ann Gordon, Kimberly Hamlin, Nancy Hewitt, Anya Jabour, Martha Jones, Lori Lalaum, Allyson Lange, Katherine Marino, Robyn Muncy, Laura Prieto, Molly Rozum, Katherine Sklar, Lisa Tetrault, Lauren McGyver Thompson, and Judy Wellman. I'm grateful to Jane Kamensky, who invited me to participate in early conversations at Radcliffe, and to Kate Lemay, who invited me to the discussions at the National Portrait Gallery.

My editor, Mark Simpson-Vos, saw the potential in this project from the beginning and has been essential in helping me shape it into what it could be. I worked with an incredible team at UNC Press, including Cate Hodorwicz, Dominique Moore, and Julie Bush.

I started thinking about many of the issues in this book in graduate school with Kathy Conzen, Amy Stanley, Julie Saville, and Catherine Brekus. I remain indebted to them and all of my teachers for their guidance and skills.

I'm grateful to all the people and institutions that help to preserve the past. I could not have written this book without assistance from Rosemary Clifford McDaniels, Ray Djuff, Mary and Nora Lukin, and Tim Tseng who all kindly responded to request for information from a stranger. I promise to pay that forward. Bayer Lee, Robert Gee, and Gary Quan of the First Chinese Baptist Church of New York have been beyond generous in their willingness to share church history and memories of Dr. Mabel Lee, as well as food and fellowship. Many thanks to the librarians at the American University Washington College of Law, the Barnard and Columbia College archives, the Library of Congress, the L. Tom Perry Special Collections of the Harold B. Lee Library at Brigham Young University, the National Archives and Records Administration branches in Denver and New York City, the National Personnel Records Center in St. Louis, the New Mexico State Archives, the Center for Southwest Research at the University of New Mexico, Clara Drummond and the other librarians at Penn State University Libraries, and the Princeton University Libraries. Thanks also go to Peter Blodget of the Huntington Library for tracking down Anna Howard Shaw's banner for me to see it in color. The Newberry Library is always an amazing site of scholarship and friendship. I'm grateful to so many people there, but especially Patricia Norby and Jim Ackerman. Also a huge thank you goes to Toby Higby for pointing me to Gertrude Bonnin's chart in the May Walden Papers and to Ben Johnson and Michelle Nickerson, who always make Chicago such a lovely place to visit.

Michael Davis supplied the fantastic author photograph and is part of a great group of friends here in State College. That group also includes Lara and Gordan Kaufmann, Michelle Marchetti and Ryan Jones, Gosia and Neil Sullivan, and Jen and Chris Rand, friends who reminded me to enjoy life outside the library.

I can't thank my family enough. It is a great gift to have such an amazing group of people in my corner, including Cathy and Ron Maher, Megan and Chris Belcastro, Matt and Shawna Maher, Maureen and Fred Sundberg, Micki Davis, and Mark Moore. My Grandma Edie was born before the Nineteenth Amendment was passed, a reminder that this history wasn't really that long ago. I have never doubted the love and enthusiastic support of Pam Cahill, Christine and Bill Disbrow, Kevin and Christine Cahill, and all the cousins. They are thoughtful hosts, generous listeners, and all-around excellent people. The times we are able to all get together have been restorative visits full of beautiful walks in the redwoods and on the coast, excellent meals, and lots of laughter. My Mom has always reminded me to be grateful for those who fought for the rights I have now, and I am so proud to include her in that number. My Dad didn't get to see this book completed, but he always told me how proud he was of me, and I liked to think he would have enjoyed reading it as much as he did the first one.

My life is immeasurably better for being shared with Andrew K. Sandoval-Strausz. He is a friend, colleague, and sweetie who shares my passion for studying the past and my hope that our work shapes a better future. This book benefited from his meticulous eye for editing, his steadfast encouragement, and infectious enthusiasm. The best thing we've done, though, is bring Cecilia and Lincoln into the world. They inspire me, make me laugh, and teach me everyday. This book is dedicated to them and their future, which I hope will be a just one. I am also grateful for the newest member of our family, fierce puppy Piña, who could be counted on to always know just when I needed a break to throw a tennis ball or go outside to take a walk.

[NOTES]

ABBREVIATIONS

CSM   *Chinese Students' Monthly*

Bonnin Collection   Gertrude Bonnin Collection, L. Tom Perry Special Collections Library, Harold B. Lee Library, Brigham Young University, Provo, Utah

Denver NARA   National Archives and Records Administration, Denver, Colorado

Du Bois Papers   W. E. B. Du Bois Papers (MS 312), Special Collections and University Archives, University of Massachusetts Amherst Libraries (accessed via http://credo.library.umass.edu/view/collection/mums312)

LOC   Library of Congress, Washington, D.C.

NAACP Papers   NAACP Papers, Part 4: Voting Rights Campaign, 1916–50, File Suffrage-Woman's, March 15–November 11, 1920, February 8–April 3, 1921, and April 4–May 17, 1921 (accessed via Proquest History Vault)

NWP Papers   National Woman's Party Papers, Part 1: 1913–74, series 2: Minutes, Legal Papers, and Financial Records, 1912–72, folder: Conference and Convention Proceedings; and Part 2: The Suffrage Years, 1913–20, series 2: Administrative Files, Printed Matter, and Photographs, 1889–1936 (accessed via Proquest History Vault)

NYC NARA   National Archives and Records Administration, New York City

PF NPRC   Personnel Folder, National Personnel Records Center, St. Louis, Missouri

Suffrage Parade   U.S. Congress, Senate, Committee on the District of Columbia, *Suffrage Parade: Hearings before a Subcommittee of the Committee on the District of Columbia United States Senate*, 63rd Cong., Special-[first] Sess. (Washington, D.C.: Government Printing Office, 1913)

INTRODUCTION

1. "Mobs at Capital Defy Police; Block Suffrage Parade," *Chicago Tribune*, March 4, 1913.

2. Higham, "Indian Princess and Roman Goddess"; Le Corbeiller, "Miss America and Her Sisters"; Genetin-Pilawa, "Indians' Capital City."

3. "Women Lawyers, in Academic Robes, to Be Pageant Feature," February 1913, in Ella M. Platt Scrapbook, 1896–1913, p. 301, Washington College of Law Historical Collection, American University Digital Research Archive, https://auislandora.wrlc.org/islandora/object/wcl%3A16 295#page/1/mode/1up (accessed February 15, 2020). Anishinaabe refers to the group of culturally related people. Anishinaabeg refers to speakers of Anishinaabemowin. Americans at the time used "Chippewa" or "Ojibwe." I have primarily used Ojibwe, but all three periodically appear.

4. "5,000 Women March, Beset by Crowds," *New York Times*, March 4, 1913; "Woman's Beauty, Grace, and Art Bewilder the Capital," *Washington Post*, March 4, 1913.

5. See *Crowd Breaking Parade up at 9th St., Mch [i.e., March] 3, 1913*, Taylor-Wash., D.C., photographic print (postcard), LOT 5541, LOC, https://lccn.loc.gov/pictures/item/91794900 (accessed January 14, 2020).

6. "Woman's Beauty, Grace, and Art Bewilder the Capital," *Washington Post*, March 4, 1913; "5,000 Women in Suffrage Parade," *Baltimore Sun*, March 4, 1913.

7. Terrell, *Colored Woman in a White World*, 212.

8. Clifford, "Suffrage Paraders," *Crisis*, April 1913, 296.

9. See photograph *Suffrage Parade, Inez Milholland*, March 1913, George Grantham Bain Collection, LOC, https://cdn.loc.gov/master/pnp/ggbain/11300/11399u.tif (accessed January 12, 2020). See also L. Barber, *Marching on Washington*, 44–74; and Lemay, *Votes for Women*, 167–86.

10. The term "Women of color" encompasses women from a range of racial and ethnic groups and nationalities. I acknowledge that it is generally imperfect but a necessary way to talk about all of the women I discuss in the book together in one category. I prefer it to the term "non-white women" as it emphasizes their identity as women first and then their racial or ethnic identity and is not a negative descriptor. I use specific terms whenever possible.

11. Edward Bracklin, "Prophecy of the Class of '14," *Carlisle (Penn.) Arrow* 10, no. 37 (May 22, 1914): 9–11; "Votes for Women," *Crisis*, August 1915, 175–92; "A Woman's Suffrage Symposium," *Crisis*, September 1912, 240–47.

12. Jones, *All Bound Up Together*; Higginbotham, *Righteous Discontent*.

13. Simpson, *Mohawk Interruptus*; Crandall, *These People Have Always Been a Republic*; Kantrowitz, "'Not Quite Constitutionalized'"; Goeman and Denetdale, "Native Feminisms"; Barker, *Critically Sovereign*; Garceau, "'Right to Help Make the Laws.'"

14. Yung, *Unbound Feet*; Ruiz, *From Out of the Shadows*. See also E. DuBois, "Woman Suffrage."

15. Vickery, "After the March, What?"

16. E. DuBois, *Feminism and Suffrage*; Terborg-Penn, *African American Women in the Struggle for the Vote*; Ginzberg, *Elizabeth Cady Stanton*; Feimster, *Southern Horrors*; Tetrault, *Myth of Seneca Falls*; Gidlow, "Sequel."

17. Mitchell, "Borderlands/La Familia"; Kantrowitz, "White Supremacy, Settler Colonialism, and the Two Citizenships of the Fourteenth Amendment"; Kantrowitz, "'Not Quite Constitutionalized'; Atkinson, "Slaves, Coolies, and Shareholders. Beth Lew Williams suggests we use "Restriction Act" rather than "Exclusion Act," as it is more accurate. Williams, *Chinese Must Go*, 8–9. I use the Exclusion Act only because of its familiarity to readers.

18. I hope to move conversations beyond the stories that lead from the Seneca Falls convention of 1848 to the Nineteenth Amendment in 1920, a narrative that was the creation of a specific historical moment and specific historical actors. Tetrault, *Myth of Seneca Falls*. I've also been deeply influenced by feminist scholars of color, both through their academic work and in the vibrant public sphere of the internet. There has also been an outpouring of recent literature reassessing the topic for the centennial. On the term "Hispana": In New Mexico, Spanish speakers preferred "Hispano" (male) or "Hispana" (female) as it emphasized European ancestry and distinguished them from Mexicans or Mexican Americans. I follow their preference in the book. See Mitchell, *Coyote Nation*, 11–13.

19. Terrell's 1921 statement before the NWP Resolutions Committee, April 4–May 17, 1921, NAACP Papers.

CHAPTER 1

1. Lewandowski, *Red Bird*, 17–22; Dominguez, "Gertrude Bonnin Story." The Yankton Sioux Tribe describes themselves as the Ihanktanwan nation.

2. Zitkala-Ša (Gertrude Bonnin), *American Indian Stories*, 7–80; Cahill, *Federal Fathers and Mothers*.

3. Cahill, *Federal Fathers and Mothers*, 54.

4. Adams, *Education for Extinction*, 56–57.

5. Rozum, "Citizenship, Civilization, and Property."

6. "Proposed Amendment to the Constitution of the State of South Dakota," *Black Hills Daily Times* (Deadwood, S.Dak.), September 21, 1890. See also *Black Hills Daily Standard*, September 19, 1890, and September 2, 1890.

7. Mumford, "Métis and the Vote"; Witgen, "Seeing Red."

8. *Laws Passed at the First Session of the Legislature of the State of South Dakota*, 117–19; Robinson, *History of South Dakota*, 601; Clem, *South Dakota Political Almanac*, "Table 7. Results of Elections Concerning State Constitutional Amendments and Initiated and Referred Laws, 1889–1968," 31–32. See also Van Voris, *Carrie Chapman Catt*, 23. Van Voris cites Catt's article "South Dakota Women," *Women's Standard*, November 1890.

9. *Daily Deadwood (S.C.) Pioneer Times*, November 8, 1890; Rozum, "Citizenship, Civilization, and Property."

10. Van Voris, *Carrie Chapman Catt*, 20.

11. Van Voris, 20; Robinson, *History of South Dakota*, 597, which states that in 1887 more than one-third of the land was held by women.

12. Van Voris, *Carrie Chapman Catt*.

13. Gustafson, *Women and the Republican Party*; Shaw, "Indians Versus Women," 146; Van Voris, *Carrie Chapman Catt*, 21.

14. According to Gunter, the Supreme Court used these laws to reject women's argument that citizenship conferred suffrage in *Minor v. Happerstett* in 1875. The Dakotas were the last two states to include such laws in their constitution, and a number of states repealed them during World War I. Gunter, "'Alien Enemies' and 'Loyal American Women.'" See also Egge, *Woman Suffrage and Citizenship*; and Van Voris, *Carrie Chapman Catt*.

15. "Indian Suffrage Mistake," *Daily Deadwood Pioneer Times*, November 8, 1890. See also "Ghost Dance and Tomahawks vs. Women" *Woman's Journal* 21, no. 48 (November 29, 1890): 380.

16. Ostler, *Plains Sioux*, 345–46.

17. Ostler, 345–46.

18. "Red Treachery," *Fall River (Mass.) Globe*, December 30, 1890; "The Scheming Reds," *Morning Oregonian* (Portland), January 1, 1891; "Hot Times at Pine Ridge," *Daily Inter Ocean* (Chicago), December 30, 1890; "Indian War at Last," *Boston Daily Advertiser*, December 30, 1890.

19. E. DuBois, *Feminism and Suffrage*, 92–96; Ginzberg, *Elizabeth Cady Stanton*; Tetrault, *Myth of Seneca Falls*.

20. Terborg-Penn, *African American Women in the Struggle for the Vote*; E. Brown, "To Catch a Vision of Freedom."

21. Anna Howard Shaw, "Indians versus Women," *Woman's Tribune*, May 9, 1891, 146. This source is used in the next two paragraphs.

22. Solomon, *Voice of Their Own*.

23. The name was an abbreviation of the first letters of the words "wives," "mothers," "daughters," and "sisters." Cooper, *Voice from the South*, 56.

24. A. Cooper, *Voice from the South*, 56; May, *Anna Julia Cooper*, 73–74.

25. Cooper, *Voice from the South*, 125 and 123.

26. Dominguez, "Gertrude Bonnin Story," 99.

27. Lewandowski, *Red Bird*, 22.

28. Quoted in Lewandowski, 23.

29. For the full speech, see Lewandowski, 3–6, 23.

30. Zitkala-Ša, *American Indian Stories*, 102–3; Lewandowski, *Red Bird*, 23.

31. Chapman and Mills, *Treacherous Texts*, 117.

32. Catt (1926) quoted in Mead, *How the Vote was Won*, 90–91.

33. It had never been held west of Des Moines, Iowa. Organizers invited suffragists. Harper, *History of Woman Suffrage*, 117.

34. *Speech of Hon. Binger Hermann*, 40.

35. Blee, "Completing Lewis and Clark's Westward March," 248; *Speech of Hon. Binger Hermann*, 37. On race and world's fairs, see Rydell, *All the World's a Fair*.

36. It was later referenced in the National Woman's Party's magazine. See "Monuments for Indian Women," *Suffragist* 7, no. 28 (July 19, 1919): 4.

37. Harper, *History of Woman Suffrage*, 124.

38. "Bigamists and Paupers on Level With Women," *Woman's Journal* 47, no. 2 (January 8, 1916): 9 and 15; Stapler, *Woman Suffrage Yearbook*, 168–75.

39. E. Brown, "To Catch the Vision of Freedom"; Gidlow, "Sequel"; McCool, Olson, and Robinson, *Native Vote*.

40. On borrowing, see Lozano, *American Language*.

41. Quoted in Stapler, *Woman Suffrage Yearbook*, 168–75.

CHAPTER 2

1. "Vast Suffrage Host Is on Parade Today," *New York Times*, May 4, 1912; "Suffrage Hosts Mounted and on Foot Impress the Metropolis," *Washington Post*, May 6, 1912.

2. "Chinese Approve Women Ballot," *St. Louis Star and Times*, March 19, 1912; "Votes for Chinese Women," *Evening Times-Republican* (Marshalltown, Iowa), March 21, 1912; and "Chinese Suffragettes," *Atchinson (Kans.) Daily Globe*, March 21, 1912. The situation was confusing: the provincial government had allowed each province to determine woman suffrage. Canton, where many of the Chinese in the United States were from, had in fact enfranchised women. Other provinces had not. Edwards, *Gender, Politics, and Democracy*.

3. Edwards, "Tang Qunying"; Pao-Tao, "Qiu Jin"; Edwards, *Gender, Politics, and Democracy*.

4. "The Chinaman's Better Half?," *New York Daily Tribune*, January 21, 1912; "China—A Company of Women Soldiers," *Brooklyn (N.Y.) Daily Eagle*, February 20, 1912; "Chinese Women Warriors," *Dayton (Ohio) Herald*, February 23, 1912; "Chinese Women Awaking," *Pittsburgh Post-Gazette*, February 27, 1912; "How Women Soldiers Won a Battle," *Journal and Tribune* (Knoxville, Tenn.) March 11, 1912; and "Tells How Chinese Girls Broke Out of School to Go To War," *Muskogee (Okla.) Times-Democrat*, March 11, 1912.

5. Spencer Talbot, "Chinese President Plans Reforms: Women Want Electoral Franchise," *Salt Lake Tribune*, February 18, 1912.

6. "Suffragists Feel Like Going to China," *New York Times*, March 23, 1912; "Chinese Suffragists Rage," *New York Times*, March 23, 1912; *Outlook*, April 21, 1915, 907.

7. William M. Ivins, year: 1920; census place: Manhattan Assembly District 15, New York, New York; roll: T625_1212; page: 10B; enumeration district: 1052 (accessed via ancestry.com, January 20, 2020).

8. "Suffragists Feel Like Going to China"; "Surprise from China: Local Suffragists Astounded but Pleased at Outbreak," *New York Daily Tribune*, March 23, 1912; "Suffrage Given Chinese Women Pleases Suffragettes," *Ft. Worth (Tex.) Star-Telegram*, March 22, 1912.

9. Ngai, "Western History and the Pacific World"; Shah, *Contagious Divides*; E. Lee *At America's Gates*, 26; Johnson, *Roaring Camp*, 125–27.

10. Quoted in E. Lee, *At America's Gates*, 26.

11. Americans described coolie labor as subjects from "China, Japan or any oriental country, without their free and voluntary consent, for the purpose of holding them to a term of service." Peffer, "Forbidden Families," 282–88; E. Lee, *At America's Gates*, 100. See also Atkinson, "Slaves, Collies, and Shareholders."

12. Quoted in E. Lee, *At America's Gates*, 100; Ngai, *Impossible Subjects*; Williams, *The Chinese Must Go*.

13. Rev. E. C. Scott, "Ordination of Lee To," *Home Mission Monthly* 25, no. 8 (August 1903): 214–15.

14. Arrived June 22, 1901, and admitted June 27, 1901. Mabel states that she was admitted as the daughter of a teacher in her June 8, 1929, statement to immigration officials in ML Chinese

Exclusion File, NYC NARA; "Missionaries among the Italians, Chinese, Mexicans and Indians," 67; Pascoe, *Relations of Rescue*, 13–17.

15. Rev. E. C. Scott, "Ordination of Lee To," *Baptist Home Missionary* 25, no. 8 (August 1903): 214–15.

16. "Mabel Lee, Applicant for an Immigration Return Permit (Form 632)," June 6, 1929, ML Chinese Exclusion File, NYC NARA; "Missionaries among the Italians, Chinese, Mexicans and Indians," 67.

17. Lui, *Chinatown Trunk Mystery*, 33.

18. On western violence see Williams, *Chinese Must Go*.

19. Campbell, "Chinese Work on the Pacific Coast," 102.

20. Song, *Shaping and Reshaping Chinese American Identity*, 35. See also Lui, *Chinatown Trunk Mystery*; and Kwong, *New Chinatown*.

21. Riis, *How the Other Half Lives*, 92–103; Beck, *New York's Chinatown*. On the West, see Shah, *Contagious Divides*; and Johnson, *Roaring Camp*.

22. Chapman and Mills, *Treacherous Texts*, 117.

23. "Suffragists Feel Like Going to China."

24. In Portland, Oregon, Kate Chan, women's rights activist, doctor of Chinese medicine, and wife of Rev. Chan Sing Kai, along with her daughter, Bertie, spoke to a suffrage gathering on women's rights in China. "Chinese Women Dine with White," *Oregonian*, April 12, 1912; "Dine Chinese Women," *Los Angeles Times*, April 12, 1912; "Chinese women at Banquet," *Billings (Mont.) Weekly Gazette*, April 12, 1912; "Chinese Women at Suffragette Banquet Twitt Oregon Men," *Fort Worth (Tex.) Star-Telegram*, April 12, 1912. See also "Chan Sing Kai Concert," *Morning Astorian* (Astoria, Ore.), June 28, 1907; and "Will Teach in New Chinese Government," *Oregon Daily Journal* (Portland), October 9, 1912. On Mrs. Wong Yie in Cincinnati, Ohio, see "Laid Down Lives for Freedom: Chinese Woman Tells of Loss of Friends—Why She Wants Suffrage," *Woman's Journal* 43, no. 2 (December 28, 1912): 416. Miss Pimsga Hu of Shanghai, a student from Wellsley, addressed a Boston suffrage group. See "One Standard for Courage," *Boston Globe*, April 23, 1912. See also "Chinese Women Will Vote in Los Angeles," *San Francisco Call*, March 29, 1912; "Chinese Women Want Ballot," *Leader-Tribune* (Englewood, Kans.), September 26, 1912. On Chinese Canadian suffragist Sue Sin Far, see Chapman, "Edith Eaton/Sui Sin Far's 'Revolution in Ink.'"

25. "Chinatown Awakens," *New York Tribune*, April 14, 1912.

26. "Chinatown Awakens."

27. "Woman Suffrage in China," *Oriental Review* 2, no. 7 (May 1912): 422.

28. "Chinese Girls in Original Drama by Grand-Niece of Li Hung Chang," *Brooklyn (N.Y.) Daily Eagle*, December 10, 1911; "Chinese Parade Ends Festive Week," *New York Times*, April 9, 1911; "Money Given to New China," *Boston Globe*, January 1, 1912 .

29. For speaker's platform, see "Woman Suffrage in China," 422. See image accompanying "Chinese Talk Suffrage," *New York Tribune*, April 11, 1912.

30. Mabel Lee's name was spelled multiple ways. It is listed as Lai Beck in her immigration file. See Mabel Lee Statement, March 10, 1923, in ML, Chinese Exclusion File, NYC NARA. It is listed as Ly Beck on Mabel Lee's tombstone, which was placed by members of the Chinese Baptist Church at the Kensico Cemetery in Westchester, New York. "Woman Suffrage in China," 421; "Chinese Girl Wants Vote," *New York Tribune*, April 13, 1912.

31. Mabel Lee, year: 1910; census place: Manhattan Ward 6, New York, New York; roll: T624_1005; page: 6B; enumeration district: 0047; FHL microfilm: 1375018; Mabel Lee, year: 1920; census place: Manhattan Assembly District 1, New York, New York; roll: T625_1185; page: 34A; enumeration district: 73 (accessed via ancestry.com, January 7, 2020).

32. Pearl Mark Loo, Chinese Exclusion File, Case Numbers 32 and 121, NYC NARA. She also went by the name Mai Zhouyi.

33. "Madame Mai's Speech: How Can It Be That They Look upon Us as Animals?," in Yung, *Unbound Voices*, 188–93.

34. "Suffrage Notes," *Dobbs Ferry (N.Y.) Register*, April 17, 1912; "Chinese Women to Parade for Woman Suffrage," *New York Times*, April 14, 1912; Marie Jenney Howe, "The Tables Turned: New York Congratulates China upon Its Progressive Democracy," *The Woman Voter*, May 12, 1913, in Delap, Dicenzo, and Ryan, *Feminism and the Periodical Press*; Tseng, "Unbinding Their Souls."

35. "Suffrage Notes"; "Education of the Chinese Women," *Buffalo (N.Y.) Enquirer*, April 12, 1912; "Chinese Women Complain," *Des Moines Register*, April 17, 1912.

36. DuBois, *Harriot Stanton Blatch*, 106.

37. DuBois, 106; Finnegan, *Selling Suffrage*; "NYC Suffrage Parade Largely Exceeds Expectations," *New York Times*, May 6, 1911.

38. "Chinese Women to March," *New York Tribune*, March 26, 1912; "New York Suffragists March in Great Parade," *Atlanta Constitution*, May 5, 1912; "Suffrage Notes," *Topeka State Journal*, April 27, 1912; "Chinese Girl Wants Vote," *New York Tribune*, April 13, 1912; "Hail Columbia Happy Land of the Suffragettes," *Baltimore Evening Sun*, May 4, 1912; "Chinese Girl in Parade," *San Bernardino County Sun*, April 28, 1912; "Chinese Girl Suffragist," *Los Angeles Evening Express*, May 6, 1912; "Chinese Women to Parade for Woman Suffrage," *New York Times*, April 14, 1912; Notes About Women: Chinese Girls Will Ride," *Des Moines Register*, April 19, 1912.

39. "Suffragettes on Parade: 20,000 Women in 28-Cent Hats in Line; Cavalrymen, Negroes and Chinese, Ten Abreast Are Viewed by 2,000,000 New Yorkers." *Centralia (Ill.) Evening News*, May 4, 1912. The *Mt. Pleasant (Iowa) Daily News*, *Sheboygan (Wis.) Press*, *Oelwein (Iowa) Daily Register*, and *Norwalk (Ohio) Daily Reflector* all ran the same story.

40. "Chinese Women to Ride," *New York Times*, May 4, 1912.

41. "Suffrage Army Out on Parade," *New York Times*, May 5, 1912.

42. "Suffrage Army Out on Parade."

43. United Press, "Gotham Turned Out to Jeer but Remained to Cheer," *Lima (Ohio) News*, May 5, 1912; "More than 20,000 in Big Suffrage Parade," *Standard Union (Brooklyn, N.Y.)*, May 5, 1912.

44. "Suffrage Army Out on Parade."

45. "20,000 Parade under Banners of Suffragists," *Washington Times*, May 4, 1912.

46. "Vast Suffrage Host is on Parade Today," *New York Times*, May 4, 1912; "Chinese Girl Wants Vote."

47. The banner is currently held by the Huntington Library in Pasadena, California. See Chapman and Mills, *Treacherous Texts*, 165–66. Thanks to Peter Blodgett for sending me a photo.

48. "Big Carnegie Hall Rally Ends Parade," *New York Times*, May 5, 1912.

49. "Suffragettes on Parade"; "Vast Suffrage Host is on Parade Today."

50. Terborg-Penn, *African American Women in the Struggle for the Vote*, 100; Goodier and Pastorello, *Women Will Vote*.

51. "Suffragettes on Parade."

52. "Vast Suffrage Host is on Parade Today"; Scharff, *Taking the Wheel*, 79–88.

53. "Suffrage Army Out on Parade."

54. "Suffrage Army Out on Parade."

55. "Big Carnegie Hall Rally." See also Shah, *Contagious Divides*; and Lui, *Chinatown Trunk Mystery*.

56. DuBois, "Woman Suffrage."

57. "To Ask Suffrage Plank: Women Will March upon Both National Conventions," *New York Tribune*, June 13, 1912; "Cheer 14-Month Baby and Aged Suffragette," *New York Tribune*, May 5, 1912.

58. Florence Goff Schwars, "Men of Ohio, Vote No!," *Cincinnati Enquirer*, September 1, 1912; "Suffragists Strike at All Candidates," *New York Times*, March 22, 1912.

59. "Bring It to Pass in the Year," in Rayé-Smith, *Equal Suffrage Song Sheaf*, 10.

60. "Says Suffragists Go on Barnum's Theory," *Detroit Free Press*, July 14, 1912; Bettie Wilson, "Advance or Retreat," *Cincinnati Enquirer*, August 11, 1912.

61. Mrs. Robert McVicker, "American Women Do Not Want to Catch Up with China," *Cincinnati Enquirer*, September 1, 1912.

62. Carrie Chapman Catt, "The New China: She Sits in the Gallery and Looks Down on China's Ten Women Legislators, Who Had Been Called a Myth," *Woman's Journal* 43, no. 40 (October 5, 1912): 314; Ida Husted Harper, "Suffrage in China Upheld," *New York Tribune*, October 12, 1912.

63. Catt, "The New China," 314.

64. Catt, 314.

65. Van Voris, *Carrie Chapman Catt*, 96–98; Catt, "She Sits in the Gallery," 314; Harper, "Suffrage in China Upheld."

66. Also known by Zhang Zhaohan, Luo Feiya, Zi Shu Fang, and Sophie M. K. Chang. Edwards, "Zhang Mojun"; Boorman, "Chang Mo-Chün," 85–87; Judge, *Republican Lens*, 284.

67. "China's Suffragists Ready to Use Force," *New York Times*, November 17, 1912.

68. Harper, *History of Woman Suffrage*, 715–19.

69. Yasutake, "Re-franchising Women of Hawai'i"; Sneider, *Suffrage in an Imperial Age*, 123, 128–29.

70. Yasutake, "Re-franchising Women of Hawai'i," 114, 118–19; Silva, *Aloha Betrayed*; Thigpen, *Island Queens and Missionary Wives*.

71. Yasutake, "Re-franchising Women of Hawai'i."

72. His name is also rendered Ching Yau Hung. *Territory of Hawaii v Mrs. Lum Yip.*

73. "Chinese Women Editor Beaters Tried in Court," *Evening Bulletin* (Honolulu), June 25, 1912; "Chinese Editor and Suffragists Appeared in Court," *Honolulu Star-Bulletin*, July 9, 1912; *Territory of Hawaii v. Mrs. Lum Yip.*

74. *Territory of Hawaii v. Mrs. Lum Yip*; Lum, *Sailing for the Sun*, 80–81.

75. *Territory of Hawaii v. Mrs. Lum Yip.*

76. Edwards, "Tang Qunying," 506.

77. "China's Suffragists Ready to Use Force."

78. "American Woman's Club," *North-China Herald and Supreme Court and Consular Gazette*, September 7, 1912.

CHAPTER 3

1. The Oteros' story is drawn from C. Whaley, *Nina Otero-Warren*. See also Wilson, Polyzoides, and Gandert, *Plazas of New Mexico*; and Blackhawk, *Violence over the Land*.

2. Montoya, *Translating Property*; Deutsch, *No Separate Refuge*.

3. The 1790 Naturalization Act limited naturalization to "free white" individuals. Gomez, *Manifest Destinies*; Lozano, *American Language*, 25. See also Mitchell, "Borderlands/La Familia."

4. Crandall, *These Peoples Have Always Been a Republic*.

5. Lozano, *American Language*, 38–66; B. Jensen, "Colorado Woman Suffrage Campaigns," 269.

6. Montoya, *Translating Property*; González, *Refusing the Favor*; Deutsch, *No Separate Refuge*; Lamar, *Far Southwest*.

7. C. Whaley, *Nina Otero-Warren* 30. On family education strategies, see Hyde, *Empires, Nations, and Families*.

8. C. Whaley, *Nina Otero-Warren*, 54.

9. C. Whaley, 59–62.

10. C. Whaley, *Nina Otero-Warren*, 61–66; Perez, *Colonial Intimacies*.

11. Holtby, *Forty-Seventh Star*; Aurora Lucero, "A Plea for the Spanish Language," in Kanellos, *Herencia*, 135–36; Lozano, *American Language*.

12. Ponce, "Lives and Works of Five Hispanic New Mexican Women Writers," 40.

13. Aurora Lucero, "Shall the Spanish Language Be Taught in the Schools of New Mexico?," *Fort Sumner Review* March 18, 1911 (the source of the quotes in the next several paragraphs unless otherwise noted); Lucero, "A Plea for the Spanish Language," in Kanellos, *Herencia*, 135–36. For the Spanish version, see "Defensa de Nuestro Idioma," *La Voz del Pueblo*, February 25, 1911. See also "Oratorical Contest," *Las Vegas (N.Mex.) Optic*, December 28, 1910; and "Officers Elected by Educational Association," *Albuquerque Journal*, December 30, 1910.

14. Lucero used the language of family to discuss statehood, especially sisterhood, but also detailed a vision of "amalgamation" of the "Castillian" and "Anglo-Saxon" in New Mexico's future. Lucero, "Shall the Spanish Language Be Taught in the Schools of New Mexico?"

15. During the 1876 Colorado Constitutional Convention, Agipeta Vigil, a Spanish-speaking Democratic delegate from southern Colorado (he had moved there from Taos, New Mexico), cowrote a minority report in favor of woman suffrage. B. Jensen, "Colorado Woman Suffrage Campaigns," 264 and 269.

16. The *Woman's Journal* similarly celebrated Queen Isabella and Columbus. See "The Woman Behind," "Columbus and Isabella," and "Columbus," *Woman's Journal* 43, no. 41 (October 1912): 321, 324, and 326.

17. English papers included *Las Cruces (N.Mex.) Citizen* cited in *La Voz del Pueblo*, February 18, 1911, and *Fort Sumner Review*, March 18, 1911.

18. "Locales" and "Gracias, Colega!," *La Voz del Pueblo*, February 18, 1911. The El Paso Times purported to reprint it, but it is a different version and contains factual errors. "Miss Lucero's Oration, Which Won Second Place in New Mexico Interscholastic Contest," *El Paso Times*, November 26, 1911.

19. Quoted in Larson, *New Mexico's Quest for Statehood*, 274.

20. Larson, 276.

21. J. Jensen, "'Disenfranchisement Is a Disgrace,'" 7.

22. Image #415, *Silver City, Fourth of July Parade*, 1911, from Silver City Museum, accessed via New Mexico Digital Collection, University of New Mexico Center for Southwest Research, Albuquerque; *Silver City (N.Mex.) Enterprise*, July 7, 1911; *Silver City Independent*, July 11, 1911. My thanks to Stephen Fox of Silver City for sharing the articles that helped me put this image in context. "Fancy Chickens Will Be on Exhibition," *Las Vegas Optic*, December 28, 1910.

23. "Proceeds from Plaza Fete $757.57," *Santa Fe New Mexican*, June 29, 1907.

24. J. Jensen, "'Disenfranchisement Is a Disgrace,'" 7; Larson, *New Mexico's Quest for Statehood*, 275. See also Holtby, *Forty-Seventh Star*, 406; "Lobbyists Flock to Santa Fe in Droves: Prohibition and Woman's Suffrage Advocates Plan Active Campaign," *Las Vegas Optic*, October 8, 1910; Jaffa, *Territory of New Mexico Report*, photo plate of Armijo between pages 64 and 65.

25. J. Jensen, "'Disenfranchisement Is a Disgrace,'" 7–8; Jaffa, *Territory of New Mexico Report*, 74–75.

26. See, for example, "Public Forum," *Albuquerque Journal*, August 20, 1910. On Texas, see Orozco, *No Mexicans, Women, or Dogs*; on Arizona, Augustine-Adams, "Where Is Their Place?"

27. Larson, *New Mexico's Quest for Statehood*, 279; B. Jensen, "Colorado Woman Suffrage Campaigns"; Crandall, *These People Have Always Been a Republic*.

CHAPTER 4
1. "Honor Mrs. Clifford," *Brooklyn (N.Y.) Times Union*, September 18, 1912; "National Session Women's Club," *Indianapolis Recorder*, August 19, 1916.

2. The opposition was argued by attorneys John D. Drake and Alvin Bates. "Woman's Suffrage," *Washington Bee*, January 1, 1913. See also "Washington Letter," *New York Age*, December 29, 1917.

3. See Clifford, "Votes for Children," as part of the symposium "Votes for Women," 185.

4. Clifford was deeply moved by Du Bois's *The Souls of Black Folk*. See advertisement, *Horizon*, December 1907, 8.

5. Tucker, "Carrie Williams Clifford's Poetic Response," 12–13; Clifford, "Business Career of Mrs. M. E. Williams," 477.

6. C. Anderson, *One Person, No Vote*; Gilmore, *Gender and Jim Crow*.

7. "The Women's World: Carrie Williams Clifford (a Sketch)," *Colored American Magazine*, February 1902, 2; Clifford, "Business Career of Mrs. M. E. Williams," 477.

8. "Death of a Remarkable Colored Woman," *Cleveland Leader*, March 21, 1903.

9. "Man in the Corner," *Colored American Magazine*, August 1902; "The Colored Voters League," *Pittsburgh Post-Gazette*, September 25, 1897; Tucker, "Carrie Williams Clifford's Poetic Response," 14–16.

10. "Women's World: Carrie Williams Clifford (a Sketch)," 2; "History of the Ohio National Association of Colored Women's Clubs," n.d., in Folder Ohio Federation of Women's Clubs, NAACP Papers, 100.

11. National Association of Colored Women's Clubs, "Minutes of the Second Convention," 7, 9, 14, 16, and 18.

12. Feimster, *Southern Horrors*; Bay, *To Tell the Truth Freely*.

13. Wells, *Southern Horrors*. See also Feimster, *Southern Horrors*; and Rosen, *Terror in the Heart of Freedom*.

14. Higginbotham, *Righteous Discontent*; Hine, "Rape and the Inner Lives of Black Women"; Lindsey, *Colored No More*.

15. B. Cooper, *Beyond Respectability*.

16. Tucker, "Carrie Williams Clifford's Poetic Response," 16. See also Clifford, "Ohio State Federation"; and "Women's World: Carrie Williams Clifford (a Sketch)."

17. I have not located any extant copies from Clifford's editorial days. "Ohio State Federation," *National Association Notes*, Tuskegee Institute Press, 7, no. 11 (July 1904): 30.

18. Tucker, "Carrie Williams Clifford's Poetic Response," 18.

19. "Women's World: Carrie Williams Clifford (a Sketch)," 2.

20. "Her Husband's Pockets," *Freeman* (Indianapolis), July 29, 1905.

21. H. B. Lyons, "Loyal Legion of Labor," *Akron Beacon*, September 28, 1904.

22. Clifford, *Sowing for Others to Reap*, 3.

23. Clifford, 3.

24. Clifford, 4; Clifford, "Ohio State Federation," 28; *Fourth Convention of the National Association of Colored Women* (n.p., 1904), 30.

25. Clifford, "Ohio State Federation," 26–29. Her poem "Marching to Conquest" was printed with that report. See also "Holiday Period in Washington," *Indianapolis Recorder*, December 31, 1910.

26. "Begins Lecture Tour," *Evening Review* (East Liverpool, Ohio), April 6, 1906; "Meeting of Round Table Club," *Evening Star* (Washington, D.C.), November 1, 1908; "A Plea to Colored Men," *Freeman*, January 11, 1908; Clifford, "Which Shall It Be?" See also Godshalk, *Veiled Visions*, 65–75.

27. Godshalk, *Veiled Visions*, 1–2.

28. Clifford, "Northern Black Point of View"; Carrie W. Clifford, "Had Her Eyes Opened," in "A Few Thousand Letters from Our Friends," *Voice of the Negro*, November 1906.

29. "Why Mr. Barber Left Atlanta," *Voice of the Negro*, November 1906; Barber, "Atlanta Tragedy." See also Godshalk, *Veiled Visions*.

30. "Why Mr. Barber Left Atlanta," 471–72; Barber, "Atlanta Tragedy."

31. "Shall the Press Be Free?," *Voice of the Negro*, October 1906, 392; "Why Mr. Barber Left Atlanta," 471–72; Clifford, "Atlanta's Shame," *Voice of the Negro*, February 1907, 72; Clifford, "Letter to the Editor," *Voice of the Negro*, February 1907.

32. Clifford, "Had Her Eyes Opened," 500.

33. Clifford, *Race Rhymes*, 7.

34. Clifford, "Atlanta's Shame," in *Race Rhymes*, 12; Clifford, "Atlanta's Shame," *Voice of the Negro*, 72.

35. See Watson, "Mary Church Terrell vs. Thomas Nelson Page."

36. "Racial Self-Restraint," *Outlook*, October 6, 1906, 308–10.

37. Clifford, "Northern Black Point of View"; Feimster, *Southern Horrors*; Bay, "The Battle for Womanhood Is the Battle for Race," 78–79.

38. Clifford, "Which Shall It Be?"; Bay, *White Image in the Black Mind*, 187–218.

39. Page, "Great American Question," 565, 568–69. This is the source of the quotes in the next paragraph as well. A few years earlier Thomas Nelson Page had clashed with Mary Church Terrell. See Watson, "Mary Church Terrell vs. Thomas Nelson Page."

40. Quoted in Drew, *Black Stereotypes*, 30–32.

41. David Blight asserts, "Page both invented and rode the crest of a sentimental national reunion fashioned out of literary enterprise and his own silky brand of genteel minstrelsy." Blight, *Race and Reunion*, 227.

42. Clifford, "Great American Question," 370–72. On black women talking about sexual violence, see Hine, "Rape and the Inner Lives of Black Women"; and Armstrong, "'The People . . . took exception to her remarks.'"

43. Clifford, "Great American Question."

44. Tucker, "Carrie Williams Clifford's Poetic Response," 20; "City Paragraphs," *Colored American Magazine*, February 1902, 16; "Information Card," n.d., William H. Clifford, PF NPRC. He initially earned $1,000. "Promoting the Negroes," *Indianapolis News*, August 13, 1908.

45. "Banquet at Cleveland," *New York Age*, November 14, 1912.

46. "The Week in Society," *Washington Bee*, September 7, 1907.

47. Advertisements, *Colored American Magazine*, June 1906, 85; Tucker, "Carrie Williams Clifford's Poetic Response," 24.

48. See Ayscough, *First Impressions in America*; d'Estournelles de Constant, *America and Her Problems*; de Bryas and de Bryas, *Frenchwoman's Impressions of America*. All three were French authors.

49. I. Anderson, *Presidents and Pies*, 4–5.

50. Ayscough, *First Impressions in America*; d'Estournelles de Constant, *America and Her Problems*; de Bryas and de Bryas, *Frenchwoman's Impressions of America*. See also C. Green, *Washington*.

51. Terrell, "What It Means to Be Colored in the Capital," 181.

52. "Thompson's Review," *Freeman*, January 4, 1908.

53. Terrell, "What It Means to Be Colored in the Capital," 181.

54. Masur, *Example for All the Land*.

55. Lindsey, *Colored No More*, 94.

56. Genetin-Pilawa, *Crooked Paths to Allotment*, 73–93.

57. Masur, *Example for All the Land*.

58. Lindsey, *Colored No More*; Masur, *Example for All the Land*; Yellin, *Racism in the Nation's Service*.

59. There were 94,446 African Americans in the city, and 22,540 of them were government employees. Walker, "Struggles and Attempts to Establish Branch Autonomy," 5–6. See also Yellin, *Racism in the Nation's Service*.

60. Terrell, "What It Means to Be Colored in the Capital," 212.

61. *Colored American Magazine*, August 16, 1902, 2.

62. "Holiday Period in Washington," *Indianapolis Recorder*, December 31, 1910; Tucker, "Carrie Williams Clifford's Poetic Response," 24. See also Allgor, *Parlor Politics*.

63. "Holiday Period in Washington."

64. "The Niagara Movement Declaration of Principles, 1905," Niagara Movement (Organization), Du Bois Papers.

65. Niagara Movement, Second Annual Meeting, August 17, 1906, Du Bois Papers. Thanks to Rosemary Clifford McDaniels for pointing out the dues information.

66. D. Lewis, *W. E. B. Du Bois*, 220.

67. Nahal and Matthews, "African American Women and the Niagara Movement," 65; W. E. B. Du Bois, report, March 14, 1908, Du Bois Papers.

68. Welke, "When All the Women Were White."

69. George Crawford, "Civil Rights Circular," April 15, 1907, Du Bois Papers; Du Bois, "Membership Letter No. 4," April 10, 1907, Du Bois Papers.

70. Advertisement, *Horizon*, December 1907, 8. See ads each subsequent month through September 1908; and F. H. M. Murray, "The In-Look," *Horizon*, October 1907, 30.

71. "Treasurer's Report of Niagara Movement," December 1908, Du Bois Papers. EH.net was used for conversion.

72. Clifford, "Relation of Full Freedom to a Full Stomach."

73. Clifford, "Plea to Colored Men"; Clifford, "Shall We Fight the Jim Crow Car," in *Race Rhymes*, 15.

74. Clifford, "Reply to Thos. Dixon," in *Race Rhymes*, 11.

75. M. W. Gilbert, Carrie W. Clifford, L. Joseph Brown, E. Burton Ceruti, G. W. Ford, and N. B. Marshall, "Report of the Niagara Movement Committee of Organization," 1906, Du Bois Papers.

76. "The National Association for the Advancement of Colored People," *Crisis*, October 1911, front matter.

77. "The NAACP," *Crisis*, April 1912, 259; "Will Hold Monster Mass Meeting," *Baltimore Afro-American*, March 16, 1912. Terrell was elected vice president and Clifford was on the executive board. See "Branch Is Formed Here," *Evening Star* (Washington, D.C.), April 13, 1912, 16.

78. "Women's Committee," *Crisis*, March 1913, 238.

79. "Honor Mrs. Clifford," Brooklyn (N.Y.) *Times Union*, September 18, 1912; "Reception to Mrs. Clifford," Brooklyn (N.Y.) *Daily Eagle*, September 22, 1912.

CHAPTER 5

1. "Young Squaws to Ride in Suffragist's Parade," *Inter Ocean* (Chicago), February 9, 1913; "Ten Indian Maidens in Suffragist Parade," *Pittsburgh Daily Post*, February 10, 1913; "Indian Girl in Parade," *Ogden (Utah) Standard*, February 10, 1913; "Dawn Mist, Indian Girl, to Ride as Suffragist," Buffalo (N.Y.) *Evening News*, February 24, 1913; "Indian Maid to Lead," *Washington Post*, February 9, 1913; "Dawn Mist to Lead Troops," *Los Angeles Times*, February 9, 1913; "Indian Maidens to Ride in Parade," *Atlanta Constitution*, February 9, 1913. One reported that Beula Benton Edmonson (Cherokee) was also planning to march. "Beautiful Indian Girl of Muskogee to March with Suffragists Monday," *Wichita (Kans.) Daily Eagle*, March 2, 1913.

2. "Indian Maid to Lead."

3. "Parade Will Be Mass of Color," *Woman's Journal* 65, no. 5 (February 1, 1913): 38.

4. After the parade, some article celebrated the "Squaw Suffragette's" ride down Pennsylvania Avenue—but the photo used was a Great Northern Railway publicity photo. See "Three Prominent Figures in Yesterday's Parade," *Morning Oregonian*, March 4, 1913.

5. R. Green, "Pocahontas Perplex"; Deloria, *Playing Indian*; Hutchinson, *Indian Craze*; Bederman, *Manliness and Civilization*; Jacobson, *Barbarian Virtues*; Burke, *From Greenwich Village to Taos*; Newman, *White Women's Rights*.

6. M. Spence, *Dispossessing the Wilderness*. White suffragists used these methods as well; see Finnegan, *Selling Suffrage*; and Lange *Picturing Political Power*.

7. Sanders, *White Quiver*, xiii, ix; Graybill, *White and the Red*; Garceau, "'Right to Help Make the Laws'"; advertisement, *Bookseller, Newsdealer and Stationer* 39 no. 5 (September 1, 1913): 172.

8. See photo by Roland Reed, *Blackfoot woman, Daisy Norris Gilham with cradleboard on her back 1915*, and description of Negative 4708, National Anthropological Archives. This same print was also a colored postcard, #5841, from Glacier National Park, Montana, labeled "Dawn Mist, Queen of the Blackfeet." Postcard in author's collection.

9. Sanders, *White Quiver*; *Bookseller, Newsdealer and Stationer*, September 1, 1913, 172.

10. Correspondence with journalist Ray Djuff of Montana, April 31, 2020.

11. He often sent his work to Louis Hill, head of the Great Northern. See, for example, his letters, including Hoke Smith to L. W. Hill, April 27, 1923, at the Minnesota Historical Society, Saint Paul.

12. M. Spence, *Dispossessing the Wilderness*.

13. M. Spence.

14. Deloria, *Indians in Unexpected Places*, 3–11; photograph of Mrs. Many Horse, LOC, https://lccn.loc.gov/2003665487 (accessed January 14, 2020).

15. *Fish Wolf Robe, ca. 1900*, photographer unknown, Elmo Scott Watson Photographs, ca. 1860–1936, box 87, Ayer Collection, Newberry Library, Chicago.

16. "Indian Guests Are Having Big Revel; Witness Sights," *Oregon Daily Journal*, June 11, 1913; "Cheering Thousands to See PowWow Opening Today," *Spokane Review*, June 16, 1913; "Indians to Attend Shriners' Meeting," *Jackson (Mich.) Daily News*, February 27, 1914; "Indian Maid Bids Tepee Good-Bye; She'll Be Chief Telegraph Operator in White Man's Hotel," *Lansing (Mich.) State Journal*, June 18, 1913; "Society Notes From Indians — Dawn Mist to Be Wed," *Daily Times* (Davenport, Iowa), June 26, 1914.

17. Hungry Wolf, *Pikunni Biographies*, 1054–55.

18. Underwood and Underwood, "Pres. Calvin Coolidge posed with Commissioner of Indian Affairs Burke and Blackfeet Indians," September 17, 1927, LOC, https://lccn.loc.gov/96519601 (accessed January 14, 2020).

19. Hungry Wolf, *Pikunni Biographies*, 1055.

20. R. Green, "Pocahontas Perplex."

21. Wagner, *Sisters in Spirit*, 32. On Cherokee women's influence on white women's political activism, see Hershberger, "Mobilizing Women"; and Miles, "'Circular Reasoning.'"

22. On Pueblo feminists, see Jacobs, *Engendered Encounters*; and Burke, *From Greenwich Village to Taos*. See also Wagner, *Sisters in Spirit*.

23. Joseph Keppler, *Savagery to "Civilization"* (graphic) (New York: Puck Publishing Corporation, May 16, 1914), in LOC, https://lccn.loc.gov/97505624 (accessed January 14, 2020). Udo Keppler, or Joseph Keppler Jr., was an activist for Native rights, especially the Iroquois of upstate New York. See Descriptive Summary, Joseph Keppler Jr. Iroquois Papers, 1882–1944, Cornell University Library, Division of Rare and Manuscript Collections, http://rmc.library.cornell.edu/EAD/htmldocs/RMM09184.html (accessed January 14, 2020).

24. There was also a 1914 film starring Mona Darkfeather and directed by Frank Montgomery titled *Indian Suffragettes*. Darkfeather's character is named "Dishwater — an Indian suffragette." Internet Movie Database (IMDB), http://www.imdb.com/title/tt0199631/ (accessed January 14, 2020). Friar and Friar, *Only Good Indian*, 108; Waggoner, *Starring Red Wing*; Sloan, "Sexual Warfare in the Silent Cinema."

25. "Interesting Early Arizona History," *Coconino (Ariz.) Sun*, December 15, 1922, 14. See also Deloria, *Indians in Unexpected Places*. The dismissive stereotype of Native women as "squaws" was often juxtaposed to suffragettes. See "The New Woman," *Daily Ardmoreite* (Ardmore, Okla.), July

27, 1913, 9; and "Poor Lo Is Becoming Civilized" and "Now for the Indian Suffragettes," *Monroe City (Mo.) Democrat*, March 25, 1915, 2.

26. See "Chinese Suffragists Go on the Warpath," *Evening Herald* (Klamath Falls, Ore.), March 22, 1912. For examples of reportage on British suffragists, see "Women Take Warpath: English Female Suffragists Make a Wild Break for the Emancipation of the Sex," *Emporia (Kans.) Gazette*, January 17, 1908, 4; no title, *Rock Island (Ill.) Argus*, February 5, 1908, 4; and "Suffragists Demand Proves Live Wire," *Indianapolis Star*, March 7, 1909, 17. See also "Mrs. Clarence MacKay on the Warpath," *Evening Journal* (Wilmington, Del.), September 3, 1909, 8; and "a suffragette is a woman who goes on the warpath for political rights," in "Telegraphic Briefs," *Coats (Kans.) Courant*, December 24, 1908.

27. J. J. Gallagher and B. A. Koellhoffer, "Oh! You Suffragettes" (Irvington, N.J.: B. A. Koellhoffer, 1912), Lester S. Levy Sheet Music Collection, box 154, item 34, Johns Hopkins University, digital format, https://jscholarship.library.jhu.edu/handle/1774.2/2085 (accessed June 24, 2014).

28. "Ladies Literary Club," *Ogden Standard*, January 27, 1916.

29. "Channing Pollock's Review of the New Plays," *Green Book Magazine*, December 1915, 983–86. For more on the revue, which ran into money trouble and played only about sixty-eight shows, see Gushee, *Pioneers of Jazz*, 157–59.

30. Rabia Belt, "Outcasts from the Vote: Woman Suffrage and Mental Disability," paper in author's possession.

31. Nettie Bacon Christian, "Citizens Who Cannot Vote" (Chicago: Thompson Music, Co., 1885); W. G. Fortney, "Is It Right?" (San Francisco: Macdonald Music Co., 1911), both on Woman Suffrage Memorabilia at http://womansuffragememorabilia.com/woman-suffrage-memorabilia/sheet-music/ (accessed June 25, 2014).

32. Advertisement for Royal Theater, *Bisbee (Ariz.) Daily Review*, October 2, 1913, 5. See *The Suffragette Minstrels* at Internet Movie Database, http://www.imdb.com/title/tt0383649. There was also the *Coontown Suffragettes* (1914), http://www.imdb.com/title/tt0212891; *The Suffragette* (1913), http://www.imdb.com/title/tt0203959/; *Billy the Suffragette* (1913), also known as *The Shan Suffragette*, http://www.imdb.com/title/tt0341275; *The Suffragette Sheriff* (1912), http://www.imdb.com/title/tt0234826; *The Suffragette's Battle in Nuttyville* (1914), http://www.imdb.com/title/tt0004655; *Oh You Suffragette* (1911), http://www.imdb.com/title/tt1165319; *The Suffragette's Dream* (1909), http://www.imdb.com/title/tt1726027; *A Cure for Suffragettes* (1913), http://www.imdb.com/title/tt0256713/; and *The Clamshell Suffragettes* (1915), http://www.imdb.com/title/tt2999182/. Dorothy Gish starred in many of these. The Charlie Chaplin film *The Busy Day* (1914) had that title instead of *The Militant Suffragette* because that name had been used by another film in 1912; http://www.imdb.com/title/tt0002363/plotsummary?ref_=tt_ov_pl (all accessed February 29, 2016).

33. The cover image depicts an African American man on a banjo. Charles McCarron and Nat Vincent, "When Old Bill Bailey Plays the Ukalele [sic]" (New York: Broadway Music, 1915), Duke University Library Digital Collections, http://library.duke.edu/digitalcollections/hasm_b0183/ (accessed June 25, 2014). For a discussion of the political implications of actual hula, see Imada, *Aloha America*; and Liliuokalani, *Hawaii's Story by Hawaii's Queen*.

34. Witgen, *Infinity of Nations*.

CHAPTER 6

1. Viola, *Diplomats in Buckskin*; Genetin-Pilawa, "Indians' Capital City."

2. Anishinaabe refers to the group of culturally related people. To be more specific, Anishinaabeg refers to the people who speak Anishinaabemowin.

3. Witgen, *Infinity of Nations*; Sleeper-Smith, *Indian Women and French Men*; Hogue, *Metis and the Medicine Line*.

4. Mumford, "Métis and the Vote"; Witgen, "Seeing Red."

5. Application form, Marie L. B. Baldwin, PF NPRC; Houghton, *Our Debt to the Red Man*.

6. Richotte, "We the Indians of Turtle Mountain," 76; Hogue, *Metis and the Medicine Line*, 23 and 49; affidavit, Laura Bottineau Grey, 1932, Rootsweb, http://sites.rootsweb.com/~mnhubbar /images/LauraBottineauGrey0001.pdf (accessed January 14, 2020). On clans, see J. B. Bottineau, "Laws of Ojibwa Descent in the Mixed Blood, July 10, 1894," MS 1180, National Anthropological Archives, Smithsonian Institution.

7. "Indian Woman Works for Uncle Sam," *Evening Star* (Washington, D.C.), December 4, 1910; affidavit, Laura Bottineau Grey. On clans, see Warren, *History of the Ojibway People*, 17–25.

8. Affidavit of Joseph E. Perrault from August 28, 1916, Becker County, Minn., Rootsweb, http://www.rootsweb.ancestry.com/~mnhubbar/images/JosephPerrault0001.pdf (accessed January 20, 2020).

9. "Indian Woman Works for Uncle Sam"; Hogue, *Metis and the Medicine Line*.

10. "Minneapolis News," *Saint Paul Globe*, September 22, 1878; "Greenback Convention" and "Minneapolis News," *Saint Paul Globe*, September 28, 1879; "Minneapolis News," *Saint Paul Globe*, September 21, 1880; "Democratic Caucuses," *Saint Paul Globe*, March 20, 1883.

11. Most Minnesota Métis in the 1850s were known as "Moccasin Democrats." Mumford, "Métis and the Vote," 41–42.

12. Service record, July 1, 1911, Marie L. B. Baldwin, PF NPRC. See Anne F. Hyde, "Hard Choices."

13. "Indian Women as Fair Exhibitors," *Native American* 15, no. 31 (September 26, 1914): 427; "Minneapolis News," *Daily Globe* (Minneapolis), July 31, 1881, 6.

14. "Social Happenings," *St. Paul Daily Globe*, Sunday a.m., June 5, 1887, 10.

15. Marie L. Baldwin, year: 1920; census place: Washington, Washington, District of Columbia; roll: T625_209; page: 14A; enumeration district: 138 (accessed via ancestry.com, January 20, 2020).

16. Information card, January 3, 1922, Marie L. B. Baldwin, PF NPRC.

17. Richotte, "We the Indians of Turtle Mountain," 76.

18. "A Correction," *Saint Paul Globe*, November 16, 1883.

19. White Weasel, *Pembina and Turtle Mountain Ojibway (Chippewa) History*, 143; Murray, "Turtle Mountain Chippewa," 21; Camp, "Dispossessed."

20. In 1900 they lived at 315 A NE. John D. Bottineau, *Boyd's Directory of the District of Columbia* (Washington, D.C.: William H. Boyd, 1900), 110 (accessed via ancestry.com, January 7, 2020); "Mrs. Marie Bottineau Dead," *Washington Post*, May 22, 1900.

21. In 1898 his home and office address was 62 C NW. See John B. Bottineau, 1898 Washington, D.C., U.S. City Directories, 1822–1995 (accessed via ancestry.com, June 23, 2017).

22. At 212 A St. NE. in 1910. J. B. Bottineau to Hon. Charles Curtis U.S.S., February 16, 1910, in MS 1647, History of the B.A.E., National Anthropological Archives, Smithsonian Institution.

23. Visenor and Doerfler, *White Earth Nation*.

24. *Chippewa Indians of Northern Dakota Territory*, 1–4.

25. *Turtle Mountain Band of Pembina Chippewa Indians*, 26; *Congressional Record*, Senate (1907), 1427.

26. "Bottineau's Big Claim," *St. Paul Sunday Globe*, January 24, 1892; "North Dakota News," *Jamestown (N.Dak.) Weekly Alert*, August 17, 1899.

27. Maddux v. Bottineau, 125–26.

28. Norgren, *Belva Lockwood*, 81–83, 86–88, 106; Babcock, *Woman Lawyer*.

29. Klebanow and Jones, *People's Lawyers*, 32–35. See also Norgren, *Belva Lockwood*.

30. Maddux v. Bottineau, 119–30.

31. Maddux v. Bottineau, 119–30.

32. Bottineau settled into the intellectual life of Washington and began to reminisce about

his early life. He started to collaborate with J. N. B. Hewitt, a linguist of Tuscarora and Scotch heritage who worked for the Smithsonian's Bureau of Ethnology. J. B. Bottineau to J. N. B. Hewitt, August 4, 1909, MS 3968; Albert S. Gatschet Notebook with Vocabularies, Texts, Notes, MS 68; and J. B. Bottineau, "Chippewa Mythology," MS 3968, all in National Anthropological Archives, Smithsonian Institution.

33. Her sister, Lillian, had remarried a white printer named William Whitney. Bottineau Baldwin's nephew, Earl, who had been living with her in Washington, returned to home.

34. Cahill, *Federal Fathers and Mothers*.

35. Robertson, *Temple of Invention*, 64–65.

36. Evaluation, Marie M. L. Baldwin, PF NPRC.

37. See evaluations in Marie L. B. Baldwin, PF NPRC. See also Viola, *Diplomats in Buckskin*.

38. See note 15 above.

39. I. Anderson, *Presidents and Pies*, 43–44. She also describes Chinese-themed parties.

40. "Preface," *Report of the Executive Council on the Proceedings of the First Annual Conference of the Society of American Indians* (Washington, D.C., 1912), 3.

41. Kellogg, *Our Democracy*; Deloria, "Four Thousand Invitations."

42. Kellogg, *Our Democracy*; Kiel, "Competing Visions of Empowerment," 6.

43. Quoted in Lewandowski, *Red Bird*, 60–61.

44. Deloria, "Four Thousand Invitations," 24.

45. See *Report of the Executive Council on the Proceedings of the First Annual Conference of the Society of American Indians*, 58.

46. "J. B. Bottineau, Indian Representative, Is Dead," *Washington Times*, December 2, 1911; "John B. Bottineau Dead: Funeral of Attorney for Indian Tribes to Be Held Tomorrow," *Washington Post*, December 3, 1911.

47. Clarke, *Sex in Education*, 132–33, 137–44.

48. Ellen Spencer Mussey, "The Law and the Lady," *Suffragist* 8, no. 5 (June 1920): 93–94. See Clark, "Founding of the Washington College of Law," 82; and Hathaway, *Fate Rides a Tortoise*.

49. The school also received applications from Jewish and Spanish-speaking students; see Washington College of Law Library, American University, box 118, folder "Applications for Admission."

50. *Sanborn Fire Insurance Map from Washington, District of Columbia* (New York: Sanborn Map Company, 1903), vol. 1, sheets 11 and 13.

51. Marie L. B. Baldwin, PF NPRC.

52. Applications file, Washington College of Law Library, American University, box 118, folder "Applications for Admission 1915–1916, Mrs. Winifred E. Ayers-Allen recommended by Florence Etheridge and Mrs. M. L. B. Baldwin"; and folder "Applications for Admission 1915–1916, Miss Ida Prophet Riley recommended by M. L. B. Baldwin (Marie Bottineau) and Florence Etheridge." See also Ida Prophet Riley, census No. 136; 1923 Quapaw Agency Census; 1923; roll: M595_413; line: 33; agency: Quapaw, U.S., Indian Census Rolls, 1885–1940 (accessed via ancestry.com, January 14, 2020).

53. Lindsey, *Colored No More*.

54. "Washington College of Law," *Evening Star* (Washington, D.C.), December 5, 1915, 13; "Widow's Mite for Woman's Might." *Washington Evening Star*, August 12, 1914.

55. Florence Etheridge, PF NPRC.

56. Efficiency report, December 31, 1914, Florence Etheridge, PF NPRC.

57. See *Hearings before the Subcommittee on Parcel Post*, 756; "Florence Etheridge," 120; Harper, *The History of Woman Suffrage*, 106; "City Suffragists Will Have Part in Baltimore Parade," *Washington Times*, June 25, 1912, in Ellen Spencer Mussey Scrapbook, 21, Washington College of Law Library, American University.

58. See "Reception to Graduates," *Washington Post*, May 5, 1914, and "Women Lawyers in D.C. to Organize."

CHAPTER 7

1. See *Official Program Woman Suffrage Procession*, Washington, D.C., March 3, 1913, LOC, http://hdl.loc.gov/loc.rbc/rbpe.20801600 (accessed March 31, 2020).

2. This is according to Alice Paul. See "Suffragist Oral History Project, Conversations with Alice Paul: Woman Suffrage and the Equal Rights Amendment," interview conducted by Amelia R. Fry at the University of California's Calisphere, http://content.cdlib.org/view?docId=kt6f59n89c&doc.view=entire_text (accessed March 12, 2020)).

3. See "Suffragist Oral History Project, Conversations with Alice Paul."

4. See *Official Program Woman Suffrage Procession*, 7; and "Suffragist Oral History Project, Conversations with Alice Paul," 75.

5. See *Official Program Woman Suffrage Procession*, 2.

6. *Suffrage Parade*, 103.

7. See "Suffragist Oral History Project, Conversations with Alice Paul."

8. "Parade Will Be a Mass of Color," *Woman's Journal* 65, no. 5 (February 1, 1913); "Militants in Favor," *Baltimore Sun*, February 8, 1913; "Equal Suffrage among Indians," *Los Angeles Times*, January 31, 1913.

9. Kiel, "Competing Visions of Empowerment"; Stanciu and Ackley, "Introduction," 9.

10. Lonetree, "Visualizing Native Survivance"; Cahill, "Marie Louise Bottineau Baldwin."

11. In the congressional hearings that followed the parade, one marcher said that a young woman who "wore the robes and costume of an Indian" also participated. She was "a friend of Senator Owen's wife, and the wife of another senator from Oklahoma," and claimed she "had some Indian blood in her." *Suffrage Parade*, 377. The non-Native women of the Montana delegation were dressed as Indians. Mead, *How the Vote Was Won*, 156. See also photograph *Suffrage Parade*, Bain News Service, 1913, https://lccn.loc.gov/2014691441 (accessed January 15, 2020). One paper also reported that there were Native observers. See "Washington Sees Big Spree," *Chicago Tribune*, March 4, 1913.

12. *Official Program Woman Suffrage Procession*, 8.

13. The *Washington Herald* stated that the women would carry "the great, golden dragon, the emblem of China, in their midst, and a banner inscribed 'Catching up with China.'" "Suffrage Story to Be Told in Pageant," *Washington Herald*, January 19, 1913, 26. On Columbia, see "Dr. Shaw's Birthday," *Evening Star* (Washington, D.C.), February 14, 1913, 10.

14. Nellie M. Quander to Alice Paul, February 17, 1913, National Woman's Party Papers, LOC, in Sklar and Dais, "How Did the National Woman's Party Address the Issue?"

15. Lindsey, *Colored No More*, 102–3.

16. On black women's participation, see "Politics," *Crisis*, April 1913, 267. On the NAWSA response, see Anna Howard Shaw to Alice Paul telegram, March 5, 1913, quoted in Linda J. Lumsden, *Rampant Women*, 221n174.

17. Clifford, "Suffrage Paraders," *Crisis*, April 1913, 296.

18. *Suffrage Parade*, 222–44.

19. *Suffrage Parade*, 274.

20. See Daughters of the American Revolution Headquarters History at http://www.dar.org/national-society/about-dar/dar-history/dar-national-headquarters-building-history (accessed January 4, 2017). The hall was at Seventeenth and D Streets. For route, see the *Suffrage Parade*, 8.

21. In the newspaper they are described as "trig stoles." "Illinois Participants in Suffrage Parade; This State Was Well Represented in Washington," *Chicago Daily Tribune*, March 5, 1913. I am assuming the colors on the basis of the iconography, which matches the Illinois flag.

22. Image from *Chicago Daily Tribune*, March 5, 1913. Their banners announced their affiliations, and the city of Chicago was strongly represented: the Suffrage Alliance of Cook County, the Cook County Woman's Association, and the Chicago Political Equity League; see "Mobs at Capital Defy Police; Block Suffrage Parade," *Chicago Daily Tribune*, March 4, 1913. For color, see "Suffragists Off for Washington," *Decatur (Ill.) Herald*, March 2, 1913, 1; and "Suffrage Spirit Runs High When Paraders Depart," *Inter Ocean* (Chicago), March 2; "Chicago Women's Special Reaches National Capital," *Inter Ocean* (Chicago), March 3, 1913. The March 2 *Inter Ocean* article states that Ida B. Wells-Barnett was on the special train, too. See Materson, *For the Freedom of Her Race*.

23. All quotations and descriptions in this section are from "Illinois Women Feature Parade," *Chicago Daily Tribune*, March 4, 1913.

24. "Off to War; Chicago Sufragists Leaving for Washington to Parade," *Chicago Tribune*, March 2, 1913, 1; "Suffragists Off for Washington," 1; "Chicago Suffragist Hike Is Abandoned by Leaders," *Inter Ocean* (Chicago), March 1, 1913, 3; "Suffrage Spirit Runs High When Paraders Depart."

25. "Chicago Women's Special Reaches National Capital," *Inter Ocean* (Chicago), March 3, 1913, 2 (236 Delaware Ave.).

26. All quotations in this section are from "Illinois Women Feature Parade." See also Bay, *To Tell the Truth Freely*.

27. This was likely Genevieve Stone, the wife of Illinois congressman Claude U. Stone and chairman of delegations from non-suffrage states. *Official Program Woman Suffrage Procession*, 13.

28. Giddings, *In Search of Sisterhood*, 28–38.

29. Rohulamin Quander, *Nellie Quander, an Alpha Kappa Alpha Pearl: The Story of the Woman Who Saved an International Organization*, 6–7, in Sklar and Dais, "How Did the National Woman's Party Address the Issue?"

30. Julius F. Taylor, "The Equal Suffrage Parade Was Viewed by Many Thousand People from All Parts of the United States," *Broad Ax* (Chicago), March 8, 1913, 1.

31. Giddings, *In Search of Sisterhood*, 30; and Lindsey, *Colored No More*. At the NACW's 1913 meeting, President Margaret Washington made this statement on suffrage:

> Our attitude toward the suffrage is one of the conservative kind. We have not blown up any houses with dynamite nor have we been engaged in parading in the streets in men's attire. We are reading and studying the great questions which are to make for the good of the country and when the vote is given to woman as it surely will be where it is not already done, we shall be ready to cast our votes intelligently and there shall not be the general accusation that our votes are for sale for all the way from a drink of liquor to two dollars ("Women Opposed to Turkey Trot," *New York Age*, March 13, 1913, 5).

32. One exception was the *Chicago Daily Tribune*; see "Illinois Women Feature Parade," 3; and "Illinois Women Participants in Suffrage Parade," *Chicago Daily Tribune*, March 5, 1913, 5.

33. "The Teacher's College Alumni," *Howard University Record* 6, no. 1 (January 1912): 23.

34. "Women of the Hour: May Howard Jackson" (with picture), *LaFollette's Weekly Magazine*, June 22, 1912, 10; "Music and Art," *Crisis*, August 1912, 169; "Music and Art," *Crisis*, January 1913, 117; "Jackson, May Howard," in Aberjhani and West, *Encyclopedia of the Harlem Renaissance*, 169.

35. Shannon Erickson, "Harriet Gibbs Marshall (1868–1941)," BlackPast.org, http://www .blackpast.org/aah/marshall-harriet-gibbs-1868-1941 (accessed March 25, 2020); Clair A. Taft, "Anna Evans Murray," in Smith, *Notable Black Women*, 492–93; "Gray, Amanda V." and "Gray, Arthur Smith," in Mather, *Who's Who of the Colored Race*, 119.

36. Carrie W. Clifford, "Suffrage Paraders," *Crisis*, April 1913, 296; and "Mary Elenora Delaney McCoy," in Mather, *Who's Who of the Colored Race*, 188.

37. Terborg-Penn, *African American Women in the Struggle for the Vote*.

38. *To Prevent and Punish the Crime of Lynching: Hearings Before the United States Senate Committee on the Judiciary, Subcommittee on S. Butler 121, Sixty-Ninth Congress, First Session* (Washington, D.C.: Government Printing Office, 1926), February 16, 1926, 111.

39. Clifford, "My Baby," in *Race Rhymes*, 24.

40. B. Cooper, *Beyond Respectability*, 11.

41. May Martel, "Colored Women in Demonstration," *New York Age*, March 13, 1913, 5.

42. Clifford, preface to *Race Rhymes*.

43. Clifford, "Duty's Call," in *Race Rhymes*, 22.

44. On crowd, see *Suffrage Parade*, M[ar]ch 3/1913, National Photo Company Collection, LOC, https://www.loc.gov/resource/npcc.20233/ (accessed January 14, 2020).

45. "Mobs at Capital Defy Police, Block Suffrage Parade," *Chicago Tribune*, March 4, 1913.

46. "Illinois Women Feature Parade."

47. Description in "Huge Mob Blocks Suffrage Parade," *Chicago Tribune*, March 4, 1913. See also the photographs in *Suffrage Parade*.

48. "Some of the Suffragists Who Have Been Active in Arranging Tomorrow's Big Demonstration," *Evening Star* (Washington, D.C.), March 2, 1913.

49. *Suffrage Parade*, 60–61.

50. *Suffrage Parade*, 59.

51. *Suffrage Parade*, 43–44.

52. *Suffrage Parade*, 57, 70–71, and 178–80.

53. *Suffrage Parade*, 62–63.

54. *Suffrage Parade*, 34–41, 72, and 80.

55. *Suffrage Parade*, 64–66.

56. *Suffrage Parade*, 63–64.

57. *Suffrage Parade*, 52.

58. *Suffrage Parade*, 93–94.

59. "Women Battle Hostile Mobs in Capital Parade," *New York Tribune*, March 4, 1913, 1.

60. "Women from All Over Land March in Suffrage Parade," *Montgomery (Ala.) Advertiser*, March 4, 1913.

61. The Daughters of the American Revolution was famously segregated in the 1930s.

62. *Suffrage Parade*, 402–3.

63. "Five Thousand Women March at Capital / Glorious Pageant Strong Appeal for Ballot / Jeers and Insults Greet Suffrage Marchers," *San Francisco Examiner*, March 4, 1913; "Score the Police for Inefficiency," *Evening Star* (Washington, D.C.), March 4, 1913.

64. *Suffrage Parade*, 5.

65. *Suffrage Parade*, 402–3.

66. In 1904 Representative Heflin shot at a black man seated with white streetcar riders and accidentally hit a bystander. He was reelected to Congress. Elbert L. Watson, "J. Thomas Heflin," *Encyclopedia of Alabama* online, http://www.encyclopediaofalabama.org/article/h-2952 (accessed January 20, 2020).

67. *Suffrage Parade*, 67–69.

68. *Suffrage Parade*, 6–7.

69. Clifford, "Suffrage Paraders," 296. The *New York Age*, an African American weekly, reported that the New York Suffrage Pilgrims marching to Washington were met in Wilmington, Delaware, by a "'delegation of Southern gentlemen,' who demanded to know if [their leader] was in favor of giving the ballot to Negro women." She responded that it was a question for the states to decide and they replied, "Remember, if you are in favor of votes for Negro women you are to pass through the enemy's country." When the Pilgrims passed out of Baltimore, "they were met at Winans ... 'by a large group of Negro men and women carrying a big yellow banner,

lettered "Votes for Women." The [suffrage] army received the greeting in embarrassed silence and slid through the village as swiftly as possible.' Of course! Why not? Had they not been warned at Wilmington that Maryland was the enemy's country for them if they favored 'votes for Negro women?'" "Southerners War on Womanhood," *New York Age*, March 6, 1913.

70. Taylor, "Equal Suffrage Parade Was Viewed by Many Thousand People from All Parts of the United States" *Broad Ax*, March 8, 1913; James C. Waters Jr., [no title], *Broad Ax*, March 8, 1913.

71. Zahniser and Fry, *Alice Paul*, 160.

72. Zahniser and Fry, 160.

73. The *Suffragist* debuted on November 15, 1913. Zahniser and Fry, *Alice Paul*, 174.

74. Zahniser and Fry, *Alice Paul*, 174.

75. Zahniser and Fry, 178–84.

76. Zahniser and Fry, 188.

77. "Suffragists on Warpath," *New York Times*, January 12, 1914; "Suffragists on the Warpath," *Baltimore Sun*, August 18, 1914; "Suffragists on the Warpath," *Reading (Pa.) Times*, September 22, 1914; "American Suffragists on Warpath to Defeat Democratic Candidates," *Salt Lake Telegram*, September 24, 1914. See also Zahniser and Fry, *Alice Paul*, 193. A movie called *When Women Go on the Warpath* was advertised in November; see *News-Herald* (Franklin, Penn.), November 17, 1913.

CHAPTER 8

1. Cassidy, *Mr. President*, 58–59.

2. Gaines, "Political Reward and Recognition."

3. Watson, "Mary Church Terrell vs. Thomas Nelson Page."

4. Yellin, *Racism in the Nation's Service*.

5. "Service Record Card, William H. Clifford" file, William H. Clifford, PF NPRC.

6. Yellin, *Racism in the Nation's Service*; Berg, *Wilson*; J. Cooper, *Woodrow Wilson*, 204–6.

7. Terrell, *Colored Woman in a White World*, 250–59 and 414–15.

8. I am indebted to John Hope Franklin for this portrait of Dixon. Franklin, "The Birth of a Nation: Propaganda as History," in *Race and History*, 10–23.

9. Quoted in Stokes, *D. W. Griffith's "The Birth of a Nation,"* 105, 122, 124, 178.

10. Foner, *Reconstruction*.

11. See "Birth of a Nation," *Crisis*, October 1915, 295–96.

12. Clifford, "A Reply to Thos. Dixon" in *Race Rhymes*, 11.

13. "President William H. Taft Will Not Recommend to Congress," *Broad Ax*, June 10, 1911.

14. "The NAACP," *Crisis*, April 1912, 259.

15. "Women's Committee," *Crisis*, March 1913, 238.

16. "Department of Education," *National Notes*, April 1923, 5.

17. See illustration of the pageant committee in *Crisis*, December 1915, 94.

18. "Items of Interest in and about Town: Gives Benefit Play," *Washington Times*, April 13, 1917.

19. Mrs. C. W. Clifford, "Vierge Noire De Notre-Dame," *Crisis*, April 1916, 318.

20. The *Crisis* ran a symposium in 1912 that Clifford surely read: "A Woman's Suffrage Symposium," *Crisis*, September 1912, 240–47.

21. "Votes for Women," *Crisis*, August 1915, 175–92.

22. "Votes for Women," 179 and 178.

23. On the "New citizen," see section "Votes for Philanthropy," under "Votes for Women," 191.

24. "Votes for Women," 188–89.

25. "Votes for Women," 179 and 188.

26. "Votes for Women," 187.

27. "Votes for Women," 185.

28. "Votes for Women," 184–85.

29. "Votes for Women," 183.

30. "Votes for Women," 180.

31. "Votes for Women," 191. *The Crisis* often had brief notes regarding suffrage activism. For example, the front matter included snippets such as "Bernice Hartley is the first colored woman to register as a voter in Nevada." "Social Uplift," *Crisis*, August 1915, 165.

32. Gidlow, "Sequel"; E. Brown, "To Catch a Vision of Freedom."

CHAPTER 9

1. On layered citizenship, see Lomawaima, "Mutuality of Citizenship." See, for example, Visenor and Doerfler, *White Earth Nation*; Miles, *Ties That Bind*; Witgen, *An Infinity of Nations*.

2. Mumford, "Métis and the Vote"; Echo-Hawk, *In the Courts of the Conqueror*, 161–88; Crandall, *These People Have Always Been a Republic*; Simpson, *Mohawk Interruptus*; Bruyneel, *Third Space of Sovereignty*.

3. Kantrowitz, "'Not Quite Constitutionalized'"; Kantrowitz, "White Supremacy, Settler Colonialism, and the Two Citizenships of the Fourteenth Amendment"; "Mumford, "Métis and the Vote," 42–44.

4. Marie Baldwin to Arthur C. Parker, November 18, 1913, Papers of the Society of American Indians (microfilm).

5. Edward Davis, year: 1870; census place: Greenville, Greenville, South Carolina; roll: M593_1498; page: 644A; family history library film: 552997 (accessed via ancestry.com, January 7, 2019).

6. Edward J. Davis, year: 1910; census place: Zuni Indian Reservation, McKinley, New Mexico; roll: T624_915; page: 1A; enumeration district: 0124; FHL microfilm: 1374928 (accessed via ancestry.com, January 7, 2019); E. J. Davis, year: 1920; census place: St. Louis Ward 17, St. Louis (Independent City), Missouri; roll: T625_956; page: 14B; enumeration district: 340 (accessed via ancestry.com, January 7, 2019); Ed. J. Davis, year: 1930; census place: St. Louis, St. Louis (Independent City), Missouri; page: 16A; enumeration district: 0138; FHL microfilm: 2340975 (accessed via ancestry.com, January 14, 2020).

7. Collier to Davis, 1931, Edward J. Davis, PF NPRC.

8. Dr. Davis to Superintendent Zuni Training School, October 27, 1904, and Zuni Indian Agency, Press Copies of Letters Sent ("Miscellaneous Letters") 1899–1905, 1906–14, National Archives and Records Administration, Denver.

9. Cahill, "Marie Louise Bottineau Baldwin."

10. Clark, "James Carroll Napier."

11. The SAI did not like the term "squaw." "Editorial Comment: The Word 'Squaw' an Out-of-date-Expression," *Quarterly Journal of the Society of American Indians* 11, no. 4 (October–December 1914): 256.

12. "Members of Congress of American Indian Lineage," *Washington Times*, July 28, 1911; Mrs. Norman Galt, "Now, Lo's Name Leads All the Rest: 'First Families' in the Social Register Now Proud to Trace Descent from Pocahontas and the Other Real First Families," *Washington Herald*, November 14, 1915.

13. None were descendants of the local Indigenous people.

14. Terrell, *Colored Woman in a White World*, 417.

15. Arthur C. Parker, "The Editor's Viewpoint: The Road to Competent Citizenship," *Quarterly Journal of the Society of American Indians* 2, no. 3 (July–September 1914): 182.

16. "Platform of Fourth Annual Conference, Society of American Indians," *Quarterly Journal of the Society of American Indians* 2, no. 3 (July–September 1914): 231.

17. Arthur C. Parker, "The Awakened American Indian: An Account of the Washington Meeting," *Quarterly Journal of the Society of American Indians* 2, no. 4 (October–December 1914): 269.

18. "The Washington Meeting and Memorial to the President," *Quarterly Journal of the Society of American Indians* 2, no. 4 (October–December 1914): 249–50.

19. "Washington Meeting and Memorial to the President," 271.

20. Cahill, "Marie Louise Bottineau Baldwin."

21. "Mrs. Marie L. B. Baldwin, Attorney," *Quarterly Journal of the Society of American Indians* 2, no. 2 (April–June 1914): 155.

22. Bottineau Baldwin, "Need of a Change in the Legal Status."

23. Washington College of Law, American University, "Washington College of Law Announcements, 1911–1912," box 103, course catalogues 1897–1925.

24. Bottineau Baldwin, "Need of a Change in the Legal Status," 63–64.

25. Bottineau Baldwin, 66.

26. Bottineau Baldwin, 63, 2, 65.

27. Surprisingly, her thesis rarely ventures into the experiences of the Ojibwe, despite her years of work on the Turtle Mountain Chippewa treaty with her father and their research.

28. Bottineau Baldwin, "Need of a Change in the Legal Status," 44.

29. Bottineau Baldwin, 37–38.

30. Bottineau Baldwin, 39.

31. "Indians of Today Realize the Value of Education as Principal Asset of the Race," *Washington Times*, March 20, 1916. Another Native lawyer was Wyandotte Lydia Conley. "Admitted to Supreme Court," *Kansas City Sun*, October 29, 1915.

32. "In the Editorial Sanctum: Powers O'Malley," *American Indian Magazine* 4, no. 2 (June 30, 1916): 174–75; for the image, see Ellinghaus, *Taking Assimilation to Heart*, 43.

33. "Editorial Comments: Our Chippewa Women Work," *Quarterly Journal of the Society of American Indians* 2, no. 3 (July–September 1914): 169; 2, no. 1 (January–March 1914): 93.

34. See Rosa Bourassa La Flesche, PF, NPRC; and Cahill, *Federal Fathers and Mothers*.

35. "Our Chippewa Women Work," 169.

36. Letter to Gabe Parker, Papers of the Society of American Indians, microfilm reel 5, series 1, #913. The other signers were Charles Dagenett, Ida Riley, Rilla Meek, and H. Doxtater. Baldwin visited Hampton with Mrs. Riley, Miss Rilla Meek, and two other Indians in 1916. *Southern Workman* (Hampton, Va.) 65, no. 7 (July 1916): 436.

37. Waggoner, *Fire Light*; Hutchison, *Indian Craze*.

38. Her relatives included nieces Anna Roulette, Mary Belgard, and Emerald Bottineau and cousin Ernestine Venne. "General School News," *Carlisle (Penn.) Arrow* 8, no. 31 (April 12, 1912): 3; "General School News," *Carlisle (Penn.) Arrow* 7, no. 30 (March 31, 1911): 3.

39. "Susan Society vs Mercer Society" and "The Susan Longstreth Literary Society," *Carlisle (Penn.) Arrow* 9, no. 7 (October 18, 1912): 3, 2; Esthel Martell, "The Susans," *Carlisle (Penn.) Arrow* 10, no. 26 (February 27, 1914): 3; Henry Hayes, "The Standards," *Carlisle (Penn.) Arrow* 10, no. 28 (March 13, 1914): 3. See also "General School News," *Carlisle (Penn.) Arrow* 10, no. 6 (October 10, 1913): 2; "For Indian Legislation," *Carlisle (Penn.) Arrow* 10, no. 9 (October 31, 1913), 5; "A Delightful Party in the Interest of Suffrage," *Carlisle (Penn.) Arrow* 10, no. 19 (January 9, 1914), 5; James Welch, "The Standard Society," *Carlisle (Penn.) Arrow* 10, no. 10 (November 7, 1913), 4; "General School News," *Carlisle (Penn.) Arrow* 11, no. 16 (December 18, 1914).

40. Edward Bracklin, "Prophecy of the Class of '14," *Carlisle (Penn.) Arrow* 10, no. 37 (May 22, 1914): 9–11.

41. Lomawaima, "Mutuality of Citizenship"; Simpson, *Mohawk Interruptus*; Bruyneel, *Third Space of Sovereignty*.

42. Crandall, *These People Have Always Been A Republic*, 188; see also 177–225.

CHAPTER 10

1. Crandall, *These People Have Always Been a Republic*; Holtby, *Forty-Seventh Star*, 260.

2. The *Albuquerque Morning Journal* reported somewhat sympathetically, and the *Santa Fe New Mexican* very much so.

3. "New Mexico Governor Says He Is for Ratification," *Suffragist* 7, no. 25 (June 28, 1919): 8; "Suffragists Entertain Hope for New Mexico," *Carlsbad Current-Argus*, October 29, 1915.

4. Lozano, *American Language*. On the gendered dimensions of Hispanic responses to American colonization, see Perez, *Colonial Intimacies*; and Hyde, *Empires, Nations, and Families*. Margie Brown-Coronel's work on California suffragist Lucretia del Valle in California has many parallels. "'Born a Leading Lady': The Political Trajectory of Lucretia del Valle," forthcoming in *Journal of the Gilded Age and Progressive Era*, draft in author's possession.

5. "Organizer for Suffs at Work in New Mexico," *Albuquerque Journal*, February 28, 1916.

6. "Only the Vice and Liquor Interests, Ultra Conservatives and Fearful Politicians Are Opposed to Woman Suffrage, National Congressional Organizer Declares Here," *Santa Fe New Mexican*, October 19, 1915.

7. "Will Teach Spanish," *Tucumcari (N.Mex.) News and Tucumcari Times*, September 21, 1916; "Pan-Americans Get Baltimore Welcome," *Baltimore Sun*, January 11, 1916; Lozano, *American Language*. See also Marino, *Feminism for the Americas*.

8. Quoted in J. Jensen, "'Disenfranchisement Is a Disgrace.'"

9. "Only the Vice and Liquor Interests"; Pereles, "'Who Has a Greater Job Than a Mother?'"

10. "Only the Vice and Liquor Interests"; "Good Addresses at Suffrage Meeting," *Santa Fe New Mexican*. October 16, 1915.

11. "150 Santa Fe Suffragists," *Santa Fe New Mexican*, October 21, 1915.

12. Lola Armijo was the state librarian. Trinidad C. de Baca was the state game and fish warden. James W. Chavez was a state house member from Torrance County. See New Mexico Secretary of State, *New Mexico Blue Book*, 1915, 124; and "New Mexico's Game Warden Now Makes His Home in El Paso," *El Paso Times*, January 3, 1952. The C. de Bacas owned the third car in Santa Fe. Mrs. C. de Baca served as New Mexico's committeewoman to the national party. See "A Contract with the People: Platform of the Progressive Party Adopted at Its National Convention, St. Louis, April 13, 1917," New York: Progressive National Committee, 1917, 2, NWP Papers, part 2.

13. The Romeros made up a powerful political dynasty with Secundino Romero at its head. See "Papa y Los Muchachos Han Tenido Como Tres Quartos de Un Millon de Pesos de Las Oficinas Publicas," *El Nuevo Mexico* (Santa Fe, N.Mex.), October 26, 1916.

14. "150 Santa Fe Suffragists," *Santa Fe New Mexican*, October 21, 1915; "Suffragist Deputation in Automobile Parade." *Santa Fe New Mexican*, October 20, 1915.

15. "150 Santa Fe Suffragists."

16. "150 Santa Fe Suffragists"; "Let the Women Stay at Home, Have Children, and Wash Dishes, Catron Idea," *Santa Fe New Mexican*, October 22, 1915.

17. J. Jensen, "'Disenfranchisement Is a Disgrace,'" 18.

18. J. Jensen, 18.

19. "Organizer for Suffs at Work in New Mexico," *Albuquerque Morning Journal*. February 28, 1916; "Mrs. Raynolds Named Head of Suffrage Union," *Albuquerque Journal*. February 29, 1916; "Talent Imported by Suffs to Help Fight for Ballot," *Albuquerque Journal*, September 15, 1916.

20. "Organizer for Suffs at Work in New Mexico"; "Miss Doris Stevens to Arrive Tonight," *Santa Fe New Mexican*, February 25, 1916; "Suffrage Rally at Capital Monday Starts Campaign," *Santa Fe New Mexican*, February 26, 1916.

21. "Big Benefit Entertainment," *Santa Fe New Mexican*, May 1, 1906.

22. "Big Benefit Entertainment"; "Plaza Fete to Be Postponed," *Santa Fe New Mexican*, June 17, 1907; "Leap Year Frolic Proves Gorgeous State Pageant," *Santa Fe New Mexican*, March 7, 1916.

23. Wilson, *Myth of Santa Fe*.

24. "435 National Lawmaker-Politicians Hard to Control, Suffrage Leader Finds: Telling Blows for Ballots for Women," *Santa Fe New Mexican*, February 29, 1916; "Congressional Union Is Organized in New Mexico," *Suffragist* 4, no. 11 (1916): 7.

25. Quoted in J. Jensen, "'Disenfranchisement Is a Disgrace,'" 16.

26. C. Whaley, *Nina Otero-Warren*, 87–88.

CHAPTER 11

1. T. V. Soong, "Eastern Conference at Amherst, Mass.," *CSM*, October 1, 1914, 30.

2. Peffer, "Forbidden Families"; Ngai, "Western History and the Pacific World"; E. Lee, *At America's Gates*; Williams, *Chinese Must Go*.

3. Beth Lew Williams suggests that calling it the "Restriction Act" is more precise. Deliberately narrow in scope, it was not designed to completely exclude. Williams, *Chinese Must Go*, 51–52.

4. "All Wore Gowns at Erasmus Hall," *Brooklyn (N.Y.) Daily Eagle*, January 31, 1913; Barnard College transcripts, Mabel Lee, enrolled 1913–16.

5. Barnard had a branch in 1908–9. "College Equal Suffrage League Nationalize Their Organization, Become Part of National American Woman Suffrage Association," Miller NAWSA Suffrage Scrapbooks, 1897–1911, Scrapbook 7 (1908–1909), National American Woman Suffrage Association Collection, Library of Congress, http://hdl.loc.gov/loc.rbc/rbcmil.scrp5003301 (accessed January 15, 2020).

6. Rosenberg, *Changing the Subject*, 58.

7. Rosenberg, 58.

8. Rosenberg, 4, 143–47; Hauptman, *Seven Generations of Iroquois Leadership*, 248. According to Rosenberg, Columbia first admitted African American students in 1906, but Teachers College did not have the racial restrictions and "under the leadership of James Earl Russell and Mabel Carney prepared more black students for careers in higher education than any other school in the country."

9. Fass, *Damned and the Beautiful*.

10. *Mortarboard* yearbook (1913), Barnard College, New York, 165, https://digitalcollections .barnard.edu/yearbook (accessed January 20, 2020). When Lee appears in the 1915 yearbook, the cover image is an Indian in a headdress described as the "earliest known native inhabitant of America, strong, courageous, benevolent, hospitable, indifferent to pain, fond of war but very cautious, eloquent, of great dignity and self-respect." *Mortarboard* (1915), 165, https:// digitalcollections.barnard.edu/yearbook (accessed January 20, 2020).

11. Bieler, *Patriots or Traitors*, 28–33.

12. Bieler, 28–33.

13. Bevis, *History of Higher Education Exchange*, 101.

14. Bevis, 97. For one of Lee's contemporaries at Vassar, see Gulliver, *Modern Women in China and Japan*, especially the chapter on Sophia Chen Zen (1890–1976), 78–97.

15. Bieler, *Patriots or Traitors*, 209. See also Hsu, *Good Immigrants*.

16. Four were at Barnard, while three women were at Teachers College and one was at Horace Mann, the lab school of the Teachers College. "Many Chinese Students at Columbia," *Columbia (N.Y.) Daily Spectator*, September 29, 1913.

17. Joy Resmovits, "Barnard President Spar Forges Ties in China," *Columbia (N.Y.) Daily Spectator*, June 28, 2014, http://columbiaspectator.com/2009/03/30/barnard-president-spar-forges -ties-china (accessed January 14, 2020).

18. The Huies' mother was a white woman named Louise Van Arnam. Kin, *Reminiscences*.

19. Barnard College transcripts, Anna Fo Jin Kong, enrolled 1912–15.

20. "Cosmopolitan Group in Brooks Hall," *Columbia (N.Y.) Daily Spectator*, July 12, 1917.

21. *Mortarboard* (1916), 52, https://digitalcollections.barnard.edu/yearbook (accessed January 20, 2020); *Barnard Bulletin*, May 18, 1928, 53.

22. "Personal Notes," *CSM*, January 1, 1916, 122. On swimming, see "Club News: Columbia," *CSM*, January 1, 1915, 255–56.

23. "Church Club Play," *Barnard Bulletin*, January 22, 1914; "Student Forum," *Barnard Bulletin*, October 13, 1913; "Another Aspect of International Obligations," *Barnard Bulletin*, March 29, 1917.

24. "China's Submerged Half (1914)," reprinted in the 92nd Anniversary Celebration Program for the First Chinese Baptist Church, New York City, August 12, 2018, edited by Rev. Bayor Lee (copy in author's possession). Despite Yuan Shikai's increasing crackdown on feminists, she continued to believe that the Chinese women would win the vote but that "disturbed conditions" in their country had kept them from that goal for the moment.

25. It irritated her that woman suffrage was considered a joke. She had been in many situations where if one man or another "should wish to be considered witty, all that either would have to do would be to mention woman suffrage, and they may be sure of laughter and merriment in response." The fight for suffrage was not funny to Mabel. See M. Lee, "Meaning of Woman Suffrage," 526.

26. Cott, *Grounding of Modern Feminism*; M. Lee, "Meaning of Woman Suffrage," 526.

27. Barnard women had marched in the 1912 suffrage parade, but their parents complained and the student newspaper was conspicuously quiet about it. Rosenberg, *Changing the Subject*, 123; *Barnard Bulletin*, May 1912 issues.

28. See the following in the *Barnard Bulletin*: "Lecture by Mrs. Beard," January 11, 1915; "Feminist Forum Lecture," January 4, 1915; "Mrs. Gilman to Speak for Feminist Forum Friday," January 10, 1916; "Mrs. Gilman Addresses the Feminist Forum," January 24, 1916; "Moving Pictures at Barnard," December 7, 1914.

29. "Feminist Forum Meeting," *Barnard Bulletin*, December 5, 1914.

30. "Feminist Forum," *Barnard Bulletin*, November 2, 1914.

31. "Social Science League," *Barnard Bulletin*, November 23, 1915; "Academic Chapel: In Re Social Science League," *Barnard Bulletin*, December 6, 1915.

32. In 1917 she was listed as "Miss Lee of Canton" speaking on "Feminism in China" in "Religious Activities on the Campus for the Coming Week," *Columbia (N.Y.) Daily Spectator*, March 31, 1917.

33. Barnard College transcripts, Mabel Lee, enrolled 1913–16.

34. M. Lee, "Meaning of Woman Suffrage." For example, Professor William Montague used a similar chronology of rights. "Feminist Forum Meeting," *Barnard Bulletin*, November 16, 1914.

35. Rosenberg, *Changing the Subject*, 107–14.

36. Cited in Ye, *Seeking Modernity in China's Name*, 144.

37. Helen Maclay to Mabel Lee, February 1, 1915, Mabel Lee Papers, private collection, First Chinese Baptist Church, New York.

38. "Chinese Girl for Suffrage," *New York Times*, January 30, 1915; "Suffrage Shop Talks," *New York Tribune*, January 18, 1915; "Human Interest Stories," *Middletown (N.Y.) Daily Argus*, February 1, 1915; Finnegan, *Selling Suffrage*.

39. "Suffrage Line Thrills East Side," *New York Tribune*, September 5, 1915; "Big Parade of Suffrage Party," *Standard Union* (Brooklyn, N.Y.), September 4, 1915.

40. "A Campaign of Interest for Suffrage," *Ithaca (N.Y.) Journal*, October 12, 1915.

41. "International Division in Suffrage Parade," *Brooklyn (N.Y.) Daily Eagle*, September 9, 1915; *Suffragette Parading in NYC 1915*, United Press International Photo in author's possession.

42. "Tramp, Tramp, Tramp Girls Are Marching; Cheered along Way," *Brooklyn (N.Y.) Daily*

Eagle, October 23, 1915; "Suffrage Parade from East Side," *Poughkeepsie (N.Y.) Eagle-News*, October 25, 1915.

43. "Columbia News," CSM, December 10, 1913, 148.

44. "Columbia Club," CSM, November 1, 1914, 107. In 1913–14 there were a total of 644 CSA members nationwide out of an estimated 1,000 Chinese students in the United States. "Alliance and Sectional Business. Report of President Chang Loy for 1913–14," CSM, November 1, 1914, 111–14.

45. "Club News: Columbia Club," CSM, December 1, 1914, 186–87; T. I. Dunn, "The 11th Annual Conference of the Eastern Section," CSM, June 1, 1915, 599–603.

46. For example, see "Chinese Students to Entertain Japanese," *Columbia (N.Y.) Daily Spectator*, March 1, 1912.

47. Yoeh-Liang Tong, "Chairman Tong's Report for October and November," CSM, December 10, 1913, 163.

48. M. Lee, "Meaning of Woman Suffrage," 531; Bieler, *Patriots or Traitors*, 187–92.

49. Soong, "Eastern Conference at Amherst, Mass.," 30–33.

50. Soong, 30–33.

51. "The Rise of Yuan Shi-Kai: Columbia Chinese Students Write Play of Chinese History, Showing Development from Ancient Times," *Columbia (N.Y.) Daily Spectator*, May 17, 1912, 6.

52. Soong, "Eastern Conference at Amherst, Mass."; Mabel Lee, "Chinese Patriotism: Winning Oration at Amherst Conference," CSM, October 1, 1914, 30–33.

53. Soong, "Eastern Section Conference at Amherst, Mass."; "Many Chinese Are Studying at T.C.," *Columbia (N.Y.) Daily Spectator*, January 31, 1916.

54. "159 New Alliance Members," CSM, January 1, 1915, 239–41; Fass, *Damned and the Beautiful*.

55. H. K. Kwong, "Alliance President's Message," CSM, December 1, 1915, 127.

56. Resolutions Committee, CSM, June 1, 1915, 602; CSM, December 1915.

57. "Spectator's Directory of T. C. Activities," *Columbia (N.Y.) Daily Spectator*, December 11, 1916, 6.

58. M. Lee, "Moral Training in Chinese Schools," 544–45.

59. M. Lee, 545.

60. M. Lee, 545–46.

61. M. Lee, "Meaning of Woman Suffrage," 527.

62. Bieler, *Patriots or Traitors*, 186–87.

63. Hahn, *Soong Sisters*.

64. M. Lee, "Meaning of Woman Suffrage," 526.

CHAPTER 12

1. The two organizations merged in 1917 into the NWP. I will use NWP from here on.

2. From "Historical Timeline of National Woman's Party," Women of Protest: Photographs from the Records of the National Woman's Party, LOC, https://www.loc.gov/collections/women -of-protest/articles-and-essays/historial-timeline-of-the-national-womans-party/1915-to-1916/ (accessed February 15, 2020).

3. "Jones, If Elected, to Head Public Lands Committee," *Santa Fe New Mexican*, June 16, 1916.

4. "Jones, Andrieus Aristieus (1862–1927)," *Biographical Dictionary of the United States Congress, 1774–Present*, http://bioguide.congress.gov/scripts/biodisplay.pl?index=J000210 (accessed January 14, 2020).

5. "New Mexico Men in Congress Get Places; Mr. Jones Draws Suffrage," *Albuquerque Journal*, April 16, 1917.

6. Hamlin, *Free Thinker*, 234; Stevens, *Jailed for Freedom*.

7. Capozzola, *Uncle Sam Wants You*, 54.

8. C. Green, *Washington*, 234–35.

9. C. Green, 234–35; Marie L. B. Baldwin, PF NPRC. Her boarders were a mother and daughter working as clerk and stenographer. Marie L. Baldwin, year: 1920; census place: Washington, Washington, District of Columbia; roll: T625_209; page: 14A; enumeration district: 138 (accessed via ancestry.com, January 14, 2020).

10. Hamlin, *Free Thinker*, 236–37; Park, *Front Door Lobby*; Flexner and Fitzpatrick, *Century of Struggle*, 269–87.

11. Linkugel and Griffin, "Distinguished War Service," 374. See also "A Formidable Array of Sunday Features, Both Instructive and Entertaining," *Evening Star* (Washington, D.C.), June 2, 1917.

12. "Women to Be Taught Conservation of Food," *Evening Star* (Washington, D.C.), June 2, 1917.

13. Efficiency Records, October 20, 1917, and April 1, 1918, Marie Baldwin, PF NPRC.

14. C. Whaley, *Nina Otero-Warren*, 88–89.

15. "Food Conservers and School Pupils Show How Fruit Waste Is Averted," *Santa Fe New Mexican*, September 29, 1917; "Personal Gossip of the Old Town," *Santa Fe New Mexican*, July 16, 1917; "Mrs. Collins Heads Local Navy Chapter," *Santa Fe New Mexican*, July 3, 1917.

16. "Confederate Armies March on Washington," *Evening Star* (Washington, D.C.), June 1, 1917; "Veterans Arriving Ahead of Schedules," *Evening Star* (Washington, D.C.), June 2, 1917.

17. "Greetings of President to Confederate Veterans," *Evening Star* (Washington, D.C.), June 5, 1917; "Welcome of Blue to Gray Cited by Gen. Harrison as Evidence of United Nation," *Evening Star* (Washington, D.C.), June 5, 1917. See also Capozzola, *Uncle Sam Wants You*.

18. "Greetings of President to Confederate Veterans."

19. P. Bernstein, *First Waco Horror*.

20. P. Bernstein.

21. Sutherland, *African Americans in War*; Maurice Cecil Clifford, WWI draft registration card, and Joshua Williams Clifford, WWI draft registration card, both in U.S. World War II Draft Registration Cards, 1917–18, registration state: District of Columbia; registration county: Washington; roll: 1556838; draft board: 08 (accessed via ancestry.com, January 15, 2020).

22. Grossman, *Land of Hope*.

23. Black women in Illinois could vote in presidential and educational elections as of 1913. Materson, *For the Freedom of Her Race*.

24. "The Negro Silent Parade," *Crisis*, September 1917, 241–44; "The Massacre of East St. Louis," *Crisis*, September 1917, 219–38; Armstrong, *Mary Turner*, 70.

25. Clifford, "Race-Hate," in *Widening Light*, 15.

26. "Negro Silent Parade," 241.

27. Clifford, "Silent Protest Parade," in *Widening Light*, 16–18. See photographs in "Negro Silent Parade," 241–44.

28. The idea of "Silent Sentinels" came from New York suffragists picketing the state capitol. Flexner and Fitzpatrick, *Century of Struggle*, 275. See also "Negro Silent Parade," 241.

29. "Negro Silent Parade"; "Massacre of East St. Louis"; Armstrong, *Mary Turner*, 70.

30. Clifford, "Silent Protest Parade," 16–18.

31. See Clifford, "Little Mother: Upon the Lynching of Mary Turner" in *Widening Light*, 19.

32. Maurice C. Clifford in Ohio Soldiers in WWI, 1917–1918 (accessed via ancestry.com, January 15, 2020).

33. Hunton and Johnson, *Two Colored Women*, 123.

34. "Oath of Office and Personal History," September 18, 1923, Joshua W. Clifford, PF NPRC; Joshua W. Clifford in Ohio Soldiers in WWI, 1917–1918 (accessed via ancestry.com, January 14,

2020). As an officer, Joshua may have been one of the men to receive additional training in the American Training School at Gondre Court. Hunton and Johnson, *Two Colored Women*, 53.

35. Hunton and Johnson, *Two Colored Women*, 52–55. See also Scott, *Scott's Official History*, especially "German Propaganda among the Negros" and "Negro Women in War Work," written by Alice Dunbar-Nelson, 344 and 367.

36. Jenkins, Peck, and Weaver, "Between Reconstructions," 66.

37. On the flu, see Hunton and Johnson, *Two Colored Women*, 150–51.

38. Clifford, "Mothers of America," in *Widening Light*, 2. Several of her poems addressed the war, including "Deceived," "The Black Draftee from Dixie," and "Our Women of the Canteen," in Clifford, *Widening Light*, 21–22, and 26.

39. Clifford, "Our Women of the Canteen," 26; Hunton and Johnson, *Two Colored Women*. Suffragists also continued to work for state suffrage. Flexner and Fitzpatrick, *Century of Struggle*, 300–306.

CHAPTER 13

1. Hamlin, *Free Thinker*, 220–79; Park, *Front Door Lobby*; Flexner and Fitzpatrick, *Century of Struggle*, 269–87.

2. Park, *Front Door Lobby*, 109.

3. Park, 64–65. She did urge all women to write letters, noting that congressmen often compared the size of the piles of letters for and against to determine their vote. Park, 93.

4. Park, 192.

5. The 1916 elections in New Mexico brought two pro-suffrage Democrats to Congress: Representative William Walton, who promised (though he needed some prodding from Otero-Warren) to vote for the amendment and did when it passed in the House in January 1918, and Senator A. A. Jones. J. Jensen, "'Disenfranchisement Is a Disgrace,'" 21.

6. Yasutake, "Re-franchising Women of Hawai'i"; Silva, *Aloha Betrayed*; Sneider, *Suffragists in an Imperial Age*.

7. King David Kalākaua conferred the title of prince on Kalaniana'ole and his brother. For more, see Prince Jonah Kūhiō Kalaniana'ole, 1872–1922, at Royal Family of Hawaii Official Website, https://www.keouanui.org/kuhio (accessed January 20, 2020).

8. Silva, *Aloha Betrayed*; Yasutake, "Re-franchising Women of Hawai'i," 118–19.

9. Yasutake, "Re-franchising Women of Hawai'i," 126; Peterson, "Kalanianaole." Elizabeth Kahanu Kalaniana'ole did live in D.C. at times during her husband's tenure. In 1919, she was in Hawaii and gave a pro-suffrage speech to the territorial legislature. In 1922, she became the head of the Women's Republican Auxiliary in Hawaii.

10. "Hawaii Wants Statehood," *Fall River (Mass.) Daily Evening News*, September 18, 1912; "Favor Woman Suffrage," *Ottawa (Kans.) Daily Republic*, April 14, 1913.

11. Harper, *History of Women Suffrage*, 715–19; Yasutake, "Re-franchising Women of Hawai'i ."

12. Delegate Kūhiō had returned to Hawaii for business, but his secretary attended the hearings. Park, *Front Door Lobby*, 104, 187.

13. Yasutake, "Re-franchising Women of Hawai'i," 129–30.

14. Flexner and Fitzpatrick, *Century of Struggle*, 169–86.

15. Stevens, *Jailed for Freedom*, 173.

16. Flexner and Fitzpatrick, *Century of Struggle*, 169–86; Hamlin, *Free Thinker*, 240–43.

17. Stevens, *Jailed for Freedom*, 155–56. See also the photograph *Negro Women Prostitutes Were Brought to This Sleeping Room and Placed in Beds Alternating with Suffrage Prisoners*, 1917, LOC, http://hdl.loc.gov/loc.mss/mnwp.160047 (accessed February 15, 2020).

18. Stevens, *Jailed for Freedom*; Flexner and Fitzpatrick, *Century of Struggle*, 279.

19. Stevens, *Jailed for Freedom*; Hamlin, *Free Thinker*, 245–67.

20. "Council Announces New Fellowships," *Columbia (N.Y.) Daily Spectator*, April 19, 1917; "Lee, Mabel Pinghua," in Tung, *Who's Who of Chinese Students in America*, 52.

21. Franceschi, "Women in the Field."

22. *Columbia University in the City of New York Catalogue* (New York City), 1917–18, 225, Columbia University Archives.

23. "Ching Ching Chinatown," *Barnard Bulletin*, October 15, 1920. Columbia also had what looks like a repeating tour; for a similar ad, see *Columbia (N.Y.) Daily Spectator*, April 30, 1915.

24. Y. C. Chang, "Club News: Columbia," *CSM*, December 1, 1918, 137.

25. From J. Spence, *Search for Modern China*, 284–85.

26. "Chinese Club Cables China," *Columbia (N.Y.) Daily Spectator*, April 30, 1915.

27. Lorraine Boissoneault, "The Surprisingly Important Role China Played in WWI," *Smithsonian Magazine*, August 17, 2017, https://www.smithsonianmag.com/history/surprisingly-important-role-china-played-world-war-i-180964532 (accessed February 15, 2020).

28. Bevis, *History of Higher Education Exchange*, 97; Edwards, "Zhang Mojun" and Boorman, "Chang Mo-Chün," 85–87.

29. Chang, "Club News: Columbia," 137.

30. This article describes her as principal of the Tseng Chow Girl-School in Shanghai, but I used Shenchou for consistency. "Club News: Columbia," *CSM*, May 1, 1919, 446.

31. "Club News: Harvard," *CSM*, February 1, 1919, 253; "Club News: Columbia," *CSM*, May 1, 1919, 446.

32. "Club News: Harvard," 253; "The Annual Conference of the Kuo Fong Hui," *CSM*, March 1, 1919, 338–42.

33. I. Lewis, *Education of Girls in China*, 4–5.

34. "Club News: Columbia," 446.

35. Boissoneault, "Surprisingly Important Role China Played in WWI." Historian Bruce Ellman argues that this unresolved issue led the Chinese down the road to communism.

36. Ta Chen, "Personal News," *CSM*, February 1, 1921, 305.

37. Rosenberg, *Changing the Subject*, 107–17.

38. *Columbia University in the City of New York Catalogue*, 1917–18, 100; Rosenberg, *Changing the Subject*, 107–17.

39. M. Lee, "Economic History of China," 16–17.

40. M. Lee, 16–17; Mencken, *American Language*, 513–14.

41. M. Lee, 14.

42. Quoted in Cott, *Grounding of Modern Feminism*, 227.

43. Alice Huie, Application for registration—Native citizen, U.S., Consular Registration Applications, 1916–, roll #: 32734_1220705228_0235, page: 304 (accessed via ancestry.com, February 15, 2020).

44. Kin, *Reminiscences*, 113–14.

45. Brooks, *American Exodus*, 62.

CHAPTER 14

1. *Tomahawk* (White Earth, Minn.), June 21, 1917. Her address is listed at 707 20th Street NW in Washington.

2. Zitkala-Ša, "Among the Ute Tribe of Indians (October–December, 1916)," in *American Indian Stories*, 168; Lewandowski, *Red Bird*, 65–101.

3. D. Welch, "Gertrude Simmons Bonnin."

4. On candy, see Marie Bottineau Baldwin to Arthur C. Parker, June 2, 1917, in Papers of the Society of American Indians (microfilm). On Bonnin's interpersonal relationships, see D. Welch, "Gertrude Simmons Bonnin."

5. See Marie Bottineau Baldwin to Arthur C. Parker, June 2, 1917.

6. "Indian Woman in Capital to Fight Growing Use of Peyote Drug by Indians," *Washington Times*, February 17, 1918.

7. D. Welch, "Gertrude Simmons Bonnin," 42.

8. "Indians Will Lobby before State Solons: Redmen Seek Passage of Peyote Bill at Next Session," *Salt Lake Telegram*, December 10, 1916.

9. Zitkala-Ša, "The Menace of Peyote," in *American Indian Stories*, 239–41.

10. "Would Put Ban on Peyote," *Evening Star* (Washington, D.C.), December 5, 1917.

11. Zitkala-Ša, "Menace of Peyote," 239–41; Barnett, "Politics of Peyote."

12. "Rely on Free Press: It Is Best Aid to National Prohibition, Miss Rankin Says," *Topeka State Journal*, December 5, 1917; "Miss Bonnin Talks at Hut," *Evening Star* (Washington, D.C.), August 20, 1918.

13. Vigil, *Indigenous Intellectuals*, 205.

14. Davidson and Norris, introduction to *American Indian Stories*, xxiii.

15. James Mooney criticized her outfit, accusing her of being inauthentic. See Carpenter, "Detecting Indianness," 150–51.

16. "Indian Woman in Capital to Fight."

17. "Indian Woman in Capital to Fight."

18. Krouse, *North American Indians in the Great War*.

19. "Personal News of Capital's Secret and Fraternal Societies: Improved Order of Red Men," *Washington Herald*, May 26, 1918.

20. "Among the Clubs: Anthony League," *Sunday Star* (Washington, D.C.), April 28, 1918; "Society in Washington," *Washington Herald*, April 24, 1918; "Mrs. Bonnin to Address Committee," *Evening Star* (Washington, D.C.), April 23, 1918.

21. "Society," *Evening Star* (Washington, D.C.), February 21, 1918. See also "Society in Washington," *Washington Herald*, February 22, 1918; "Personal News of Capital's Secret and Fraternal Societies"; and "Among the Clubs: The Mount Pleasant WCTU," *Sunday Star* (Washington, D.C.), May 19, 1918.

22. "Miss Bonnin Talks at Hut: Tells of American Indians' Patriotism at Camp Meigs," *Evening Star* (Washington, D.C.), August 20, 1918; "Indian Woman in Capital to Fight Growing Use of Peyote Drug by Indians"; "Indians Seek Closer Touch with Congress," *Evening Star* (Washington, D.C.), February 9, 1918.

23. Carpenter, "Detecting Indianness."

24. "Indian Woman to be Speaker," *Washington Post*, June 2, 1918. The NWP headquarters moved to 14 Jackson Place NW in January 1918 when Bonnin was testifying at the peyote hearings. See "Historical Timeline of National Woman's Party," Women of Protest: Photographs from the Records of the National Woman's Party, LOC, https://www.loc.gov/collections/women -of-protest/articles-and-essays/historial-timeline-of-the-national-womans-party/1915-to-1916/ (accessed February 15, 2020).; and Terrell, *Colored Woman in a White World*, 316.

25. "Break the Shackles Now, — Make Us Free"; Chauncey Yellow Robe, "The Fighting Sioux"; Charles Eastman, "The Sioux of Yesterday and Today," *American Indian Magazine* 5, no. 4 (Winter 1917): 213–15, 227, 239. For an example, see Archambault, "Man of Two Worlds."

26. See Cahill, "Marie Louise Bottineau Baldwin." Only thirty members attended. Bonnin claimed the low attendance was because of the war, but the pro-peyote group boycotted. Others were disappointed by the society's seeming inability to change federal policy. See D. Welch, "Gertrude Simmons Bonnin," 46.

27. Zitkala-Ša, "Address by the Secretary-Treasurer, Society of American Indians Annual Convention, Summer 1919," in *American Indian Stories*, 217–18.

28. Zitkala-Ša, "America, Home of the Red Man," in *American Indian Stories*, 193–95.

29. Zitkala-Ša, 184.

30. Zitkala-Ša, "Editorial Comment (Winter 1919)," in *American Indian Stories*, 192.

31. Zitkala-Ša, "Editorial Comment (Summer 1919)," in *American Indian Stories*, 208.

32. From Zitkala-Ša, "Editorial Comment (Winter 1919)," 191–92. Approximately 12,000 Natives had served in the war. About 6,500 of them had been drafted and another 6,000 volunteered. Approximately 20–30 percent of all adult Native men served, giving them a higher rate of service than American men. At least 5 percent of Native soldiers died in action. Many of those who died did not have U.S. citizenship. Krouse, *North American Indians in the Great War*, 80; Barsh, "American Indians in the Great War."

33. From Zitkala-Ša, "Editorial Comment (Winter 1919)," 191–92.

34. Krouse, *North American Indians in the Great War*, 148–64.

35. Krouse, 148–64.

CHAPTER 15

1. Special Correspondent, "Mrs. Otero-Warren Aids in Lobby Work for Suffrage Cause," *Santa Fe New Mexican*, March 15, 1916; "President Opposed to Using Guard," *Carlsbad (N.Mex.) Current-Argus*, March 24, 1916; "Personals," *Santa Fe New Mexican*, April 17, 1916; "Mr. and Mrs. White Entertained in East," *Santa Fe New Mexican*, March 14, 1916; "Congressional Union Is Organized in New Mexico," *Suffragist*, 4 no. 11 (March 11, 1916): 7. It is possible she also attended a meeting of educators in Atlantic City. See "Personal Gossip of the Old Town," *Santa Fe New Mexican*, February 6, 1918; "Personal Gossip of the Old Town," *Santa Fe New Mexican*, March 18, 1918.

2. "The City's Social Side," *Washington Times*, February 23, 1918; "Society," *Washington Post*, February 14, 1918; *San Francisco Chronicle*, March 3, 1918.

3. Correspondencia Especial, "Una Candidata para el Senado," *La Voz del Pueblo*, March 23, 1918. The two women also traveled to Wisconsin via New York to visit Otero-Warren's sister, Estella Bergere, who was married to ecologist Aldo Leopold. "Personals"; Burke, *A Land Apart*, 155–57.

4. "Meet of State Bankers Enlivens Society in Ancient City; Kings of Finance are Royally Entertained," *Albuquerque Journal*, September 15, 1918; "Suffrage League Meeting," *Albuquerque Journal*, June 16, 1918. Aurora Lucero moved to Tucumcari to teach high school and was therefore out of the main suffrage work. See "Will Teach Spanish," *Tucumcari (N.Mex.) News and Tucumcari Times*, September 21, 1916; "Local Items, *Albuquerque Morning Journal*, October 17, 1917. But she was elected to a committee in November 1917; see "Wants to Back Up Ballots at Polls, Suffrage Leaguers Serve Refreshments," *Santa Fe New Mexican*, November 2, 1917. She embarked with Mrs. Benito Baca on a statewide anti-saloon league tour in October visiting Tucumcari, Clovis, Albuquerque, Socorro, Deming, and Silver City, among others. "Local Items," *Albuquerque Morning Journal*, October 19, 1917; "Personal Gossip of the Old Town," *Santa Fe New Mexican*, October 29, 1917. In June 1919 she married a Denver man and moved to Latin America. "Miss Aurora Lucero Is Wed to Garner D. White," *Albuquerque Journal*, June 25, 1919.

5. "Republican Candidates of the County of Santa Fe," *Santa Fe New Mexican*, November 2, 1918.

6. "Eight Counties to Have Women Superintendents," *Albuquerque Morning Journal*, November 29, 1918. See also "Women Win Offices in Several States," *Los Angeles Times*, November 9, 1918.

7. "Mrs. Adelina Otero-Warren Is to Head Victory Organization," *Santa Fe New Mexican*, October 31, 1918; "Mrs. Warren May Go Abroad," *Albuquerque Journal*, November 25, 1918.

8. C. Whaley, *Nina Otero-Warren*, 90–91.

9. "Club Women Map Out Program for New Legislation," *Albuquerque Journal*, January 30, 1919; "New Mexico Clubwomen Want Delinquent Girls Looked After, Movies Censored, Public Health Board," *Santa Fe New Mexican*, January 29, 1919.

10. "Club Women Map Out Program for New Legislation"; "Executive Reception Brilliant," *Santa Fe New Mexican*, February 1, 1919.

11. "Notes of the Week: Republican Woman's Committee," *Suffragist* 7, no. 50 (January 4, 1919): 3.

12. "Mrs. Warren Given Bursum's Place on State Health Board," *Santa Fe New Mexican*, April 25, 1919; "State Department of Health Holds Initial Meeting," *Santa Fe New Mexican*, April 26, 1919; "New Mexico Has Only Woman in US on a State Health Board," *Albuquerque Journal*, April 27, 1919.

13. "Women to Confer on G.O.P Policies," *Evening Star* (Washington, D.C.), May 18, 1919; "Republican Women Meet at Washington," *Standard Union* (Brooklyn, N.Y.), May 22, 1919, 11; "Delegates Named," *Santa Fe New Mexican*, May 24, 1919; "New Mexico to Be Well Represented at Educational Meet," *Santa Fe New Mexican*, February 21, 1919.

14. "Suffrage Jubilee," *Albuquerque Journal*, June 1, 1919.

15. "Suffrage Jubilee"; "Suffrage Meeting to Hear Miss Winsor Non-Partisan Affair," *Santa Fe New Mexican*, June 12, 1919. See also Harper, *History of Woman Suffrage*, 647.

16. He did not do so until February of the following year. Harper, *History of Woman Suffrage*, 605–7 and 642; J. Jensen, "'Disenfranchisement Is a Disgrace,'" 22–23.

17. Catt had proposed the league at the NAWSA conference in St. Louis that March, and it would be officially founded at the NAWSA conference the following year. It initially had a "scattershot" approach to politics but soon settled into a good government organization. Cott, *Grounding of Modern Feminism*, 86. On the LWV's postradification work, see Gidlow, *Big Vote*.

18. They were Marjorie Shuller, Jessie Haver, and Dr. Valeria Parker.

19. "Mrs. Catt Arrives for Conference of Women Voters," *Albuquerque Morning Journal*, December 4, 1919, 2; "Women Decide to Organize Voters' League," *Evening Herald* (Albuquerque), December 5, 1919; "Mrs. Catt Given Big Ovations at Three Meetings," *Albuquerque Journal*, December 5, 1919; "Want to Vote before National Election in 1920," *Albuquerque Morning Journal*, November 24, 1919; "Women of New Mexico Are Preparing for the Ballot," *Deming (N.Mex.) Headlight*, December 23, 1919; "New Mexico Women Have Great Chance to Be of Service to Suffrage Cause, Says Mrs. Catt," *Santa Fe New Mexican*, December 14, 1919.

20. "Legislature Urged to Ratify Suffrage Amendment Promptly," *Albuquerque Journal*, January 18, 1919.

21. Washington Street was closely connected to women's activism in the city. It included the county library, which women had funded and which had employed the state's first female civil servant, Lola Armijo.

22. "GOP Women's Division ... Homey Headquarters Opened Not Much Like the Old Style," *Santa Fe New Mexican*, February 15, 1920.

23. "Suffrage Totters on Edge of Defeat by Pledge-Breakers," *Santa Fe New Mexican*, February 17, 1920; "Ratify," *Santa Fe New Mexican*, February 16, 1920; "Is New Mexico Going to Line Up with Texas?," *Santa Fe New Mexican*, February 17, 1920. Texas ratified the amendment in June 1919, but the author seems to be using New Mexican fears of white supremacist immigrants from Texas.

24. "Society Divided," *Albuquerque Journal*, February 22, 1920; "Hurry Call Sent Out to Republican Leaders to Break Opposition Line Up," *Santa Fe New Mexican*, February 17, 1920.

25. "Women May Not Vote in NM Next November," *Albuquerque Journal*, February 27, 1920.

26. See pictures from 1919 at LOC, https://www.loc.gov/resource/hec.12742/ and https://www.loc.gov/resource/mnwp.150012/ (accessed January 15, 2020).

27. July: Iowa, Missouri, Arkansas; August: Montana, Nebraska; September: Minnesota, New Hampshire; October: Utah; November: California, Maine.

28. December: North Dakota, South Dakota, Colorado; January: Kentucky, Rhode Island, Oregon, Indiana, Wyoming.

CHAPTER 16

1. Catt and Shuler, *Woman Suffrage*, 428. See also Weiss, *Woman's Hour*.
2. Catt and Shuler, 442.
3. Catt and Shuler, 445.
4. Van Voris, *Carrie Chapman Catt*.
5. "Stream of Colors Fill State Capital," *Chattanooga News*, August 18, 1920.
6. "Federal Amendment to the Constitution Granting Universal Suffrage to Women Adapted by State General Assembly—50 to 46," *Chattanooga News*, August 18, 1920; "News Received with Wild Enthusiasm," *Chattanooga News*, August 18, 1920.
7. Catt and Shuler, *Woman Suffrage*, 449.
8. Boyd, *Tennessee Statesman Harry T. Burn*, 53.
9. Catt and Shuler, *Woman Suffrage*, 456.
10. Van Voris, *Carrie Chapman Catt*, 162.
11. Catt and Shuler, *Woman Suffrage*, 455–56.
12. Kellogg, *Our Democracy*, 86.
13. "Will Address Women Tonight," *Wausau (Wis.) Daily Herald*, September 6, 1920.
14. "Mrs. Kellogg at Plymouth Wednesday," *Sheboygan (Wis.) Press*, September 21, 1920, 6; "Will Speak to Women," *Oshkosh (Wis.) Northwestern*, September 16, 1920, 4; "Woman's Defense Ass'n Speaks Here on Friday," *Daily Tribune* (Wisconsin Rapids), September 9, 1920.
15. Hauptman, *Seven Generations of Iroquois Leadership*, 147.
16. "Woman's Defense Ass'n Speaks Here on Friday"; "Will Address Women Tonight."
17. "Woman's Defense Ass'n Speaks Here on Friday," 1.
18. See "Wisconsin and the 19th Amendment," National Park Service https://www.nps.gov/articles/wisconsin-women-s-history.htm (accessed January 15, 2020).
19. Wisconsin currently has eleven federally recognized tribes.
20. The 1923 Wisconsin laws stated that "civilized persons of Indian decent" who no longer lived in tribal relations or those who had been made citizens by an act of Congress could vote. *Wisconsin Blue Book*, 691–92 and 715–16.
21. The census enumerator said it was not by allotment; none of the Oneida citizens on the page were. Minnie Cornelious, year: 1900; census place: Oneida Indian Reservation, Outagamie, Wisconsin; page: 40; enumeration district: 0161; FHL microfilm: 1241779 (accessed via ancestry.com, January 7, 2020).
22. Kellogg, *Laura Cornelius Kellogg*, 43–46.
23. Paul R. Mallon, "Princess White Deer Predicts Squaws Will Have Something to Say at Polls," *News-Herald*, March 19, 1921; Galperin, *In Search of Princess White Deer*, 167–68. See also Crandall, *These People Have Always Been a Republic*.
24. Hauptman and McLester, *Oneida Indians*, 249–52.
25. "Indian Women on War Path to Get Equal Suffrage," *Daily Ardmoreite* (Ardmore, Okla.), June 6, 1922, 4; for an earlier article on the Chippewa enfranchising women, see "News to Date in Paragraphs," *Carrizozo (N.Mex.) Outlook*, July 20, 1917, 4.
26. Mrs. Peter Nicolar to Percival P. Baxter, February 21, 1921, in *Sprague's Journal of Maine History* 9, no. 1 (January–March 1921), 44; Lucien Thayer, "Woman Suffrage Fight Isn't Won Yet: Maine Indians Won't Let Squaws Vote," *Boston Globe*, March 13, 1921; "Indian Women Start on Warpath for Rights," *Daily Ardmoreite* (Ardmore, Okla.), February 28, 1921; "Indian Women Want Right to Vote in Tribal Elections," *Albuquerque Morning Journal*, February 27, 1921. On Penobscot women's history of petitioning and their participation in governance, see Pawling, "'Labyrinth of Uncertainties.'"
27. In most cases, formal inclusion would not occur until the passage of the Indian Reorganization Act in 1933 that created federally recognized tribal governments. The IRA guar-

anteed Native women the right to vote and to hold tribal office. See A. Bernstein, "Mixed Record."

28. Giddings, *Ida*, 615. At the Republican National Convention in the spring of 1920, white women ousted Robert Terrell from his position as delegate, which "ruined any chance for their receiving support from the colored people in the suffrage fight." Secretary NAACP to Miss Paul, July 9, 1920, NAACP Papers.

29. C. Anderson, *One Person, No Vote*; Gidlow, "Sequel"; Gilmore, *Gender and Jim Crow*; Terborg, *African American Women in the Struggle for the Vote*.

30. Anna A. Clemons to Emma Wold, October 10, 1920, National Woman's Party Papers, 1913–74, LOC (microfilm 19279, reel 5). See also Sklar and Dias, "How Did the National Woman's Party Address the Issue."

31. Emma Wold to Anna A. Clemons, October 20, 1920, National Woman's Party Papers, 1913–74, LOC (microfilm 19279, reel 5).

32. Anna A. Clemons to Emma Wold, October 24, 1920, National Woman's Party Papers, 1913–74, LOC (microfilm 19279, reel 5).

33. Emma Wold to Anna A. Clemons, October 28, 1920, and November 2, 1920, National Woman's Party Papers, 1913–74, LOC (microfilm 19279, reel 5). See also Gidlow, "Sequel."

34. "NAACP History: Dyer Anti-Lynching Bill," NAACP.org https://www.naacp.org/naacp-history-dyer-anti-lynching-bill/ (accessed May 7, 2019); Mungarro and Anderson, "How Did Black Women?"; Zangrando, *NAACP Crusade Against Lynching*.

35. Jenkins, Peck, and Weaver, "Between Reconstructions."

36. "Suffrage to Be Celebrated at Noon on Saturday," *Albuquerque Morning Journal*, August 27, 1920.

37. "Women Here Plan Suffrage Jubilee," *Evening Herald* (Albuquerque), August 20, 1920.

38. "Women Getting Share in Work of Demo Party at Convention," *Albuquerque Morning Journal*, August 25, 1920; "Women's Place in Republican State Organization Fixed at Albuquerque; Given Third of Central Committee," *Santa Fe New Mexican*, September 7, 1920.

39. "Woman Suffrage," *Deming (N.Mex.) Headlight*, September 7, 1920.

40. "Woman Suffrage," *Deming (N.Mex.) Headlight*, September 7, 1920; J. Jensen, "'Disenfranchisement Is a Disgrace,'" 23–24.

41. "Women to Play Important Part at Convention," *Albuquerque Morning Journal*, September 7, 1920; "Women Get Tips on Inside Politics," *Evening Herald* (Albuquerque), September 10, 1920. Not all Hispanas agreed with her; see Luz Clena Ortiz's letter to the editor, "Women Want Reduction in Taxes and Less Officeholders, One Says," *Santa Fe New Mexican*, September 14, 1920.

42. "County Sends 68 Delegates—But Mrs. Warren Is Not One of Them," *Santa Fe New Mexican*, August 18, 1921. Female delegates with Spanish surnames included Mrs. Benito Alarid, Mrs. Kate Alarid, and Mrs. Manuel Salazar. Margie Brown-Coronel, "'Born a Leading Lady': The Political Trajectory," forthcoming in *Journal of the Gilded Age and Progressive Era*, draft in author's possession. An African American, Annie Simms Banks of Winchester, served as a delegate to the Republican convention in Kentucky in 1920 as well. See *New York Age*, March 31, 1920, in NAACP Papers.

43. "Women Voters Hold Balance of Power in Coming Election Is Leader's Belief," *Santa Fe New Mexican*, August 22, 1920.

44. "Governor Mechem Stands by Party Platform," *Santa Fe New Mexican*, January 12, 1921.

45. "Governor Mechem Stands by Party Platform"; "Governor Mechem's Address," *Las Vegas Optic*, January 12, 1921; "Governor Mechem's Message to Legislature Recommends Party Pledges of Campaign," *Las Vegas Optic*, January 12, 1921; "Short Ballot Urged, Abolish Sinecures," *Santa Fe New Mexican*, January 12, 1921.

46. "Proposal to Permit Women to Hold Public Office Ratified; Up to Governor for Signa-

ture," *Albuquerque Morning Journal*, February 10, 1921; "Bill for County Budgets and One Creating Office of State Education Auditor Pass House," *Albuquerque Morning Journal*, March 13, 1921.

47. "Platforms Adopted by the Democratic and Republican State Conventions," *Alamogordo (N.Mex.) News*, August 25, 1921.

48. "To the Women Voters of New Mexico," *Albuquerque Morning Journal*, September 18, 1921.

49. "The Amendments," *Lordsburg (N.Mex.) Liberal*, September 29, 1921; "The Journal's Recommendations," *Albuquerque Morning Journal*, September 12, 1921.

50. "The First Amendment Went Over and Hereafter Women May Hold Office in the State of New Mexico," *Alamogordo (N.Mex.) News*, October 13, 1921.

CHAPTER 17

1. "Woman's Ballot: What Shall Be Done With It?," *Shanghai Times* (China), March 28, 1921; "Honor Pioneer Suffragists at Nation's Capital," *Chicago Daily Tribune*, February 16, 1921.

2. "Woman's Ballot: What Shall Be Done With It?"

3. For a partial list, see "Stenographic Report National Convention of the National Women's Party" (Washington, D.C.: Roger Calvert, n.d.), NWP Papers, 4–6; Eva Wright, "Our Women Take Part in Suffrage Memorial Ceremonies," *Competitor* (Pittsburgh, Pa.), April 1921, 30–31; and "Noted Women Leaders Coming," *Washington Herald*, January 3, 1921. The NWP sent a fundraising letter for the statue to the NAACP. See Alice Paul to Dear Fellow Voter, November 11, 1920, in NAACP Papers.

4. When Kelley pointed out that the Consumers League was not explicitly feminist, Paul said she was making an exception because Kelley was on the NWP's advisory council. Kelley to Miss Ovington, December 22, 1920; Emma Wold to Mrs. Blatch, December 29, 1920; Chairman to Mrs. Talbert, December 30, 1920; Talbert to Miss Mary W. Ovington, January 5, 1921; Chairman to Mrs. W. Spencer Murray, January 12, 1921, all NAACP Papers. See also N. Brown, *Private Politics and Public Voices*, 143–44.

5. For more on Hunton, see Lutz, "Addie W. Hunton." Black women did sometimes work with the NWP branches; see photograph *Suffragists Demonstrating against Woodrow Wilson in Chicago, 1916*, in which two African American women are present. LOC, http://hdl.loc.gov/loc.mss /mnwp.276016 (accessed February 15, 2020).

6. A. W. Hunton to Dear Friends, February 8, 1921, NAACP Papers.

7. Alice Dunbar Nelson to Mrs. Addie W. Hunton, February 8, 1921; A. W. Hunton to Mr. Johnson, February 10, 1921; A. W. Hunton to Dear Friends, February 8, 1921; A. W. Hunton to Dear Friends, February 11, 1921; Clifford to James Weldon Johnson, February 20, 1921; NAACP Secretary to Clifford, February 23, 1921, all in NAACP Papers.

8. See Memorial in NAACP Papers; and Freda Kirchwey, "Alice Paul Pulls the Strings," *The Nation*, March 2, 1921, 332–33, https://www.thenation.com/article/alice-paul-pulls-strings/ (accessed October 26, 2017).

9. Kirchwey, "Alice Paul Pulls the Strings."

10. A. W. Hunton to James Weldon Johnson, February 15, 1921, NAACP Papers; Kirchwey, "Alice Paul Pulls the Strings," 7.

11. On Bonnin, see "Five Factions Seek Support of Woman Party," *Washington Herald*, February 18, 1921. The NWP stenographer listed her as "Bonnan" representing "the National Indian Society." See "Stenographic Report National Convention of the National Women's Party," 78.

12. "Women Led by Mrs. Catt Disavow Capital Statue," *New York Herald*, February 15, 1921; "Five Factions Seek Support of Woman Party"; Butler, *Two Paths to Equality*.

13. Adams and Keene, *After the Vote Was Won*, 4; "Woman Delegates from 30 States," *Evening Star* (Washington, D.C.), February 15, 1921.

14. On Hotel Washington, see U.S. Department of Interior National Park Service, National

Register of Historic Places registration form for Hotel Washington," https://npgallery.nps.gov /pdfhost/docs/NRHP/Text/95000352.pdf (accessed February 15, 2020); and Sandoval-Strausz, *Hotel*, 249.

15. Kirchwey, "Alice Paul Pulls the Strings." Cott notes that black delegates from Virginia were worried about segregation and inquired about the "arrangements . . . for the colored delegates in this convention," and were told that they would have "the same arrangements as white women and would be seated with their state delegations." Cott, "Feminist Politics in the 1920s," 51.

16. "Five Factions Seek Support of Woman Party"; "Indian Princess Attends Women's Suffrage Convention," *Boston Post Sun*, March 13, 1921. Regardless of the Nineteenth Amendment, the women like Bonnin who lived in Washington, D.C., could not vote in federal elections.

17. See "Stenographic Report National Convention of the National Women's Party," 78.

18. Also spelled Wei Ling Sze. See "Large Attendance at Missionary Conference Here," *Sedalia (Mo.) Democrat*, April 9, 1920.

19. "Stenographic Report National Convention of the National Women's Party," 46–47 and 80.

20. Hallie Quinn Brown had raised similar themes at the statue ceremony on the first day. See Wright, "Our Women Take Part in Suffrage Memorial Ceremonies," 30–31.

21. Mary Church Terrell's statement before the Resolutions Committee and its memorial petition that Kirchwey quoted (Hunton sent her the memorial) are in the NAACP Papers. See also Hunton to Kirchwey, February 19, 1921, NAACP Papers.

22. This omission was conceded by the NWP in a letter of apology. See "Dear Madam," February 11, 1921, NAACP Papers.

23. "Stenographic Report National Convention of the National Women's Party," 61 and 78–79. Abby Scott Baker, who had organized the foreign women's section of the 1913 parade, also urged the organization to "fight for justice for the negro" (116). Murray wrote a report of the meeting for the *Crisis*. Ella Rush Murray, "The Woman's Party and the Violation of the 19th Amendment," *Crisis*, April 1921, 259–61.

24. "Stenographic Report National Convention of the National Women's Party," 134–35.

25. On Terrell see Rupp and Taylor, *Survival in the Doldrums*, 154.

26. Addie W. Hunton to Mrs. Maggie L. Walker, February 23, 1921, NAACP Papers.

27. Quoted in Cott, "Feminist Politics in the 1920s"; Terrell, *Colored Woman in a White World*.

28. Terrell, *Colored Woman in a White World*, 316–17; Cott, "Feminist Politics in the 1920s, 53"; Ware, *Why They Marched*, 237–50.

29. Terrell, *Colored Woman in a White World*, 332–33.

30. Carrie W. Clifford to James Weldon Johnson, February 20, 1921, NAACP Papers.

31. Lutz, "Addie Hunton."

32. Field organizer [likely Addie W. Hunton] to Mrs. Maud Wood Park, April 4, 1921, NAACP Papers.

33. Telegram from Maud Wood Park to Addie W. Hunton, April 7, 1921, NAACP Papers.

34. Addie W. Hunton to James Weldon Johnson, April 20, 1921, NAACP Papers.

35. She mentions the loss of her bag in her letter to Mrs. B. M. Grady, April 26, 1921, NAACP Papers. She also was excited and saw this as "a positive step forward in understanding and cooperation with the women of the convention."

36. Addie W. Hunton to James Weldon Johnson, April 20, 1921, NAACP Papers.

37. *National Woman's Party Headquarters Is Sold to the United States*, Wide World Photos, 1929, LOC, https://www.loc.gov/item/mnwp000324/ (accessed January 15, 2020).

38. "Make the Old Capitol Shrine for Women," *Washington Post*, May 22, 1922; see also "Dedicate Woman's Party Home Today," *Washington Post*, May 21, 1922.

39. "The National Woman's Party Dedicates New Home Opposite the Capitol," *Washington Post*, May 22, 1922.

40. "President to Be at Dedication by National Woman's Party," *Evening Star* (Washington, D.C.), May 21, 1922.

41. The next several paragraphs are drawn from these sources: "Make Old Capitol Shrine for Women"; "Woman's Party Chiefs to Discuss New Home," *Washington Post*, May 23, 1922; "The New Era for Women," *Washington Post*, May 23, 1922; "Dedicate Woman's Party Home Today"; "National Woman's Party Dedicates New Home Opposite the Capitol."

42. "Making the Old Capitol Shrine for Women."

43. Wright, "Our Women Take Part in Suffrage Memorial Ceremonies," 30–31.

CHAPTER 18

1. C. Anderson, *One Person, No Vote*; Gidlow, "Resistance after Ratification."

2. Jenkins, Peck, and Weaver, "Between Reconstructions," 67; Feimster, *Southern Horrors*, 212–33; Zangrando, *NAACP Crusade Against Lynching*. Wells continued her work as well, writing her pamphlet *The Arkansas Race Riot* in 1920.

3. "President William H. Taft Will Not Recommend to Congress," *Broad Ax*, June 10, 1911.

4. Jenkins, Peck, and Weaver, "Between Reconstructions"; Feimster, *Southern Horrors*, 220; Materson, *For the Freedom of Her Race*.

5. Jenkins, Peck, and Weaver, "Between Reconstructions," 67–69. The other two were Representative Frederick Dallinger of Massachusetts and Merrill Moores of Indiana.

6. There was also one socialist who voted for the bill. Jenkins, Peck, and Weaver argue that this was the beginning of partisan realignment as black electoral mobilization and advocacy threatened certain northern Democrats, especially after 1922, leading them to realize the importance of black voting power in the North, though the national party would not actively court northern blacks until Al Smith's 1928 campaign. Jenkins, Peck, and Weaver, "Between Reconstructions," 71. On realignment, see Grant, *Great Migration and the Democratic Party*.

7. Jenkins, Peck, and Weaver, 71–73; Materson, *For the Freedom of Her Race*, 118–22.

8. "Negro 'Silent Parade' Protests Lynchings," *Evening Star* (Washington, D.C.), June 15, 1922.

9. Murphy, "African American Women's Politics," 328; Mungarro and Anderson, "How Did Black Women?"

10. Murphy, 332. For conversion I used the calculator tool at Measuring Worth, measuring worth.com (accessed March 25, 2020).

11. "Negro 'Silent Parade' Protests Lynchings" and "Plan Lynching Protest Parade," *Washington Herald*, June 11, 1922.

12. For a full description of organizations, see Murphy, "African American Women's Politics," 334–35.

13. Terrell, *Colored Woman in a White World*, 108.

14. Northeastern Federation of Colored Women's Clubs, *Terrible Blot on Civilization*, Washington, D.C., 1922, http://hdl.loc.gov/loc.rbc/rbpe.20803600 (accessed January 15, 2020); "5,000 Parade in D.C. as Lynching Protest," *Baltimore Afro-American*, June 16, 1922; Murphy, "African American Women's Politics," 334–35.

15. "Colored Parade a Demonstration against Lynching," *Brooklyn (N.Y.) Daily Eagle*, July 5, 1922, 30; Corbould, "Streets, Sounds, and Identity," 865.

16. Northeastern Federation of Colored Women's Clubs, *Terrible Blot on Civilization*.

17. Alice Dunbar Nelson, "The Negro Woman and the Ballot," *Messenger* (New York), April 1, 1927, 111.

18. Clifford, *Widening Light*, 16, 22, 15, 3, 2; Murphy, "African American Women's Politics," 73.

19. By 1922 Clifford was serving as chair of the NACW's Education Committee and the Department of Literature; "Department of Education," *National Notes*, April 1923, 5. See also Cahill, "A Matter of History," in *Women Claiming Freedom* (forthcoming).

20. Quigley, *Just Another Southern Town*.

21. E. Brown, "To Catch a Vision of Freedom."

CHAPTER 19

1. Mary Kinimaka Ha'aheo Atcherley ran for office in Hawaii in both 1920 and 1922. Yasutake, "Re-franchising Women of Hawai'i," 134.

2. "Mrs. Warren Is Candidate for Congress Seat," *Albuquerque Journal*, August 5, 1922; "Mrs. Otero-Warren's Work in the Field of Social Service," *Alamogordo (N.Mex.) News*, October 12, 1922.

3. "Mrs. Nina Otero-Warren," *La Revista*, October 6, 1922; "Lanza su Candidatura la Sra. Otero-Warren," *La Revista*, August 25, 1922.

4. "Republican Party Adds Three Women to Congressional Candidate List," *Morning Call* (Allentown, Pa.), October 15, 1922; "Washington View of Prospects for Women Candidates for House and Senate," *Standard Union* (Brooklyn, N.Y.), October 21, 1922.

5. "Spanish Don's Daughter among 4 Women in Race for Congress," *New York Tribune*, September 14, 1922; "Washington View of Prospects for Women Candidates for House and Senate," *Standard Union* (Brooklyn, N.Y.), October 21, 1922; "Three Women Candidates for Congress on the GPO Ticket," *Courier-Journal* (Louisville, Ky.), October 11, 1922; "Daughter of Spain Runs for Congress," *Daily Herald* (Rutland, Vt.), October 2, 1922.

6. "Mrs. Nina Otero-Warren"; "Boleta Republicana," *La Revista*, October 6, 1922.

7. "Daughter of Spain Runs for Congress"; *Roswell (N.Mex.) Daily Record*, October 31, 1922.

8. "Miss Aurora Lucero Is Wed to Garner D. White," *Albuquerque Journal*, June 25, 1919, 5.

9. "Convention Is Told about Swope's Innocent Infancy and Life as a Working Man," *Santa Fe New Mexican*, September 4, 1926; "Miss Eckles Not to Serve on Committee Draw Dem. Platform," *Roswell Daily Record*, September 9, 1930.

10. Andrés, "Chacón, Soledad Chávez"; Chávez, *Soledad Chávez Chacón*, 5–6.

11. Leonard, "Dennis Chavez," 107; on Chávez de Chacón, see Chávez, *Soledad Chávez Chacón*; Andrés, "Chacón, Soledad Chávez," 143. See also Enciso and North, "Dennis Chávez," 15–17.

12. Lozano, *American Language*.

13. "Democrats Fill Ticket without Hard Contests," *Albuquerque Journal*, September 3, 1922.

14. They lived on 1st Street and NJ Avenue in a boardinghouse. Most of their neighbors were also government workers. The census did not list Spanish as one of their languages. Dennis Ch[á]vez, year: 1920; census place: Washington, Washington, District of Columbia; roll: T625_209; page: 15A; enumeration district: 143 (accessed via ancestry.com, February 15, 2020).

15. "Three Go to Women Voters State Meet," *Albuquerque Journal*, October 4, 1922.

16. "Woman May Be Governor of New Mexico," *Boston Globe*, June 1, 1924.

17. Chávez, *Soledad Chávez Chacón*, 11.

18. Soledad C. Chac[ó]n, year: 1930; census place: Albuquerque, Bernalillo, New Mexico; page: 6A; enumeration district: 0006; FHL microfilm: 2341127 (accessed via ancestry.com, January 7, 2020).

19. Susie Chavez, year: 1930; census place: Las Vegas, San Miguel, New Mexico; page: 5A; enumeration district: 0031; FHL microfilm: 2341134 (accessed via ancestry.com, January 7, 2020).

20. Andrés, "Chacón, Soledad Chávez," 143–44.

21. Chávez, *Soledad Chávez Chacón*, 6–7; Dennis Chavez, "Congressional Reflections," *Gallup (N.Mex.) Independent*, June 12, 1934.

22. Andrés, "Chacón, Soledad Chávez," 143–44.

23. S. Welch, "Women in State Legislatures."

24. C. Whaley, *Nina Otero-Warren*.

25. Quoted in C. Whaley, 120. See also "Woman Indian Inspector Is for Education," *La Crosse (Wis.) Tribune*, June 1, 1923; and "Mothers and Babies First!," *Modesto (Calif.) Evening News*, June 2, 1923.

26. C. Whaley, *Nina Otero-Warren*, 121.

27. She had also endorsed Bursum for election. "To the Women Voters of New Mexico," *Albuquerque Morning Journal*, September 18, 1921; "Mrs. Otero-Warren in the Field of Education," *Roswell Daily Record*, October 17, 1922; "Women Taking Keen Interest in Indian Work," *Albuquerque Journal*, October 25, 1923.

28. Huebner, "Unexpected Alliance"; Wenger, *We Have a Religion*; Vigil, *Indigenous Intellectuals*; Philip, *John Collier's Crusade*; Kelly, *Assault on Assimilation*.

29. "Women Taking Keen Interest in Indian Work."

30. Wenger, *We Have a Religion*; Daily, *Battle for the BIA*, 45–47; entry, September 6, 1924, notebook, 1924, box 3, folder 28, A. M. Berge Family Papers, New Mexico State Archives, Santa Fe. See also Walden, "The Pueblo Confederation's Political Wing," 24–44.

31. "Interesting Is Statement of Case Given Out by John Collier," *Santa Fe New Mexican*, January 24; "Collier Indian Delegation Leaves on Wild Goose Chase," *Santa Fe New Mexican*, January 24, 1924; Crandall, *These People Have Always Been A Republic*.

32. Entry, June 10, 1924, notebook, 1924, box 3, folder 28, A. M. Berge Family Papers; Tessie Stringfellow Read, "The Club Woman—Here, There And Everywhere," *Wisconsin State Journal*, September 28, 1924.

33. Entry, June 11 and June 12, 1924, notebook, 1924, box 3, folder 28, A. M. Berge Family Papers.

34. Wenger, *We Have a Religion*, 133. See also Daily, *Battle for the BIA*.

35. Otero-Warren served as interpreter for the All Pueblo Council when it met with inspectors for the Meriam Report in 1927. Meriam, *Problem of Indian Administration*, 310.

CHAPTER 20

1. One account states her original title was *The Failure of American Democracy*. Her editors suggest the publisher changed it. Kellogg, *Our Democracy*, 260n73. According to the Library of Congress's copyright office, it received a copyright in February 1920. Library of Congress, *Catalogue of Copyright Entries*, 371.

2. Hauptman, *Iroquois and the New Deal*, 70–73.

3. She pointed to the European model of the garden city and to Mormons as comparable examples. Kellogg, *Our Democracy*, 96.

4. Lomawaima, "Mutuality of Citizenship," 334, 345; Kellogg, *Our Democracy*, 267n8 and 89–98; Stanciu, "Americanization on Native Terms."

5. Kellogg, *Our Democracy*, 91–92.

6. Simpson, *Mohawk Interruptus*; Weaver, *Red Atlantic*.

7. Reed, *Serving the Cherokee Nation*; Rosier, *Serving Their Country*.

8. Cott, *Grounding of Modern Feminism*, 72–74.

9. "Woman's Defense Ass'n Speaks Here on Friday," *Daily Tribune*, September 9, 1920; "Will Address Women Tonight," *Wausau (Wis.) Daily Herald*, September 6, 1920.

10. Kellogg, *Our Democracy*, 205 and 73. For more on Haudenosaunee philosophy, see Hill, *The Clay We Are Made Of*.

11. Lewandowski, *Red Bird*.

12. See "Stenographic Report National Convention of the National Women's Party," 78; Zitkala-Ša, "America's Indian Problem," in *American Indian Stories*, 185.

13. "Women of Two States are Hostesses," *Salt Lake Telegram*, June 16, 1921; Lewandowski, *Red Bird*.

14. "Women of Two States are Hostesses."

15. Quoted in Lewandowski, *Red Bird*, 159; "Council of General Federation of Women's Clubs Will Convene Today," *Salt Lake Tribune*, June 14, 1921. See also Vigil, *Indigenous Intellectuals*, 197–99.

16. "For First Time," *News-Press* (Fort Meyers, Fla.), March 30, 1926; "Woman Pleads to Give Indians the Right of Vote," *San Francisco Chronicle*, October 19, 1922. See also Lomawaima, "Mutuality of Citizenship"; and Lewandowski, *Red Bird*, 164–65.

17. Vigil, *Indigenous Intellectuals*, 165–233.

18. For the diagram, see Zitkala-Ša (Gertrude Bonnin), "Indian Study," box 8, folder 201, in the May Walden Papers, 1870–1972, Newberry Library, Chicago. See also *Americanize the First American*, Bonnin Collection, box 1, Folder 4.

19. Posthumus, *All My Relatives*, 37–38.

20. Carpenter, "Detecting Indianness," 153.

21. Zitkala-Ša, "America's Indian Problem," 185.

22. Zitkala-Ša, "Indian Study"; Means, "'Indians shall do things in common.'"

23. Bonnin, *Americanize the First Americans*.

24. Huebner, "Unexpected Alliance."

25. Bonnin, Fabens, and Sniffen, *Oklahoma's Poor Rich Indians*.

26. Thorne, *World's Richest Indian*; Harmon, *Rich Indians*.

27. Bonnin, Fabens, and Sniffen, *Oklahoma's Poor Rich Indians*, 3.

28. Bonnin, Fabens, and Sniffen, 23–24, 26, 31; Deer, *Beginning and the End of Rape*.

29. Leslie S. Read, "The Clubwoman—Here, There and Everywhere," *Atlanta Constitution*, April 13, 1924. On Native women's continued involvement in the GFWC, see Ramirez, *Standing Up to Colonial Power*, 196–205.

30. Kellogg, *Our Democracy*, 101–2.

31. For a fuller account, see Lewandowski, *Red Bird*, 165–72.

32. "Kaw Indians Elect Woman for Chief," *New Castle (Pa.) Herald*, December 28, 1922.

33. The Seminole chief was listed as Alice B. Davis. Edith E. Moriarty, "With the Women of Today," *Sioux City (Iowa) Journal*, February 12, 1923; "Kaw Indians Follow Example of Other Tribes and Elect Woman as Chief at Great Meeting" and "Claims against Government Will Be Pushed," *Daily Oklahoman*, November 19, 1922.

34. "Kaw Indians Rally to Their Woman Chief," *Vicksburg (Miss.) Herald Sun*, December 31, 1922; "College Woman Trained Nurse Tribal Chief of Kaw Indians," *Daily Advance* (Elizabeth City, N.C.), December 29, 1922; "Kaw Indians Elect Woman for Chief"; "A Woman Who Sits on the Top of the World," *Buffalo (N.Y.) Courier*, March 11, 1923.

35. "Red Feminist," *La Crosse (Wis.) Tribune*, February 10, 1923, 10.

36. "Kaw Indian Tribe Has Squaw Chief," *Scranton (Pa.) Republican*, July 2, 1923; "Woman Chief to Entertain Tribe," *Haskell (Kans.) News*, November 16, 1922. On Indigenous feminists focusing on cultural traditions, see Risling Baldy, *We Are Dancing for You*.

37. Another senator of Native heritage, Robert Owen of Oklahoma, supported suffrage legislation and worked with suffragists. He taught in a suffrage school in 1913, for example. "Suffrage School," *Suffragist* 1, no. 2 (November 11, 1913): 11.

38. Amar, *America's Constitution*.

39. Changed in 1943 to today's unratified amendment: "Equality of rights under the law

shall not be denied or abridged by the US or by any state on account of sex." Amar, *America's Constitution.* On U.S. territories, see Prieto, "Votes for Colonized Women."

40. E. DuBois, *Feminism and Suffrage,* 79–105; Tetrault, *Myth of Seneca Falls,* 23–27.

41. The Equal Rights Amendment was reintroduced in every session of Congress for forty-nine consecutive years, although Paul revised the original 1923 wording in 1943. "Detailed Chronology National Woman's Party History," American Memory, LOC, https://www.loc.gov /collections/static/women-of-protest/images/detchron.pdf (accessed February 15, 2020).

42. Bieler, *Patriots or Traitors,* 152–54; Brooks, *American Exodus,* 66–67. Louise Huie regained her citizenship in 1933 before she went to China for a second time. On the Cable Act, see Bredbenner, *Nationality of Her Own.*

43. News photo of Curtis at NWP headquarters in author's possession; Unrau, "Charles Curtis/Kaw."

44. Unrau, "Charles Curtis, Kaw"; William Atherton Du Puy, "Kaw Indian Now Leader of the Senate," *New York Times,* December 27, 1924.

45. "The Next Vice-President," *New York Herald,* December 9, 1928.

46. At one point he was dropped from the Kaw tribal roll and he requested reinstatement. Unrau, "Charles Curtis, Kaw," 25; Parman, *Indians and the American West,* 48. His half sister Dolly Curtis Gann helped minimize his heritage for posterity, writing in her memoir that his mother had a mere "stain" of "Indian blood" from her great grandfather, White Plume. Gann, *Dolly Gann's Book,* 3.

47. For example, he set up the 1911 NAACP's presentation of an anti-lynching petition to President Taft and supported a movement for pensions for former enslaved people. "President William H. Taft Will Not Recommend to Congress," *Broad Ax,* June 10, 1911; "The Maury County Ex-slave Convention Flyer, 1899," Correspondence and Case Files of the Bureau of Pensions Pertaining to the Ex-Slave Pension Movement, 1892–1922, microfilm M2110, 1 roll, Records of the Veterans Administration, Record Group 15, National Archives and Records Administration, Washington, D.C. (accessed via ancestry.com, February 15, 2020).

48. The Curtis Act abolished tribal courts and subjected people to federal law. Unrau, "Charles Curtis, Kaw," 25–27. An Indian census of the Kaw tribe in 1931 actually listed him as a ward.

49. Hertzberg, *Search for an American Indian Identity,* 187.

50. Benton-Cohen, *Inventing the Immigration Problem.*

51. Ngai, *Impossible Subjects.*

52. Simpson, *Mohawk Interruptus;* Lewandowski, *Red Bird,* 171–72. In 1923 a delegation of Mohawk traveled to Europe to ask for international recognition of their sovereignty from the League of Nations. Weaver, *Red Atlantic,* 183–88.

53. Vigil, *Indigenous Intellectuals,* 210–12.

54. "National Council of American Indians," 20th ed., *Congressional Record* 67 (1926): 8152–58; Dominguez, "Gertrude Bonnin Story," 277–97; Lewandowski, *Red Bird.*

55. Gertrude Bonnin to Mr. Joseph R. Kettle, March 14, 1926, box 3, folder 3, Gertrude Bonnin Collection, L. Tom Perry Special Collections Library, Harold B. Lee Library, Brigham Young University, Provo, Utah.

56. "National Council of American Indians," 8152–58; Hertzberg, *Search for an American Indian Identity,* 187. On the backers for the first year, see Wise, *Red Man in the New World Drama,* 574. The Bonnins financed the second year and Raymond was appointed to a Senate investigation for the third. See Dominguez, "Gertrude Bonnin Story," 277–97; and Sen. Lyman Frazier to Capt. R. T. Bonnin, May 16, 1928, box 4, folder 13, Gertrude Bonnin Collection.

57. Gertrude Bonnin to George Flesch, December 19, 1926, box 3, folder 12, Gertrude Bonnin Collection.

58. In 1912 she wrote, "Were I a man, I'd gather together all the Indian votes in our United States—then perhaps—my appeal for justice would have some consideration." Quoted in Lewandowski, *Red Bird*, 178–79. Gertrude Bonnin to Mr. F. W. Magnuson, December 24, 1916, box 12, folder 3; NCAI pamphlet, *Information Service for Indian Citizen Voters on Scattered Indian Reservations*, box 4, folder 5; *Representative William Williamson and the Indians*, box 1, folder 4, all in Gertrude Bonnin Collection.

59. Wise suggests the events of the next two years also indicated awareness of Indians as a political force from both politicians and Native people themselves. After Senator Harreld's defeat, the Committee on Indian Affairs "was now alive to the importance of the Indian vote." Wise, *Red Man in the New World Drama*, 570–74.

60. There were multiple articles about the "Indian vote" in 1926. See, for example, "Nevada Wages Hot Campaign: Personalities, Bids for Indian Vote Make for Color in Politics," *Racine (Wis.) Journal-News*, November 1, 1926; "Registration Coming in Slowly; Now 1,701—Will Indians Vote," *Casa Grande (Ariz.) Dispatch*, July 16, 1926; "Indian Vote Is Big Factor in Alaska," *Sioux City Journal*, October 4, 1926; and "Official Election Returns, Nov. 2, 1926: Showing Total Registration, Indian Registration, Total Indian Vote, Totals in Precincts and County, Total Vote Cast," *Hardin (Mont.) Tribune*, December 31, 1926.

61. *Survey of Conditions of Indians*, 876; Lewandowski, *Red Bird*, 176–83.

62. "Indian Powwow Favors Curtis for President," *Baltimore Sun*, November 9, 1927.

63. "Curtis, of Kaw Indian Ancestry, Lived as a Boy in Prairie Tepee," and "Curtis Acceptable Both East and West," both in *Boston Globe*, June 16, 1928.

64. Cott, "Feminist Politics in the 1920s," 62–63; "'Charlie' Curtis Home Again after Triumph," *Boston Globe*, June 16, 1928. Republican Party platform of 1928 via Kenneth Janda's PoliTxts, http://janda.org/politxts/PartyPlatforms/listing.html (accessed January 15, 2020).

65. The Democratic platform also had a plank declaring "for equality with men in all political and governmental matters," as well as for equal pay for equal services. It did not address Native people but did have separate planks for the territories of Alaska, Hawaii, Puerto Rico, and the Philippines. Republican Party platform of 1928 and Democratic Party platform of 1928, via Kenneth Janda's PoliTxts, http://janda.org/politxts/PartyPlatforms/listing.html (accessed January 15, 2020).

66. Jennings Wise drafted the language, worked closely with the NCAI, and was likely a member. He was tribal attorney for the Yankton Sioux in 1925 when Raymond Bonnin went to Washington with the tribal delegation. Wise, *Red Man in the New World Drama*, 558, 570–80.

67. "Kaw Tribe to Honor Curtis," *Morning Post*, July 18, 1928; "Kaw's College-Bred Woman Chief to Boss Curtis Home-Coming," *News Review* (Roseburg, Ore.), July 27, 1928; "Kaw Indian Tribe Wants 15 Million," *Detroit Free Press*, December 18, 1930; "Kaws Awaiting 'Cousin Charlie,'" *Miami Daily News-Record*, September 28, 1932.

68. "Montana Women Registered in the Kitchens to Aid Hoover," *New York Times*, September 19, 1928; "Host of Indians Will Vote Here This Year," *Independent Record* (Helena, Mont.), September 13, 1928.

69. Nelson, "Eunice Woodhull Stabler," 55–56; "Indian Powwow Favors Curtis for President," *Baltimore Sun*, November 9, 1927; "Curtis Ends His First Campaign with Dry Talk," *Sedalia (Okla.) Weekly Democrat*, October 5, 1928; "Chief Delivers Hoover-Curtis Call to Indians," *New York Herald Tribune*, September 10, 1928; "Crow Indians Adopt Curtis in Montana," *New York Times*, September 23, 1928.

70. Draft of letter prepared by John Collier for signature of Al Smith, presidential candidate, 1928, box 4, folder 8, Gertrude Bonnin Collection.

71. "Mrs. Edison to Pose Here to Aid Hoover," *New York Times*, September 10, 1928; "Ancient Indian Foes Bid Curtis Welcome," *Daily Boston Globe*, September 23, 1928; "Smith Calls Corrup-

tion Republican Party Burden; Attacks Hoover's Silence," *New York Times*, September 25, 1928; "Smith at Helena Hits Hoover on '24 'Corruption' Issue," *New York Herald Tribune*, September 25, 1928.

72. "Hoover Public Utility Tool, Hoosier Says," *News-Palladium* (Benton Harbor, Mich.), October 24, 1928, 13.

73. Gertrude Bonnin to Senator Charles Curtis, September 14, 1928, box 4, folder 17, and Gertrude Bonnin to My Dear Indian Kinsmen, October 10, 1928, box 18, folder 4, both in Gertrude Bonnin Collection.

74. "Racial Pride of Indians Is Hope of GOP," *Amarillo (Tex.) Globe-Times*, September 28, 1928; "Indian Vote May Carry Oklahoma," *St. Louis Post-Dispatch*, August 19, 1928; "Permits 3,000 Indians Vote at the Polls," *Ithaca Journal*, September 18, 1928. It seemed as though this issue may have also driven some white voters out of the party. In 1926 the "Republican Fair Play League of McKinley County" ran the ad "An Appeal to Good Citizens" that asked, "Do You Want the Blanket Indians to control New Mexico? Let Your Ballot Say No. Vote the Straight Democratic Ticket," *Albuquerque Journal*, October 30, 1926. See Francis-Fallon, *Rise of the Latino Vote*.

75. Svingen, "Jim Crow, Indian Style"; Clow, "Crossing the Divide from Citizen to Voter."

76. McCoy, "Hidden Citizens"; Phelps, "Representation without Taxation."

77. Gertrude Bonnin, "What It Means to Be an Indian Today," *Friend's Intelligencer*, January 19, 1929, 46–47.

78. McCool, Olson, and Robinson, *Native Vote*, 14–16.

79. Wilma Mankiller (Cherokee), Elizabeth Bender Cloud (Ojibwe), and Leta Meyers Smart (Omaha) are three of many examples. Ramierez also mentions Roberta Campbell Lawson, Louie LeFlore, and Ida Collins Goodale. Carpio, *Indigenous Albuquerque*; Mankiller and Wallis, *Mankiller*; Ramirez, *Standing Up to Colonial Power*, 196; Genetin-Pilawa, "Curious Removal."

EPILOGUE

1. See, for example, Tetrault, *Myth of Seneca Falls*; Brown, "To Catch a Vision of Freedom"; Gidlow, "Resistance after Ratification"; Jones, *Vanguard*; Lindsey, *Colored No More*; and Ware, *Why They Marched*.

2. White, "Frederick Jackson Turner and Buffalo Bill"; O'Brian, *Firsting and Lasting*; Hoganson, *Fighting for American Manhood*; Benton-Cohen, *Inventing the Immigration Problem*.

3. Ulrich, *Age of Homespun*; O'Brian, *Firsting and Lasting*; White, "Frederick Jackson Turner and Buffalo Bill"; Prescott, *Pioneer Mother Monuments*.

4. Blight, *Race and Reunion*; Cox, *Dixie's Daughters*.

5. Lange, *Picturing Political Power*.

6. Tetrault, *Myth of Seneca Falls*.

7. Correspondence with Steve Carney, Arlington National Cemetery Command Historian, August 16, 2019; Lewandowski, *Red Bird*, 187–88.

8. See "They Rode with Custer: Arlington National Cemetery," http://www.arlingtoncemetery .net/custer.htm; and "Ernest Albert Garlington," http://www.arlingtoncemetery.net/garling .htm (both accessed January 11, 2020).

9. Lewandowski, *Red Bird*, 188.

10. Lewandowski, 188. Dominguez asserts that the Native community in New York City memorialized her at a powwow soon after her death and that her memory was kept alive in the Yankton community in South Dakota. Dominguez, "Gertrude Bonnin Story," 315–16.

11. On Red Power and Native Studies, see Blansett, *Journey to Freedom*. Scholars have certainly discussed Bonnin's writings on citizenship broadly. See Carpenter, "Detecting Indianness"; Maddox, *Citizen Indians*; and Vigil, *Indigenous Intellectuals*. P. Jane Hafen's newest anthology has reprinted a number of her later writings. See Zitkala-Ša, *Help Indians Help Themselves*.

12. Carrie W. Clifford to W. E. B. Du Bois, n.d. [1927?], Du Bois Papers.

13. Carrie W. Clifford to W. E. B. Du Bois, March 11, 1932, Du Bois Papers.

14. "Mrs. C. W. Clifford Dead," New York Age, November 17, 1934, 2. See also "Carrie W. Clifford," at Find A Grave, https://www.findagrave.com/memorial/82906847/carrie-williams-clifford (accessed May 1, 2018).

15. Tucker, "Carrie Williams Clifford's Poetic Response."

16. Information listed by the Woodland Cemetery Foundation and accessed through Find A Grave, https://www.findagrave.com/memorial/82906847/carrie-williams-clifford#view-photo =63529224 (accessed May 1, 2018).

17. Waggoner, Fire Light, 250.

18. It is worth thinking about Native collectors. Gladys Tantaquidgeon also developed a collection during her time as an Indian Service employee. The collection became the core of the Mohegan nation of Connecticut tribal museum. For more, see the article by Gladys Tantaquidgeon's niece Rachel Sayet, "From the Mohegan Tribal Museum to Harvard to NMAI: An Intern's Journey (So Far)," NMAI (blog), May 20, 2011, https://blog.nmai.si.edu/main/2011/05/rachel-sayet -akitusu-mohegan-tribal-member-and-nmai-intern.html (accessed February 15, 2020).

19. Gretchen Smith, "Indian Collection Work of 30 Years," Evening Star (Washington, D.C.), April 15, 1929.

20. Retirement Card, Bottineau-Baldwin, PF NPRC; "Bottineau Field Retains Name after Hearing" and "Bottineau versus Pulaski Fight Ends 'No Decision,'" Star Tribune (Minneapolis), April 4, 1933.

21. "Bottineau Field Retains Name"; "Bottineau versus Pulaski Fight Ends."

22. "60 Territorial Pioneers Chat over Old Days," Star Tribune, June 1, 1933. On remembering and American innocence, see Cothran, Remembering the Modoc War.

23. Accessions, Historical Society Notes (Minnesota Historical Society, 1929), 339.

24. Correspondence with Lindsey Geyer, Park Board Archivist, Minneapolis, June 13, 2019.

25. Houghton, Our Debt to the Red Man; Bottineau and Hewitt, "Jean Baptiste Bottineau: In Memoriam."

26. On her sister's death, see "Whitney, Mrs. Lillie Ann," Minneapolis Star, January 3, 1949. On LA, see Rosenthal, Reimagining Indian Country; on her desire to fly, see Smith, "Indian Collection Work of 30 Years." On her death, see "Marie Lillian [sic] Bottineau Baldwin," death certificate, State of California, courtesy of Linda Waggoner.

27. "Vital Records," Los Angeles Times, May 19, 1952.

28. Lozano, American Language. See also "Peace and Goodwill Message of South American Tourists Here for Day of Entertainment," Santa Fe New Mexican, October 21, 1939.

29. Burke, From Greenwich Village to Taos.

30. Otero, "My People," 150.

31. Otero, 150.

32. Otero, 151.

33. Otero, 150.

34. Lea, Literary Folklore of the Hispanic Southwest, ix. On Anglo appropriation of this imagery, see Kropp, California Vieja; and Deverell, Whitewashed Adobe.

35. Lea, Literary Folklore of the Hispanic Southwest, 241–43; Rebolledo and Márquez, Women's Tales, 441; Weigle and Powell, "From 'Alice Corbin's Lines Mumbled in Sleep' to 'Eufeia's Sopapillas.'"

36. According to Ponce, Otero-Warren was second cousin to Cleofas Martinez Jaramillo. "Lives and Works of Five Hispanic New Mexican Women Writers," 36. See the following from the Santa Fe New Mexican: "Gowns of Last Century Worn in Fascinating Style Show of Sociedad Folklorica Sunday," September 16, 1936; "Sociedad Folklorica Meets Next Feb. 19," January 15, 1937; "Sociedad Folklorica Plans Big Participation in 1937 Fiesta," June 10, 1937; "Sociedad Folk-

lorica Aids Fiesta," August 29, 1938; "Gowns and Finery Will Appear at Folklorica Merienda," August 30, 1940; "Lace, Blue, and Pink, Transform Seth Hall for Baile," August 30, 1944.

37. Wilson, *Myth of Santa Fe*. This continues to be a contested issue as an Indigenous group, the Red nation, has protested the fiesta as revisionist history that does not address the violent conquest of Native people in New Mexico by the Spanish. The Red nation, https://therednation .org/2017/08/10/pueblo-resurgence-white-revisionism-the-bloody-truth-about-the-santa-fe -entrada/ (accessed February 15, 2020).

38. I'm grateful to Judy Tzu-Chun Wu for conversations and presentations about her forth-coming biography of Patsy Mink.

39. Kiel, "Competing Visions of Empowerment"; Stanciu and Ackley, "Introduction."

40. Kiel, "Competing Visions of Empowerment," 435.

41. This echoed her 1913 arrest in Oklahoma for "obtaining money under false pretenses and impersonating United States officials." In that case, Kellogg, at the time head of the edu-cational division of the SAI, claimed she was working indirectly for Thomas Sloan, another SAI member, who was on a committee investigating the frauds being committed in Osage country. She was acquitted, but her reputation was damaged. She was asked to leave the SAI, the organi-zation of which she was a co-founder. Kiel, "Competing Visions of Empowerment"; "Kelloggs are Arrested," *Wichita (Kans.) Beacon*, October 13, 1913; "Oneida Princess in Trouble," *Sheboygan (Wis.) Press*, October 31, 1913. See also Hauptman, *Seven Generations of Iroquois Leadership*, 143–64.

42. Hauptman, *Seven Generations of Iroquois Leadership*, 121–22; "After 600 Years, Tribe at Oneida Has No Chief," *Post-Crescent* (Appleton, Wis.), April 8, 1935.

43. They are joined in this by the Cultural Heritage Department of the Oneida Nation of Wis-consin. See also Hauptman, *Seven Generations of Iroquois Leadership*.

44. "Supplementary statements made by the applicant, Miss Mabel Lee," form 431, March 12, 1923, ML Chinese Exclusion File, NYC NARA. The inspector then went to Columbia to con-fer with those witness to confirm her residence. Report, March 12, 1922, ML Chinese Exclusion File, NYC NARA.

45. Lee kept a short travel journal of the first few weeks of the trip. It is held by the First Chi-nese Baptist Church in New York City. I thank Bayor Lee for giving me access to it.

46. Huie Kin discussed his return experience in *Reminiscences*, 85.

47. Quoted in Tseng, "Dr. Mabel Lee."

48. See stationery in Mabel Lee Papers, private collection, First Chinese Baptist Church, New York.

49. Mabel Lee, "Chinese Patriotism," CSM, October 1, 1914, 23–26.

50. Author correspondence with Gary Quan, church member.

51. The plaque lists the Lin Sing Association, Hok San Society, Chung San Association, Tai Pun Welfare Association, Yu San Club, Tung On Association, Nam Shun Associations, and Lee Kung Yoke.

52. Tseng, "Dr. Mabel Lee."

53. Hu Shih visited New York in the fall of 1936 during a trip to Harvard where he spoke at the dedication of a memorial stele donated to the school by its Chinese alumni on the occasion of its three hundredth anniversary. See Harvard Tercentenary Stele, Fairbanks Center for Chi-nese Studies, Harvard University, https://fairbank.fas.harvard.edu/300th-anniversary-stele/ (ac-cessed October 10, 2019).

54. Hu Shih to Mabel Lee, November 19, 1936, quoted in *The First Chinese Baptist Church: Our Congregation*, 75th Anniversary Commemoratory Journal (n.p., 2001), 18.

55. Application for Return Permit, Form 12/943, June 18, 1937, in ML Chinese Exclusion File, NYC NARA.

56. Marie Proctor, Dist. Comm. Seattle Dist., to Dist. Dir. INS Ellis Island, October 16, 1937,

in ML Chinese Exclusion File, NYC NARA; J. Spence, *Search for Modern China*; Brooks, *American Exodus*.

57. See Tseng, "Dr. Mabel Lee," for further details.

58. Ngai, *Impossible Subjects*; Hsu, "Disappearance of America's Cold War Chinese Refugees."

59. I am especially indebted to Gary Quan and Robert Gee as well as to Pastor Bayer Lee for talking about Mabel Lee and church history with me and inviting me to church events honoring Dr. Lee. I am particularly grateful to Gary Quan for taking me to visit her final resting place.

60. "Mabel Lee Memorial Post Office" dedication ceremony program, December 3, 2018, in author's possession.

61. The exhibits and social media posts around the centennial of the Nineteenth Amendment have included some of these women, though the larger context this book offers is required for a full picture.

62. Increased interest in a more inclusive national history came out of the civil rights movements of the 1960s and 1970s when many of the same battles from the turn of the century were being fought. This interest brought many, though not all, of these women back into a wider public awareness, but their place in American history was sometimes limited to a narrow conception of their contributions.

63. The descendants of these women and others continue their work, including Rosemary Clifford Wilson, Carrie Clifford's granddaughter; Michelle Duster, Ida B. Wells's great-granddaughter; A'Lelia Bundles, Madam C. J. Walker's great-great-granddaughter; and Adele Logan Alexander, Adella Hunt Logan's granddaughter, who just published her story, *Princess of Hither Isles: A Black Suffragist's Story from the Jim Crow South*.

64. Clifford, *Sowing for Others to Reap*, 4.

[BIBLIOGRAPHY]

PRIMARY SOURCES
Manuscript Sources
A. M. Berge Family Papers, New Mexico State Archives, Santa Fe

Gertrude Bonnin Collection, L. Tom Perry Special Collections, Harold B. Lee Library, Brigham Young University, Provo, Utah

Columbia University Archives, New York

Mabel Lee Papers, Private Collection, First Chinese Baptist Church, New York

Minnesota Historical Society, Saint Paul

National Anthropological Archives, Smithsonian Institution, Washington, D.C.

National Personnel Records Center, Personnel Folders, St. Louis, Missouri

Papers of the Society of American Indians (microfilm)

University of New Mexico Center for Southwest Research, Albuquerque, New Mexico

May Walden Papers, 1870–1972, Newberry Library, Chicago

Washington College of Law, American University, Washington, D.C.

Elmo Scott Watson Photographs, ca. 1860–1936, Ayer Collection, Newberry Library, Chicago

Government Documents
Chippewa Indians of Northern Dakota Territory Jno. B. Bottineau (Member of the Tribe) before the Hon. Secretary of the Interior, February 16, 1878. Washington, D.C.: Government Printing Office, 1878.

Congressional Record, Senate (1907).

Congressional Record, Senate (1926).

Hearings before the Subcommittee on Parcel Post of the Senate Committee on Post Office and Post Roads under S. Res. 56. Washington, D.C.: Government Printing Office, 1912.

Laws Passed at the First Session of the Legislature of the State of South Dakota: Begun and Held at Pierre, the Temporary Capital of Said State, on Tuesday, the Seventh Day of January, A.D. 1890, and Concluded March 7th, A.D. 1890. Pierre, S.Dak.: State Bindery, 1890.

Maddux v. Bottineau. In *Reports of Cases Adjudged in the Court of Appeals of the District of Columbia from November 2, 1909, to April 5, 1910*. Edited by Charles Cowles Tucker, 119–30. Vol. 34 (34 App. D.C.). Washington, D.C.: Lawyers Co-operative Publishing Co., 1910.

New Mexico Secretary of State. *New Mexico Blue Book or State Official Register*. Santa Fe, 1915–26.

Speech of Hon. Binger Hermann, of Oregon, in the House of Representatives of the United States. Lewis and Clark Exposition, 58th Cong., March 4, 1904. Washington, D.C.: Government Printing Office, 1904.

Survey of Conditions of Indians in the United States: Hearings before a Subcommittee of the Committee of Indian Affairs U.S. Senate, 70th Congress, 2nd session pursuant to S. Res 79. Washington, D.C.: Government Printing Office, 1926.

The Territory of Hawaii v Mrs. Lum Yip, Mrs. Wong How Fee, Mrs. Hee Tong, Mrs. Choy Sing, Wong Moo Kow Moo, Chock Kim Moo, and Loo Tau Moo. June 18, 1912, Federal District Court of Honolulu, Hawaii.

Turtle Mountain Band of Pembina Chippewa Indians: Mr. Kyle Presented the Following Petition and Memorial of Turtle Mountain Band of Chippewa Indians, in the State of North Dakota, Praying for the Reference of Their Claim to the Court. Senate Document No. 154, 55th Cong., 2nd Sess. Washington, D.C.: Government Printing Office, 1898.

U.S. Congress. Senate. Committee on the District of Columbia. *Suffrage Parade: Hearings before a Subcommittee of the Committee on the District of Columbia United States Senate*. 63rd Cong., Special-[first] Sess. Washington, D.C.: Government Printing Office, 1913.

Akron Beacon

Alamogordo (N.Mex.) News

Albuquerque Journal

Albuquerque Morning Journal

Amarillo (Tex.) Globe-Times

American Indian Magazine. Published as the
Quarterly Journal of the Society of American
Indians (Washington, D.C., 1916–20,
accessed via the American Indian Digital
History Project, http://www.aidhp.com)

Atchison (Kans.) Daily Globe

Atlanta Constitution

Baltimore Afro-American

Baltimore Evening Sun

Baltimore Sun

Baptist Home Missionary

Barnard Bulletin

Billings (Mont.) Weekly Gazette

Bisbee (Ariz.) Daily Review

Black Hills Daily Standard (Deadwood, S.Dak.)

Black Hills Daily Times (Deadwood, S.Dak.)

Bookseller, Newsdealer and Stationer

Boston Daily Advertiser

Boston Globe

Boston Post Sun

Broad Ax (Chicago)

Brooklyn Daily Eagle

Brooklyn Times Union

Buffalo (N.Y.) Courier

Buffalo (N.Y.) Enquirer

Buffalo (N.Y.) Evening News

Carlisle (Penn.) Arrow (accessed via Carlisle
Indian School Digital Resource Center)

Carlsbad (N.Mex.) Current-Argus

Carrizozo (N.Mex.) Outlook

Casa Grande (Ariz.) Dispatch

Centralia (Ill.) Evening News

Chattanooga News

Chicago Daily Tribune

Chicago Tribune

Chinese Students' Monthly (New York, 1909–29,
accessed via American Periodicals from
the Center for Research Libraries via
ProQuest)

Cincinnati Enquirer

Cleveland Leader

Coats (Kans.) Courant

Coconino (Ariz.) Sun

Colored American Magazine

Columbia (N.Y.) Daily Spectator

Competitor (Pittsburgh, Pa.)

Courier-Journal (Louisville, Ky.)

The Crisis (New York: National Association
for the Advancement of Colored People,
1910–22, accessed via Modernist Journals
Project, https://modjourn.org/journal
/crisis)

Daily Advance (Elizabeth City, N.C.)

Daily Ardmoreite (Ardmore, Okla.)

Daily Boston Globe

Daily Deadwood (S.C.) Pioneer Times

Daily Globe (Minneapolis)

Daily Herald (Rutland, Vt.)

Daily Inter Ocean (Chicago)

Daily Oklahoman

Daily Times (Davenport, Iowa)

Daily Tribune (Wisconsin Rapids)

Decatur (Ill.) Herald

Deming (N.Mex.) Headlight

Des Moines Register

Detroit Free Press

Dobbs Ferry (N.Y.) Register

El Nuevo Mexico (Santa Fe, N.Mex.)

El Paso Times

Emporia (Kans.) Gazette

Evening Bulletin (Honolulu)

Evening Herald (Albuquerque)

Evening Herald (Klamath Falls, Ore.)

Evening Journal (Wilmington, Del.)

Evening Review (East Liverpool, Ohio)

Evening Star (Washington, D.C.)

Evening Times-Republican (Marshalltown, Iowa)

Fall River (Mass.) Daily Evening News

Fall River (Mass.) Globe

Fort Sumner Review

Fort Worth (Tex.) Star-Telegram

Freeman (Indianapolis)

Friend's Intelligencer

Gallup (N.Mex.) Independent

Green Book Magazine

Hardin (Mont.) Tribune

Haskell (Kans.) News

Historical Society Notes (Minneapolis, Minn.)

Home Mission Monthly

Honolulu Star-Bulletin

Horizon

Howard University Record (Washington, D.C.)
Independent Record (Helena, Mont.)
Indianapolis News
Indianapolis Recorder
Indianapolis Star
Inter Ocean (Chicago)
Ithaca (N.Y.) Journal
Jackson (Miss.) Daily News
Jamestown (N.Dak.) Weekly Alert
Journal and Tribune (Knoxville, Tenn.)
Kansas City (Kans.) Sun
La Crosse (Wis.) Tribune
Las Cruces (N.Mex.) Citizen
LaFollette's Weekly Magazine
Las Vegas (N.Mex.) Optic
La Voz del Pueblo
Lansing (MI) State Journal
Lima (Ohio) News
Lordsburg (N.Mex.) Liberal
Los Angeles Evening Express
Los Angeles Times
Messenger (New York)
Miami Daily News-Record
Middletown (N.Y.) Daily Argus
Minneapolis Star
Modesto (Calif.) Evening News
Montgomery Advertiser
Monroe City (Mo.) Democrat
Morning Astorian (Astoria, Ore.)
Morning Call (Allentown, Pa.)
Morning Oregonian (Portland)
Morning Post (Camden, N.J.)
Mt. Pleasant (Iowa) Daily News
Muskogee (Okla.) Times-Democrat
National Notes (Kansas City, Mo.)
Native American
New Castle (Pa.) Herald
News-Herald (Franklin, Penn.)
News-Palladium (Benton Harbor, Mich.)
News-Press (Fort Meyers, Fla.)
News Review (Roseburg, Ore.)
New York Age
New York Daily Tribune
New York Herald Tribune
New York Times
New York Tribune
New York World
North-China Herald and Supreme Court and
    Consular Gazette

Norwalk (Ohio) Daily Reflector
Oelwein (Iowa) Daily Register
Ogden (Utah) Standard
Oregon Daily Journal (Portland)
Oregonian
Oriental Economic Review
Oriental Review
Oshkosh (Wis.) Northwestern
Ottawa (Kans.) Daily Republic
The Outlook
Piitsburgh Daily Post
Pittsburgh Post-Gazette
Post-Crescent (Appleton, Wis.)
Poughkeepsie (N.Y.) Eagle-News
Racine (Wis.) Journal-News
Reading Times
La Revista
Rock Island (Ill.) Argus
Roswell (N.Mex.) Daily Record
Saint Paul Globe
Salt Lake Telegram
Salt Lake Tribune
San Bernardino County Sun
San Francisco Call
San Francisco Chronicle
Santa Fe New Mexican
Scranton (Pa.) Republican
Sedalia (Mo.) Democrat
Sedalia (Okla.) Weekly Democrat
Shanghai Times (China)
Sheboygan (Wis.) Press
Silver City (N.Mex.) Enterprise
Silver City Independent
Sioux City (Iowa) Journal
Southern Workman (Hampton, Va.)
Spokane (Wash.) Review
Sprague's Journal of Maine History
Standard Union (Brooklyn, N.Y.)
Star Tribune (Minneapolis)
St. Louis Post-Dispatch
St. Louis Star and Times
St. Paul Daily Globe
St. Paul Sunday Globe
Suffragist
Sunday Star (Washington, D.C.)
Tomahawk (White Earth, Minn.)
Topeka State Journal
Tucumcari (N.Mex.) News and Tucumcari Times
Vicksburg (Miss.) Herald Sun

Voice of the Negro
Washington Bee
Washington Herald
Washington Post
Washington Times
Wausau (Wis.) Daily Herald
Wichita (Kans.) Beacon

Wichita (Kans.) Daily Eagle
Wisconsin State Journal
Woman's Journal (Boston: George Brewster
 Gallup, 1870–1912, accessed at http://id
 .lib.harvard.edu/alma/99011724747020
 3941/catalog)
Woman's Tribune

Other Primary Sources

Anderson, Isabel. Presidents and Pies: Life in Washington, 1897–1919. Boston: Houghton Mifflin,
 1920.
Ayscough, John. First Impressions in America. London: John Long, 1921.
Barber, Max. "The Atlanta Tragedy." Voice of the Negro, November 1906, 471–72.
Beck, Louis. New York's Chinatown: An Historical Presentation of Its People and Places. New York:
 Bohemia Publishing Co., 1898.
Bonnin, Gertrude. See Zitkala-Ša.
Bonnin, Gertrude, Charles H. Fabens, and Mathew K. Sniffen. Oklahoma's Poor Rich Indians: An
 Orgy of Graft and Exploitation of the Five Civilized Tribes—Legalized Robbery. Philadelphia: Office
 of the Indian Rights Association, 1924.
Bottineau Baldwin, Marie Louise. "The Need of a Change in the Legal Status of the North
 American Indian in the United States." Master's thesis, Washington College of Law,
 American University Archives, Washington, D.C., 1915.
Bottineau Baldwin, Marie Louise, and J. N. B. Hewitt, "In Memoriam: Jean Baptiste Bottineau,
 Obit Dec. 1st, 1911." Washington, D.C., 1911.
Campbell, Rev. Geo. "Chinese Work on the Pacific Coast." In Seventy-Second Annual Report of the
 American Baptist Home Mission Society, 101–3. New York: American Baptist Home Mission
 Society, 1904.
Catt, Carrie Chapman, and Nettie Rogers Shuler. Woman Suffrage and Politics: The Inner Story of the
 Suffrage Movement. New York: Charles Scribner's Sons, 1923.
Clarke, Edward H. Sex in Education; or, A Fair Chance for Girls. 2nd ed. Boston: Houghton, Mifflin,
 1884.
Clifford, Carrie Williams. "Atlanta's Shame." Voice of the Negro, February 1907, 72.
———. "The Business Career of Mrs. M. E. Williams." Colored American Magazine, September
 1905, 477.
———. "The Great American Question." Colored American Magazine, May 1, 1907, 370–72.
———. "A Northern Black Point of View." Outlook, November 3, 1906, 562.
———. "Ohio State Federation." National Association Notes, Tuskegee Institute Press, 7, no. 11
 (July 1904): 26–29.
———. "A Plea to Colored Men." Freeman (Indianapolis, Ind.), January 11, 1908.
———. Race Rhymes. Washington, D.C.: R. L. Pendleton, 1911.
———. "Relation of Full Freedom to a Full Stomach." New York Age, April 25, 1907.
———. "Votes for Children," The Crisis 10, no. 4 (1915): 185.
———. "Which Shall It Be?" Colored American Magazine, January 1907, 33–34.
———. The Widening Light. Boston: Walter Reid Co., 1922.
———, ed. Sowing for Others to Reap. Boston: Charles Alexander, 1900.
Cooper, Anna Julia. A Voice from the South. Xenia, Ohio: Aldine Printing House, 1892.
De Bryas, Comtesse Madeleine, and Jacqueline de Bryas. A Frenchwoman's Impressions of America.
 New York: Century, 1920.
D'Estournelles de Constant, Paul H. B. America and Her Problems. New York: Macmillan, 1915.

Gann, Dolly Curtis. *Dolly Gann's Book.* New York: Doubleday, 1933.

Harper, Ida Husted, ed. *The History of Woman Suffrage, 1900–1920.* Vol. 5. New York: J. J. Little and Ives, 1922.

Houghton, Louise Seymour. *Our Debt to the Red Man: The French Indians in the Development of the United States.* Boston: Stratford, 1918.

Hunton, Addie W., and Kathryn M. Johnson. *Two Colored Women with the American Expeditionary Forces.* New York: Brooklyn Eagle Press, 1920.

Jaffa, Nathan. *Territory of New Mexico Report of the Secretary of the Territory, 1909–1910 and Legislative Manual.* Santa Fe: New Mexican Printing Co., 1911.

Kellogg, Laura Cornelius. *Laura Cornelius Kellogg: Our Democracy and the American Indian and Other Works.* Edited by Cristina Stanciu and Kristina Ackley. Syracuse: Syracuse University Press, 2015.

Kin, Huie. *Reminiscences.* Peiping, China: San Yu Press, 1932.

Lea, Aurora Lucero-White. *Literary Folklore of the Hispanic Southwest.* San Antonio, Tex.: Naylor, 1953.

Lee, Mabel Ping-Hua. "The Economic History of China: With Special Reference to Agriculture." Ph.D. diss., Columbia University, 1921.

———. "The Meaning of Woman Suffrage." *Chinese Students' Monthly,* May 12, 1914, 526–31.

———. "Moral Training in Chinese Schools." *Chinese Students' Monthly,* June 1, 1916, 543–47.

Lewis, Ida Bell. *The Education of Girls in China.* Teachers College publication #104.

Library of Congress. *Catalogue of Copyright Entries.* Part 1: Books. Group 1, vol. 17, nos. 1–136. Washington, D.C.: Government Printing Office, 1920.

Liliuokalani. *Hawaii's Story by Hawaii's Queen.* Boston: Lee and Shepard, 1898.

Mankiller, Wilma, and Michael Wallis. *Mankiller: A Chief and Her People.* New York: St. Martin's Griffin, 1993.

Marquis, Albert Nelson, ed. "Florence Etheridge." In *Who's Who in America: A Biographical Dictionary of Notable Living Men and Women of the United States.* Vol. 9, 1916–1917. Chicago: A. N. Marquis, 1916.

Mather, Frank Lincoln, ed. *Who's Who of the Colored Race: A General Biographical Dictionary of Men and Women of African Descent.* Vol. 1. Chicago, 1915.

Mencken, H. L. *American Language.* New York: Alfred A. Knopf, 1919.

Meriam, Lewis. *The Problem of Indian Administration.* Washington, D.C.: Brookings Institute, 1928.

"Missionaries among the Italians, Chinese, Mexicans and Indians." In *Seventieth Annual Report of the American Baptist Home Mission Society,* 1–24. New York: American Baptist Home Missionary Society, 1902.

National Association of Colored Women's Clubs. *Minutes of the Second Convention of the National Association of Colored Women Held at Quinn Chapel 24th Street and Wabash Ave., Chicago, Ill. August 14th, 15th, and 16th, 1899.* Chicago, 1899.

Otero, Adelina. "My People." *Survey Graphic* 66, no. 3 (May 1, 1931): 149–51.

Page, Thomas Nelson. "The Great American Question: The Special Plea of a Southerner." *McClure's,* March 1907, 565–72.

Park, Maud Wood. *Front Door Lobby.* https://www.loc.gov/item/93838361/.

Rayé-Smith, Eugénie M. *Equal Suffrage Song Sheaf.* N.p., 1912.

Report of the Executive Council on the Proceedings of the First Annual Conference of the Society of American Indians. Washington, D.C., 1912.

Riis, Jacob A. *How the Other Half Lives: Studies among the Tenements of New York.* New York: Charles Scribner's Sons, 1914.

Robinson, Doane. *History of South Dakota.* Vol. 1. N.p.: B. F. Bowen, 1904.

Sanders, Helen Fitzgerald. *The White Quiver*. New York: Duffield, 1913.

Simkhovitch, Vladimir G. "Rome's Fall Reconsidered." *Political Science Quarterly* 31, no. 2 (June 1916): 201–43.

Scott, Emmett J. *Scott's Official History of the American Negro in the World War*. Chicago: Homewood Press, 1919.

Stevens, Doris. *Jailed for Freedom*. New York: Boni and Liveright, 1920.

Stapler, Martha G., ed. *The Woman Suffrage Yearbook*. New York: National Woman Suffrage Publishing Co., 1917.

Terrell, Mary Church. *A Colored Woman in a White World*. Washington, D.C.: Ransdelling, 1940.

———. "What It Means to Be Colored in the Capital of the United States." *Independent*, January 24, 1907, 181–86.

Tung, Hsin Chia, ed. *Who's Who of Chinese Students in America*. Berkley: Lederer, Street and Zeus Company, 1921.

Wells, Ida B. *The Arkansas Race Riot*. Chicago, Illinois, 1920.

———. *Southern Horrors: Lynch Law in All Its Phases*. New York: New York Age Print, 1892.

Wisconsin Blue Book. State Printing Board, 1923.

Wise, Jennings C. *The Red Man in the New World Drama*. Washington, D.C.: W. F. Roberts Company, 1931.

Zitkala-Ša [Gertrude Bonnin]. *American Indian Stories, Legends, and Other Writings*. Edited by Cathy N. Davidson and Ada Norris. New York: Penguin Books, 2003.

Zitkala-Ša [Gertrude Bonnin]. *Help Indians Help Themselves: The Later Writings of Gertrude Simmons Bonnin (Zitkala-Ša)*. Edited by P. Jane Hafen. Lubbock: Texas Tech University Press, 2020.

SECONDARY SOURCES

Aberjhani and Sandra L. West. *Encyclopedia of the Harlem Renaissance*. New York: Facts on File, 2003.

Adams, David Wallace. *Education for Extinction: American Indians and the Boarding School Experience, 1875–1928*. Lawrence: University of Kansas Press, 1995.

Adams, Katherine H., and Michael L. Keene. *After the Vote Was Won: The Later Achievements of Fifteen Suffragists*. Jefferson, N.C.: McFarland, 2010.

Alexander, Adele Logan. *Princess of Hither Isles: A Black Suffragist's Story from the Jim Crow South*. New Haven, Conn.: Yale University Press, 2019.

Allgor, Catherine. *Parlor Politics: In Which the Ladies of Washington Help Build a City and a Government*. Charlottesville: University Press of Virginia, 2000.

Amar, Akhil Reed. *America's Constitution: A Biography*. New York: Random House, 2005.

Anderson, Carol. *One Person, No Vote: How Voter Suppression Is Destroying Our Democracy*. New York: Bloomsbury, 2018.

Andrés, Benny, Jr. "Chacón, Soledad Chávez (1890–1936)." In *Latinas in the United States: A Historical Encyclopedia*, edited by Vicki L. Ruiz and Virginia Sánchez Korrol, 143–44. Bloomington: Indiana University Press, 2006.

Archambault, JoAllyn. "A Man of Two Worlds: Joseph Archambault." *North Dakota History* 68, no. 2 (2001): 24–26.

Armstrong, Julie Buckner. *Mary Turner and the Memory of Lynching*. Athens: University of Georgia Press, 2011.

———. "'The People . . . took exception to her remarks': Meta Warrick Fuller, Angelina Weld Grimké, and the Lynching of Mary Turner." *Mississippi Quarterly* 61, no. 1/2 (Winter 2008): 113–41.

Atkinson, Evelyn., "Slaves, Coolies, and Shareholders: Corporations Claim the Fourteenth Amendment." *Journal of the Civil War Era* 10, no. 1 (March 2020): 54–80.

Augustine-Adams, Kif. "Where Is Their Place? Mexican-Origin Women, Citizenship, and Suffrage in the Arizona Borderlands." *Journal of Arizona History* 61, no. 2 (Summer 2020): 241–48.

Babcock, Barbara. *Woman Lawyer: The Trials of Clara Foltz*. Stanford, Calif.: Stanford University Press, 2011.

Barber, Lucy Grace. *Marching on Washington: The Forging of an American Tradition*. Berkeley: University of California Press, 2004.

Barker, Joanne, ed. *Critically Sovereign: Indigenous Gender, Sexuality, and Feminist Studies*. Durham, N.C.: Duke University Press, 2017.

Barnett, Lisa Dawn. "The Politics of Peyote: The Construction of Religious and Racial Identities in the Creation of the Native American Church, 1880–1937." Ph.D. diss., Texas Christian University, 2017.

Barsh, Russel Lawrence. "American Indians in the Great War." *Ethnohistory* 38, no. 3 (Summer 1991): 276–303.

Bay, Mia E. "The Battle for Womanhood Is the Battle for Race." In *Toward an Intellectual History of Black Women*, edited by Mia E. Bay, Farah J. Griffin, Martha S. Jones, and Barbara D. Savage, 75–92. Chapel Hill: University of North Carolina Press, 2015.

——— . *To Tell the Truth Freely: The Life of Ida B. Wells*. New York: Hill and Wang, 2010.

——— . *The White Image in the Black Mind: African-American Ideas about White People, 1830–1925*. New York: Oxford University Press, 2000.

Bederman, Gail. *Manliness and Civilization: A Cultural History of Gender and Race in the United States, 1880–1917*. Chicago: University of Chicago Press, 1995.

Benton-Cohen, Katherine. *Inventing the Immigration Problem: The Dillingham Commission and Its Legacy*. Cambridge, Mass.: Harvard University Press, 2018.

Berg, A. Scott. *Wilson*. New York: Simon & Schuster, 2013.

Bernstein, Alison. "A Mixed Record: The Political Enfranchisement of American Indian Women during the Indian New Deal." *Journal of the West* 23, no. 3 (1984): 13–20.

Bernstein, Patricia. *The First Waco Horror: The Lynching of Jesse Washington and the Rise of the NAACP*. College Station: University of Texas A&M Press, 2006.

Bevis, Teresa Brawner. *A History of Higher Education Exchange: China and America*. New York: Routledge, 2014.

Bieler, Stacey. *Patriots or Traitors: A History of American Educated Chinese Students*. New York: Routledge, 2004.

Blackhawk, Ned. *Violence over the Land: Indians and Empires in the Early American West*. Cambridge, Mass.: Harvard University Press, 2008.

Blansett, Kent. *Journey to Freedom: Richard Oakes, Alcatraz, and the Red Power Movement*. New Haven, Conn.: Yale University Press, 2018.

Blee, Lisa. "Completing Lewis and Clark's Westward March: Exhibiting a History of Empire at the 1905 Portland World's Fair." *Oregon Historical Quarterly* 106, no. 2 (2005): 232–53.

Blight, David W. *Race and Reunion: The Civil War in American Memory*. Cambridge, Mass.: Belknap Press, 2002.

Boorman, Howard, L. "Chang Mo-Chün." In *Biographical Dictionary of Republican China*. Vol. 1, edited by Howard L. Boorman, 85–87. New York: Columbia University Press, 1967.

Boyd, Tyler L. *Tennessee Statesman Harry T. Burn: Woman Suffrage, Free Elections and a Life of Service*. Charleston, S.C.: History Press, 2019.

Bredbenner, Candice Lewis. *A Nationality of Her Own: Women, Marriage, and the Law of Citizenship*. Berkeley: University of California Press, 1998.

Brooks, Charlotte. *American Exodus: Second-Generation Chinese Americans in China, 1901–1949*. Berkeley: University of California Press, 2019.

Brown, Elsa Barkley. "To Catch a Vision of Freedom: Reconstructing Southern Black Women's Political History, 1865–1880." In *African American Women and the Vote, 1837–1960*, edited by Ann Gordon, Bettye Collier-Thomas, John H. Bracey, Arlene Avakian, and Joyce Berkman, 66–99. Amherst: University of Massachusetts Press, 1997.

Brown, Nikki. *Private Politics and Public Voices: Black Women's Activism from World War I to the New Deal*. Bloomington: Indiana University Press, 2006.

Bruyneel, Kevin. *The Third Space of Sovereignty: The Postcolonial Politics of US–Indigenous Relations*. Minneapolis: University of Minnesota Press, 2007.

Burke, Flannery. *From Greenwich Village to Taos: Primitivism and Place at Mabel Dodge Luhan's*. 2nd ed. Lawrence: University Press of Kansas, 2016.

———. *A Land Apart: The Southwest and the Nation in the Twentieth Century*. Tucson: University of Arizona Press, 2017.

Butler, Amy E. *Two Paths to Equality: Alice Paul and Ethel M. Smith in the ERA Debate, 1921–1929*. Albany: SUNY Press, 2002.

Cahill, Cathleen D. *Federal Fathers and Mothers: A Social History of the United States Indian Service, 1869–1933*. Chapel Hill: University of North Carolina Press, 2011.

———. "Marie Louise Bottineau Baldwin: Indigenizing the Federal Indian Service." *Studies in American Indian Literatures* 25, no. 2 (Summer 2013): 63–86.

———. "A Matter of History: Carrie W. Clifford Claiming Freedom through History." In *Women Claiming Freedom: Slavery, Race, and Resistance Across the Americas*. Edited by Erica L. Ball, Tatiana Seijas, and Terri L. Snyder. New York: Cambridge University Press, forthcoming.

Camp, Gregory S. "The Dispossessed: The Ojibwa and Métis of Northwest North Dakota." *North Dakota History* 69, nos. 2–4 (2002): 62–80.

Capozzola, Christopher. *Uncle Sam Wants You: World War I and the Making of the Modern American Citizen*. New York: Oxford University Press, 2008.

Carpenter, Cari. "Detecting Indianness: Gertrude Bonnin's Investigation of Native American Identity." *Wicazo Sa Review* 20, no. 1 (Spring 2005): 139–59.

Carpio, Myla Vincenti. *Indigenous Albuquerque*. Lubbock: Texas Tech University Press, 2011.

Cassidy, Tina. *Mr. President, How Long Must We Wait? Alice Paul, Woodrow Wilson, and the Fight for the Right to Vote*. New York: 37 Ink, 2019.

Chapman, Mary. "Edith Eaton/Sui Sin Far's 'Revolution in Ink'": Print Culture Alternatives to U.S. Suffrage Discourse." *American Quarterly* 60, no. 4 (December 2008): 975–1001.

———. *Making Noise, Making News: Suffrage Print Culture and U.S. Modernism*. New York: Oxford University Press, 1914.

Chapman, Mary, and Angela Mills, eds. *Treacherous Texts: An Anthology of U.S. Suffrage Literature, 1846–1946*. New Brunswick: Rutgers University Press, 2011.

Chávez, Dan D. *Soledad Chávez Chacón: A New Mexico Political Pioneer, 1890–1936*. Albuquerque: University of New Mexico Printing Services, 1996.

Child, Brenda. *Holding Our World Together: Ojibwe Women and the Survival of Community*. New York: Viking Penguin, 2012.

Clark, Herbert L. "James Carroll Napier: National Negro Leader." *Tennessee Historical Quarterly* 49, no. 4 (Winter 1990): 243–52.

Clark, Mary L. "The Founding of the Washington College of Law: The First Law School Established by Women for Women." *American University Law Review* 47, no. 3 (April 1998): 613–76.

Clem, Alan L. *South Dakota Political Almanac*. Vermillion, S.Dak.: Dakota Press, 1969.

Clow, Richmond, L. "Crossing the Divide from Citizen to Voter: Tribal Suffrage in Montana, 1880–2016." *Montana* 69, no. 1 (Spring 2019): 35–54.

Cooper, Brittney C. *Beyond Respectability: The Intellectual Thought of Race Women*. Urbana: University of Illinois Press, 2017.

Corbould, Clare. "Streets, Sounds, and Identity in Interwar Harlem." *Journal of Social History* 40, no. 4 (2007): 859–82.

Cothran, Boyd. *Remembering the Modoc War: Redemptive Violence and the Making of American Innocence*. Chapel Hill: University of North Carolina Press, 2014.

Cott, Nancy. "Feminist Politics in the 1920s: The National Woman's Party." *Journal of American History* 71, no. 1 (June 1984): 43–68.

———. *The Grounding of Modern Feminism*. New Haven, Conn.: Yale University Press, 1987.

Cox, Karen L. *Dixie's Daughters: The United Daughters of the Confederacy and the Preservation of Confederate Culture*. Gainesville: University Press of Florida, 2019.

Crandall, Maurice S. *These People Have Always Been a Republic: Indigenous Electorates in the U.S.–Mexico Borderlands, 1598–1912*. Chapel Hill: University of North Carolina Press, 2019.

Daily, David W. *Battle for the BIA: G. E. E. Lindquist and the Missionary Crusade against John Collier*. Tucson: University of Arizona Press, 2004.

Davidson, Cathy N., and Ada Norris. Introduction to *American Indian Stories, Legends, and Other Writings*, by Zitkala-Ša. New York: Penguin, 2003.

Deer, Sarah. *The Beginning and the End of Rape: Confronting Sexual Violence in Native America*. Minneapolis: University of Minnesota Press, 2015.

Delap, Lucy, Maria Dicenzo, and Leila Ryan, eds. *Feminism and the Periodical Press, 1900–1918*. Vol. 3. New York: Routledge, 2006.

Deloria, Philip. "Four Thousand Invitations." *American Indian Quarterly* 37 no. 3 (Summer 2013): 25–43.

———. *Indians in Unexpected Places*. Lawrence: University Press of Kansas, 2004.

———. *Playing Indian*. New Haven, Conn.: Yale University Press, 1998.

Deutsch, Sarah. *No Separate Refuge: Culture, Class, and Gender on an Anglo-Hispanic Frontier in the American Southwest, 1880–1940*. New York: Oxford University Press, 1989.

Deverell, William F. *Whitewashed Adobe: The Rise of Los Angeles and the Remaking of Its Mexican Past*. Berkeley: University of California Press, 2004.

Dominguez, Susan Rose. "The Gertrude Bonnin Story: From Yankton Destiny into American History, 1804–1938, Volume 1." Ph.D. diss., Michigan State University, 2005.

Drew, Bernard A. *Black Stereotypes in Popular Series Fiction, 1851–1955: Jim Crow Era Authors and Their Characters*. Jefferson, N.C.: McFarland, 2015.

DuBois, Ellen Carol. *Feminism and Suffrage: The Emergence of an Independent Women's Movement in America, 1848–1869*. 2nd ed. Ithaca: Cornell University Press, 1999.

———. *Harriot Stanton Blatch and the Winning of Woman Suffrage*. New Haven, Conn.: Yale University Press, 1999.

———. *Suffrage: Women's Long Battle for the Vote*. New York: Simon & Schuster, 2020.

———. "Woman Suffrage: The View from the Pacific." *Pacific Historical Review* 69, no. 4 (November 2000): 539–51.

Echo-Hawk, Walter R. *In the Courts of the Conqueror: The 10 Worst Indian Law Cases Ever Decided*. 2nd ed. Golden, Colo.: Fulcrum, 2012.

Edwards, Louise P. *Gender, Politics, and Democracy: Women's Suffrage in China*. Stanford: Stanford University Press, 2008.

———. "Tang Qunying." In *Biographical Dictionary of Chinese Women: The 20th Century, 1912–2000*, edited by Lily Xiao Hong Lee and A. D. Stefanowska, 506. Hong Kong: Hong Kong University Press, 2002.

———. "Zhang Mojun." In *Biographical Dictionary of Chinese Women: The 20th Century, 1912–2000*, edited by Lily Xiao Hong Lee and A. D. Stefanowska, 685–87. Hong Kong: Hong Kong University Press, 2002.

Egge, Sara. *Woman Suffrage and Citizenship in the Midwest, 1870–1920.* Iowa City: University of Iowa Press, 2018.

Ellinghaus, Katherine. *Taking Assimilation to Heart: Marriages of White Women and Indigenous Men in the United States and Australia, 1887–1937.* Lincoln: University of Nebraska Press, 2006.

Enciso, Carmen E., and Tracy North, eds. "Dennis Chávez." In *Hispanic Americans in Congress, 1822–2012.* Washington, D.C.: Government Printing Office, 1995.

Estes, Nick. *Our History Is the Future: Standing Rock versus the Dakota Access Pipeline and the Long Tradition of Indigenous Resistance.* New York: Verso, 2019.

Fass, Paula S. *The Damned and the Beautiful: American Youth in the 1920s.* New York: Oxford University Press, 1977.

Feimster, Crystal N. *Southern Horrors: Women and the Politics of Rape and Lynching.* Cambridge, Mass.: Harvard University Press, 2009.

Finnegan, Margaret Mary. *Selling Suffrage: Consumer Culture and Votes for Women.* New York: Columbia University Press, 1999.

Flexner, Eleanor, and Ellen Fitzpatrick. *Century of Struggle: The Woman's Rights Movement in the United States.* 2nd ed. Cambridge, Mass.: Belknap Press of Harvard University Press, 1996.

Foner, Eric. *Reconstruction: America's Unfinished Revolution.* New York: Harper and Row, 1988.

Franceschi, Zelda Alice. "Women in the Field: Writing the History, Genealogies and Science in Margaret Mead's Autobiographical Writings." In *Writing about Lives in Science: (Auto)Biography, Gender, and Genre,* edited by Paola Govoni and Zelda Alice Franceshi, 161–86. Gottingen, Ger.: V&R Unipress, 2014.

Francis-Fallon, Benjamin. *The Rise of the Latino Vote.* Cambridge, Mass.: Harvard University Press, 2019.

Franklin, John Hope. *Race and History: Selected Essays, 1938–1988.* Baton Rouge: Louisiana State University Press, 1989.

Friar, Ralph F., and Natasha A. Friar. *The Only Good Indian: The Hollywood Gospel.* New York: Drama Book Specialists, 1972.

Gaines, Anne-Rosewell J. "Political Reward and Recognition: Woodrow Wilson Appoints Thomas Nelson Page Ambassador to Italy." *Virginia Magazine of History and Biography* 89, no. 3 (July 1981): 328–40.

Galperin, Patricia O. *In Search of Princess White Deer: The Biography of Esther Deer.* Sparta, N.J.: Flint and Feather Press, 2012.

Garceau, Dee. "'A Right to Help Make the Laws': Helen Piotopowaka Clarke, Virginia Billedeaux, and Blackfeet Empowerment." In *Equality at the Ballot Box: Votes for Women on the Northern Great Plains,* edited by Lori Ann Lahlum and Molly P. Rozum, 240–63. Pierre: South Dakota Historical Society Press, 2019.

Genetin-Pilawa, C. Joseph. *Crooked Paths to Allotment: The Fight over Federal Indian Policy after the Civil War.* Chapel Hill: University of North Carolina Press, 2012.

———. "A Curious Removal: Leta Myers Smart, The Rescue, and The Discovery of America." *The Capital Dome: A Magazine of History Published by the United States Capital Historical Society* 51, no. 1 (Spring 2015): 2–9.

———. "The Indians' Capital City: Diplomatic Visits, Place, and Two-Worlds Discourse in Nineteenth-Century Washington, D.C." In *Beyond Two Worlds: Critical Conversations on Language and Power in Native North America,* edited by James Joseph Buss and C. Joseph Genetin-Pilawa, 117–36. Albany: SUNY Press, 2014.

Giddings, Paula J. *Ida: A Sword among Lions: Ida B. Wells and the Campaign against Lynching.* New York: HarperCollins, 2008.

———. *In Search of Sisterhood: Delta Sigma Theta and the Challenge of the Black Sorority Movement*. New York: Perennial, 1988.

Gidlow, Liette. "Resistance after Ratification: The Nineteenth Amendment, African American Women, and the Problem of Female Disfranchisement after 1920." In *Women and Social Movements in the United States, 1600–2000*. Alexandria, Va.: Alexander Street, 2017. Retrieved from Women and Social Movements in the United States, 1600–2000, database at docu ments.alexanderstreet.com. Accessed February 15, 2020.

———. "The Sequel: The Fifteenth Amendment, the Nineteenth Amendment, and Southern Black Women's Struggle to Vote." *Journal of the Gilded Age and Progressive Era* 17, no. 3 (July 2018): 433–49.

Gilmore, Glenda Elizabeth. *Gender and Jim Crow: Women and the Politics of White Supremacy in North Carolina, 1896–1920*. Chapel Hill: University of North Carolina Press, 1996.

Ginzberg, Lori D. *Elizabeth Cady Stanton: An American Life*. New York: Hill and Wang, 2009.

Godshalk, David Fort. *Veiled Visions: The 1906 Atlanta Race Riot and the Reshaping of American Race Relations*. Chapel Hill: University of North Carolina Press, 2005.

Goeman, Mishuana R. *Mark My Words: Native Women Mapping Our Nations*. Minneapolis: University of Minnesota Press, 2013.

Goeman, Mishuana R., and Jennifer Nez Denetdale, eds. "Native Feminisms." Special issue, *Wicazo Sa Review* 24, no. 2 (Fall 2009).

Gomez, Laura E. *Manifest Destinies: The Making of the Mexican American Race*. New York: New York University Press, 2007.

González, Deena J. *Refusing the Favor: The Spanish-Mexican Women of Santa Fe, 1820–1880*. New York: Oxford University Press, 2001.

Goodier, Susan, and Karen Pastorello. *Women Will Vote: Winning Suffrage in New York State*. Ithaca: Cornell University Press, 2017.

Grant, Keneshia N. *The Great Migration and the Democratic Party: Black Voters and the Realignment of American Politics in the 20th Century*. Philadelphia: Temple University Press, 2020.

Graybill, Andrew R. *The White and the Red: A Family Saga of the American West*. New York: Liveright, 2013.

Green, Constance McLaughlin. *Washington, Capital City 1879–1950*. Princeton, N.J.: Princeton University Press, 1963.

Green, Rayna. "The Pocahontas Perplex: Images of American Indian Women in American Culture." *Massachusetts Review* 16, no. 4 (Autumn 1975): 698–714.

Grimshaw, Patricia. *Women's Suffrage in New Zealand*. Auckland: Auckland University Press, 2013.

Grossman, James R. *Land of Hope: Chicago, Black Southerners, and the Great Migration*. Chicago: University of Chicago Press, 1989.

Gulliver, Katrina. *Modern Women in China and Japan: Gender, Feminism and Global Modernity*. New York: I. B. Tauris, 2012.

Gunter, Rachel. "'Alien Enemies' and 'Loyal American Women': Woman Suffrage, Alien Suffrage, and Contested Meanings of Citizenship." *Journal of the Gilded Age and Progressive Era*, forthcoming. Manuscript in author's possession.

Gushee, Lawrence. *Pioneers of Jazz: The Story of the Creole Band*. New York: Oxford University Press, 2010.

Gustafson, Melanie Susan. *Women and the Republican Party, 1854–1924*. Champaign-Urbana: University of Illinois Press, 2001.

Hahn, Emily. *The Soong Sisters: The Revealing Biography of Madame Chiang Kai-shek and Her Sisters*. New York: Doubleday, Doran, 1943.

Hamlin, Kimberly A. *Free Thinker: Sex, Suffrage, and the Extraordinary Life of Helen Hamilton Gardener*. New York: W. W. Norton, 2020.

Harmon, Alexandra. *Rich Indians: Native People and the Problem of Wealth in American History*. Chapel Hill: University of North Carolina Press, 2010.

Hathaway, Grace. *Fate Rides a Tortoise: A Biography of Ellen Spencer Mussey*. Philadelphia: John C. Winston, 1937.

Hauptman, Laurence M. *The Iroquois and the New Deal*. Syracuse: Syracuse University Press, 1988.

———. *Seven Generations of Iroquois Leadership*. Syracuse: Syracuse University Press, 2008.

Hauptman, Laurence M., and L. Gordon McLester III, eds. *The Oneida Indians in the Age of Allotment*. Norman: University of Oklahoma Press, 2006.

Hershberger, Mary. "Mobilizing Women, Anticipating Abolition: The Struggle against Indian Removal in the 1830s." *Journal of American History* 86, no. 1 (June 1999): 15–40.

Hertzberg, Hazel W. *Search for an American Indian Identity: Modern Pan-Indian Movements*. Syracuse: Syracuse University Press, 1971.

Higginbotham, Evelyn Brooks. "Clubwomen and Electoral Politics in the 1920s." In *African American Women and the Vote, 1837–1965*, edited by Ann D. Gordon and Bettye Collier-Thomas, 134–55. Amherst: University of Massachusetts Press, 1997.

———. *Righteous Discontent: The Women's Movement in the Black Baptist Church, 1880–1920*. Cambridge, Mass.: Harvard University Press, 1993.

Higham, John. "Indian Princess and Roman Goddess: The First Female Symbols of America." *Proceedings of the American Antiquarian Society* 100, pt. 1 (1990): 59–66.

Hill, Susan M. *The Clay We Are Made Of: Haudenosaunee Land Tenure of the Grand River*. Winnipeg: University of Manitoba Press, 2017.

Hine, Darlene Clark. "Rape and the Inner Lives of Black Women in the Middle West: Preliminary Thoughts on the Culture of Dissemblance." *Signs: Journal of Women in Culture and Society* 14, no. 4 (Summer 1989): 912–20.

Hoganson, Kristen. *Fighting for American Manhood: How Gender Politics Provoked the Spanish-American and Philippine-American Wars*. New Haven, Conn.: Yale University Press, 2000.

Hogue, Michel. *Metis and the Medicine Line: Creating a Border and Dividing a People*. Chapel Hill: University of North Carolina Press, 2015.

Holtby, David V. *The Forty-Seventh Star: New Mexico's Struggle for Statehood*. Norman: University of Oklahoma Press, 2012.

Hsu, Madeline Y. "The Disappearance of America's Cold War Chinese Refugees, 1948–1966." *Journal of American Ethnic History* 31, no. 4 (Summer 2012): 12–33.

———. *The Good Immigrants: How the Yellow Peril Became the Model Minority*. Princeton, N.J.: Princeton University Press, 2015.

Huebner, Karin L. "An Unexpected Alliance: Stella Atwood, the California Clubwoman, John Collier, and the Indians of the Southwest, 1917–1934." *Pacific Historical Review* 78, no. 3 (August 2009): 337–66.

Hungry Wolf, Adolf. *Pikunni Biographies*. Vol. 4 of *The Blackfoot Papers*. Browning, Mt.: Blackfoot Heritage Center and Art Gallery, 2006.

Hutchinson, Elizabeth. *The Indian Craze: Primitivism, Modernism and Transculturation in American Art, 1890–1915*. Durham, N.C.: Duke University Press, 2009.

Hyde, Anne F. *Empires, Nations, and Families: A New History of the American West: A History of the North American West, 1800–1860*. Lincoln: University of Nebraska Press, 2011.

———. "Hard Choices: Mixed-Race Families and Strategies of Acculturation in the U.S. West after 1848." In *On the Borders of Love and Power: Families and Kinship in the Intercultural American Southwest*, edited by David Wallace Adams and Crista DeLuzio, 93–118. Berkeley: University of California Press, 2012.

Imada, Adria L. *Aloha America: Hula Circuits through the U.S. Empire*. Durham, N.C.: Duke University Press, 2012.

Jacobs, Margaret D. *Engendered Encounters: Feminism and Pueblo Cultures, 1879–1934.* Lincoln: University of Nebraska Press, 1999.

Jacobson, Matthew Frye. *Barbarian Virtues: The United States Encounters Foreign Peoples at Home and Abroad, 1876–1917.* New York: Hill and Wang, 2000.

Jenkins, Jeffry A., Justin Peck, and Vesla M. Weaver. "Between Reconstructions: Congressional Action on Civil Rights, 1891–1940." *Studies in American Political Development* 24, no. 1 (April 2010): 57–89.

Jensen, Billie Barnes. "Colorado Woman Suffrage Campaigns of the 1870s." *Journal of the West* 12, no. 1 (April 1973): 254–71.

Jensen, Joan M. "'Disenfranchisement Is a Disgrace': Women and Politics in New Mexico, 1900–1940." *New Mexico Historical Review* 56, no. 1 (January 1981): 5–35.

Johnson, Susan Lee. *Roaring Camp: The Social World of the California Gold Rush.* New York: W. W. Norton, 2000.

Jones, Martha S. *All Bound Up Together: The Woman Question in African American Public Culture, 1830–1900.* Chapel Hill: University of North Carolina Press, 2007.

———. *Vanguard: How Black Women Broke Barriers, Won the Vote, and Insisted on Equality for All.* New York: Basic Books, 2020.

Judge, Joan. *Republican Lens: Gender, Visuality, and Experience in the Early Chinese Periodical Press.* Los Angeles: University of California Press, 2015.

Kanellos, Nicolás, ed. *Herencia: The Anthology of Hispanic Literature of the United States.* New York: Oxford University Press, 2002.

Kantrowitz, Stephen. "White Supremacy, Settler Colonialism, and the Two Citizenships of the Fourteenth Amendment." *Journal of the Civil War Era* 10, no. 1 (March 2020): 29–53.

Kantrowitz, Stephen. "'Not Quite Constitutionalized': The Meanings of 'Civilization' and the Limits of Native American Citizenship." In *The World the Civil War Made*, edited by Gregory P. Downs and Kate Masur, 75–105. Chapel Hill: University of North Carolina Press, 2015.

Kelly, Lawrence, C. *The Assault on Assimilation: John Collier and the Origins of Indian Policy Reform.* Albuquerque: University of New Mexico Press, 1983.

Kiel, Doug. "Competing Visions of Empowerment: Oneida Progressive-Era Politics and Writing Tribal Histories." *Ethnohistory* 61, no. 3 (2014): 419–44.

Klebanow, Diana, and Franklin L. Jones. *People's Lawyers: Crusaders for Justice in American History.* New York: Routledge, 2002.

Kropp, Phoebe S. *California Vieja: Culture and Memory in a Modern American Place.* Berkeley: University of California Press, 2006.

Krouse, Susan Applegate. *North American Indians in the Great War.* Lincoln: University of Nebraska Press, 2007.

Kwong, Peter. *New Chinatown.* 2nd ed. New York: Hill and Wang, 1996.

Lamar, Howard. *The Far Southwest: A Territorial History, 1846–1912.* New Haven, Conn.: Yale University Press, 1966.

Landsman, Gail H. "The 'Other' as Political Symbol: Images of Indians in the Woman Suffrage Movement." *Ethnohistory* 39, no. 3 (Summer 1992): 247–84.

Lange, Allison K. *Picturing Political Power: Images in the Women's Suffrage Movement.* Chicago: University of Chicago Press, 2020.

Larson, Robert W. *New Mexico's Quest for Statehood.* 2nd ed. Albuquerque: University of New Mexico Press, 2013.

Le Corbeiller, Clare. "Miss America and Her Sisters: Personifications of the Four Parts of the World." *Metropolitan Museum of Art Bulletin* 19, no. 8 (April 1961): 209–23.

Lee, Erika. *At America's Gates: Chinese Immigration during the Exclusion Era, 1882–1943.* Chapel Hill: University of North Carolina Press, 2004.

Lemay, Kate Clarke. *Votes For Women: A Portrait of Persistence*. Princeton, N.J.: Princeton University Press, 2019.

Leonard, Kevin Allen. "Dennis Chavez: The Last of the Patrones." In *The Human Tradition in America between the Wars, 1920–1945*, edited Donald W. Whisenhunt, 105–20. Wilmington, Del.: Scholarly Resources, 2002.

Lewandowski, Tadeusz. *Red Bird, Red Power: The Life and Legacy of Zitkala-Ša*. Norman: University of Oklahoma Press, 2016.

Lewis, David Levering. *W. E. B. Du Bois: A Biography, 1868–1963*. New York: Henry Holt, 2009.

Lindsey, Treva. *Colored No More: Reinventing Black Womanhood in Washington, D.C*. Urbana: University of Illinois Press, 2017.

Linkugel, Wil A., and Kim Griffin. "The Distinguished War Service of Dr. Anna Howard Shaw." *Pennsylvania History: A Journal of Mid-Atlantic Studies* 28, no. 4 (1961): 372–85.

Lomawaima, Tsianina. "The Mutuality of Citizenship and Sovereignty: The Society of American Indians and the Battle to Inherit America." *American Indian Quarterly* 37, no. 3 (2013): 331–51.

Lonetree, Amy. "Visualizing Native Survivance: Encounters with My Ho-Chunk Ancestors in the Family Photographs of Charles Van Schaick." In *People of the Big Voice: Photographs of Ho-Chunk Families by Charles Van Schaick, 1879–1942*, 13–22. Madison: Wisconsin Historical Society Press, 2011.

Lozano, Rosina. *An American Language: The History of Spanish in the United States*. Oakland: University of California Press, 2018.

Lui, Mary Ting Yi. *The Chinatown Trunk Mystery: Murder, Miscegenation, and Other Dangerous Encounters in Turn-of-the-Century New York City*. Princeton, N.J.: Princeton University Press, 2007.

Lum, Arlene, ed. *Sailing for the Sun: The Chinese in Hawaii, 1789–1989*. Honolulu: University of Hawaii Press, 1988.

Lumsden, Linda J. *Rampant Women: Suffragists and the Right of Assembly*. Knoxville: University of Tennessee Press, 1997.

Lutz, Christine. "Addie W. Hunton: Crusader for Pan Africanism and Peace." In *Portraits of African American Life since 1865*, edited by Nina Mjagki, 109–27. Lanham, Md.: Rowman and Littlefield, 2003.

Maddox, Lucy. *Citizen Indians: Native American Intellectuals, Race & Reform*. Ithaca: Cornell University Press, 2005.

Marino, Catherine M. *Feminism for the Americas: The Making of an International Human Rights Movement*. Chapel Hill: University of North Carolina Press, 2019.

Massmann, Ann M. "Adelina 'Nina' Otero-Warren: A Spanish-American Cultural Broker." *Journal of the Southwest* 42, no. 4 (2000): 877–96.

Masur, Kate. *An Example for All the Land: Emancipation and the Struggle over Equality in Washington, D.C*. Chapel Hill: University of North Carolina Press, 2010.

Materson, Lisa G. *For the Freedom of Her Race: Black Women and Electoral Politics in Illinois, 1877–1932*. Chapel Hill: University of North Carolina Press, 2009.

May, Vivian M. *Anna Julia Cooper, Visionary Black Feminist*. New York: Routledge, 2007.

McCool, David, Susan M. Olson, and Jennifer L. Robinson. *Native Vote: American Indians, the Voting Rights Act, and the Right to Vote*. New York: Cambridge University Press, 2007.

McCoy, Matthew G. "Hidden Citizens: The Courts and Native American Voting Rights in the Southwest." *Journal of the Southwest* 58, no. 2 (2016): 293–310.

McKeown, Adam. *Chinese Migrant Networks and Cultural Change: Peru, Chicago, Hawaii, 1900–1936*. Chicago: University of Chicago Press, 2001.

McLester, L. Gordon, III, and Laurence M. Hauptman, eds. *The Oneida Indians in the Age of Allotment, 1860–1920*. Norman: University of Oklahoma Press, 2006.

McVeigh, Brian J. *The History of Japanese Psychology: Global Perspectives, 1875–1950*. London: Bloomsbury, 2017.

Mead, Rebecca J. *How the Vote Was Won: Woman Suffrage in the Western United States, 1868–1914*. New York: New York University Press, 2004.

Means, Jeffrey D. "'Indians shall do things in common': Oglala Lakota Identity and Economics during the Early Reservation Era, 1868–1889." *Montana: The Magazine of Western History* 60, no. 3 (Fall 2011): 3–21.

Miles, Tiya. "'Circular Reasoning': Recentering Cherokee Women in the Antiremoval Campaigns." *American Quarterly* 61, no. 2 (June 2009): 221–43.

———. *Ties That Bind: The Story of an Afro-Cherokee Family in Slavery and Freedom*. Berkeley: University of California Press, 2006.

Mitchell, Pablo. "Borderlands/La Familia: Mexicans, Homes, and Colonialism in the Early Twentieth-Century Southwest." In *On the Borders of Love and Power*, edited by David Wallace Adams and Crista DeLuzio, 185–208. Berkeley: University of California Press, 2012.

———. *Coyote Nation: Sexuality, Race, and Conquest in Modernizing New Mexico, 1880–1920*. Chicago: University of Chicago Press, 2005.

Montoya, Maria E. *Translating Property: The Maxwell Land Grant and Conflict over Land in the American West, 1840–1900*. Lawrence: University Press of Kansas, 2005.

Mumford, Jeremy. "Métis and the Vote in 19th-Century America." *Journal of the West* 39, no. 3 (July 2000): 38–45.

Mungarro, Angelica, and Karen Anderson. "How Did Black Women in the NAACP Promote the Dyer Anti-Lynching Bill, 1918–1923?" In *Women and Social Networks*. Binghampton: State University of New York, 2003. Retrieved from Women and Social Movements in the United States, 1600–2000, database at documents.alexanderstreet.com. Accessed February 15, 2020.

Murphy, Mary-Elizabeth B. "African American Women's Politics, Organizing, and Activism in 1920s Washington, D.C." Ph.D. diss., University of Maryland, College Park, 2012.

Murray, Stanley N. "The Turtle Mountain Chippewa, 1882–1905." *North Dakota History* 51 (Winter 1984): 14–27.

Nahal, Anita, and Lopez D. Matthews Jr. "African American Women and the Niagara Movement, 1905–1909." *Afro-Americans in New York Life and History* 32, no. 2 (July 2008): 65–84.

Nelson, Elaine M. "Eunice Woodhull Stabler, Omaha Indian Writer, 1885–1963." M.A. thesis, University of Nebraska-Lincoln, 2004.

Newman, Louise Michele. *White Women's Rights: The Racial Origins of Feminism in the United States*. New York: Oxford University Press, 1999.

Ngai, Mae M. *Impossible Subjects: Illegal Aliens and the Making of Modern America*. Princeton, N.J.: Princeton University Press, 2005.

———. "Western History and the Pacific World." *Western Historical Quarterly* 43, no. 3 (Autumn 2012): 282–88.

Nieto-Phillips, John. *The Language of Blood: The Making of Spanish-American Identity in New Mexico, 1880s–1930s*. Albuquerque: University of New Mexico Press, 2004.

Norgren, Jill. *Belva Lockwood: The Woman Who Would Be President*. New York: New York University Press, 2007.

O'Brian, Jean M. *Firsting and Lasting: Writing Indians Out of Existence in New England*. Minneapolis: University of Minnesota Press, 2010.

Orozco, Cynthia E. *No Mexicans, Women, or Dogs Allowed: The Rise of the Mexican American Civil Rights Movement*. Austin: University of Texas Press, 2009.

———. *Agent of Change: Adela Sloss-Vento, Mexican-American Civil Rights Activist and Texas Feminist*. Austin: University of Texas Press, 2020.

Ostler, Jeffrey. *The Plains Sioux and U.S. Colonialism from Lewis and Clark to Wounded Knee.* New York: Cambridge University Press, 2004.

Pao-Tao, Chia-lin. "Qiu Jin." In *Biographical Dictionary of Chinese Women: The Qing Period, 1644–1911,* edited by Lily Xiao Hong Lee, Clara Lau, and A. D. Stefanowska, 175–76. Hong Kong: Hong Kong University Press, 1998.

Parman, Donald L. *Indians and the American West in the Twentieth Century.* Bloomington: Indiana University Press, 1994.

Pascoe, Peggy. *Relations of Rescue: The Search for Female Moral Authority in the American West, 1874–1939.* New York: Oxford University Press, 1993.

————. *What Comes Naturally: Miscegenation Law and the Making of Race in America.* New York: Oxford University Press, 2010.

Pawling, Micah A. "A 'Labyrinth of Uncertainties': Penobscot River Islands, Land Assignments, and Indigenous Women Proprietors in Nineteenth-Century Maine." *American Indian Quarterly* 42, no. 4 (Fall 2018): 454–87.

Peffer, George Anthony. "Forbidden Families: Emigration Experiences of Chinese Women under the Page Law, 1875–1882." *Journal of American Ethnic History* 6, no. 1 (Fall 1986): 28–46.

Pereles, Monica. "'Who Has a Greater Job than a Mother?' Defining Mexican American Motherhood on the U.S.–Mexico Border in the Early Twentieth Century." In *On the Borders of Love and Power,* edited by David Wallace Adams and Crista DeLuzio, 163–84. Berkeley: University of California Press, 2012.

Perez, Erika. *Colonial Intimacies: Interethnic Kinship, Sexuality, and Marriage in Southern California.* Berkeley: University of California Press, 2018.

Peterson, Barbara Bennett. "Kalanianaole, Princess Elizabeth Kahanu Kaleiwohi-Kaauwai." In *Notable Women of Hawaii,* edited by Barbara Bennett Peterson, 186–89. Honolulu: University of Hawaii Press, 1984.

Phelps, Glenn A. "Representation without Taxation: Citizenship and Suffrage in Indian Country." *American Indian Quarterly* 9, no. 2 (Spring 1985): 135–48.

Philip, Kenneth R. *John Collier's Crusade for Indian Reform, 1920–1954.* Tucson: University of Arizona Press, 1977.

Ponce, Merrihelen. "The Lives and Works of Five Hispanic New Mexican Women Writers, 1878–1991." Albuquerque: University of New Mexico Southwest Hispanic Research Institute Working Paper no. 119 (Summer 1992).

Posthumus, David C. *All My Relatives: Exploring Lakota Ontology, Belief, and Ritual.* Lincoln: University of Nebraska Press, 2018.

Prescott, Cynthia Culver. *Pioneer Mother Monuments: Constructing Cultural Memory.* Norman: University of Oklahoma Press, 2019.

Prieto, Laura. "Votes for Colonized Women." *Process: A Blog for American History.* Organization of American Historians, May 28, 2020. http://www.processhistory.org/prieto-votes-colonized.

Quigley, Joan. *Just Another Southern Town: Mary Church Terrell and the Struggle for Racial Justice in the Nation's Capital.* New York: Oxford University Press, 2016.

Ramirez, Renya K. *Standing Up to Colonial Power: The Lives of Henry Roe and Elizabeth Bender Cloud.* Lincoln: University of Nebraska Press, 2018.

Rebolledo, Tey Diana, and María Teresa Márquez, eds. *Women's Tales from the New Mexico WPA: La Diabla a Pie.* Houston, Tex.: Arte Público Press, 2000.

Reed, Julie. *Serving the Cherokee Nation: Cherokee Sovereignty and Social Welfare, 1800–1907.* Norman: University of Oklahoma Press, 2016.

Richotte, Keith Steven, Jr. "We the Indians of Turtle Mountain: Rethinking Tribal Constitutionalism beyond the Colonialist/Revolutionary Dialectic." Ph.D. diss., University of Minnesota, 2009.

Risling Baldy, Cutcha. *We Are Dancing for You: Native Feminisms and the Revitalization of Women's Coming-of-Age Ceremonies.* Seattle: University of Washington Press, 2018.

Robertson, Charles F. *Temple of Invention: History of a National Landmark.* London: Scala Publishers, 2006.

Rosen, Hannah. *Terror in the Heart of Freedom: Citizenship, Sexual Violence, and the Meaning of Race in the Postemancipation South.* Chapel Hill: University of North Carolina Press, 2009.

Rosenberg, Rosalind. *Changing the Subject: How the Women of Columbia Shaped the Way We Think about Sex and Politics.* New York: Columbia University Press, 2004.

Rosenthal, Nicolas G. *Reimagining Indian Country: Native American Migration and Identity in Twentieth-Century Los Angeles.* Chapel Hill: University of North Carolina Press, 2012.

Rosier, Paul. *Serving Their Country: Indian Politics and Patriotism in the Twentieth Century.* Cambridge, Mass.: Harvard University Press, 2009.

Rozum, Molly P. "Citizenship, Civilization, and Property: The 1890 South Dakota Vote on Woman Suffrage and Indian Suffrage." In *Equality at the Ballot Box: Votes for Women on the Northern Great Plains,* edited by Lori Ann Lahlum and Molly P. Rozum, 240–63. Pierre: South Dakota Historical Society Press, 2019.

Ruiz, Vicki. *From Out of the Shadows: Mexican Women in Twentieth-Century America.* 2nd ed. New York: Oxford University Press, 2008.

Rupp, Leila J., and Verta Taylor. *Survival in the Doldrums: The American Women's Rights Movement, 1945 to the 1960s.* New York: Oxford University Press, 1987.

Rydell, Robert W. *All the World's a Fair: Visions of Empire at American International Expositions, 1876–1916.* Chicago: University of Chicago Press, 1987.

Sandoval-Strausz, Andrew K. *Hotel: An American History.* New Haven, Conn.: Yale University Press, 2008.

Scharff, Virginia. *Taking the Wheel: Women and the Coming of the Motor Age.* Albuquerque: University of New Mexico Press, 1999.

Shah, Nayan. *Contagious Divides: Epidemics and Race in San Francisco's Chinatown.* Berkeley: University of California Press, 2001.

Silva, Noenoe K. *Aloha Betrayed: Native Hawaiian Resistance to American Colonialism.* Durham, N.C.: Duke University Press, 2004.

Simpson, Audra. *Mohawk Interruptus: Political Life across the Borders of Settler States.* Durham, N.C.: Duke University Press, 2014.

Sklar, Kathryn Kish, and Jill Dais. "How Did the National Woman's Party Address the Issue of the Enfranchisement of Black Women, 1919–1924?" Binghamton: State University of New York, 1997. Retrieved from Women and Social Movements in the United States, 1600–2000, database at documents.alexanderstreet.com. Accessed February 15, 2020.

Sleeper-Smith, Susan. *Indian Women and French Men: Rethinking Cultural Encounter in the Western Great Lakes.* Amherst: University of Massachusetts Press, 2011.

Sloan, Kay. "Sexual Warfare in the Silent Cinema: Comedies and Melodramas of Woman Suffragism." *American Quarterly* 33, no. 4 (Autumn 1981): 412–36.

Smith, Jessie Carney, ed. *Notable Black Women.* Book 2. New York: Gale Research, 1999.

Sneider, Allison L. *Suffragists in an Imperial Age: U.S. Expansion and the Woman Question.* New York: Oxford University Press, 2008.

Solomon, Martha M., ed. *A Voice of Their Own: The Woman Suffrage Press, 1840–1910.* Tuscaloosa: University of Alabama Press, 1991.

Song, Jingyi. *Shaping and Reshaping Chinese American Identity: New York's Chinese during the Depression and World War II.* Plymouth, UK: Lexington Books, 2010.

Spence, Jonathan D. *The Search for Modern China.* New York: W. W. Norton, 2012.

Spence, Mark David. *Dispossessing the Wilderness: Indian Removal and the Making of the National Parks.* New York: Oxford University Press, 1999.

Stanciu, Cristina. "Americanization on Native Terms: The Society of American Indians, Citizenship Debates, and Tropes of 'Racial Difference.'" *Native American and Indigenous Studies* 6, no. 1 (2019): 111–48.

Stanciu, Cristina, and Kristina Ackley. "Introduction: Laura Cornelius Kellogg: Haudenosaunee Thinker, Native Activist, American Writer." In *Laura Cornelius Kellogg: Our Democracy and the American Indian and Other Works,* 1–64. Syracuse: Syracuse University Press, 2015.

Stokes, Melvyn. *D. W. Griffith's "The Birth of a Nation": A History of "the Most Controversial Motion Picture of All Time."* Oxford: Oxford University Press, 2007.

Sutherland, Jonathan D., ed. *African Americans in War: An Encyclopedia.* Santa Barbara, Calif.: ABC-CLIO, 2003.

Svingen, Orlan J. "Jim Crow, Indian Style." *American Indian Quarterly* 11, no. 4 (1987): 275–86.

Terborg-Penn, Rosalyn. *African American Women in the Struggle for the Vote, 1850–1920.* Bloomington: Indiana University Press, 1998.

Tetrault, Lisa. *The Myth of Seneca Falls: Memory and the Women's Suffrage Movement, 1848–1898.* Chapel Hill: University of North Carolina Press, 2017.

Thigpen, Jennifer. *Island Queens and Missionary Wives: How Gender and Empire Remade Hawai'i's Pacific World.* Chapel Hill: University of North Carolina Press, 2014.

Thorne, Tanis C. *The World's Richest Indian: The Scandal over Jackson Barnett's Oil Fortune.* Oxford: Oxford University Press, 2003.

Tseng, Timothy. "Dr. Mabel Lee: The Intersticial Career of a Protestant Chinese American Woman, 1924–1950." Paper presented at the 1996 OAH meeting. Accessed via https://timtsengdotnet.files.wordpress.com/2013/11/mabel-lee-paper-1996.pdf. Accessed October 10, 2017.

———. "Unbinding Their Souls: Chinese Protestant Women in Twentieth-Century America." In *Women and 20th Century Protestantism,* edited by Margaret Lamberts Bendroth and Virginia Lieson Brereton, 136–63. Urbana: University of Illinois Press, 2002.

Tucker, Vernitta Brothers. "Carrie Williams Clifford's Poetic Response to Racial Injustice: A Call to Action and a Demand for Justice." Master's thesis, Morgan State University, 2013.

Ulrich, Laurel Thatcher. *Age of Homespun: Objects and Stories in the Creation of an American Myth.* New York: Vintage, 2002.

Unrau, William E. "Charles Curtis/Kaw." In *The New Warriors: Native American Leaders since 1900,* edited by R. David Edmunds, 17–34. Lincoln: University of Nebraska Press, 2001.

———. *Mixed Bloods and the Dispossession: Charles Curtis and the Quest for Indian Identity.* Lawrence: University Press of Kansas, 1989.

Van Voris, Jacqueline. *Carrie Chapman Catt: A Public Life.* New York: Feminist Press, 1987.

Vickery, Amanda Elizabeth. "After the March, What? Rethinking How We Teach the Feminist Movement." *Social Studies Research and Practices* 13, no. 3 (2018): 402–11.

Vigil, Kiara M. *Indigenous Intellectuals: Sovereignty, Citizenship, and the American Imagination, 1880–1930.* Cambridge: Cambridge University Press, 2015.

Viola, Herman J. *Diplomats in Buckskin: A History of Indian Delegations in Washington City.* Bluffton, S.C.: Rivilo Books, 1995.

Visenor, Gerald, and Jill Doerfler, eds. *The White Earth Nation: Ratification of a Native Democratic Constitution.* Lincoln: University of Nebraska Press, 2012.

Waggoner, Linda M. *Fire Light: The Life of Angel De Cora, Winnebago Artist*. Norman: University of Oklahoma Press, 2008.

———. *Starring Red Wing: The Incredible Career of Lillian M. St. Cyr, the First Native American Film Star*. Lincoln: University of Nebraska Press, 2019.

Wagner, Sally Roesch. *Sisters in Spirit: Haudenosaunee (Iroquois) Influence on Early Suffragists*. Summertown, Tenn.: Native Voices, 2001.

Walden, Robin S. "The Pueblo Confederation's Political Wing: The All Indian Pueblo Council, 1920–1975." Ph.D. diss., University of New Mexico, 2011.

Walker, Lewis Newton, Jr. "The Struggles and Attempts to Establish Branch Autonomy and Hegemony: A History of the District of Columbia Branch National Association for the Advancement of Colored People, 1912–1942." Ph.D. diss., University of Delaware, 1979.

Ware, Susan. *Why They Marched: Untold Stories of the Women Who Fought for the Right to Vote*. Cambridge, Mass.: Belknap Press of Harvard University Press, 2019.

Warren, William Whipple. *History of the Ojibway People*. 2nd ed. Minneapolis: Minnesota Historical Society Press, 2009.

Watson, Martha Solomon. "Mary Church Terrell vs. Thomas Nelson Page: Gender, Race, and Class." *Rhetoric and Public Affairs* 12, no. 1 (2009): 65–90.

Weaver, Jace. *The Red Atlantic: American Indigenes and the Making of the Modern World, 1000–1927*. Chapel Hill: University of North Carolina Press, 2014.

Weigle, Marta, and Mary Powell. "From 'Alice Corbin's Lines Mumbled in Sleep' to 'Eufeia's Sopapillas': Women and the Federal Writers' Project in New Mexico." *New America* 4, no. 3 (1981): 54–76.

Weiss, Elaine. *The Woman's Hour: The Great Fight to Win the Vote*. New York: Penguin Books, 2018.

Welch, Deborah. "Gertrude Simmons Bonnin (Zitkala-Ša)/Dakota." In *The New Warriors: Native American Leaders since 1900*, edited by R. David Edmunds, 35–54. Lincoln: University of Nebraska Press, 2001.

Welch, Susan. "Women in State Legislatures from the Gilded Age to the Global Age." In *100 Years of the Nineteenth Amendment: An Appraisal of Women's Political Activism*, edited by Holly J. McCammon and Lee Ann Banaszak, 151–71. New York: Oxford University Press, 2018.

Welke, Barbara Y. "When All the Women Were White, and All the Blacks Were Men: Gender, Class, Race, and the Road to Plessy, 1855–1914." *Law and History Review* 13, no. 2 (Autumn 1995): 261–316.

Wenger, Tisa. *We Have a Religion: The 1920s Pueblo Indian Dance Controversy and American Religious Freedom*. Chapel Hill: University of North Carolina Press, 2009.

Whaley, Charlotte. *Nina Otero-Warren of Santa Fe*. Santa Fe: Sunstone Press, 2007.

Whaley, Deborah Elizabeth. *Disciplining Women: Alpha Kappa Alpha, Black Counterpublics, and the Cultural Politics of Black Sororities*. Albany: SUNY Press, 2010.

White, Richard. "Frederick Jackson Turner and Buffalo Bill." In *The Frontier in American Culture*, edited by James R. Grossman, 7–66. Berkeley: University of California Press, 1994.

White Weasel, Charlie. *Pembina and Turtle Mountain Ojibway (Chippewa) History: From the Personal Collections and Writings of Charlie White Weasel*. Madison: University of Wisconsin Press, 2010.

Williams, Beth Lew. *The Chinese Must Go: Violence, Exclusion, and the Making of the Alien in America*. Cambridge, Mass.: Harvard University Press, 2018.

Wilson, Chris. *The Myth of Santa Fe: Creating Modern Regional Tradition*. Albuquerque: University of New Mexico Press, 1997.

Wilson, Chris, Stefanos Polyzoides, and Miguel Gandert. *The Plazas of New Mexico*. San Antonio: Trinity University Press, 2011.

Witgen, Michael J. *An Infinity of Nations: How the Native New World Shaped Early North America*. Philadelphia: University of Pennsylvania Press, 2012.

———. "Seeing Red: Race, Citizenship, and Indigeneity in the Old Northwest." *Journal of the Early Republic* 38, no. 4 (Winter 2018): 581–611.

Yasutake, Rumi. "Re-franchising Women of Hawai'i, 1912–1920." In *Gendering the Trans-Pacific World*, edited by Catherine Ceniza Choy and Judy Tzu-Chun Wu Leiden, 114–39. The Netherlands: Koninklijke Brill, 2017.

Ye, Weili. *Seeking Modernity in China's Name: Chinese Students in the United States, 1900–1927*. Stanford: Stanford University Press, 2001.

Yellin, Eric S. *Racism in the Nation's Service: Government Workers and the Color Line in Woodrow Wilson's America*. Chapel Hill: University of North Carolina Press, 2013.

Yung, Judy. *Unbound Feet: A Social History of Chinese Women in San Francisco*. Berkeley: University of California Press, 1995.

———, ed. *Unbound Voices: A Documentary History of Chinese Women in San Francisco*. Berkeley: University of California Press, 1999.

Zahniser, Jill D., and Amelia R. Fry. *Alice Paul: Claiming Power*. New York: Oxford University Press, 2014.

Zangrando, Robert L. *The NAACP Crusade against Lynching, 1909–1950*. Philadelphia: Temple University Press, 1980.

[INDEX]

Page numbers in italics refer to illustrations.

Abeita, Pablo, 241
abolitionism, 18
Ackley, Kristina, 274
Addams, Jane, 59, 97, 124, 276
Alabama, 197
Alarid, Mrs. Benito, 315n42
Alarid, Mrs. Kate, 315n42
Alaska, 23
Alcott, Louisa May, 35
Alexander, Adele Logan, 327n63
Alexander's Magazine, 61
alien suffrage, 15
Allen, Charles, 57
Allen, Martha, 57
Allen, Mary E., 58, 59
All Pueblo Council, 240, 241
Alpha Kappa Alpha, 102–3, 107
Alpha Suffrage Club, 104, 128
American Baptist Home Mission Society,
   275
"American Citizens Who Cannot Vote"
   (song), 80
American Federation of Labor, 27
American Horse, 16
American Indian Defense Association, 249,
   256
American Indian Magazine, 189
American Indian Stories (Bonnin), 245–46
The American Language (Mencken), 181
American Woman and Her Political Peers (Briggs-
   Wall), 80
American Woman Suffrage Association
   (AWSA), 17–18
Anderson, Isabel, 90
Anderson, Larz, 90
Anishinaabe (Ojibwe), 83
Anthony, Daniel, 252–53
Anthony, Susan B., 19, 22, 55, 76, 213, 263;
   Hawaiian suffrage and, 43–44, 174; racist
   tendencies of, 17, 53, 252; in South Dakota
   referendum campaign, 11, 14
Anthony League, 188
Apache, 48, 49, 142
Arizona, 23, 24, 49, 52, 199, 239, 260

Armijo, Carlos, 47
Armijo, George W., 54
Armijo, Lola C., 54, 145
Asplund, Julia, 144
"Atlanta's Shame" (Carrie Williams Clifford),
   62–63, 69
Atwood, Stella, 240, 241, 246–47
Austin, Mary, 270
Aztecs, 53–54

Baca, Ida, 196
Baca, Pablo, 47
Baca, R. I., 142
Baca, Ramona (Mona), 142, 146, 195
Baker, Abby Scott, 111–13
Baldwin, Fred S., 85–86
Baldwin, Maria L., 128
Banks, Annie Sims, 315n42
Barber, J. Max, 62
Barnard College, 32, 148–53, 156, 158
Barnes, Mrs. R. P., 194
Barton, Clara, 35
Battle of Little Big Horn (Battle of the Greasy
   Grass, 1876), 16
Beard, Charles, 178, 180
Beard, Mary, 152–55
Beck, Louis, 29
Belgard, Mary, 303n36
Belmont, Alva, 29, 38, 110, 222, 224
Bergere, Alfred M., 49–50, 194
Bergere, Dolores, 146, 195
Bergere, Luna, 194
Bergere, Rosina, 146, 195
Bernstorff, Johann Heinrich, Graf von, 165
Big Foot, 14, 16
The Birth of a Nation (film), 124, 232
Blackfeet, 73
Blackwell, Antoinette Brown, 35
Blackwell, Henry, 17
Blatch, Harriet Stanton, 25, 32–35, 38, 39,
   113, 154, 215
Blight, David, 292n41
Boas, Franz, 177–78, 180, 181
Bolshevik Revolution (1917), 244

Bonnin, Gertrude Simmons (Zitkala-Ša), 4, 20–21, 91–92, 187, 217, 218, 252; congressional testimony by, 186, 188; disenfranchisement assailed by, 260; early years of, 11–12; during election of 1928, 259–60; gravesite of, 264; Kellogg compared with, 249–50; legacy of, 264–65, 273; Native citizenship viewed by, 189, 191–92, 245–49, 256; as NCAI co-founder, 256–58; peyote use opposed by, 185–86; as SAI secretary, 184–85, 190

Bonnin, Raymond, 184, 185, 188, 256, 257, 264

Bottineau, Alvina Clementa, 85, 94

Bottineau, Emerald, 303n38

Bottineau, Jean Baptiste, 83, 85, 86–88, 93–94, 269

Bottineau, Lillian, 85, 269

Bottineau, Marie Renville, 83, 94

Bottineau, Pierre, 84, 85, 268–69

Bottineau Baldwin, Marie Louise, 1, 222; Bonnin and, 184–85, 266; death of, 269; early years of, 83–84, 85; Indigenous citizenship backed by, 137–38, 141, 192; as law clerk, 86–89; as law student, 94–95, 137, 138; marriage of, 85–86; Native artwork collected by, 266–67; racist sentiments of, 132–33; retirement of, 267–68; as SAI leader, 90–92, 96, 99, 136–39, 266; in segregated civil service, 131–32; social network of, 139–40; suffrage procession (1913) and, 100–102, 121; tribe membership of, 84–85; during wartime, 165, 166; in Washington society, 90, 134–35

Bourassa (La Flesche), Rosa, 89, 139

Boxer Rebellion (1889), 151

Bracklin, Edward, 140

Bradley, Harriet, 181

Brandt, Mrs. Schuyler Coe, 105

Bread, Daniel, 91

Brookings Institution, 259

Brooks, Virginia, 104, 105, 106

Brown, Hallie Quinn, 213, 214, 317n20

Brownsville Affair, 69

Brown v. Board of Education (1954), 232

Bundles, A'Lelia, 327n63

Bureau of Indian Affairs, 76, 136, 184, 244, 246, 256, 261

Burke, Charles, 240

Burleson, Mary Jane Walker, 111

Burn, Harry, 204

Burns, Lucy, 99, 116, 176, 177

Bursum, Holm, 198, 212, 239, 240

Bursum Bill, 240, 249, 250, 259

Butcher, Harriet (Shadd), 109

Butler, Marion, 109

Butler, Nicholas Murray, 274

Bynner, Witter, 270

Cabeza de Baca, Trinidad, 145

Cable Act (Married Women's Citizenship Act; 1922), 253

California, 21, 23, 239; Mexican Americans in, 49; voting restrictions in, 24

California Workingmen's Party, 28

Carlisle Indian Industrial School, 3

Carney, Mabel, 305n8

Carrere and Hastings (architectural firm), 217

Carter, Charles D., 89, 134

Carter, Italy, 134

Carter, Julia, 134

Carter, Stella, 134

Catron, Thomas, 144–46

Catt, Carrie Chapman, 4, 11, 45–46, 113, 116, 173, 176, 237, 263; Hawaii visited by, 174, 175; immigrants disparaged by, 21; in South Dakota referendum campaign, 14; suffrage tours by, 41–44, 179, 196, 203; at Tennessee ratification vote, 203–4; war backed by, 165

Chacón, Eduardo (Ed), 237–38

Chacón, Felipe, 237

Chan, Bertie, 287n24

Chan, Kate, 287n24

Chang, Sophia (Zhang Mojun), 42–43, 179–80, 289n66

Chaplin, Charlie, 295n32

Chávez, David, 236

Chávez, Dennis (Dionisio), 236, 237, 239

Chavez, James, 145

Chávez, Paz, 236

Chávez, Susie, 238

Chávez, Ymelda Espinoza, 236, 237

Chávez de Chacón, Adelina (Lena), 238

Chávez de Chacón, Santiago (Jim), 238, 239

Chávez de Chacón, Soledad, 4, 236, 237–38

Cherokee, 255

Chiang, Mei-Ling Soong, 160
Chiang Kai-shek, 160
Chinese Baptist Church, 274–77
Chinese Consolidated Benevolent Association, 29
Chinese Exclusion Act (1882), 5, 28, 121, 148–49, 255, 284n17
Chinese Ladies Mutual Helping Society (Shenzhou Women's United Assistance Society), 42
Chinese Restriction Act (1882). See Chinese Exclusion Act
Chinese Revolution (1911), 1–2, 25–26, 32, 45, 46, 102, 157, 218
Chinese Students' Alliance (CSA), 156–60, 178–80
Chinese Students' Monthly (CSM), 156–57, 158, 160
Chinese Women's Club for Mutual Encouragement, 30
Choctaw, 255
Christian, Nettie Bacon, 80
Chung You Hung, 44, 45
citizenship: birthright, 5, 27, 121, 131, 148, 149, 253; martial, 26, 170, 189, 191–92; naturalized, 15, 149, 253; tribal, 86, 121, 131, 132, 141, 205, 244, 247, 251, 264, 314n21
Civilian Conservation Corps, 271
Civil War, 18, 263
The Clansman (Thomas Dixon), 69, 124
Clarke, Edward, 94
Clarke, Helen, 72
Clemons, Anna, 207–8
Cleveland Magazine, 61
Clifford, Carrie Williams, 4, 70, 127, 129, 172, 216, 223, 225, 278; African American critics of, 63–64; death and burial of, 265–66; Dixon denounced by, 125–26; early years of, 57–59; Hunton backed by, 220–21; lynching ban backed by, 228–29; maternalism stressed by, 128; as NACW member, 60–62; in Niagara Movement, 67–68, 69; as poet, 61, 62–63, 69, 110, 111, 126, 170, 171, 232; racial violence and, 167, 169, 170; in suffrage procession (1913), 2–3, 108, 109–11, 115, 117; in Washington society, 67; white southerners denounced by, 62–63, 65, 66; Wilson viewed by, 166–67

Clifford, Joshua, 168, 170–71, 172, 265
Clifford, Maurice, 168, 170, 172, 265
Clifford, William H., 59, 65, 122–23, 266
Cloud, Elizabeth Bender, 324n79
Colby, Bainbridge, 209
College League, 38
Collier, John, 133, 240–41, 249, 256, 259, 264
Coloquios de los Pastores (Aurora Lucero), 272
Colorado, 21, 49, 53, 239
Colored American Magazine, 61, 63, 64, 65
Colored Women's Republican League, 228–29
Columbia University, 150–51, 158, 177
Comanche, 48
Committee of One Hundred, 228–29
Congressional Union (CU), 115–17, 142, 144, 146–47, 163
Cook, Coralie Franklin, 129, 228
Coolidge, Calvin, 76
Cooper, Anna Julia, 19, 219
Cooper, Brittney, 110
Cornplanter, Jesse, 77
Craig, George, 198
Cree, 83
Creek, 255
Crisis, 3, 69, 109–10, 126–29, 167–69, 227–28
Curtis, Charles, 89, 126, 173, 186, 224–25, 252–55, 258–59
Curtis, Oren, 254
Curtis, Permelia, 254
Curtis Act (1898), 137, 255, 259
Custer, George Armstrong, 16

Dagenett, Charles, 89, 91, 139
Dakota Territory, 12, 14
Dakota War (1862), 85, 268
Dallinger, Frederick, 318n5
Dance Circular (Circular #1665), 240–41, 249
Darkfeather, Mona, 78
Daughters of the American Revolution, 263
Davids, Sharice, 261
Davis, Alice B., 321n33
Davis, Edward J., 132–33
Dawes Act (General Allotment Act; 1887), 12, 13, 137
Dawn Mist, 71–78, 81–82
DeCora, Angel, 89, 139–40, 266
Deer, Esther, 206

New Jersey, 199, 232

New Mexico, 24, 47–48, 209; anti-Asian sentiment in, 212; female candidates in, 233–36, 237–39; female officeholding questioned in, 210–12; Mexican Americans in, 48–49; Native Americans in, 132, 141, 207, 260; Nineteenth Amendment ratified by, 199; statehood for, 4, 23, 49, 52, 78, 142

New Mexico Federation of Women's Clubs, 54

New York Age, 110

New York City Baptist Missionary Society, 275

New York State, 198, 239

New York Sun, 54

New York Times, 33, 36, 117

New York Tribune, 41

New York World, 62

Niagara Movement, 67–68, 69

Nichols, Earl, 269

Nicolar, Mrs. Peter, 207

Nightingale, Florence, 35

Nineteenth Amendment (1920), 14, 253; circumvention of, 208, 215, 216, 219, 222; ratification of, 199, 203–7; uneven impact of, 5–6, 205–9, 214–22, 243–49; in U.S. territories, 176

Nixon, Frances, 237

Normand, Mabel, 78

Norris, Daisy, 76

North Dakota, 12, 23, 261

Núñez Cabeza de Vaca, Alvar, 133

Nyi, Z. T., 157

Occoquan Workhouse, 177

O'Grady, M. E., 87

Ohio, 40, 198

Ohio Federation of Colored Women's Clubs (OFCWC), 61–62

Ojibwe (Anishinaabe), 83

O'Keeffe, Georgia, 270

Oklahoma, 23, 199, 207, 249–50, 255, 260

Old Indian Legends (Bonnin), 245

Old Spain in Our Southwest (Otero-Warren), 50, 271, 272

Oneida, 91, 205–6, 243–44, 273

Oregon, 23, 239

Organic Acts, 43, 44, 174

Ortiz y Pino, Concha, 238–39

Osage, 207, 250

Otero, Eduardo, 195, 198

Otero, Eloisa Luna, 49–50

Otero, Josefita, 210

Otero, Manuel, 47–48, 49

Otero, Miguel, 50, 234

Otero-Warren, Adelina "Nina" Luna, 4, 147, 166, 174, 198; death of, 272; early years of, 47, 49–50; elite background of, 142–43; language rights defended by, 56, 269–70; marriage of, 50–51; in New Mexico suffrage fight, 52, 55, 56, 144, 146, 193–94, 196–98; Nuevomexicano identity viewed by, 270–71; in Republican politics, 195–98, 210–11, 212, 233–35, 240; as schools inspector, 239–42

"Our Debt to Suffragists" (Robert H. Terrell), 128

Our Debt to the Red Man (Houghton), 269

Our Democracy and the American Indian (Kellogg), 243, 272

"Our Women of the Canteen" (Carrie Williams Clifford), 171

Outlook, 63

Ovington, Mary White, 214

Owen, Dorothy, 134

Owen, Narcissa Chisholm, 134

Owen, Robert L., 89, 134, 136, 321n37

Page, Horace, 27–28

Page, Thomas Nelson, 63, 64–65, 110, 122, 130

Page Act (1875), 27, 121

Paiute, 15

Pankhurst, Emmeline, 3, 32, 97, 116, 140

Pappen, Julie, 254

Park, Caddie, 109

Park, Maud Wood, 149, 173–76, 217, 218, 221–22, 236, 263

Parker, Arthur C., 77, 132, 135–37, 139, 185, 189, 266

Parker, Ely S., 66

Parker, Gabriel E., 134, 136, 139

Parker, Georgia, 134

Parker, Lucille, 134

Parsons, Elsie Clews, 76, 154, 178

Patterson, Lindsay, 234

Paul, Alice, 4, 108, 113, 147, 193, 198, 204, 225; African American voting rights slighted by, 215–16, 220, 222; arrest and conviction of, 177; Congressional Union formed by, 116–17, 142; growing radicalism of, 188–89; national amendment backed by, 115–16; as pacifist, 176; suffrage procession (1913) organized by, 70, 97–99, 102–4, 107; Wilson targeted by, 164

Peck, Mrs. Charles, 29–30
Pedregon, Cesario, 54
Pennsylvania, 198
Penobscot, 207
Perkins, Alice J. G., 34–35
Persons, Ell, 168, 226
Philippines, 22, 50, 53
Pierce, Charlotte, 225
Pitman, Almira Hollander, 175
Pitman, Benjamin, 175
"A Plea to Colored Men" (Carrie Williams Clifford), 68–69
Plessy v. Ferguson (1896), 59
Pocahontas, 134, 218
Poindexter, Miles, 114
Political Equality Association, 36, 38
Pollock, Channing, 80
poll taxes, 24, 41, 59, 211, 226
Pope, Barbara, 68
Porter v. Hall (1928), 260
Presidents and Pies (Anderson), 90
Price, Harriet, 59
Progressive Council of Indians, 241
Progressive movement, 128
Prohibition, 186, 203
prostitution, 27, 176
Pueblos, 48, 141, 240–42
Puerto Rico, 53, 235, 255
Purvis, Robert, 128

Quander, Nellie, 102–3, 107, 121
Queen's Garden (newspaper), 61

Race Congress, 229
Race Rhymes (Carrie Williams Clifford), 69, 110, 126
racial stereotypes, 5, 55, 264; of African Americans, 60, 80, 108, 122–24, 132, 146; of Chinese, 25, 27–29, 34, 102, 121, 146, 148, 150; of Hawaiian women, 81; of Native Americans, 71–75, 81–82, 90, 92–93, 294n25, 302n12; of Spanish speakers, 53

Rankin, Jeannette, 163, 165, 186, 237
Raynolds, Sarah, 147
Read, Leslie S., 250
Reavis, C. Frank, 227
Reconstruction, 66, 122, 124–25, 130, 263
Red Rock (Thomas Nelson Page), 122
Red Scares, 244
Red Summer (1919), 209
Reel, Estelle, 88
"A Reply to Thos. Dixon" (Carrie Williams Clifford), 69, 126
Republican Party, 14, 66, 228–29; in New Mexico, 54, 195–98, 210–11, 212, 233–35, 240
Revista (newspaper), 233–34
Revista Católica (newspaper), 54
Riis, Jacob, 29
Riley, Ida Prophet, 95, 139
Riley, Mrs. Bell I., 57
Rivera, Diego, 270
Rogers, Will, 80
Romero, Cleofas, 145
Romero, Marie, 145
Romero, Secundino, 145
Roosevelt, Franklin D., 133, 234–35, 271
Roosevelt, Theodore, 164, 197
Ross, Eva, 109
Ross, Nellie, 238
Rough Feather, 16
Roulette, Anna, 140
Ruffin, Josephine St. Pierre, 60, 128
Russell, James Earl, 305n8

Sacagawea, 22
Saíz, Mrs. P., 238
Salazar, Mrs. Manuel, 315n42
Sanders, Helen Fitzgerald, 72, 75
Santa Fe Railroad, 78
Santee Dakota, 11
"Savagery to 'Civilization'" (Keppler), 102
Second Sino-Japanese War, 276
Seminole, 251, 255
Seneca Falls Convention (1848), 17, 76, 149–50, 225
Seventeenth Amendment (1912), 115, 253–54
Sex in Education (Clarke), 94
Shadd (Butcher), Harriet, 109
Shadows of the Past (Jaramillo), 272
Shafroth, John, 175

"Shall We Fight the Jim Crow Car?" (Carrie Williams Clifford), 69

Shaw, Anna Howard, 4, 22–23, 31, 37, 116–17, 175, 218; Anthony and, 14, 15; racist tendencies of, 18–19, 21, 29; in South Dakota referendum campaign, 11, 15, 17; suffrage parades and, 36, 39, 40, 103, 113, 156; wartime operation overseen by, 165–66

Shelton, Carolyn, 238

Shenzhou Women's United Assistance Society (Chinese Ladies Mutual Helping Society), 42

silent anti-lynching parades: in Brooklyn (1922), 230; in New York City (1917), 169–70; in Washington, D.C. (1922), 228–31

"Silent Protest Parade" (Carrie Williams Clifford), 170

Simkhovitch, Mary, 153–54

Simkhovitch, Vladimir, 153, 180, 181

Simpson, Georgia, 109

Sioux Agreement (1889), 12–13

"The Sioux Past and Present" (Eastman), 189

"A Sioux Woman's Love for Her Grandchild" (Bonnin), 189

Sixteenth Amendment (1909), 115

Sloan, Thomas, 326n41

Smart, Leta Myers, 324n79

Smith, Alfred E., 259–60, 318n6

Smith, Ethel, 217

Smith, Hoke, 73–76

Smith, Marcus Aurelius, 174

Snyder, Homer, 250

Sociedad Folklórica, 272

Society of American Indians (SAI), 92–93, 150, 186, 273; Bonnin's work with, 184–85, 190; Bottineau Baldwin's work with, 90–92, 96, 99, 136–39, 266; founding of, 90–92; Native citizenship and, 135, 137, 141; stereotypes facing, 100; Wilson's meeting with, 136–37

Songab, Marguerite Ahdick, 85

Sons of the American Revolution, 263

Soong, T. V., 159–60

Soong Ching-Ling, 160

The Souls of Black Folk (Du Bois), 68

South Dakota, 11–15, 21, 189, 260

Southern Horrors (Wells), 60

sovereignty, tribal, 5, 86, 131, 135–38, 206–7, 244–49, 256, 264, 272–73

Sowing for Others to Reap (ed. Carrie Williams Clifford), 61, 278

Spanish-American War (1898), 50

Spencer, Anna Garlin, 39–40

Spencer, Ellen, 223

Spencer, Herbert, 94

Squire, Belle, 104, 106

Stabler, Eunice, 259

Stanciu, Cristina, 274

Standing Rock Reservation, 16, 20, 192, 258

Stanton, Elizabeth Cady, 17, 32, 76, 213, 252, 263

Stanton Suffrage Club, 96

The Star of Ethiopia (Du Bois), 127

Stevens, Doris, 116–17, 146, 177, 263

Stevenson, Matilda Coxe, 90

Steward, Charlotte, 108

Stokes, Ora B., 215

Stone, Genevieve, 106

Stone, Lucy, 17

Stowe, Harriet Beecher, 35

Stroup, Mrs. A. B., 209–10

suffrage parades: in New Mexico, 55, 71, 145; in New York City (1912), 25, 32–39, 153 (see also "Votes for Women" parade); in New York City (1915), 155; in Washington, D.C. (1913), 1–2, 97–117, 121, 122, 142, 217, 223 (see also National Inaugural Suffrage Procession)

The Suffragette Minstrels (film), 80

The Sun Dance Opera (Bonnin and Hanson), 184, 264

Sun Yat-sen, 25–26, 45, 160

Sylvester, Richard, 114, 115, 116

Sze, Betty, 223

Sze, Wai Ling, 217, 218, 223

Taft, William Howard, 126, 227

Talbert, Mary B., 129, 215, 227

Taney, Roger, 131

Tang Qunying, 26, 42, 45

Tantaquidgeon, Gladys, 325n18

Taylor, James (cook), 133

Taylor, Jim (Cherokee litigant), 87

Taylor, Paul, 270

Teachers College, 150, 151, 158, 179, 183

Teapot Dome Scandal, 250